BOOKS BY *H. R. Hays*

In the Beginnings   (1963)

From Ape to Angel   (1958)

The Envoys   (1953)

The Takers of the City   (1947)

Lie Down in Darkness   (1944)

Stranger on the Highway   (1943)

TRANSLATIONS

The Selected Writings of Juan Ramón Jiménez   (1957)

Twelve Spanish American Poets   (1943)

FROM *Ape* TO *Angel*

H. R. HAYS

FROM *Ape* TO *Angel*

AN INFORMAL HISTORY OF

Social Anthropology

Drawings by Sue Allen

NEW YORK *Capricorn Books*

L. C. Catalog card number: 58-7713   © H. R. Hays, 1958

———————————

CAPRICORN BOOKS EDITION, 1964

———————————

TO MY WIFE *Juliette*

Preface

■ It has not, of course, been possible within the scope of one volume to discuss the work of all the scientists who have made valuable contributions to the study of man; in recent decades in particular the growth of teamwork and the multiplicity of specialized approaches have made it necessary to be somewhat arbitrary in the choice of figures to represent trends. It has been felt, however, that by selectivity, however arbitrary, a clearer picture could be drawn for the general reader than by cluttering the pages with lists of names, titles, and brief references.

In addition, it must be pointed out that the significance of contributions made by contemporary scientists is bound to be a highly controversial matter. Time is still in the process of determining their stature. Consequently, the final chapters of this book must be considered a sketch of work in progress in which all judgments are tentative.

The author wishes to express his gratitude to Dr. Robert Redfield of the University of Chicago, to Dr. Hortense Powdermaker of Queens College, to Dr. Helen Codere of Vassar College, to Dr. Rhoda Metraux, and to Lisa Delza for advice and helpful suggestions. To Dr. Margaret Mead of the American Museum of Natural History and Dr. Allan Holmberg of Cornell University, who were kind enough to read a draft of the entire book in manuscript, the author is particularly indebted for expert criticism, and to Stewart Richardson for painstaking and creative editing.

Introduction

■ This book attempts to tell the hitherto untold story of social anthropology. It sketches the extraordinary world of curious ethical, religious, and marital custom revealed by the research of field workers who went to live among primitive and exotic tribes. It also traces the inception and development of various schools of ethnological thought in terms of the lives and activities of the leading scholars who forged the science. In telling the story an effort has been made to set these scholars in the intellectual backgrounds of their times and to show how their insights have played a dramatic role in the making of the modern mind.

Social anthropology has only recently attained such status that it has been called upon for advice in wartime. It was on the advice of the social anthropologist that the Japanese Emperor was not deposed, with the result that the Japanese armies were induced to lay down their arms almost as one man. The general public is not aware of such achievements and perhaps does not have a clear idea of what social anthropology is. We shall begin, therefore, with a working definition of the scope and aims of the study.

Ever since man left his inarticulate animal ancestry behind him, he has been living in groups varying in size from the family to the village or tribe, to the nation or federation of states. These groups, at every level, have developed shared beliefs and customs. Out of such communal heritage, civilizations and cultures have emerged.

The study of social anthropology is an attempt to describe, analyze, compare, understand, and evaluate group behavior and the products of group behavior. Man as a member of society is a different sort of creature from man considered as an isolated individual. As a member of society he is no longer free. In fact, when we study folkways impartially we become aware that the social animal is capable of the most fantastic beliefs, the most shocking and cruel activities, and subscribes to the most insane prohibitions, all of which, in one part of the world or another, are solemnly justified by tradition and ritual. Philosophers, saints, and teachers of ethics have set up systems, have left us legacies of theory and maxim, which, if heeded, would make the world a better place to live in. But, although the great moralists are praised and honored, the peoples of the earth continue to follow tradition and doggedly stick to customs that have no connection with the lessons of their teachers.

Social anthropology tries to discover how all this comes about, tries to extend human consciousness, tries to provide man with the means for understanding his irrational and unconscious drives. By eating the apple, Adam was destined to become as one of the angels. But the apple was not an elixir. It opened man's eyes and perhaps symbolized the dawn of consciousness, but the job of civilizing himself was his own problem. As we look at man's present plight, we see that if he is to become as one of the angels, he has a long way to go. If he fails to push on, however, he may soon find himself extinct with the protoapes from which he sprang.

Social anthropology, because it is the general study of man, occupies a unique position that requires it to borrow points of view and make use of methods developed by related sciences. Thus the study of man as an animal involves biology. The study of his past requires reference to archeology and history. Any examination of his mental and emotional processes invades the field of psychology. An inquiry into language, written and spoken, borrows from the study of linguistics and literary criticism. The investigation of man's ideas leads into religion and philosophy. In consequence, social anthropology has to endure the charge that it possesses no clearly defined field of its own, that it poaches on others' preserves. If this is a defect, it is also a virtue. Time will tell whether the study of anthropology can achieve a synthesis.

Although anthropology is now fully accepted in the family of social studies, it is one of the youngest of the scientific professions. It can look back on roughly one hundred years of development. The public is acquainted with some important anthropologists, but the leading figures in this field have never been dramatized as have, for example, the pioneers of medicine. The study of man is, nevertheless, essentially rich in human interest. In the past, as the area of investigation has been gradually defined, the emphasis has been upon the behavior of primitive peoples. For this there are two reasons. It was thought that primitives were simpler than contemporary civilized men, and it was also believed that savages preserved stages in human development which would throw light on the prehistory of the race.

To the surprise of investigators, even the simple Indian or naked South Sea Islander revealed complicated patterns of thought and custom. The man who lives in a crude hut and subsists by primitive techniques of hunting and fishing has been driven by ambition and fear to construct elaborate forms of art, myth, and ritual. He has tried by all sorts of techniques to control his environment and his fellows and to come to grips with a world he never made. Sometimes his successes and his failures parallel our own, sometimes they are weirdly different, but the likenesses and differences hold lessons for all of us: when fully understood, they should aid us in shaping our own future.

The story emerges piecemeal. The scholars who first concerned themselves with the origin and meaning of society and culture were men of their era, limited by the prejudices of their time. Yet, in spite of such handicaps, they arrived at new insights, and their achievements are a fascinating chapter in the history of modern thought.

If we are still far from the angels, we can at least, as we look back, perceive with hope that we have traveled some distance from the ape.

If social anthropology be crudely defined as an objective study of the physical and mental habits of men living in groups, it follows that the initial impetus for such a study had to arise from the contact of people with strikingly different cultures. It is therefore in books written by travelers to unfamiliar countries that we find the first anthropological data. It would be a waste of time to pick details from Herodotus or Marco Polo in order to prove them precursors of the modern social scientist. The historical process that truly fathered social anthropology was Europe's gradual domination of the world through successive waves of exploration and colonization.

We find much important anthropological source material in the Portuguese and Spanish chronicles of the conquest of parts of Africa and the New World in the fifteenth and sixteenth centuries. These narratives, however, were distorted and lacking in objectivity because of the fierce theological partisanship of the Church fathers and the soldiers who were their authors. There was less interest in recording the habits of the natives than in pointing out their sins. One shining exception is the great liberal Bartolomé de Las Casas, who wrote of the Mayan religion with extraordinary objectivity, remarking that the Quiché were, in their way, more pious than the Spaniards. Garcilaso de la Vega, a half-Inca, also wrote a valuable book about his own people. On the whole, this early anthropological material was set down by voyagers who liked to tell tall tales or by missionaries whose interest in the habits of their native charges had to overcome their prejudices against them.

The Renaissance, the inductive reasoning of the seventeenth century, and the ensuing rationalism of the eighteenth century produced a loosening of authoritarian religious dogma and encouraged exact observation. In addition, a fresh wave of colonization and exploration took place as the newly emerging powers England and France began to jockey for position in the unexploited areas of the world. Each produced a great sailor-explorer, and the writings of these two circumnavigators are another step in the direction of our science. Their attitudes and observations are typical of the European point of view toward alien cultures in the eighteenth century.

Oddly enough, these two men almost faced each other at the siege of Quebec. The Frenchman, Louis, Comte de Bougainville (1729–1811), a clever and polished young aristocrat, was a colonel in Montcalm's army and one of his most important aides. The young man had been a favorite of Mme de Pompadour and looked forward to a brilliant military career. The surrender of Quebec in 1756 and the collapse of the French colonial aims in Canada shocked and sobered him. He felt the necessity of circumventing the British on a global scale. The Falkland Islands, off the coast of Argentina, seemed to him an important base. He raised the funds himself, received a captain's commission and the royal blessing of Louis XV, and set sail to found a colony. The Falklands were already claimed by the British, but were inhabited only by "penguins looking like choirboys in surplices." Bougainville planted a colony on one of these bleak, eroded dots on the map which support only seals and sea birds. Sailing on through the Strait of Magellan, he encountered the Patagonians, who refused wine when it was offered to them and were coached by the French to shout (not very articulately) "*Vive le roi!*" Bougainville noted that the female Patagonians plucked their eyebrows and allowed the French sailors to stroke their breasts. Their husbands were content to receive presents of tobacco.

This voyage was completed in 1765. The following year Bougainville, who was a more imaginative imperialist than his king, set out to circumnavigate the earth. He commanded a frigate and a supply ship. Louis XV, that same year, had already ceded the Falklands to Spain, but Bougainville, the sailor-explorer, was now concerned with the islands of the Pacific. When he passed through the Strait of Magellan once again, he made contact with the inhabitants of Tierra del Fuego. Bougainville's interest in natives dated from his residence in Canada, where the French Jesuits had also done some pioneer anthropological work. The explorer had read Rousseau, and was ready to believe that people in a state of nature might lead idyllic lives, uncorrupted by society. The Fuegians, however, did not bear out this theory. He wrote that they were small, thin, and ugly, and stank abominably.

Tahiti was a different story. This island, which he named New Cytherea, seemed indeed Rousseau's imagined paradise. The French sailors were greatly affected by the splendid proportions of the women. The French entertained the natives with fireworks, which produced fear and delight. The Tahitians brought provisions and offered wives. They were indeed a beautiful people living in sweet idleness. The French explorer remarked that a painter could have found no finer models for a Hercules or a Mars. The most serious occupation of the women was "the art of pleasing."

Bougainville subsequently tried to land on New Guinea, where he was attacked by the natives and repulsed, and suffered from scurvy and lack of water. He returned to France in 1769 by way of the New Hebrides and the Solomon Islands. A species of convolvulus was named after him, the bougainvillea, which now adorns most tropical gardens. It was he who created the traditionally romantic picture of the South Seas as an erotic Eden which continues to our own day.

He had a long career in France during which he just missed the guillotine, but his significance for our science lies in his travel book published in 1771.

Bougainville's English counterpart was James Cook (1728–1779), a poor boy who fortunately learned to read and write, was apprenticed to a grocer on the Yorkshire coast, and at fourteen took service on a collier. By the time he was twenty-four he was the mate of a four-hundred-ton collier. During the French and Indian War, when Bougainville was defending Quebec, Cook was taking soundings in the St. Lawrence to discover whether the English fleet could advance up the river. His maps proved so useful and accurate that he was given the post of master of the frigate *Northumberland* in 1762, at the age of thirty-four.

In this period the English were not active in the Pacific. As Spanish colonial vitality waned, the Dutch had swarmed into Batavia. On top of this, Bougainville's voyage of 1765 was a distinct challenge. Britain was not inclined to let her rival get ahead of her. In 1767 the British Royal Society wanted to observe the transit of Venus from one of the South Sea islands. Thus science and imperial ambition went hand in hand, and Cook, whose reputation as a navigator had not ceased to grow, was chosen to head the expedition. His secret instructions ordered him to explore new areas that could be annexed by the British Crown.

Cook, when he reached the South Seas, also succeeded in maintaining fairly good relations with the Tahitians, though he was less concerned with the beautiful proportions of the women than with their propensity to steal. Although intensely property-conscious, the British never succeeded in changing the South Sea islanders' habits in this respect. Cook tried his best to control the amorous activities of the sailors, who promptly introduced venereal disease to Tahiti, but in this he was also unsuccessful. He was not impressed by native culture. A nose-flute concert pleased him most when it came to an end. Of the Society Islands, which he annexed, he said: "Neither the music nor the dancing was calculated to please a European." The warlike Maori of New Zealand fought him tooth and nail, and seldom allowed him to land. Nevertheless, he added these islands to the British Empire. He landed on the southeast coast of Australia, where he was received with spears, and annexed this last habitable, unclaimed continent to Great Britain. His voyage around the world took three years.

In 1772 Cook was sent out a second time with two ships to explore the Antarctic and to seek a legendary southern land mass. After many months of hardship and adventure in the Antarctic, he returned to New Zealand. He had discovered Easter Island with its enigmatic statues, beaten his own men and the natives for stealing, and spread venereal disease over several newly discovered archipelagoes.

In 1775 he set off on another voyage, bearing domestic animals that he intended to give to the natives. On all of his voyages he carried astronomers, botanists, and geographers; social anthropology, however, was not yet born. Cook's itinerary included Tasmania and the Sandwich Islands (all added to the Empire), and even the west coast of North America, where the Indians offered to sell him roasted human hands. In Tahiti, when he had an attack of sciatica, a whole battalion of Tahitian beauties arrived, laid him flat, and subjected him to the local school of osteopathy. He was well in a couple of days.

Cook was an honest, fair-minded man who hated bloodshed. His attitude toward South Sea native peoples was curiously ambivalent. On the one hand they fascinated him, and on the other they shocked him by such practices as cannibalism. Of New Zealand he could write: "The women were not impregnable but the terms and manner of compliance were as decent as those in marriage among us and, according to their notions, the agreement was innocent." He objected to the "deformity" of their tattooing, but was capable of admiring the grace of the spirals. The difference between his Anglo-Saxon caution and the warm admiration of Bougainville is seen in Cook's pronouncement on the Tahitians: "Yet, if we admit that they are on the whole happier than we, we must admit that the child is happier than the man."

His tragic death in Hawaii in 1779 somehow stems from this ambivalence. The natives had a myth concerning a god who had left them and would again return (we are reminded of Quetzalcoatl and the Aztecs). Cook was received with divine honors and hailed as the returning god. On the one hand, he very sensibly allowed himself to be garlanded with leis and put through the ritual of the cult; on the other, he stupidly tried to use as firewood the sacred fence surrounding a ritual center. He had speculated on the mystical word *taboo*, and thus ignorance could not be his excuse. Hostility between the natives and the whites reached a point at which Cook attempted to take hostages to protect himself. While he was on shore his men, against his orders, fired on the native canoes. Cook, cut off on the beach and unable to swim, faced the angry natives alone. He was desperately ordering the boats from his ship to cease fire when a warrior's stone knife struck him in the back.

So ended the first contacts of the Europeans with the South Sea islanders. In the remorseful words of Cook (he had honestly tried to check the spread of venereal infection): "I own I cannot avoid expressing it as my real opinion that it would have been better for these poor people never to have known our superiority . . . indeed they can not be returned to that happy mediocrity in which they lived before we discovered them." Over one hundred and fifty years later we are still ruefully discussing the same problem.

The writing of these travelers and many others, and the speculations of Rousseau concerning the noble primitive were a part of the intellectual climate of the beginning of the nineteenth century.

Man's view of man is likewise conditioned by his view of the external world. By 1822, the date at which we have arbitrarily chosen to begin our story, the habit of exact observation was fully formed and the universe had already lost its simple and arbitrary mythological character as its nature began to be revealed by new techniques of measurement. Laplace had been studying the solar system, calculating the orderly relationship between the sun and the planets. Count Rumford was asking: "What is heat?" He set about analyzing it experimentally. Fresnel was demonstrating the wave theory of light. Lyell had not yet published his epoch-making geology, but a certain Dr. Hutton had made a geological map of England and suggested that the way to know how rocks had been formed in the past was to study their formation in the present.

From the investigation of the universe it was easy to turn to a more precise observation of living things. The microscope, by then good enough to permit the detailed scrutiny of anatomy, had already proved that Harvey's theory of the circulation of the blood was correct. Linnaeus, a new Adam, had developed a two-name system for plants and animals and was classifying their species. Our own Audubon, in 1820, had gone down the Mississippi in flight from his wife and his general store to dedicate himself to that brightly colored record of American birds which he was to publish in the next decade. Only a few years before, that tireless traveler Alexander von Humboldt had explored the Orinoco, dispelling the myth that the river Indians had mouths where their navels should be, and had watched the Quechua of Cajamarca dancing sadly to their mountain pan pipes.

As the interest in nature and the external world grew, and as every cultured man became something of an amateur naturalist, the concept of laws and systems applying to all of life also grew. The medieval synthesis had been challenged by Protestantism, and now the authoritarianism of the Calvinists was an irksome restriction. In America, old-line Calvinists such as Lyman Beecher were trying to stem the tide of liberal Unitarian views that held man's nature to be good and perfectible and rejected the blackmail of hell and heaven. There was a need for a new and unified intellectual attitude. The human mind was breaking through boundaries on all sides and seeking for new formulations.

The humanitarian spirit, a complement of the industrial revolution, also possessed importance for the science of man. The evils of wage slavery and Negro slavery, and the desire to improve man's social situation suggested the need for a study of his nature. Indeed, such reformers as Fanny Wright were soon to create controversy and scandal. It was significant that she chose America for a laboratory in which to set up her utopian interracial colony. In America a new society was taking shape, in America there was room for change and experiment.

In America, too, sharply contrasting cultures were coexistent. The white colonists from Europe had conquered an aboriginal race and were pushing it steadily out of its hunting-grounds. The frontier was the point of contact between the two peoples. Out of this contact, which led to trading and treaty-making, a closer relationship was bound to develop; antagonism could give way to curiosity and interest. Fortunately for the science of social anthropology, into this strategic area came a man sensitive to new intellectual trends who was both a humanitarian and a scholar.

Contents

Contents

Drawings in the Text

PART *One*

The Classical Evolutionists

Chapter 1

FRONTIER ANTHROPOLOGIST

Concerning Henry Rowe Schoolcraft

■ In the summer of 1822 Henry Schoolcraft, a round-faced, spectacled, scholarly young man of twenty-nine from Oneida, New York, sailed into the little river port of Ste. Marie on the river of the same name, which joins Lake Michigan to Lake Huron. The sails came rattling down upon the booms, the anchor splashed into the blue water, and Schoolcraft stared at the frontier settlement that was to be his home for almost twenty years. There was not much to see: a scattering of dilapidated wooden buildings, a stockade containing a detachment of soldiers, and, behind this, the virgin forest. But Chippewa Indians were running down to the shore, the Indians who had brought him to Ste. Marie. He strained his eyes to see what they were like.

Presently, when boats had been lowered and carpetbags stowed in their bows, he was taken ashore. One of the first people to clap him on the shoulder was a hearty Irishman, John Johnson, a leading settler and a successful fur-trader. Schoolcraft soon learned that Johnson was far from the average frontier type. He possessed a well-stocked library, was something of a poet, and had married O-she-wash-co-da-wa (Woman of the Green Valley), the daughter of the leading Chippewa chief of the region. Accompanying Johnson were his charming and cultivated daughters, one of whom had been educated in England.

Among the white settlers were Chippewa chiefs wearing calico shirts, red cloth leggings, eagles' feathers in frontlets on their fore-heads, and blue broadcloth togas flung over their shoulders.

The young Indian agent drank in the colorful and barbaric scene. Near by were the domed lodges of his charges, in front of them medicine poles with bright strands of cloth and beads flutter-ing from their tops. He wondered what they signified. The chiefs stared at him with silent curiosity. Schoolcraft looked into their dark faces with emotions uncommon for a member of a conquer-ing race. He did not accept the usual attitude that these were monsters to be despised and destroyed. They were men. They were men with wives and families, with beliefs and customs which they respected and to which they clung. He was filled with curiosity. Could he make friends with them, learn their language, understand their motives and aspirations as fellow human beings?

When he dined with the Johnson family, he was full of ques-tions. To his delight, Mrs. Johnson, dark-skinned and aquiline-featured, yet possessing the graces of an English lady, was able to answer them. Yes, Chippewa verbs were declined, the language had a fully developed grammar. How could he study it? There were no books. Then and there he decided to compile one.

The young ladies, too, were delighted to find the new agent a social asset. No doubt they discussed Walter Scott's novels and quoted poetry. The Chippewa Indians, too, were not without poetry. Whitefish, one of the chief foods of the Indians and settlers, was called *attiksumaig* or deer-of-the-waters. It was a pretty metaphor. Schoolcraft made a note of it.

In a very short time he was accepted as one of the family.

He hired an official interpreter, a drunken Irishman whose vocabulary was sufficient for eating, drinking, and trading but who knew little and cared less about the ideas and customs of the wild people with whom he was in daily contact. This, Schoolcraft realized, was a typical attitude and responsible for the errors con-cerning Indians which had crept into books. Although a man of literary tastes, he was also a scientist. He was interested in accurate observation, and he was becoming aware, from his attempts at communication and from his daily discussions with Mrs. Johnson, who was proud of her heritage, that the Indian was neither the yelling demon of the frontier atrocity story nor the noble savage of Chateaubriand's poetic dreams.

"I had always heard the Indian spoken of as a revengeful, bloodthirsty man who was steeled to endurance and delighted in deeds of cruelty. To find him a man capable of feeling and affection, with a heart open to the wants and responsive to the ties of social life, was amazing."

Schoolcraft's education had begun. The young man who was able to write so openmindedly of the red man was destined to be America's first social anthropologist and the first genuine field anthropologist in the world. He had taught himself Hebrew and German and matriculated at college at the age of fifteen. He was fond of natural sciences and an accomplished mineralogist. He also wrote poetry.

His father, of English stock, was a glass-manufacturer. After the War of 1812 there was a slump in American glass manufacture. Schoolcraft, who had worked for his father, found his advancement blocked and resolved to turn his scientific background to good account. In 1818 he set out to explore the west with the very practical aim of investigating its mineral resources. He traveled through Missouri and Arkansas, then continued down the Mississippi and back east by sea, having made a complete circuit of the Union, in those days measuring six thousand miles. He published a book on lead mines, was elected to the Lyceum of Natural History, and was appointed mineralogist to the expedition, led by General Lewis Cass, to the upper Mississippi and the Lake Superior region. Cass became his friend and patron. Schoolcraft published another travel book. His career was shaping up nicely. He hoped to become superintendent of the United States Bureau of Mines. Meanwhile, with Cass's backing, he got the job of Indian agent at Ste. Marie as a stopgap. He was not aware that this was to change his whole life.

In 1822, when the white race was striking into the heart of the continent, the moccasined hunting tribes were already doomed to virtual extinction. By then the conquerors could afford to use the subtler weapons of diplomacy. The year before, General Cass, then governor of the Michigan Territory, had made a treaty with the Algonquin tribes by which they relinquished five million acres in northern Illinois, Indiana, and western Michigan. One of Schoolcraft's official jobs was to see that the treaty was carried out. There was an added problem: General Cass wanted to prevent the Indians from visiting Canada, for he believed that the British were keeping alive hostile feelings toward the United States. The

War of 1812 was not yet forgotten, and the native tribes were pawns in the game of power politics.

So far, the land ceded by the Indians was no more than an acquisition on paper. The midwest was still a primeval wilderness. Chicago was a few shabby buildings, Ste. Marie a dilapidated French hamlet. Flour was still brought to Michigan from Ohio. The mineral wealth on the shores of Lake Superior was only a supposition. In spite of President Monroe's caution concerning internal improvements, roads were being built and waterways improved, and the settlements that bordered the Atlantic were turning toward the unexplored western areas so rich in romantic adventure and material promise.

Schoolcraft's Indian agency was a building thirty-six feet square, of squared timber and mortar, whitewashed on the outside. It consisted of one big room and two smaller anterooms with plastered walls. The building was heated by a big iron stove that could take three-foot logs, a necessity during the icy northern winters. In front of the agency a green, covered with Indian lodges, swept down to the river, here three quarters of a mile wide.

From his window he could look out on his charges. Their family life, their livestock, their domestic arts, their quarrels, and their games were spread before him, a living anthropological laboratory. It is no wonder he labored hard on his grammar. In fact, he grudged the time wasted by casual visitors who insisted on passing the time of day when he was working on Chippewa verbs.

His immediate task was to establish friendly relations with the Chippewa, who were considered only semi-friendly, and to perform a certain amount of what would now be called social service, which included medical attention and actual relief for the hungry. In addition he was supposed to wean them away from any political intrigues in which they might be engaged with the British across the border.

His sympathy for the Indians soon made him critical of the policies of the fur-traders, who consistently exploited the Indians' love of whisky. When the furs were all extracted and the whisky received in payment was drunk up, the Indians and their families went hungry and half naked. In this condition they came to his office to beg for rations. Schoolcraft was in the unenviable position of having to discriminate between the deserving and the undeserving poor.

To add to his problems, the soldiers were without tact or good sense in their handling of the Indians. The Chippewa were accustomed to place peeled and painted saplings, tipped with bits of red cloth or beads, outside their lodges when there was sickness. An officer obtusely appropriated one of these poles to support his tent. An angry quarrel ensued before the Indian's property was returned.

Schoolcraft, the man of good will, was obliged to steer a middle course, though his sympathies inclined more and more toward the Indians. His undeserving poor were those Indians who tried to play both ends against the middle by begging from both British and American authorities, or drunkards who bartered the rations he gave them for more whisky. He made a rule that he would interview only sober Indians. When the heavy drinkers informed him that they were his children, he scolded them like an indignant father.

He was making progress with the language when, after months of patient work, his dog got hold of his Chippewa verbs and playfully tore them up. Schoolcraft painstakingly collected the scraps and glued them together (the grammar finally became a part of a six-volume work). *Totem* was a word he heard often. Mrs. Johnson explained that it was actually pronounced "dodaim" and that it meant family mark or coat-of-arms. He thought it was derived from *odanah*, town or village. Family relationships were traced in a kind of feudal system by means of the totem. He wrote: "The institution seems to be of some importance to the several bands." This was a pioneer observation upon a subject that was to arouse decades of controversy and speculation, totemism being one of the fundamental forms of social organization of primitive men all over the world.

He had already ventured far beyond philology. As his ability to speak to the other race developed, he stepped into a new world, a world of demons and terrors where ghosts appeared in sacred dreams, where the processes of nature were surrounded with magic and mystery, where *jossakeeds*, or medicine men, were supposed to be able to plunge naked into roaring fires without being burned, where an Indian died from no visible organic ailment because he believed harmful spells had been used against him. It was all puzzling, exciting, and even poetic.

He encountered inexplicable rites. A sacred tree with a hollow trunk made a sound like a native drum when the wind blew through it. To this the Chippewa made offering. Stranger still, an Indian woman was accustomed to run naked around a newly planted cornfield at night to protect it from vermin or blight and to ensure a good crop. He discovered that articles which had been stepped over by Indian women were considered unclean and were avoided by the men. Hairs combed from a woman's head were buried in the ashes of the fire. A man would not eat out of the same dish as a woman. At menstruation, a lodge of separation was built; if the woman lacked bark to cover a dome-shaped lodge, she made a bower of branches. These were all accurate observations of sex taboo. In fact, Schoolcraft noted down fundamental facts about magic, taboo, and social organization which were to be the concern of anthropology for the next hundred years.

The greatest revelation of all came after he had made a trip into the interior and spent some time as a guest in the lodges of his Indian friends. At this point he discovered the ability of the red man to create myths. "Why have no travelers mentioned this trait? Surprise reached its acme when I found him whiling away the tedium of his long winter evenings relating tales and legends for the amusement of the social lodge. These fictions were sometimes employed, I observed, to convey instruction or to impress examples of courage, daring or right action. But they were at all times replete with wild forest notions of spiritual agencies, necromancy, and demonology. They revealed abundantly the cause of his hopes and fears, his notions of duty, and his belief in a future state."

Schoolcraft had discovered a literature! To a poet nothing could have been more exciting, and he embarked at once on a voyage of adventure into the mind of primitive man.

By this time the plan to become superintendent of mines had been forever destroyed because the federal government had sold its mining concessions. He no longer cared. He was fascinated by the new world he had discovered, and he was dedicating his life to exploring its enigmas.

Encouraging and stimulating him, Mrs. Johnson was always ready to be his guide. At the same time a closer intimacy had developed between him and her English-educated daughter. The girl was proud of her Indian blood and touched that the young scholar had come to regard her people with so much respect and sympathy. For him she became the link between the two worlds. Less than a year after his arrival at Ste. Marie they were married.

In the eighteen years that followed he came to know his Indian charges so well and was, in turn, so trusted by them that General Cass employed him to help negotiate a peace treaty between the Chippewa and their traditional enemies, the Sioux, at Prairie du Chien on the upper Mississippi. The Iowas, the Sacs, and the Fox Indians landed on the bank of the river. They came dressed as a war party, armed with spears, clubs, and guns. They wore necklaces of bears' claws and crests of horsehair which resembled Roman helmets. As they landed, beating drums and yelling, in compact ranks, Schoolcraft was thrilled by the majestic and martial sight.

He did not, however, forget his official task. Upon the necks of the Indian chiefs, who promised to maintain peace with the United States and the Sioux, he placed "silver medals of the first and second class." Class apparently indicated size. Schoolcraft dealt out his medals like merit badges. One he gave to an Indian who saved a white man from drowning.

He traveled constantly, trying to avert clashes between the always hostile Chippewa and Sioux. Near Red Cedar Lake he found the Chippewa dancing. The warriors, arrayed for war, stamped in circles to the music of their drums and rattles. With the war drums and the war cries ringing in his ears, Schoolcraft argued and pleaded for peace. The older and wiser chiefs listened. They kept the peace and accepted him as a friend.

He was indeed the Indians' friend, counselor, and historian. During the hard winters he distributed flour, pork, and tickets on the agency blacksmith which entitled them to have their kettles and axes repaired. He fought for their political rights so determinedly that he was elected to the legislative council of the Michigan Territory. The Indian agents were forbidden to give whisky to the natives, but the Hudson Bay Fur Company traders got special permits to sell it over the heads of the agents. "Little does the spirit of commerce care how many Indians die inebriated if it can be assured of its beaver skins," he wrote indignantly.

In 1832 he founded the Algic Society to collect and disseminate information concerning the Indians' language, history, traditions, customs, and character. Although his official activities and his efforts to create a better understanding of the defeated race took up much of his time, he continued to fill his notebooks with story after story gathered as he traveled the winding waterways and the blue expanses of the lakes in frail canoes and sat in the council lodges of his Indian friends. He now had a sufficient body of material to think of publishing a book. Washington Irving, whom he had come to know through his membership in learned societies, wrote condescendingly, and with a practical eye on profits, that he would be happy to edit and polish Schoolcraft's Indian lore. Schoolcraft did not like the idea. He thought the result would depart too radically from what he had noted down. Although aware of the problem of

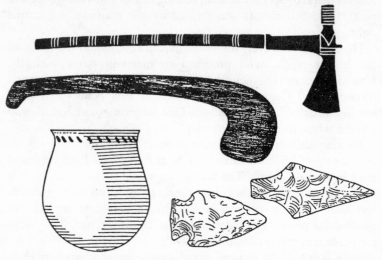

Tomahawk, fish club, storage jar, and arrowheads.

style, he was not always able to extricate himself from the literary graces of the period. In fact, he cut, censored what he considered indecent, and distorted the original stories considerably. *Algic Researches*, two volumes of myths and legends, was published in 1839. He believed the chief values of his myths consisted "in their exhibition of aboriginal opinions." He was seriously trying to give to the world something of what he had glimpsed of an alien culture in which he had been immersed for years.

Ironically enough, his work was to become famous at second hand through Longfellow's sugar-and-water rendering of his material in the poem *Hiawatha*.

In the introduction to *Algic Researches*, Schoolcraft wrote that he had examined the mythology of the Chippewa as a means of acquiring insight into their modes of thinking and reasoning, and the probable origin of their institutions. He thought that he observed traces of Oriental customs in the myths, particularly in reference to burning the dead. There was a similarity between the menstruation taboo and purification and sex taboos mentioned in the Bible. The puberty fast, he noted correctly, was equivalent to the public profession of faith in civilized religions. The visions that came to the adolescent undergoing the fast "stand in all respects in the place of a Christian's hope, with the small difference that the name [of the person or creature which appeared] is never uttered." In the story of the culture hero or inventor of civilizing arts, Manbozho, Schoolcraft thought he detected a character derived from Asiatic sources. On the whole, he subscribed to the theory that the Indian had migrated to America from the Orient. In this period, of course, the vast extent of prehistoric and geologic time, substantiated by modern science, was unimaginable. It is well to remember that the first European collection of mythology, Grimm's *Deutsche Mythologie*, which appeared in 1836, preceded Schoolcraft's book by only three years.

In 1841, because his wife was unwell and because he was eager to visit Europe, Schoolcraft left the frontier for good. By now he considered himself an anthropologist. His nineteen years had been well spent, for he took east a wealth of material which he continued to publish. In fact, few modern anthropologists could boast as long a period of field experience. In his "Plan for the Investigation of American Ethnology," which he presented to the board of regents of the Smithsonian Institution at its first meeting in 1846, he defined the province of the new science. Ethnology, he maintained, should consist of "ascertained fact and history." It was to include evidence from philosophy and archeology and utilize the methods of the exact sciences. He then listed the divisions of his proposed study, which included all of the arts, sciences, crafts, institutions, and ideas that are a part of culture. Indeed, in his little pamphlet Schoolcraft sketched out a fairly comprehensive road map for the future of the science he enthusiastically labored to create.

The following year he published *Notes on the Iroquois*, a mixture of archeology, legends, history, art, notes on language, and biographical studies of famous Indians. Most important are his observations on social organization.

11

A French Jesuit missionary, Joseph Francis Lafiteau (1671–1746), first pointed out that the Iroquois were governed on what he called an "oligarchic" basis and traced descent through the female line. He correctly noted that children in one *cabane* or family group called all their mother's sisters mothers and regarded all their mother's brothers as uncles. He wrote a pioneering book in 1724, *Mœurs des sauvages Américaines comparées aux mœurs des premiers temps,* in which he drew shrewd parallels between the customs of the American Iroquois and those of the Egyptians, Greeks, and Romans. Schoolcraft was probably not familiar with his work.

Schoolcraft pointed out that tribes were divided into clans, each distinguished by an animal, bird, or object totem, and that clan organization was the basis of the Iroquois political and tribal network. A man must marry into a clan different from his own, and descent was traced through the female line. A chief's son could not succeed him; a chief's heir was a brother's or a sister's son. Chieftainship had to be approved by the tribal council. There were six clans, a civil chief heading each one. War chiefs were independent of civil chiefs and obtained their office on the basis of ability, being appointed when needed. Warriors had the right to assemble in council to approve the action of their chiefs. In summation he wrote: "Practically considered, a purer democracy perhaps never existed."

These were amazingly objective judgments. Schoolcraft's social material is significant, for it contains the germs of ideas to be developed later by his great colleague Lewis Morgan.

The Indian in His Wigwam, which Schoolcraft published in 1848, was a popular book in which he tried to change the general attitude toward Indians. He was writing about his friends, writing with maturity and imagination. He insisted that an understanding observer "sees them acting as other men would act, if placed exactly in his condition, prepared with the education the forest has given him, and surrounded with the same wants, temptations, and dangers." This is a statement that Franz Boas, nearly one hundred years later, would have applauded.

Schoolcraft's was a lone, honorable voice raised to advocate racial tolerance at a time when the Indian was still being tricked out of his lands and harried into the virtual prison of inadequate reservations.

His monumental work was *Historical and Statistical Informa-*

*tion Respecting the History, Condition and Prospects of the In-
dian Tribes of the United States, Collected and Prepared under the
Direction of the Bureau of Indian Affairs,* published in 1851. In
six quarto volumes averaging six hundred pages he collected material on archeology, language, customs, history, and Indian art,
and endeavored to compare the material with similar evidence
from Oriental sources. The book was handsomely illustrated with
black-and-white and colored lithographs by Captain Seth Eastman.
Like all of Schoolcraft's work, it suffers from lack of organization
and system. It contains, however, a wealth of material in the rough,
a tremendous collection of ore from which other scientists were to
extract useful metal.

There was little he could do to change the condition of the
Indian, despite his visits to Washington, his lectures, and his writings. The shameful drama marched to its conclusion as the triumphant industrial civilization of the whites rode roughshod over
the remnants of the forest tribes, still refusing to recognize any
virtues in their culture. Schoolcraft's contributions to his science,
however, make him doubly a pioneer. Individually, he broke
through the white man's egocentricity. Indians were people. They
were also poets. Viewed in context, many of their customs, though
strange, possessed logic. What did they mean? How did they develop? The scientists who followed him continued to busy themselves with these problems.

It is true that by the 1840's and 1850's German scholars were
writing culture histories and collecting material from travelers' accounts, but none of them was a field worker, none of them lived
among native peoples. Theodor Waitz's *Anthropologie der Natürvolker* (*Anthropology of Nature Peoples*) did not begin to appear
until 1859. Klemm's *Allgemeine Culturgeschichte der Menschheit*
(*General History of Humanity*) began to be published in 1843;
Humboldt's semi-anthropological book *Kosmos* began to appear
in 1848. Schoolcraft's first book, published in 1839, antedates all
of these, and all of English social anthropology as well.

Thanks to the very nature of the frontier, Schoolcraft was
kept in continuous contact with an alien race and studied a particular group exhaustively. Because of his American situation he
avoided much of the fantastic speculation to which many of the
armchair scientists who followed him were prone. Moreover, his
work leads directly into that of his successor, Lewis Morgan, one

of the founders of the evolutionary school. After 1857 rheumatism and paralysis put an end to his active career. When he died in 1864 he was considered the greatest Indian scholar in America.

Henry Schoolcraft, therefore, deserves recognition as the first true field worker in the science of social anthropology. Considering his efforts to better the condition of the American Indian, it is scarcely an exaggeration to call him the first applied anthropologist.

Chapter 2

A PROUD AND PROGRESSIVE RACE

Concerning Lewis Henry Morgan (Part I)

■ Fortunately for the study of anthropology, the Indian lies heavily upon the conscience of America. Early in the nineteenth century he ceased to be an important factor in the life of the country. The pioneer and the prospector classed him as a nuisance in the same general category as the panther and the grizzly, but a sense of obligation and guilt remained, translated into a faint curiosity concerning the proud aboriginal who clung to the bow and the hunting trail. In the east, when he was no longer a serious threat to industrialization, it was possible to regard him with a certain romantic nostalgia. The drums, the war paint, and the dance rituals were picturesque. The warpath and the forest camp appealed to youthful imagination.

Lewis Henry Morgan (1818–1881) was a young and imaginative boy when the Seneca Indians of New York State came to his attention. Indeed, Morgan, who has been called the father of American anthropology, might never have merited the title if it had not been for a schoolboy prank. Cayuga Academy, which he attended, was situated in Aurora, the heart of the Iroquois country. A number of tribes, and the Seneca in particular, still preserved even on their reservation a good deal of their traditional way of life. Morgan was aware of Indians from his earliest years. He also had a passion for organizing. While still at school he inducted his friends into a secret society called the Gordian Knot. The boys used to sneak into a disused Masonic lodge and array themselves in the robes of the Masons to conduct their own rites. This playful ceremony was not forgotten. We shall hear more of the Gordian Knot.

Although in Morgan's day the archeological past was still unknown, his birthplace, the Finger Lakes region, was an ancient center of aboriginal life. The lakes and streams teemed with fish and other aquatic foods, and the forests had sheltered game that had sustained ancient man for over 5,500 years. The early hunters, who had not yet invented the bow, left behind them their javelin points, their rough stone choppers and scrapers, and their bone awls. Long before the European discovery of America they were replaced by what are now termed the Iroquois tribes, who had passed into a semi-agricultural stage, sowing corn and gathering various wild vegetable foods.

No doubt the future anthropologist played at being an Indian, as do most young Americans. Nothing more might have come of it if he had not, like Schoolcraft, been the victim of a financial depression. Having studied law, he was admitted to the bar in 1844 and moved to Rochester to set up his practice. But business was bad, and the young lawyer had no clients. Time hung heavy on his hands. He re-formed the Gordian Knot and took in some new members. Among them was a dark-skinned, heavy-featured, powerfully built young Indian named Ely Parker.

Parker was a man of character and ability. As a boy, when he had worked for some white men, he had been mocked for his defective English. Parker determined to vindicate himself and his race. He set out to obtain a white man's education. He was the son of one of the Tonawanda Seneca chiefs and proud of it. After studying law for a time, he discovered that he could never be admitted to the bar: he was an Indian, and only white men could apply.

Undaunted, he went to Rochester in the hope of becoming a civil engineer, and enrolled in the Rensselaer Polytechnic Institute. This young man, later to become a brigadier general under Grant, Grant's Commissioner of Indian Affairs, and, at the end of his life, the last Grand Sachem of the League of the Iroquois, so impressed Morgan that he decided to change the name of his society. He renamed it the New Confederation of the Iroquois and, fired by Parker's enthusiasm for the culture of his people, modeled its ceremonies on those of the Iroquois.

The initiation rites developed by Morgan were colorful, if naïve.

The whole group wore Indian costumes, carried bows and arrows, and assembled outdoors around a bonfire. The Prophet made a speech to the novice, swearing him to secrecy and warning him that the Seneca never abandoned a friend or forgave an enemy. The new member knelt before the Sachem as the bandage was removed from his eyes; the warriors stood in perfect silence, resting on their bows. The Prophet and the novice then stood in the center of the group while the head warrior led the band around them singing a war song. Each member was introduced to the recruit by his Indian name, and the latter was accepted into the society and given an Indian name. Speeches, poems, and refreshments followed. All was strictly temperance, for Morgan was a devout Presbyterian and did not touch liquor.

Parker's strong personality had a profound influence upon Morgan. Together they visited the neary-by Seneca reservation. To Morgan it was a revelation. Here was a people with a traditional wisdom that united them with nature. In spite of conquest, and isolation in the midst of an unfriendly civilization, they were sustained by a body of ritual and belief which made them remarkably self-sufficient. Far from being a crude savage, the Seneca was a poised, dignified individual, in every way the moral equal of the white man who saw fit to despise him.

Morgan's familiarity with the Seneca gradually developed into a scientific interest. The romantic, college-fraternity atmosphere of the club began to change, reflecting his growing maturity. It became a serious historical society. Its founder decided that it should seek to record the fast-disappearing Indian culture. Henry Schoolcraft, by then recognized as the outstanding Indian authority in the country, agreed to deliver one of the annual addresses, and, heartily approving of the society's aims, became a member under the name of Alhalla (he had written a poem about an Indian under that title).

Morgan's visits to the Seneca continued. He was still not seriously occupied with law practice. His Indians, however, presented him with a case. A typical swindle was being perpetrated against them. The Ogden Land Company had been intriguing to conclude a treaty with the Seneca by which they could be relieved of a large part of their reservation. Agents of the company began by paying ten chiefs three thousand dollars apiece for their signatures to the treaty. Others signed after having been provided with unlimited whisky at the company's expense. Still others signed who were not chiefs at all, having been elevated to the office in a sham election run by the company.

Land was worth $16 an acre in that area, but the Indians were being deprived of it for $1.60 an acre. The United States Senate was about to ratify the treaty over the angry protests of the members of the tribe.

Sparked by Parker, Morgan became indignant. The New Confederation had set aside thirty per cent of its funds for Indian welfare. Drawing upon this, Morgan and Parker rushed to the defense of the Seneca. They rolled up an impressive number of signatures to a petition, went to Washington, buttonholed senators, exposed the machinations of the land company, and quashed the treaty.

The grateful Seneca adopted Morgan into the Hawk Clan of the Tonawanda band at the corn-Harvest festival of 1846 under the name of Ta-ya-da-o-wuh-kuh (One-lying-across). The name signified that he lay across the boundaries of the Indian and white races.

The episode is described by Charles Porter, a fellow member of the League of the Iroquois, who spent ten days on the reservation with Morgan. In the morning Morgan filled his notebook, with Parker as mentor and interpreter. Parker was a grandson of Jimmy Johnson, the tribal Prophet, and delighted in taking down the old man's speeches for Morgan. In the afternoon the Indians put on dances and games to entertain their guests.

A Baptist missionary who was working on the reservation was much perturbed. He felt that the young anthropologists were leading the Indians back to pernicious customs and heathen ways.

In the actual ceremony Jimmy Johnson made a long speech explaining the intricacies of kinship and gave the young men their Indian names. This was perhaps the point at which Morgan became interested in the mysteries of that system of relationships with which his name will always be linked.

Each novice was led up and down the council lodge by two painted chiefs dressed in ceremonial regalia—fringed and beaded buckskin and bright feathers. They chanted the song of adoption as they marched. At the end of each verse the assembled tribe responded, singing in chorus and shaking turtleshell rattles. This ceremony was of great importance, for the Iroquois were accustomed to absorb prisoners of war into their tribes, making them a part of their extraordinarily well-knit society.

A dance followed in which women took part, the young white men being given partners. "Then for the first time my ears were regaled with Indian music," says Porter. "Two young men were seated on opposite sides of a drum which looked to me very like a nail keg. On this they pounded violently with sticks as an accompaniment to the most discordant howling. An Indian has no conception of musical intervals. But they kept good time and the dancing was animated." A bullock had been killed and made into a stew. The large kettles in which it had been boiled were taken into the council house and set in a row in the middle of the floor. The dancing went on around them, the dancers moving in pairs, facing each other, about six feet apart, one moving forward, the other backward, with a shuffling step. Every minute or so, on a signal from the leader, all changed places. Porter took part so animatedly that he nearly fell into a kettle of stew. The young men ate succotash, an Indian invention. They were also served cakes made by mixing boiled and pounded corn and black beans, which were then boiled again and eaten without salt. To wash them down they had hemlock tea.

Like Schoolcraft, Morgan became obsessed by the culture of a primitive people. He continued to study them under the auspices of Parker and in 1851 published the *League of the Ho-de-no-sausee or Iroquois*, a two-volume study that has been called the first scientific account of an Indian tribe ever given to the world. It still stands as a classic. He dedicated it to Ely Parker with a grateful acknowledgment of the latter's contribution. It is hardly fair, however, to give Morgan all the credit for investigating the Iroquois, for Schoolcraft's account, though less scholarly, certainly broke ground.

The Iroquois, or "Real Adders," as their name signified, had played a most important part in American colonial history. They had defeated both the English and French at various times, and as allies of the English settlers had swung the balance of power against the French. Before the coming of the Europeans they had federated all the tribes in their area in the interests of peace.

They lived in gabled houses made of bark laid on a frame of upright poles, "long houses" that were sometimes a hundred feet in length, with tiers of bunks along the sides and fireplaces down the center. They had false-face societies in which the members wore grotesque twisted masks representing evil spirits. A man became a member of such a society when he dreamed that he was a false face. Their special ceremonies and dances were intended to propitiate evil spirits and cure disease. They shook turtleshell rattles, sprinkled hot ashes over the patient, and danced around him.

They had thirty-two distinct dances. Morgan remarked acutely that when they ceased to dance they would no longer be Indians.

They worshipped rain gods, harvest gods, and wind gods, and gave thanks to trees, vegetables, fire, and water. They smoked tobacco as a means of communication with the spiritual world, the smoke, as incense, ascending to the Great Spirit.

Morgan believed that the Iroquois fell below the Greeks in nobility of religion, but that they had arrived at the existence of a supreme being "without revelation."

In short, they were noble savages, though not Presbyterians.

Morgan's interest in the Seneca stemmed from his own character. If Schoolcraft the poet was preoccupied with myth and primitive psychology, social organization and government appealed to the Rochester lawyer. American democracy was for him the pinnacle of human achievement. When he caught glimpses of what appeared to be democracy among his red-skinned hunters, his imagination took fire.

The American colonists had emigrated to a new world to escape the tyranny of absolute monarchs. They had founded a new type of state. But when Morgan looked closely at the Iroquois, he found untutored savages living in harmonious brotherhood, with no hereditary royalty and without benefit of a Declaration of Independence or a Constitution. They had even achieved a political federation whose aim was universal peace.

What, then, was the nature of this curious government? What mysterious forces produced the admirable character of the Iroquois? How had he achieved an organized way of life which permitted the development of dignified and impressive human beings? Above all, after shameful persecution, what gave him strength to remain an Indian?

Morgan, notebook in hand, investigated their socio-political organization.

The five Iroquois nations—Mohawk, Oneida, Onondaga, Cayuga, and Seneca—had been joined in the federation, according to

Morgan's conjecture, for a century and a half before the arrival of the Dutch. Schoolcraft thought that it had existed for a man's lifetime previous to the European colonization. Modern scholarship, on the basis of a legend in which the Indian hero Deganawidah puts out the sun in order to persuade the nations to unite peacefully, dates its origin from an eclipse in 1451. The hunting-grounds of the Iroquois were bounded by the Hudson River and Lake Erie. An Iroquois nation was divided into eight tribes. Like those of the

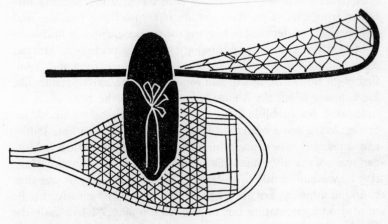

Lacrosse stick, moccasin, and snowshoe.

Romans, the Greeks, and the Hebrews, the Iroquois tribes were subdivided into family groups. There were eight of these clans: wolf, bear, beaver, turtle, deer, snipe, heron, and hawk.

"The names doubtless had emblematic significance," Morgan wrote, missing the significance of totemism. He discovered, however, that the clan was the concept that welded the whole Iroquois League together. Members of the hawk clan, for instance, whether of the Seneca, Mohawk, Oneida, Cayuga, or Onondaga nation, were all brothers. They considered themselves to be of the same family, as closely tied together as children of the same mother. Thus the clan bonds cut across the division of tribes and nations on the basis of real or supposed blood ties, all clan members being united by a network of obligation and privilege. If the political divisions of tribe and nation were the warp of the League, the clan was the woof. Theoretically, Morgan realized, the League was one great family woven together by kinship ties. This was its unique strength, so different from the elective organization of his own United States. He wrote: "It forms an enduring monument to that proud and progressive race who reared under its protection a wide-spread Indian sovereignty."

This was the crux of his observation. You could not conceive of Americans, after conquest and imprisonment, still retaining Whig or Democratic party organization. Yet here were Indians still as closely knit by mysterious bonds as they had been before the white man came. There was a structure here which was essentially different from that of modern civilization, something puzzling and unique that was destined to become the preoccupation of his life.

In 1851 the study of anthropology was not a profession. Morgan came of a solid middle-class family. In later life, earnest and dignified, with sideburns, beard, and longish hair, he looked rather like a composite of all the Victorian novelists. At the time when his first book was published he was in love with his cousin Mary Steele. As she was a woman of impeccable piety, she and her family had decided that her future husband should be a missionary. Morgan was not exactly a missionary, but he evidently convinced Mary that he was sufficiently God-fearing. She accepted him. It was time to found a family; frivolity was at an end. He saw clearly that he must drop a fascinating but unprofitable hobby. "I laid aside the Indian subject to devote myself to my profession."

This good resolution produced results. A connection with the financier Samuel P. Ely, who became his financial adviser, involved him in railroads, specifically in building a railway to the south shore of Lake Superior, a region rich in iron ore. Both Schoolcraft's and Morgan's careers reflect westward expansion—Schoolcraft prospecting for mines, Morgan making possible their exploitation. He made money from the railroad; the railroad stimulated mining. Morgan shrewdly put his capital into the newborn iron industry. By the end of his life he was worth one hundred thousand dollars.

But Morgan was not able to "put aside the Indian subject." In the process of building his railroad, he made a number of trips to the shores of Lake Superior, where Schoolcraft had preceded him as a field worker. When he visited the Chippewa reservation in 1855, his old curiosity reasserted itself. He began to ask questions. To his amazement, the Chippewa, though speaking a different language, held the same views on cousins, aunts, clan brothers and sisters, and marriage as the Iroquois. More amazing still, their tribes also were divided into totemic clans.

The puzzling organization was proving to be widespread. Perhaps it was characteristic in all of America. If so, it might be profoundly significant.

Leaving the dividends to take care of themselves for a while, in 1858 he sent out a questionnaire to all Indian agents in the United States, hoping to learn if the kinship systems and marriage customs were the same among North American Indians. In this he had the co-operation of the Smithsonian Institution. He got a few stimulating results from North Dakota, but most of the agents were too ignorant, too ill-equipped, and too uninterested to be of much help. He himself, the following year, traveled in Kansas and Nebraska and accumulated more significant data. A chance meeting with a missionary from southern India, however, was a turning-point in his life. From him he learned that a hill tribe, the Tamils, had approximately the same kinship system as the Iroquois. Morgan was delirious with excitement. A daring conjecture was framing itself in his mind. Here were a potential twenty-four million Asians who might fit into the scheme! It could be, it must be, universal!

Along with a wife, Morgan had acquired a keeper of his conscience, his wife's pastor, the Reverend James Hall McIlvaine. McIlvaine, who was something of a scholar (a member of the Smithsonian Institution), sympathized with Morgan's interests and admired his achievements, but was duty-bound to shield him from heresy. There were some disturbing theories in the air, and you never knew where untrammeled scientific speculation might lead. He suggested that Morgan's North American Indians were quite sufficient to keep him busy. McIlvaine agreed that the peculiar nature of Indian kinship might be important. He did not share the popular attitude that it reflected only "the total depravity and perversity of the Indian mind," but the universal nature of Morgan's thinking worried him.

Morgan was not to be controlled. He felt himself on the track of a great principle. Through the Smithsonian Institution he got the co-operation of General Cass, by then Secretary of State and already indoctrinated by Schoolcraft with the importance of ethnological inquiry. Cass offered the facilities of the State Department. Morgan sent out questionnaires to United States consular agents all over the world. He also sent them to leading scientists and to missionaries.

McIlvaine's anxieties were justified. At the very time when Morgan was conducting his investigation, the orthodox view of the world was being dealt some hard knocks by an inquiring student of natural sciences named Charles Darwin.

Chapter 3

DARWIN'S DREADFUL SECRET

Concerning Evolution and Anthropology

■ "And God saw everything that he had made, and, behold, it was very good. And the evening and the morning were the sixth day."

Before the dawn of the scientific attitude, the Bible was the final source and authority on the natural order of things. The Bible stated that the world had been shaped in six days. Every species of plant and animal had received God's individual attention and had been created at the same time. The mythological outlook of a group of Semitic tribes had, by the ascendancy of the Christian faith, become the official viewpoint of the western civilized world. Actually, the cultural level of these tribes had not been so different from that of some of the Indians of the Americas. Their world view, however, having been institutionalized, was to be taken literally without question. It was written down in a book, the book was divinely inspired, and that, as far as western scholars were concerned, was that. The fact that many universities were still theologically oriented in the early nineteenth century tended to preserve the *status quo*.

Geology is a study of the history of the earth. Graven in the stony crust of the earth is a record, a record of time immemorial, of ancient life forms and lost eras. The flesh decays, but the bones, the hard shells, the molded imprints of leaves, footprints, and tentacles live on. The insistent tap of the geologist's hammer was heard during the entire nineteenth century, chipping here and there, discovering layer upon layer of stone differing in composition, in formation, and in the records contained.

It was possible to explain the method of formation of the rock layers, and it became evident that an incalculable number of years had been required to build them up. By comparing the sequence of the strata at different points, the scientists were able to work out a time map. They also began to record and classify the fossilized remains of living creatures found in the earth's crust. Some did not appear in the oldest strata. Some appeared for a time and then disappeared.

This data hardly confirmed a six-day creation. True, the Bible mentioned a flood in which some species could have been wiped out. The Irish Archbishop Ussher had worked out a Biblical chronology: the world had been created in 4004 B.C. and the flood took place in 2501 B.C. But the lost species did not disappear all at once. The troubled geologists suggested a number of floods, a series of creations.

This theory did not cover the evidence too well, and it departed from the literal Biblical story, but it was the best they could do. One thing was certain. A species—that is, a particular type of animal or plant which could not interbreed with any other type—was separate and distinct. It must have come into existence full-blown, must always have remained the same, and probably would always remain the same.

In 1832 Sir Charles Lyell, in his *Principles of Geology*, noted that in the deepest geological strata remains of life were rare, that above them came shells and vegetable remains, then the bones of fishes and reptiles, the remains of birds, and finally of quadrupeds. Man was still more recent, and Lyell did not attempt to explain the discrepancy. He suggested that all the influences in the present which mold the development of living things were also present in the past. As Adam and Eve were supposed to have distributed names among the birds and the beasts in the Garden of Eden, it was disturbing that the remains of man came so late in the geological scheme of things. Lyell saw the problem, but it was a touchy subject and he did not venture to explore more deeply.

His book was read with interest by young Charles Darwin (1809–1882) while voyaging through the South Seas in the *Beagle*

Admiral Robert Fitzroy

(a trip that lasted from 1831 to 1836), observing how admirably animals and plants were adapted to their environment and meditating on the nature of species. Lyell also discussed the development theory put forth by a clever Frenchman, Jean Baptiste Lamarck (1744–1829) in 1809. Lamarck had entertained the obviously fantastic notion that one species might develop into another because of the intense desire and efforts of an individual to better adapt itself to its environment. This, of course, implied the ability to pass on a change in structure to its descendants. Lamarck's ideas were treated with polite irony that relegated them to the sphere of curiosities.

When Darwin returned from his voyage in 1836 he had already collected a great deal of data concerning the peculiar adaptation of species living on isolated islands. He continued to work over his notes and by 1842 had already sketched out his famous theory of the origin of species. For years he did not dare to publish it. He communicated his conclusions in confidence to the botanist Hooker; to Lyell, the geologist; and, some years later, to the American botanist Asa Gray. The theory of evolution was discussed behind closed doors as if it were a dangerous conspiracy. Darwin's well-reasoned arguments were indeed explosive in their time, as shattering as the activation and control of nuclear fission in ours. For if it was true that species were not God-given, but developed by some slow natural process, what became of Adam and Eve and the Flood and, indeed, the whole literal interpretation of the Bible?

The preservation of belief in religion was felt to rest upon authoritarian grounds. Without original sin, there could be no redemption, no salvation. If doubt was cast upon the origin of sin, what became of morality? What became of wicked human nature, kept from all sorts of violent excesses only by the fear of Divine retribution?

In a sense, the guardians of the *status quo* were right. Anthropology itself shows that man has been motivated chiefly by nonlogical impulses and by poetic projections of his desires. On the other hand, it also shows that, as facts fall into place, the supernatural retreats before them. The scientific revolution of the mid-nineteenth century, accentuated by Darwin's work, points up this duality of man's nature. We are still caught in a destructive conflict between these two aspects of human character.

27

Darwin was not the only rationalist thinking along such lines. Herbert Spencer (1820–1903), who took all of science and philosophy for his province, also hovered on the outskirts of anthropology. An engineer and an inventor, he had a curiously relaxed childhood during which he studied only what pleased him. Taking a dilettante interest in politics, philosophy, mathematics, and geology, he too read Lyell's *Principles of Geology* and, instead of being convinced by Lyell's refutation of Lamarck, was converted to the Frenchman's theory. Spencer enjoyed speculation, but hated monotony. He found it very difficult to read any writer whose ideas were contrary to his own. He began to apply Lamarckian thinking to the sphere of social development. In 1852 he published a paper on the development hypothesis, or "evolution," as he called it, which was to form the basis for all his thinking. In a book on the principles of psychology published two years later he held that the nervous system was continually modified by adaptation to higher and more complicated forms of society. Spencer was not, however, a scientific investigator. "It has never been my way to set before myself a problem and puzzle out an answer. The conclusions I have, from time to time, arrived at have not been arrived at as solutions of questions raised: but have been arrived at unawares—each as the ultimate outcome of a body of thought which slowly grew from a germ." Spencer attempted to be the philosopher of science, and we shall have more to say of him in connection with the beginnings of sociology.

Although there were radicals such as Spencer who by intuition believed in evolution, even so liberated a mind as that of Thomas Huxley was frankly agnostic. He found the theory of successive floods hard to take, but could see no way of disproving it.

Knowing well the opposition he would face, Darwin held back for years, patiently accumulating more evidence. To confess the theory he held was like confessing murder. The orthodox religionists were bound to consider it destructive of all order and decency, at one blow cutting away the foundation of the best of all civilizations.

Charles Darwin was one of the most cautious and meticulous of the new generation of scientists. From his botanical studies he knew of the struggle for existence among living things. To cope with the environment all sorts of special adaptations occurred. The visits of bees were necessary for the fertilization of red clover. Lacking bees, the clover died out. Some hardier species of animals were known to have replaced others: one variety of cockroach, for example, had driven out another. It was clear that some species were more successful than others in the struggle for existence.

How did they become more successful?

Species had a tendency to vary slightly. Animals that lived in the far north had thicker fur than the same species in a warmer climate. From this it was possible to assume a still greater degree of variation. The ostrich, for example, had wings that evidently at some point in the history of the breed had been used for flight.

Darwin came to the conclusion that individuals whose variations best fitted them for the struggle to survive in their particular environment would be most likely to win the battle and would reproduce most plentifully. The less well adapted would tend to die out. This was natural selection.

"With the giraffe, the continued preservation of the individuals of some extinct high-reaching ruminant, which had the longest necks, legs, etc., and could browse a little above the average height, and the continued destruction of those which could not browse so high, would have sufficed for the production of this remarkable quadruped," he wrote.

Darwin piled up evidence from all departments of botany, zoology, and entomology. Studying the development of the embryo, he was able to show that "the wings of birds and bats and the legs of horses and other quadrupeds are indistinguishable at an early embryonic period and that they become differentiated by insensibly fine steps."

This, he felt, mirrored the gradual historical process of adaptation, showing that there were no great leaps in the formation of new species. Natural selection was, as we have seen, the direct opposite of Lamarck's conception.

In 1856 Darwin began to write his epoch-making book. The idea of evolution was in the air. Before he could publish, Alfred Wallace, a naturalist who had been working in the Malay Archipelago, sent him a paper outlining similar views. Although Wallace had not supported his work by an impressive mass of evidence such as Darwin had assembled, the latter felt that both his work and Wallace's should be presented to the Linnaean Society. This was done in 1858. The opposition was caught napping. The prestige of Lyell and Hooker overawed the other members at the meeting, and the new theory was listened to without opposition.

During the years that Darwin worked on his book he became a scientific godfather to a young neighbor, John Lubbock. Lubbock came of a wealthy county family. He was a fine-featured, slender, charming boy who, as an adult, grew a delicate curling beard. He visited Darwin continually. Plants and animals fascinated him. He studied Darwin's specimens and learned scientific method from the older man. He began to study botany seriously. When *The Origin of Species* was published in 1859 and the storm broke, Lubbock was one of Darwin's ardent supporters.

The other avowed evolutionist, Herbert Spencer, commented: "Reading it gave me great satisfaction, whether there was any set-off to this satisfaction I can not say. . . . Up to that time . . . I held the sole cause of organic evolution is the inheritance of functionally produced modifications. *The Origin of Species* made it clear to me I was wrong." Spencer had his share of intellectual vanity, as will appear later, which made him eager to copyright his contributions to thought.

Everyone took sides. In the United States, battle was joined between Asa Gray (1810–1888) and Louis Agassiz (1807–1873). The former was a round-faced, shrewd, kindly Yankee whose *Manual of Botany of the Northern United States*, published in 1848, became such a best-seller that among mid-nineteenth-century young ladies pressing plants was almost as important a cultural activity as "water-color drawing" or playing the piano. The book was reprinted as recently as 1950. Agassiz was a fiery Swiss zoologist, a *Schläger* fencer, and a brilliant classifier of species who captured Boston and New York audiences when he first lectured on natural science in the fifties. As both men were teaching at Harvard, they were drawn into controversy at a meeting of the Natural History Society of Boston in 1860. Agassiz, the anti-evolutionist, was a poor debater; he grew emotional and accused his antagonist of having no training in the biological sciences. Gray, a good churchman but a logical thinker, had the better of the argument. The Harvard faculty divided into two camps, and the students of the two men cut one another in the corridors. Darwin had a high opinion of Gray and once remarked: "If I ever doubt what I mean myself, I think I shall ask him."

In England, Hooker, Lyell, and Thomas Huxley championed

the new scientific outlook. On the famous evening of the meeting of the British Association for the Advancement of Science in 1860, when Huxley met Bishop Wilberforce of Oxford in pitched battle, Lubbock (at twenty-five already a member of the Royal Society) sat on the platform and spoke in favor of Darwin, citing his own botanical experience. Students jeered, Lady Brewster fainted, and Admiral Robert Fitzroy, who had been captain of the *Beagle*, waved his Bible and screamed that Darwin was a viper.

The Bishop displayed his ignorance of Darwin's ideas and sneeringly asked Huxley if he traced his descent from a monkey through his grandfather or his grandmother. Huxley demolished "Soapy Sam," as Wilberforce's enemies called him, with cold logic. The battle over the descent of man was to go on for decades, and the Bishop's sneer was to be duplicated countless times.

An indication of the impression that the new theory soon made upon the popular mind is Jules Verne's first successful novel, *Journey to the Center of the Earth*, which was published in 1864. In it Verne sent his scientists down the crater of an Iceland volcano. As they descended through the layers of rock they traced the remains of ancient animal life backward in time in strict Darwinian sequence and even, in defiance of the law of gravity, discovered a huge cavity in the center of the earth which contained living mastodons and a twelve-foot prehistoric man! Verne's book made him world-famous and founded the genre of science fiction.

Darwin had done his work well. A new vista had opened in the future of science. If animals and plants had evolved by a slow process of adaptation, did not the same principles apply to other phases of life? Why not to human institutions?

Cradled in evolutionary theory, John Lubbock was destined to be a link between Darwinism and the infant science of anthropology. In America, Lewis Henry Morgan continued to labor over the intricacies of kinship. At the same time certain European scholars were attacking the problem of the origin of marriage and property.

Chapter 4

THREE JURISTS AND THE PRIMITIVE HORDE

Concerning Sir Henry Maine, Johan Bachofen, John McLennan

■ Law is the codification of folkways, the system of rules by which men officially agree to live. The terminology of legal archives may be dry and pedantic, but the Latin phrases are symbols of the conflict between individual impulses and social obligation. It is therefore not surprising that not only Lewis Henry Morgan, but also his three important European contemporary anthropologists were lawyers by profession.

The first of the three, Sir Henry James Sumner Maine (1822–1888), was a dignified aristocrat with Dundreary whiskers. He taught civil law at Cambridge, and was at one time a member of the government of India. Maine was an empire-builder who thought that the British conquest of India compensated happily for the crusades "by placing the foot of the most fervently believing of Christian nations on the neck of the mightiest of Mahometan dynasties."

Early in his career he complained that there was a lack of knowledge of Roman law in British law schools. English law could be better understood by an investigation of its origins. To remedy the situation he published, in 1861, *Ancient Law, Its Connection* with the Early History of Society and Its Relation to Modern Ideas.

His facts led him to a novel conclusion. "Ancient law . . . knows next to nothing of individuals. It is concerned, not with individuals but groups. . . . The life of each citizen is not regarded as limited by birth and death but as a continuation of his forefathers, and it will be prolonged in the existence of his descendants."

Once again blood ties seemed to be significant. It was clear that the primitive mind differed considerably from that of the Victorian Englishman. Sir Henry added: "In Roman law everybody is at first a citizen, then as a citizen, he is a member of his order . . . , next he is a member of a gens or clan, and lastly he is a member of a family. . . . I repeat the definition of primitive society given before. It has for its units not individuals but groups of men united by the reality or the fiction of blood relationship." The family was the key. Because he was a lawyer, property was his next concern. His investigation led to an inevitable conclusion. As the individual was not the social unit, individual rights were not paramount.

For perhaps the first time it appeared that the sacred distinction between mine and thine was not eternal. This was a shock to the European mind educated in the nineteenth-century atmosphere of individualistic, competitive capitalism. Sir Henry was probably not aware of the social and political significance of such a trend of thought. At any rate he faced his facts austerely. "It is more likely that joint ownership and not separate ownership is the really archaic institution and that the forms of property which will afford us instruction will be those which are associated with the rights of families and of groups of kindred."

Morgan had already decided independently that kinship was the explanation of much that was fundamental in ancient society. Maine, working from classical evidence and from his knowledge of primitive villages in India, was moving in the same direction.

Maine knew that in certain Indian villages property was held in common. Groups of families owned land together and tilled it co-operatively. Personal relationships and ownership of land were therefore intertwined. Sir Henry was acute enough to see that injustices often resulted when English administrators tried to separate the two. Indian communities, tracing descent through the male line, were patriarchal. Sometimes communities composed of several families assumed they were all descended from one ancestor. This was a link with the classical world. The Romans had a term for a group of families descended from one ancestor. They called it a *gens*. Tracing the relationship between the family and property, Maine found evidence of communal ownership of land in Russian villages, in Turkey, in Serbia, and in Croatia. (It also existed in Mexico and Peru.) This was as far as he was prepared to go. He concluded: "If it be true that by far the most important passage in the history of Private Property is the gradual separation from co-ownership . . . what were the motives which originally prompted man to hold together in family union? To such a question jurisprudence, unassisted by other sciences, is unable to reply."

But others were looking for anthropological answers. Both Johan Bachofen and John McLennan, also working independently, came to the conclusion that the answers had something to do with marriage.

Maine, because the Indian communities with which he was familiar were patriarchal, assumed that males had been dominant in society from time immemorial. He did realize that ancient law subordinated the woman to her blood relations, in contrast to the legal system of his time which made her dependent on her husband.

A dreamy German Swiss with a round, sensitive face, Johan Jacob Bachofen (1815–1887), had set himself the same task as Sir Henry Maine. While professor of law at Basel, he, too, began investigating ancient law. As he came of a wealthy family, he had leisure to pursue his studies throughout Europe. In 1839 he enjoyed the sophisticated delights of Paris; for several years he continued his studies in the peaceful, scholarly atmosphere of Cambridge. It was Italy, however, sensuous, sunny, pagan, which had the most profound effect upon him. Classical law led him into archeology and myth. In 1848 his studies were interrupted by the loud invasion of politics. That year Garibaldi made his triumphant entry into Rome. In the confusion that followed, Bachofen had to clear himself of the charge of being a French spy. Nevertheless he went on meditating lyrically upon the world of the ancients in elegant and melancholy prose worthy of Lamartine. He began to theorize concerning the symbolism of classical monuments and myths.

Under the brilliant southern sky he was undergoing a truly

Germanic revolution of the soul. He decided that a Christian intellectual heritage threw no light upon primitive thought. He saw in the sculptured tombs of the Greeks and Romans a symbol not of decay, but of the fecundity of the earth.

"I see more and more that one law rules everything and that early man in his earthly life was motivated by the impulses of animal instinct. It is my aspiration and goal to fathom completely this characteristic of ancient thought, especially in matters of law and the state. I am now concerned with a thoroughgoing investigation of nature."

In 1851 Bachofen published a Roman history, and in 1856 (the same year that Darwin undertook his great book) he first presented, as a lecture in Stuttgart, his theory of matriarchal society. Like Lamarck, Bachofen had an intuitive rather than a systematic mind. The book he published in 1861, *Das Mutterrecht* (*Mother Right*), is half poetry, half science. McLennan later exasperatedly called it mystical and hard to get through. It is true that Bachofen is forever sailing off into literary essays that are curiously vague, but it is also true that he was the first scholar to suggest that men had not always been dominant in society.

Historians had examined such stories as the rape of the Sabine women in the hope of finding historical fact. The picture of well-shaped females in flying draperies, stretching out their arms to husbands and brothers, was all very well when painted by David, but it did not look like actual history. The historians of the period gave up the myths as fanciful nonsense. Bachofen insisted on a new evaluation of mythology. Myths surely obeyed regular laws that could be studied to throw light on early institutions. They contained symbolic truth that could be interpreted to explain ancient thought. This was an insight ahead of his time. His method, nevertheless, was mostly speculative guesswork. The story of the rape of the Sabines was an indication that the position of women had been different in early Roman times. He brought together other bits of information. The Lycian Greeks were accustomed to give their children the mother's family name. There was female succession to the Egyptian throne. The sacrifice of Iphigenia to the gods showed that women in early times were superior to men in sanctity and religious importance. Women were associated with cults of the moon, the fecund earth as against the fecundating sea, the cult of the dead as against that of the living. All this was a consequence of the "gynocratic" spirit, Bachofen's term for the supremacy of women.

Bachofen concluded that in the most primitive society promiscuous intercourse took place. Women, being nobler and more sensitive beings than men, were disgusted by this, and, reinforced by religious aspirations, put an end to it by violence. The first marriage was thus invented and dominated by women.

He used as proof the myth of Bellerophon (containing an account of the rebellion of the Lycian women) and the myth of the Amazons. This second period of prehistory he called the Amazonian period, or that of gynocracy. "The gynocratic epoch is the poetry of history because of the sublime character, the heroic majesty and beauty, it lends to women." Women were heads of families, children were given their mothers' family names, right of inheritance descended through women. Demeter, the great mother, was the goddess of the period. Woman's religious supremacy was translated into political supremacy.

Bachofen's third historical stage was the revolution that came about with the emergence of Dionysius, who proclaimed that fatherhood alone was divine and that the mother was merely the nurse of the offspring. Women rebelled at this, but were beaten by force of arms. As proof of the conflict he cited the *Orestes* of Aeschylus. In it the chorus of furies sustains Clytemnestra and justifies her crime. Apollo defends Orestes. This symbolized the actual conflict between the matriarchate and the patriarchate. Women, he concluded, were eventually defeated, although the struggle went on spasmodically until finally settled by the codified authority of Roman law. As further proof of his theory, he found matriarchal characteristics in Babylonian, Armenian, and Persian religions.

Bachofen's method curiously foreshadows the modern psychoanalyst's approach to classic myth. Ironically enough, the repercussions of his work were strongest among the socialists. The work of this wealthy conservative was used by Marx and Engels to prove that the family was but a passing phase in the development of society.

A rather irascible Scotch advocate, John Ferguson McLennan (1827–1881), arrived at similar conclusions from different facts. McLennan, a graduate of the University of Aberdeen, studied law at Cambridge, but left without obtaining a degree. From 1855 to 1857 he remained in London, writing for George Henry Lewes's *Leader*. In this period he must have become aware of the scientific trends of the time. He was called to the bar in Edinburgh in 1857, and in the same year was commissioned to write the article on law for the eighth edition of the *Encyclopaedia Britannica*. He, too, was thus impelled to investigate ancient law, and he was struck by certain Spartan and Roman marriage customs.

When he published his book *Primitive Marriage* in 1861 he had not read Bachofen and considered his own work to be the first scientific study of marriage. It was subtitled "An Inquiry into the Origin of the Form of Capture in Marriage Ceremonies." McLennan, although he too used classical authors as a source, was a more diligent collector of facts than Bachofen. He was one of the first anthropologists to use a variety of evidence drawn from travelers' accounts of savage tribes. The chief source of his information concerning the early history of civil society, he wrote, "is the study of races in their primitive condition and the study of symbols used by advanced nations in the constitutional exercise of civil rights." The scientist should look to Central Africa, America, India, and the Pacific islands for data. When "symbolic forms" were present, it could be inferred that there had been corresponding realities in the past life of people employing them.

The symbolic form that fascinated McLennan was the element of capture in marriage ceremonies. Among the Dorian Greeks, according to Herodotus, the bridegroom or his friend went through a pretense of stealing the bride. Apuleius, in *The Golden Ass*, described a similar custom among the Romans. A British observer wrote of the Khonds in India: "I heard some loud cries proceeding from a village close at hand. Fearing some quarrel, I rode to the spot and there I saw a man bearing away upon his back something enveloped in an ample covering of scarlet cloth. He was surrounded by twenty or thirty young fellows and by them protected from the desperate attacks made upon him by a party of young women. On seeking an explanation of this novel scene, I was told that the man had just been married and his precious burden was his blooming bride, whom he was conveying to his own village. Her youthful friends, as it appears is the custom, were seeking to regain possession of her and hurled stones and bamboos at the head of the devoted bridegroom until he reached the confines of his village."

A similar sham resistance was put up by the bride and her friends among the Kalmucks, the Tartars, and the Bedouin Arabs. In Wales in McLennan's time there was a scuffle over the bride. There was also evidence from primitive groups in Africa and the Americas.

McLennan had worked out a technique for the library anthropologist which was to be used by many others: compilation of data from classical antiquity, contemporary primitives, and folk customs from contemporary Europe. A number of instances of a custom occurring in various areas indicated its distribution "just as a fossil fish in a rock on a hillside forces us to conceive of the whole surrounding country at one time under water."

McLennan's first explanation of bride-capture was that women acquired in war would be taken as wives by the victors. This did not account for peacetime bride-stealing. He noted two customs that he named *endogamy* and *exogamy*. The first term stood for a situation in which men were obliged to take wives within their tribe, the second for a situation where wives were taken from other tribes. Exogamy resulted from a shortage of women, and this, in turn, from female infanticide, which several peoples were known to practice. As, according to McLennan, savage tribes were generally in a state of hostility toward one another, the only way to obtain brides when women were scarce was by stealing them from the neighbors. Travelers in Australia described bride-stealing as still actually taking place. Some even maintained that pretty women were badly scarred from being captured many times! McLennan painted a sadistic picture: "The reader may imagine the extent to which, among these myriad hordes of savages, the women are knocked about by the men, accustomed to associate the acquisition of a wife with acts of violence and rapine."

Among the Khonds exogamy was the rule. Endogamy was considered incestuous and punished by death. The Kalmucks, the Circassians, and the Samoyeds of Siberia were unable to marry within the tribe. The Kamileroi of Australia were divided into castes with rules against marriage within them.

Exogamy arose gradually. The earliest human groups had no idea of kinship. The next step in McLennan's theory brought him into agreement with Bachofen: "The most ancient system in which the idea of blood relationship was embodied was a system of kinship through females only."

McLennan arrived at this conclusion by a system of deductive reasoning. He invented something that he called the Primitive Horde. In this Horde there was no pairing off between men and women. Its members were sexually undiscriminating. Promiscuity resulted in uncertainty of fatherhood and led to a system of kinship through the mother only. McLennan skipped rapidly over this phase because he had other ammunition up his sleeve. In India, the Aleutian Islands, and Ceylon, women were accustomed to marry several husbands at the same time. Following out his line of thought, he reasoned that female infanticide when it caused a scarcity of women could also result in such polyandry. This would be an intermediate stage between the sexual free-for-all of the Primitive Horde and monogamy. In the lower stage of polyandry, a woman took a miscellaneous group of husbands; in the second stage, which he considered higher, she married a group of brothers. The Bible supplied the custom that when a man died it was obligatory for a younger brother to marry his widow. This was an example of the symbolic survival of the second stage of polyandry. He also cited Lewis Morgan's statement (from the questionnaire the latter had sent all over the world) that among the Iroquois a man's brothers were considered equally fathers of his child. This was proof of polyandry in America.

McLennan criticized Sir Henry Maine for thinking that the patriarchal system had always existed. The Scotch lawyer was convinced that polyandry was a stage through which all of society had passed. Endogamy was harder to account for. Perhaps, he suggested, after a tribe had practiced bride-stealing for some time, and continued to reckon descent through the female line, enough spare males of largely alien blood would accumulate so that intermarriage could take place within the tribe. Family groups within the tribe might then become clans, consider themselves descended from a common ancestor, and practice an endogamy which was technically exogamy.

Although McLennan did not use the term *evolution*, his ideas suggest that he was already affected by Darwinism. He retains the distinction of being the first anthropologist to analyze the practices that he named for all time, endogamy and exogamy. His theory of marriage by capture has not stood up under later scientific investigation. In his own time he defended it violently, engaging in angry controversy. When he died in 1881 he was at work on a book that was meant to demolish Sir Henry Maine's patriarchal reasoning. *The Patriarchal Theory* was edited and published by his brother in 1885. His other chief opponent was Lewis Morgan, whose great book, *Ancient Society*, was under way in the early sixties. Morgan was developing a theory that would have bearing on all of the ideas just discussed.

Chapter 5

THE LABYRINTH OF KINSHIP

Concerning Lewis Henry Morgan (Part II)

■ By 1861 Morgan had accumulated forty-eight tables that recorded the precise terms used by as many tribes in describing their relatives.

While he was doing this the Darwinian revolution was gaining strength. Even more disturbing had been the discovery, in 1856, in the Neanderthal Valley near Düsseldorf, of a skull which resembled that of an ape in some respects and that of a man in others. Although it was waved away by many scholars as a freak, the alarming suspicion that man had not been created precisely in the Divine image began to be confirmed. The Bishop of Oxford's gibe at Huxley's grandmother no longer seemed so amusing.

Morgan, working independently, was piling up pages and pages of dry and repetitive facts. Although the man in the street might be indifferent to the exact term a central Australian applied to his maternal cousin, the Rochester lawyer was filled with fanatical enthusiasm. He was confident that by just such industrious compilation he would be able to explain the development of human society through the ages all over the world.

Schoolcraft, now no longer active, wrote encouragingly. He had tried, he said, to compare the religious heritages of the American Indian and the Asian primitives. Morgan's comparison of kinship systems in both hemispheres was a new approach that promised to be very important. The great pioneer was passing on the torch of investigation to his successor.

As we have seen, Schoolcraft believed that the Indians came originally from Asia. Other scientists such as Agassiz considered them as indigenous as the bison. Morgan inclined to agree with Schoolcraft and hoped by comparison of kinship systems to prove the Asiatic theory.

Morgan's book *Systems of Consanguinity of the Human Family* was published by the Smithsonian Institution in 1866 under the watchful eye of the Reverend Mr. McIlvaine. A six-hundred-page quarto volume, it compared all types of kinship classifications all over the world. It was not until he had nearly finished it that Morgan worked out the theory which he spent the rest of his life defending.

After comparing these kinship systems he thought he had found evidence of a series of customs and institutions which marked the development of human society "from a state of promiscuous intercourse to final civilization."

It is amusing to note with what horrified but fascinated insistence the Victorian anthropologists contemplated the sexual free-for-all that they attributed to primitive man.

Morgan maintained that every system of kinship, "spread out so as to show the several degrees of relationship, will be found to rest upon definite ideas." He held that the peoples of the world could be divided according to the method by which they described kinship. The first group used *descriptive* terms. That is, kin not in the direct line of descent had to be identified by combinations such as *brother-in-law, father-in-law,* etc. *Husband, wife, father, mother, brother, sister, son* and *daughter, grandfather, grandmother, grandson* and *granddaughter* were all descriptive of single, specific, blood or marriage relationship. This was the higher system, according to Morgan, used by Semitic peoples, some Turkish peoples, and the civilized groups of the western world.

The second division of the human race used *classificatory* kinship terms that divided their relatives into great, seemingly arbitrary classes and did not emphasize the actual facts of blood or marriage relationship. A man's clan brothers' sons were *his* sons. Likewise, the children of clan sisters and real sisters were all nephews and nieces. The races using this system included the North American Indians, some Asian Indian tribes, the Malayans, and some South Sea and Australian peoples. This whole group had remained at a fairly primitive level of culture.

Son, brother, sister, or *aunt,* in the classificatory sense, did not mean the same thing as similar words used in the western European sense. Why?

Morgan, from a point of view not unlike McLennan's, reasoned that the classificatory terms harked back to that fascinatingly dreadful state of affairs, the primitive sexual free-for-all. If a man considered all of his clan brothers' children to be his children, this must mean that at some time in the history of the human race individual paternity could not be established. Among the Iroquois, the children of clan sisters or real sisters were distinguished as nephews and nieces without regard to blood relationship. A child's mother's clan sisters were not aunts but additional mothers, and his father's clan brothers were also his fathers. It followed that at some stage all the men of one clan were permitted to sleep with all of the women in another clan. This happy state of affairs has been facetiously called "a thousand miles of wives." Morgan's hypothesis stood or fell on the assumption that the terms really meant what they said, although in his time actual pair marriage was already the rule among the Iroquois.

Following up this clue, Morgan also constructed a theoretical series.

1. *Promiscuous intercourse*
2. *Cohabitation of brothers and sisters*
3. *The communal family*
4. *Clan organization*
5. *Marriage between single pairs*
6. *The patriarchal family*
7. *Polyandry*
8. *The development of private property*
9. *Civilized marriage and the change to the descriptive system*

It went like this. Proof of primitive promiscuity was lacking, but Morgan, like McLennan, assumed that the Primitive Horde formed no permanent or distinct sexual attachments. This was followed by a series of "reforms." That brothers and sisters actually cohabited, he thought was indicated by the incestuous Egyptian royal house. Then, in the interests of eugenics, blood brothers and sisters ceased to cohabit, but a group of brothers and a group of sisters got together to form a sort of marriage club in which all of the men slept with all of the women. He believed he found evidence of this in Hawaii. Again, to avoid inbreeding and to improve the vigor of the stock, another reform took place. Clans were formed in which clan (not blood) brothers married all the clan (not blood) sisters. He had discovered that among the Iroquois a woman of the wolf clan, for example, could marry a man of any clan other than her own and that her children became members of her clan. Her sons must marry women of other clans, and were lost to her clan.

Morgan had also discovered that among the Iroquois property tended to be held not individually, but by a family group. He also knew that descent was reckoned and inheritance took place through the female line. He agreed with McLennan that this situation arose originally because in the thousand-miles-of-wives stage there was no way of identifying the individual father. He believed that after pair marriage was established, fatherhood became distinct; the males then became dominant and wished to hand down their property to their sons. Thus the patriarchal system arose. The latter also gave rise to polygamy in the case of a ruling class to which many wives stood for wealth and position. Polyandry, which Morgan called "a repulsive converse of polygamy," resulted from a scarcity of women. The final "reform" was, of course, Presbyterian monogamy.

Morgan insisted that the still existing classificatory terms could not be explained in any other way. He pointed out how obstinately the system endured and how easily it was understood by those who used it, even though it no longer had literal sexual validity.

What, then, explained its persistence?

In primitive ages family ties took the place of political organization. There was no state, no police system. A man had to depend upon his kin for the protection of both personal rights and property. The bonds between clan brothers, the ties of blood recognized through maternal descent, were the only human relationships upon which society could count. The system was democratic, and it worked. For this reason, although with the rise of pair marriage clan organization had become artificial, it nevertheless endured because it had proved its organizational value. This piece of reasoning was probably one of Morgan's most important achievements.

The distinction between classificatory and descriptive terms upon which Morgan based his theory has since been severely criticized. Although the clan organization of primitive tribes was a fact, Morgan was never able to explain the importance of the totem or animal emblem of the clan. Other scholars have denied primitive promiscuity. It has been suggested that he took too literally what was merely a symbolical extension of the meaning of words. After all, it is not unusual for a man to call a close friend a brother. The use of the term *Father* in addressing Roman Catholic priests is a similar example of a poetic metaphor.

In his own time Morgan's book created something of a sensation. Darwin, who had just published his own great work, praised it, as did Herbert Spencer. Sir Henry Maine wrote a cordial and interested letter. McLennan, whose explanation of exogamy it contradicted, called it "a wild dream, not to say nightmare of early institutions." Marriage by capture was understandable, but incest was indecent.

Morgan's hypothesis had the beauty of symmetry. He was able to place at the bottom of the ladder the types of marriage he found most distasteful. Even McIlvaine, scanning it closely for anything which might tend to weaken religious faith, announced happily that "another grand result of his labors is a demonstration that progress is a fundamental law of human society."

While writing his book, Morgan found time to run successfully for the New York State Assembly on the Republican ticket. He was a party-line politician who failed to be re-elected when his strongest backer was exposed as a participant in the Erie Railroad scandals.

After his book was published, Morgan went to Europe, met Darwin and Sir John Lubbock, and in Italy had an audience with the Pope. When the Pope held out his hand to be kissed, Morgan, the staunch Republican, said: "In America, we do not kiss a distinguished man's hand, we shake it." The Pope replied: "We will follow the American custom."

Although he had been an undiscriminating admirer of Grant all through that bewildered general's unhappy administration, after the Custer massacre in 1876 he came forward in defense of Sitting Bull. He pleaded for a sympathetic attitude toward the Indians. He felt that efforts should be made to teach them to be self-supporting and denounced a policy that either treated them as charity cases or shot them when they impeded the advance of the pioneers.

Morgan was essentially a humane person. Fond of animals, he

did not subscribe to the belief that they were created especially for the use of man. He thought they existed for their own happiness and welfare. The word *brute* offended him. "You ought not to use that word," he told McIlvaine, "it has a bad sense; you should call them mutes."

In the seventies he was working on his magnum opus. An anthropologist living in Australia, Lorimer Fison, had given him some new information, and he had extended and perfected his theory. In 1877 he published *Ancient Society or Researches in the Lines of Human Progress from Savagery through Barbarism to Civilization.*

He broke completely with the idea that savages were degenerate remnants of former civilizations, saying that this theory was not supported by fact. In his introduction he wrote: "It can now be asserted upon convincing evidence that savagery preceded barbarism in all the tribes of mankind, as barbarism is known to have preceded civilization." The degeneration theory, however, did not die easily, and we shall have more to say about it. Morgan concluded: "The history of the human race is one in source, one in experience, one in progress."

This was an evolutionary statement, but the Reverend Mr. McIlvaine congratulated himself that nowhere in the pages of the book did the word *evolution* appear. In fact, he made Morgan strike out one passage that seemed to endorse Darwin's views. For the rest, nothing in Morgan's work could offend a Christian, for nowhere in the Scriptures did McIlvaine discover "a revealed chronology."

Morgan's book contained a whole structure of social theory which, though it rested in part on the weak reed of kinship terminology, nevertheless presented new and penetrating insights. His theory of marriage remained the same except that he added much of Fison's material on the Kamileroi of Australia, who further complicated the clan system by subdividing their clans into marrying classes. Morgan stated flatly that all through the period of savagery and barbarism men were organized into tribes and clans or, as he now preferred to call them, *gentes.* He either ignored or was not familiar with those primitive groups which had a hereditary aristocracy.

Just as the family passed through various forms, the structure of property had evolved and changed. In savages the desire for possessions scarcely existed; in modern civilization it ruled humanity. "The organization of political society on a territorial basis," he wrote, "was the line of demarkation where modern civilization begins."

He then traced the Iroquois organization in great detail as the archetype of gentile or clan, non-territorial society. The word *gens* (Latin, from the root *gigno*, "to beget") was now his term for clan. It was identical with the Albanian *phrara*, the Greek *yévas*. North American Indian government rested upon the gens. The next unit was the phratry, an assemblage of related gentes united for the common welfare, next the tribe, and, finally, the confederation of tribes, all speaking the same language or nearly related languages. This was the democratic organization that had fascinated him ever since his initiation as a Seneca. There was no state, no propertied class, no hereditary aristocracy.

The characteristics of the gens were as follows:

1. *Right of electing its sachems and chiefs*
2. *Right of deposing its sachems and chiefs*
3. *Obligation not to marry within the gens*
4. *Group inheritance of property of the deceased*
5. *Obligation to help members of the gens, defend them, and redress their injuries*
6. *Right of giving names to its members*
7. *Right of adoption of strangers*
8. *Common religious rites*
9. *Common burial place*
10. *General council of the whole gens to approve or disapprove decisions of sachem and chiefs*

Because the system was matriarchal, a son could not succeed his father as chief or sachem. A sachem was a peace official, one being appointed by each gens. War chiefs were appointed for bravery, wisdom, and eloquence. A chief was the head of a tribe or group of gentes. A sachem was generally succeeded in office by his brother or his sister's son. There was normally about one chief to fifty people. A council of the gens or the entire tribe could depose a sachem or chief for unworthy conduct by "taking off the horns" with which he had been invested on election.

Children of deceased males did not inherit their property—they belonged to different gentes. Likewise, the wife did not inherit from the husband or vice versa. Property was inherited by the maternal relatives.

Such obligations as protection and revenge were assumed by the gens. War captives were often adopted into it. At the general council, every adult male and female had a vote. All chiefs took part in the tribal council and in the council of the confederacy.

The phratry was an association of two or more gentes of the same tribe mostly for social or religious purposes. The whole phratry turned out at funerals. In ball games they often formed separate teams that played against each other. By now Morgan was aware that in some tribes the gens claimed descent from the animal whose name it bore, and that its members were forbidden to eat the totem.

The tribe had a roughly defined territory of its own, spoke a dialect of the common language, and had a distinct government. The tendency of dialects to grow further apart eventually resulted in new tribes that went off to form separate colonies. Tribes, generally consisting of a few hundred or a few thousand individuals, fought fiercely with tribes of other language stocks. A tribe sometimes had a head chief, as did a confederacy. He was merely a provisional officer who functioned when the council was not in session. His authority was slight. (This was a situation never understood by the whites, and it gave rise to many tragic misunderstandings.)

There had to be unanimity in council for every public act. Vote was by tribes in council, and if there was no agreement, the matter was put aside. Agreements with foreign tribes were sealed by exchanging wampum belts. Theoretically a tribe was perpetually at war with any tribe with which it had not signed a treaty of peace.

Such was the picture of an early state of society held together by the bonds of kinship. "Liberty, equality, fraternity, though never formulated, were cardinal principles of the gens," wrote Morgan the capitalist, half regretful that the change to private property and territorial government had to come about.

He found this system operating in most North American Indian tribes and in other primitive areas, and he tried to prove its former existence in Mexico, a contention that later scholars have disputed. He also investigated classical literature and pointed out remnants of clan organization among the Greeks and the Romans. It was this clan background, he maintained, which served as a basis for Greek and Roman democracy. The Roman state degenerated when power was transferred to the upper propertied classes. However, modern governments with elective presidents and congresses were moving steadily forward in the direction of greater democracy.

Morgan's triumphant Americanism happily coalesced with his theory of social development, quaintly blind as he was to the Fisks and Goulds of his own day.

Ancient Society was an epoch-making book, the first of its kind. The reactions to it were mixed. Bachofen, the theorist of matri- archy, was naturally pleased, and dedicated his next book to Mor- gan with a cordial letter. Darwin could not accept primitive prom- iscuity, basing his objection on the sex habits of the gorilla. Maine, who had similar views on ownership of property, was delighted with the book. McLennan, who clung to marriage by capture, continued to sputter and fume. Morgan had added an appendix in which he called wife-stealing nonsense and exogamy a misunderstanding of the law of the gens. McLennan responded by insisting that Morgan's kinship terms had no meaning. They were merely "modes of addressing people" and had no sexual connotation.

Ironically enough, Friedrich Engels, the communist, used Mor- gan's book as a basis for his study *The Origin of the Family*. In- deed Morgan, the railroad magnate, because of his analysis of the evolution of property, has had more world-wide popularity among socialists and communists than among other groups.

Although his views on early marriage gave rise to decades of controversy, Morgan's distinction between kinship and territorial society was a permanent contribution and a brilliant piece of analysis. But for a certain lack of caution and objectivity, Morgan could have been the Darwin of social anthropology.

The Reverend Mr. McIlvaine, who preached Morgan's funeral sermon, remained faithful to the last, but had a few lingering doubts. During Morgan's last illness he questioned him concerning his religious convictions. Morgan, honest but tactful even in his last hours, said: "I do not claim to have freed my mind from all skeptical doubts—but my heart is with the Christian religion."

Chapter 6

DEGENERATION VERSUS
EVOLUTION

Concerning Sir John Lubbock

■ We have seen John Lubbock, the young botanist, fighting manfully at Darwin's side at the outset of his career. From botany his interest shifted to ancient remains. He wandered about the valley of the Somme collecting chipped flints, weapons which, scholars had now decided, had been shaped by men who lived before the beginning of recorded history. Lubbock also visited Switzerland, where other prehistoric men, living in lake dwellings, had tossed their garbage into the water. From the water, chipped flints, stone axes, even bits of basketry and pottery were being recovered by Swiss scholars.

He observed that some stone implements were cruder than others, and seemed, as they lay at the bottom of the deposits, to be older. He coined the terms *paleolithic* (Old Stone Age) and *neolithic* (New Stone Age). He was trying to imagine how these dim ancestors of civilized men might have looked and behaved. A crude spearhead or a club was scarcely more than an extension of the hand and arm of the ancient hunter. A smaller chipped triangle, which could be identified as an arrowhead, indicated a truly revolutionary invention, man making practical use of the fundamental laws of physics.

As a staunch pupil of Darwin he believed that civilization had developed from simpler origins. Perhaps by combining archeological evidence with observations drawn from the life of contemporary savages, a factual case could be made for the evolutionary point of view.

The argument as to whether civilization had evolved or had always existed with the primitives as miserable, sinful outcasts was not easily settled. The degeneration theory of savagery (that primitives *regressed* from the civilized state) had to be fought vigorously before social anthropology could progress.

Lubbock, the first Baron Avebury, is a convenient link between Darwin and the evolutionist or classical school of British anthropology. He is also a sympathetic example of the cultured British aristocrat. He made contributions to botany, archeology, and anthropology, found time to engage in a business career, and even stood for Parliament. In 1864, when he was already president of the Ethnological Society, he lectured at the Royal Institution on the antiquity of man. From these lectures came his book *Prehistoric Times.*

It contained pictures of the chipped flints, and the subtitle read: *As Illustrated by Ancient Remains and the Customs of Modern Savages.* The material on modern savages was taken from accounts by sea captains, travelers, and missionaries. Some of his quotations illustrate the highly colored and subjective testimony upon which early anthropologists had to rely.

"Feegeeans were the most inveterate cannibals and so fond were they of human flesh that the greatest praise they can bestow on any delicacy is to say it is as tender as a dead man. Nay, they were even so fastidious as to dislike the taste of white men, to prefer the flesh of women to that of men, and to consider the arm above the elbow and the thigh as the best joints. . . . Ra Undre-undre, chief of Raki-Raki, was said to have eaten nine hundred persons, permitting no one to share them with him."

Lubbock noted that New Zealand cannibalism was ritual. It destroyed the souls of enemies and endowed the eater with the strength and courage of the eaten. Therefore, "celebrated chiefs, however old and dry they might be, were preferred to plump young men or tender damsels." Summing up his descriptions of primitive customs, Lubbock said: "It is common opinion that savages are, as a general rule, only miserable remnants of nations once more civilized; but although there are some well established cases of national decay, there is no scientific evidence which would justify us in asserting that this is generally the case." He followed up this comment with a clear statement of his position. "The great principle of natural selection which in animals affects the body and seems to have little influence on the mind; in man affects the mind and has little influence on the body. In the first it tends mainly to the preservation of life; in the second to the improvement of the mind and consequently to the increase of happiness." Lubbock, like most of the early evolutionists, believed that the development of human society was *unilinear*, a progression upward as a whole, in a straight line

The year that his book was published he stood for Parliament. Friends had urged him to delay publication, but he refused. Because of his radical anthropological views, he was resoundingly defeated.

Undaunted, he went on to publish *The Origin of Civilization* in 1870, founded on more lectures before the Royal Society. The material in this book was drawn entirely from the study of primitive peoples, and is a summary of the state of ethnology in the late sixties. "I shall have to record many actions and ideas very abhorrent to us, so many in fact, that if I pass them without comment it is because I am reluctant to fatigue the reader by a wearisome iteration of disapproval." In comparison with Schoolcraft, Lubbock seems fairly timid. Perhaps he had been chastened by his political experience. He was aware that data reported by casual observers was not too trustworthy. He wrote: "When Labillardiere inquired of the friendly Islanders the word for 1,000,-000,000, they said 'laounouna' that is to say, 'nonsense,' while for the higher numbers, they gave him certain coarse expressions which he has gravely published in his table of numerals."

On the whole, he was inclined to accept McLennan's notion of marriage by capture (as against Morgan's theory, which he ignored). He was doubtful about early matriarchy, however, because he found most savage women in an inferior position. "The lowest races have no institution of marriage, true love is almost unknown among them." Indeed, to a Victorian the primitives seemed sadly lacking in the finer feelings. "Among savages, female virtue is, in many cases, but slightly regarded."

When it came to religion, his thinking was more original. "While savages," he wrote, "show us a melancholy spectacle of gross superstitions and ferocious forms of worship, the religious mind can not but feel a peculiar satisfaction in tracing up the gradual evolution of more correct ideas and of nobler creeds." Religions had one origin and passed through similar, if not identical stages, which he labeled as follows:

1. *Atheism—in which there is absence of any definite ideas on the subject.*
2. *Nature worship or totemism—in which natural objects are worshipped.*
3. *Shamanism—in which superior deities are more powerful than man and of a different nature, accessible to shamans (medicine men).*
4. *Idolatry—in which gods take on the nature of man, and are more powerful but amenable to persuasion.*
5. *Monotheism—in which a single deity is considered the author of creation, associated with moral ideas.*

Lubbock cited Schoolcraft for evidence of nature worship or *fetishism*, as he called it, taking the term from Auguste Comte. Shamanism he derived from material on the Eskimos, while idolatry he defined by interpreting mythology. The amount of evidence he assembled for his scheme was not, however, very impressive.

He was also interested in the origin of moral ideas. He criticized Herbert Spencer, who believed that moral feeling had been developed from inherited experience of what was useful, which, in turn, modified the nervous system. Lubbock's ethical sense recoiled at this Lamarckian explanation. Morality, he felt, was authoritarian, religious or civil, transmitted through parental authority. This was rather begging the issue. He had already committed himself to the gradual evolution of religion. Granted that moral precepts were transmitted by parental authority, how did they develop in the first place?

Lubbock continued to lecture, travel, and take part in British political life. Two years after his defeat in 1865 he again stood for Parliament and was defeated. In 1870 he tried again and was elected. Enlightened, with many interests, something of a popularizer, he was a typically well-rounded Victorian. Apart from his scientific work, he wrote agreeable books on the enjoyment of reading and the attainment of happiness. He was raised to the peerage as Baron Avebury in 1899. That he never ceased to take an interest in anthropology is proved by the publication in 1912 of *Marriage, Totemism and Religion,* only two years before his death.

It was his friend Edward Burnett Tylor (1832–1917) who put the science of anthropology on a firm basis and who once and for all destroyed the degeneration theory. Like Lubbock, he worked from a strictly evolutionary point of view. In his first anthropological book, *Researches into the Early History of Mankind and the Development of Civilization,* published in 1865, he took up the degeneration theory of primitive peoples. It had been most fully expressed by Comte Joseph de Maistre, an eighteenth-century apologist for the *ancien régime* and one of Rousseau's chief opponents. Rousseau's romantic rebellion had resulted in an uncritical admiration for the savage, who was held to live in a state of nature, superior to the conventions of civilization. Sex relations were free, and man followed the dictates of his instincts, which were sure to be benevolent. Maistre answered acidly that man could not exist in a state contrary to nature, that the nature of anything was as God wished it to be. Rousseau's "nature" was poetry without basis in fact. Society had always existed. The noble redskin, extolled by Rousseau, was a myth. The American savages, as was well known from accounts by observers, were repulsive brutes. His explanation for the condition of the savage, based on revealed religion, was as follows: "The savage represents, not a rudimentary state of society and culture, but a degraded state of both human nature and of human society, in a word, the social objectivation of original sin. Savage races came later than civilized races and represent their disintegration."

It was a simple argument; man had fallen, savages had fallen further. When Maistre attempted a more factual explanation, he lapsed into an easily disproved position. "One thing is sure, the savage is necessarily later in time than civilized man. For example, let us examine America. This country has every characteristic of a new land. But, since civilization is of great antiquity in the old countries, it follows that the savages who inhabited America at the time of the discovery descended from civilized man."

The religious opponents of evolution adhered to this line of thought. In 1856 Archbishop Whately of Dublin had published a paper, *The Origin of Civilization,* in which he said: "Men, left in the lowest or even anything approaching the lowest degree of barbarism . . . , never did and never can raise themselves unaided, into a higher condition."

Whately added that the New Zealanders, whom Tasman discovered in 1642, were found in just the same condition by Cook one hundred and twenty-seven years later. But, said Tylor, Tasman never set foot in New Zealand, and his testimony is only a page or so of hearsay evidence. Whately also mutilated a quote from Darwin on the Fuegians. The latter wrote: "Their skill in some respects may be compared to the instinct of animals—their canoe has remained the same for the last one hundred and fifty years." Whately failed to add what Darwin had also pointed out— that the Fuegians, by actually inventing the canoe, had done better than their neighbors across the strait, who were still using rafts.

It was true that the Central American Maya had declined, but Tylor believed that when the use of metals, pottery, flint and steel, higher tools and weapons was once fairly established, degeneration was an exception. Such an exception could generally be explained by conquest or some serious outside influence.

Tylor considered the issue important enough to devote some space to it in his great book, *Primitive Culture*. He argued that if stages in the evolution of tools, customs, and beliefs could be found (he later cited them), the presumption was that a chain of development was present. The degeneration theory he criticized as requiring divine revelation to explain civilization. He finally repeated that there was no reliable evidence to show that a civilized community had regressed to a truly primitive state. No prehistoric metal tools were to be found in areas where primitives now had no metal tools. Moreover, prehistoric archeology could show tools cruder than any now existing.

Tylor marshaled the arguments and the evidence against degeneration which are now accepted by anthropology. It was an important task, but only a minor facet of his work. His major contributions were in the field of religion and mythology, and his career as a whole was a highly significant one for the new science.

Chapter 7

THE HAPPY VOYAGERS

Concerning Sir Edward Burnett Tylor (Part I)

■ In 1855 a tall, blond young Englishman was riding on a Havana omnibus. The vehicle creaked and groaned over the cobbles, closely packed with talkative humanity, baskets, bundles, and even chickens. The young man listened with amused interest to the clatter of conversation, stretching his Spanish to the utmost, and tucked in his long legs as descending passengers stumbled over them. Suddenly he caught the intonations of an English voice. The speaker was using *thee* and *thou*. The young man craned his neck. He saw a slightly eccentric-looking gentleman wearing a white hat, holding a white umbrella, sitting in the rear of the bus. Presently the seat next to the man in the white hat was vacated. The young man made his way to it and introduced himself as a compatriot and a fellow Quaker.

They shook hands.

The young man was Edward Burnett Tylor. The chance meeting was the turning-point in his life.

Tylor was the son of a well-to-do Quaker liberal who owned a brass foundry. After a grammar-school education the boy went into the family business. In 1855 he was threatened with tuberculosis. His parents sent him on a trip to the United States to escape the English climate and to recover his health. He wandered about the young republic, sightseeing. From New Orleans he drifted down to Havana. The gentleman in the white hat was Henry Christy, a wealthy banker and a passionate antiquarian. He had traveled all over the Orient, and now he was exploring the new world. Remains of ancient man, seeds of rare plants, the weapons of savages, all attracted his excited attention. His life was spent collecting. At his death he left a vast assemblage of archeological specimens to the British Museum.

Lured by the remains of Aztec and Toltec civilizations, Christy was on his way to Mexico. His was a compelling personality and his enthusiasm was infectious. In a very short time he had converted young Tylor (who was twenty-four) to his interests and had persuaded him to join him on the trip to Mexico.

The two were excellent travelers. Shrewd, interested in everything, having a sense of humor, not dismayed by the discomforts of a backward country, they had a delightful time. Mexico exercises a subtle charm. Tylor recorded it in his first book, *Anahuac or Mexico and the Mexicans, Ancient and Modern*, which he published in 1856. Although not a university graduate (he used to boast that he never took an examination in his life), Tylor proved himself a born writer. *Anahuac* is a classic travel book; indeed, parts of it hold good for Mexico today.

Christy, he wrote, had been botanizing in tropic jungles, visiting copper mines and coffee estates (mixing his hobby with business, no doubt), and talking to all sorts of people from whom information could be got "from consuls to retired slave dealers and assassins." Before leaving Cuba, the two made a trip to the Isle of Pines. There was a law in Cuba at the time prohibiting a husband from leaving town without a passport containing his wife's permission. This quaint provision must have been an insurance against desertion. A Cuban got aboard the boat with what proved to be a false passport. As the boat was about to leave, the enraged wife steamed up to the pier, red in the face from running. The captain produced the passport, which she promptly tore up. The delinquent husband ran for his life. Then an obstacle race occurred around the deck while the passengers, including Tylor and Christy, shouted with laughter. The hard-pressed husband finally escaped by climbing on top of the paddlebox, and the steamer moved off, leaving the wife shaking her fist on the pier.

The travelers enjoyed the Isle of Pines. It was curious to see pines and palms growing side by side. Although the natives dressed in white and sang charmingly to the accompaniment of guitars, the romantic atmosphere was slightly marred by the fierce appetite of the mosquitoes. Tylor shot a woodpecker, intending to skin it, but a horde of army ants entered through an open window and destroyed his specimen. He also tried the unfortunate experiment of nibbling castor-oil nuts. The natives told him he must have eaten an uneven number—the second nut neutralized the effect of the first, and so on.

Tylor met a hilarious and happy Roman Catholic priest who seemed beloved by his parishioners. The Quaker tolerantly decided that the Roman missionaries were often more successful than Protestants because the latter "go to India with the best intentions and set to work at once flinging their doctrines at the natives before they have learned in the least how to understand what the natives' minds are like or how they work."

The young Quaker's own mind was remarkably objective. The Negroes of Cuba pleased him. They were said to be lazy, but he did not see why they should work harder in order to buy (doubtless British) manufactured goods. "If we measure prosperity by the enjoyment of life, their condition is an enviable one." They were a gay, musical people. To his surprise, after his experience in the United States, marriage between Negroes and whites was taken as a matter of course. He noted with indignation that the slave trade was still secretly going on, although British gunboats were trying to put an end to it.

The two Quakers took a ship for Mexico which stopped briefly at a small town in Yucatán. There Tylor saw Indians for the first time, "grave, taciturn men with their brown complexions, bright eyes and strikingly aquiline noses" which made the belief that they were the lost ten tribes of Israel seem not so far-fetched. The theory was not satisfactory, but the Indians were fascinating. He wrote: "Crude as these ideas are, one feels a good deal of interest in the first inquiry that set men thinking seriously about the origin of races, and laid the foundation of the science of ethnology."

Races and institutions, puzzling exotic ways of life—all this was a new field. The whole range of human culture bristled with tantalizing questions. Where did the Mexican race come from? How did their civilization develop? He was to visit the awe-inspiring ruins of their temples studded with great heads of serpents and cabalistic designs. Strange gods and spirits seemed to hover over this fantastic country where the past lived on beside the present. All at once European civilization seemed but a brief moment in the vast multiplicity of forms and beliefs that men had created through the ages. Above all, how did so cruel and terrifying a religion as that of the Aztecs, in which hearts were ripped from the bodies of war captives, take shape in the human mind?

When the travelers arrived at Veracruz, they found that there were two rival Mexican presidents. Comonfort, the incumbent, had decided to replenish the empty treasury by depriving the clergy of some of their privileges and wealth. Don Antonio Haro y Ra-

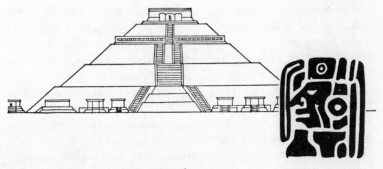

Pyramid and stamp seal: Teotihuacán.

mírez had been set up by the clergy at Puebla as a counter-president. Comonfort was conducting a rather vague siege of that town. There were false reports of battles. The air buzzed with rumors. Tylor noted them all down, slightly amused but not at all perturbed. He and Christy found cochineal insects on cactuses, specimens to them as interesting as Mexican politics.

On their way up to Mexico City past Orizaba, in a stagecoach called a *diligence*, they also observed dozens of whirling sand pillars. Thirty feet in diameter and four hundred feet high, the *molino de viento* drifted about, carrying with it small stones and leaves.

They detoured Puebla to avoid the siege. All along the route in the inns at which they stopped they were told horror stories of highway robbery. A diligence had been held up only a few days before. The two Quakers decided to be robbed docilely. At one point, seeing rough-looking men on the road, they began slipping their valuables into crevices in the cushions of the diligence, only to learn that the suspicious characters were Comonfort's soldiers.

As they climbed to the top of the sierras it began to grow chilly. The air grew thin and pure. Snowcapped peaks loomed above them. From the edge of the winding road the valleys fell away in abysses thousands of feet deep. At last they paused on the crest and looked down into the valley of Mexico. Cortés must have been in their minds as they first viewed that fruitful plain with its maguey, its cornfields, and its pink and blue churches.

Christy suddenly leaped down from his seat on top of the diligence. His sharp eye had spotted an arrowhead, a genuine Aztec relic. He was delighted with his first contact with ancient Mexican civilization.

The descent was terrifying. They plunged at a trot down a road that consisted of steps a foot deep. On top of the coach, Christy and Tylor clung to the handrails for their lives and listened to the inside passengers "howling for mercy as they were shot up to the roof which knocked them back into their seats."

From their base in Mexico City they made numerous trips to ruins situated near miserable hamlets. Tylor, like many visitors to Mexico since, was impressed by the contrast between gaudy baroque churches and the cheerless adobe huts of the people. Palm Sunday in Mexico City was an initiation into local holiday customs. Fourteen mestizos were killed in knife battles. Tylor thought that full-blooded Indians were more peaceable. He saw effigies of Judas being burned in a fiesta. "We had unexpectedly come upon an old custom of which our processions and burning of Guy Fawkes in England are merely an adaptation." Here was something to think about. A folk custom could change its outward appearance from one country to another and yet preserve something recognizable. What was the basic significance? Was it truly a Catholic festival that had somehow been modified by a political event in England, or was it still older? Were other apparently pointless folkways related to one another? What was their significance in the development of society? It was a problem not to be solved immediately, but somewhere in the back of Tylor's mind it was filed away for future reference.

At their hotel, for breakfast, they had tortillas and pulque. "Pulque . . . looks like milk and water and has a mild smell and taste of rotten eggs. Tortillas are like oat cakes but made of Indian corn meal, not crisp, but soft and leathery. We thought them dreadfully nasty for a day or two; then we could just endure them, then we came to like them, and before we left the country we wondered how we should do without them."

Christy, always the eager botanist, secured two pits of the fruit of the mamey, which was new to him. He put them in the tail pockets of his coat, from which one was stolen, the thief evidently thinking it a snuffbox. Tylor was troubled by the general dishonesty. He ascribed it to the mentality of an enslaved people and the confessional system of the Roman Church. He felt that the priests made little effort to raise the ethical level, but merely absolved their thieving parishioners with stock phrases.

The two Quakers visited a bullfight, finding that the matadors were unskillful. Lassoing and throwing the bull pleased them more. Everyone in Mexico carried a revolver. Tylor, the peaceful Quaker, had already become acquainted with the custom in the still pioneer United States. He provided himself with a five-barreled one.

On trips into the *tierra caliente* Christy wore a white turban, relic of his Oriental travels, and carried the white umbrella. The elbows of Tylor's jacket and the seat of his trousers had worn through. He bought a leather jacket and trousers and a gray felt hat, stiff as a boiler plate, with a silver serpent for a band. He wore a red silk sash around his waist which held up his trousers "and interfered with his digestion." He carried a serape, under which he slept. He was proud of his *ranchero* costume, which he found highly practical.

The travelers visited the hill of flints, a deposit of obsidian from which the Aztecs chipped sharp sacrificial knives, flints for war clubs, and even razors. Tylor compared the flint-chipping process with that used by the ancient Scandinavians of the kitchen middens and by the North American Indians, and wondered if the Mexicans had derived the craft from European sources. He and Christy studied the pyramids of Teotihuacán and sketched a corbel arch in an ancient bridge. Mexican saddles, on which they rode about the country, were a novelty to them. The basketlike design had its uses. Christy used to let his reins lie loose upon his horse's neck while he made notes.

Votive offerings of hair, teeth, rags, and ribbons hung in a tree reminded Tylor of a similar custom in Brittany, where locks of hair were hung up in chapels to charm away disease. Here, again, was an odd similarity. Brittany peasants and Mexican Indians were using parts of the body as a charm to ward off disease. This had certainly nothing to do with Catholicism. It was a kind of magic.

What did the tree have to do with it? Tylor filed it away with the Judas-burning. Someday perhaps he would work out a theory. . . . Meanwhile, he and Christy discussed the climatic theory of cultural development. This was a typically European view that only in temperate zones had progress been made in civilization. Christy and Tylor had seen vast and imposing ruins. In the United States there was nothing like them. It was nonsense to think that the Aztecs had first shaped their civilization in the United States and then transported it south. Theory did not deserve publication unless it rested upon a solid foundation of facts.

Tylor included in his book a history of the Aztecs and careful descriptions of the ruins he had seen and the specimens collected by Christy. The dauntless scientists even climbed Popocatepetl and descended into its crater.

Tylor's *Wanderjahr* was coming to an end. He and his friend had seen Mexico, studied its ruins, and observed an amateurish civil war. Tylor was beginning to be homesick, and Christy was planning to push on up to Hudson Bay.

With nostalgia, for he had been affected by Mexico's melancholy charm, Tylor embarked at Veracruz after saying good-by to his companion. His final comment has been echoed by many travelers since: "It seems hard to be always attacking the Roman clergy but of one thing we can not remain in doubt—that their influence has had more to do than anything with the doleful ignorance which remains supreme in Mexico." He was sure the country would soon be absorbed by the United States.

Tylor's American adventure ended the romantic period of his life. The threatened tuberculosis was successfully arrested. Perhaps boredom with the brass foundry had been more to blame than any organic weakness. He had sufficient means to devote himself to research. A couple of years after his return he married a Quaker girl, Anna Fox, and finally settled down to a scholarly existence at Oxford.

The Mexican episode and Henry Christy had shown him where his interests lay. In addition, contact with a remote and alien civilization had given him a breadth of outlook unlike that of students of culture who confined themselves to Biblical or classical sources. The Judas-burning and the votive offering were not forgotten. In the years that followed he became an adventurer once more, an adventurer in the uncharted regions of folk custom and prehistory.

Chapter 8

THE NATURAL HISTORY OF GHOSTS

Concerning Sir Edward Burnett Tylor (Part II)

▪ Edward Tylor in his prime was described as tall, handsome as a Greek god (he wore a Jovian beard), gentle at heart, and at the same time possessing the hard, keen, penetrating intelligence of the naturalist of genius.

His Olympian figure looms large in the history of social anthropology. He is credited with having made it into a science. All of his writing is pervaded by a warmly human outlook, a serene optimism, and a largeness of spirit typical of the great Victorians.

First of all, he formulated a definition of culture. "Culture or civilization is that complex whole which includes knowledge, belief, art, morals, law, custom, and any other capabilities and habits acquired by man as a member of society. The condition of culture among the various societies of mankind, in so far as it is capable of being investigated on general principles, is a subject for the study of the laws of human thought and action. On the one hand, the uniformity which so largely pervades civilization may be ascribed, in a great measure, to the uniform action of uniform causes; while on the other hand its various grades may be regarded as stages of development or evolution, each the outcome of previous history, and about to do its proper part in shaping the history of the future."

This expresses the idea of unlinear evolution current in his time, but a fundamental caution in all of Tylor's judgments saved him from the passionate errors of such theorists as McLennan and Morgan.

He went on to elaborate his definition of social anthropology as a branch of history. "At all times historians, so far as they have aimed at being more than mere chroniclers, have done their best to show not merely succession but connection among the events they record." German scholars such as Gustav Klemm had written what they called cultural history, but their books consisted merely of consecutive descriptions of the races of man with no attempt to analyze institutions or to point out stages in the progress of civilization. To Tylor, social anthropology was history and something more. From his time to the present this branch of knowledge has extended between the two poles of history and science without ever being able to disregard either point of view. It was Tylor who first defined this area of investigation.

His method was of far-reaching significance.

Recurrence was the test of a piece of factual evidence. If a similar belief or custom could be found in different cultures in many parts of the world, he felt that it was a valid clue to reconstructing the prehistory of human society. McLennan had had a similar notion, but no one before Tylor had seined up such vast netfuls of evidence before venturing upon an interpretation. Those who followed him did the same, and the works of this school are huge tomes in which a thread of theory is pursued through hundreds of pages of data gathered from every imaginable source. The weakness of the method lay in the evaluation of evidence plucked out of context, and in the fact that much of the material, at a time when there were almost no trained field workers, came from amateur observers. Nevertheless, recurrence was a tool that became part of the standard equipment of anthropology.

In addition to recurrence, Tylor formulated the doctrine of *survivals*. McLennan had talked of the symbolic meaning of certain social customs, but Tylor analyzed the phenomenon more closely. "Meaningless customs must be survivals, they had a practical or at least a ceremonial intention when and where they first arose, but are now fallen into absurdity from having been carried on into a new state in society where the original sense had been discarded."

His was thus a two-way approach to an area of the past for which there was no direct evidence, which had to be reconstructed by inference: first, by studying the customs of contemporary primitives whose stage of culture could be considered parallel to early society, and, second, by studying survivals still extant in contemporary folklore.

A Serbian legend, for instance, recounted the hostility of a demon who at night razed a wall that three hundred workmen built by day. It was finally decided that a workman's wife would have to be built into the wall to appease the demon. It was done, but the poor woman begged that an opening be left in the wall for her to suckle her child. The opening was left for a year. Today the tomb of the mother is marked by a stream of milky water which trickles down the wall of the fortress of Skadra. This legend indicated that these people had once practiced human sacrifice to appease the gods. Similar superstitions occurred in Scotland, Germany, and Denmark. In Bohemia it was thought unlucky to save a man from

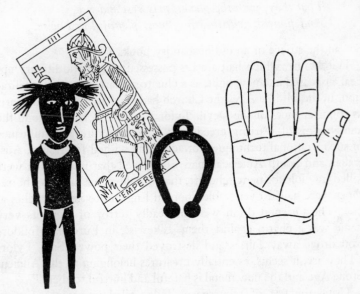

A South Seas image, a tarot card, a horseshoe, and the palm of a human hand.

drowning. Fishermen believed the water demon would spoil their luck. This also was a survival of human sacrifice, this time to a water god.

Magic, in particular, was a survival related to early forms of religion. The North American Indian placed the shoulderblade of a porcupine in the fire and interpreted the resulting cracks, a form of divination. Palmistry and Tarot fortune-telling cards were psychologically similar. The divining-rod, used to find water or precious metals, was in the same category.

Astrology was a degenerate form of early magical belief. Among its classical precepts were: "To set eggs under the hen at the new moon (waxing—growth), root up trees when the moon is on the wane, and after midday. The Lithuanian precept to wean boys on a waxing moon, no doubt to make the boys sturdy, but the girls on a waning moon to make them slim and delicate, is a fair match for the Orkney Islanders' objection to marrying except with the growing moon, while some even wish for a flowing tide."

> *Sowe peason and beans in the wane of the moon*
> *Who soweth sooner, he soweth too soon:*
> *That they, with the planet, may rest and rise,*
> *And flourish with bearing, most plentiful and wise.*

So ran the advice of an old husbandry book.

Witchcraft, which had always possessed a romantic literary appeal, appeared in a new light, as a clue to an earlier state of civilization. In the Middle Ages the Church had stigmatized the black arts as appurtenances of the Devil. Tylor was able to look beyond the antagonisms of warring creeds and trace the cultural significance of such irrational techniques for achieving wished-for results. Australian and South American natives believed that unless men were killed by violence or witchcraft, they would never die. Iron horseshoes were nailed over stable doors in England to keep witches at bay. The Oriental djinn were in deadly terror of iron; its very name was a charm against them. Likewise, in European folklore iron drove away fairies and destroyed their power. Said Tylor: "They are, it seems, essentially creatures belonging to the Ancient Stone Age and the new metal is hateful and hurtful to them."

Using the test of recurrence, Tylor piled up proof of great similarities among superstitions and apparently meaningless customs all over the world. It seemed clear that the same habits of mind persisted among the peasants and among the contemporary primitives.

Tylor's early observations in Mexico had borne fruit. He felt he had tapped a source of study which had endless possibilities. It all led toward an investigation of the nature of religion. Previously religion, in the sense of worship or belief in supernatural entities or powers, had remained in the hands of the philologists and literary critics, who contented themselves with collecting Oriental, classic, and Teutonic mythology. Lubbock's evolutionary scheme had rested mostly on speculation. Would the new tools of recurrence and survival make it possible to work out a soundly documented reconstruction of the mind of early man confronted with the mysteries of nature?

Tylor resolved to try.

He examined the nature of magic, beginning with the doll. Toys resemble real objects: dolls, wooden soldiers, Noah's arks are examples. A child's mind, more imaginative than an adult's, needs less to work with. "Bits of wood can be dragged about, representing a ship at sea or a coach on a road." To this he compared "a native woman in Van Diemen's land arranging several stones that were flat and oval and about two inches wide and marked in various directions with red and black lines." These represented absent friends. African women carried dolls in memory of dead children. From this Tylor arrived at a fundamental principle: "Men in a low stage of culture very commonly believe that between the object and the image of it there is a real connection which does not arise from a merely subjective process in the observer, and that it is accordingly possible to communicate an impression to the original through the copy." European folk believed that witches could cause disease by sticking pins into a wax figure of the victim. Algonquin medicine men made an image of a deer and shot arrows into it to insure good hunting. Primitive Catholic peasants beat the images of saints who failed to answer their prayers.

This was a first step in the investigation of primitive mentality.

In his great book, *Primitive Culture* (1871), Tylor continued along the same lines. He found evidence to show that savages endowed almost everything with life and human feelings. In old English law not only the beast that killed a man, but also the cartwheel that ran over him or the tree that fell on him and killed him was given to God by being forfeited and sold to the poor. In Germany there was a custom of "telling the bees" of the death of the master of the house. Even the beasts in the stall had to be informed, and every sack of corn had to be shaken and touched so that they might know the master or mistress was gone. This habit of mind appeared all over the world. The Eskimos called the stars of Orion's belt "The Lost Ones," seal-hunters who had lost their way. Waterspouts, which the Japanese saw often off their coast, were thought to be long-tailed dragons flying in the air. The Zulus were afraid to wash in large pools: there were rainbows in them, and if they caught a man they would eat him. Even disease, in a Russian myth, was given life in the form of the Pest Maiden.

This tendency to see life in all of the external world had been noted before and called *fetishism* by Auguste Comte in his *Philosophie de Positivisme* (1851–4). The word came from the Portuguese *feitico*, meaning a charm, and was applied to relics, rosaries, and images of the fifteenth century which were thought to have magical properties. Portuguese explorers in West Africa used it to describe stone figures and objects worshipped by the natives. It was popularized by C. de Brosses, author of *Du culte des dieux fétiches* (1760), and was used by Comte to cover his theory of early religion. "The theological period of humanity could begin no otherwise than by a complete and usually very durable state of pure Fetichism, which allowed free exercise to that tendency of our nature by which Man conceives of all external bodies as animated by a life analogous to his own with a difference of mere intensity." A savage, for instance, would believe that a watch was a live animal. Comte thought fetishism could develop as far as star-worship without a priesthood. He was convinced that it preceded polytheism and monotheism. This was a simple but purely speculative theory.

Tylor perhaps owes something to Comte, but he was working along subtler lines. Disagreeing sharply with Lubbock, he did not believe that any tribe with no religious belief or worship whatsoever could be found. The testimony of missionaries was biased. "They attribute irreligion to tribes whose doctrines are unlike theirs, in the same manner as theologians have so often attributed atheism to those whose deities differed from their own."

The tendency to see life in the external world existed among the simplest cultures. It might include deities, a doctrine of souls, and a future life, yet contain no moral attitude. Tylor was still fascinated by the phenomenon of the doll used for magical effect. The key to the problem lay in an attitude of mind, an attitude toward animate or inanimate objects outside the self. Turning it all over in his mind, he arrived at what has been called his dream theory.

Such races as the Algonquins, Zulus, and Tasmanians all had a word for the shade or ghost. West Australians, Greenlanders, and

Malays equated the soul with the breath. Contemporary Tyrolese peasants believed that a man's soul issued from his mouth like a little white cloud. The North American Indians, New Zealanders, Burmese, Zulus, and aborigines of South Guinea were visited by ghosts of ancestors during sleep. There was also the modern superstition of second sight, by which people appeared to those dear to them when dying or in peril. Homer described the twitter of ghosts. The Algonquins described a ghost's voice as having a cricket's chirp. The New Zealanders called them the whistlers.

Then, too, most savage races felt that animals had souls. The Pawnees killed a warrior's horse so that he might follow his dead master, the Arabs a camel, the Hindus a black cow at a Brahmin's funeral. A survival, the leading of an army officer's horse behind his bier, derives from the same custom.

The belief extended to inanimate things: thus an Egyptian Pharaoh's goods, a Tasmanian's spear, a Greenlander's kayak and arrows were buried in their tombs.

Death was strange and inexplicable. Something left the body. The tendency to dream of those no longer living gave rise to the idea that whatever had left the body, a projection, copy, or insubstantial essence, still existed. Tylor also believed, harking back to the image of the doll, that the highly imaginative savage mind did not distinguish clearly between the imagined and the real, the animate and the inanimate. Hence unexplained psychic phenomena *were* real.

Tylor called his theory *animism*. It differed from Comte's fetishism in that it implied a *detachable* spiritual essence. It was also concerned with the mystery and terror of death, which Comte had disregarded.

From animism came the idea of the hovering dead who might affect the living for good or evil. According to the Greeks, the souls of dead men not given proper burial would wander in a dismal crowd along the banks of Acheron. The Iroquois and the New Zealanders believed that the souls of unburied men or those killed in battle would not rest. As the Slavs put it: "Ha, with a shriek, the spirit flutters from the mouth, flies up to a tree, hither and thither, until the dead is burned."

The spirits of the dead were frightening and perhaps dangerous. The Aleutian islanders thought they walked unseen among the living and accompanied them on hunting trips. The Hottentots of

Africa abandoned a dead man's house and avoided entering lest the ghost should be inside. The Yakuts of Siberia let the hut of a dead man fall to pieces. The modern superstition of the haunted house is a survival.

The idea of the disembodied spirit developed in two directions: that of transmigration, and that of a future life.

In the first case, the Algonquins, for example, buried dead children by the wayside so that their souls might pass into potential mothers who might be traveling by that route. The African Yorubas greeted a newborn baby with the salutation "Thou art come?" because they were convinced an ancestral soul had returned. Such a belief had been known to lead African Negroes to commit suicide when enslaved, in the hope they would thus return to their own country. An Eskimo widow lived on bird's meat, refusing to touch walrus flesh, forbidden to her by the *angekok* (medicine man) because the soul of her husband had entered into a walrus. The Tlascalans of Mexico believed that after death the nobles would become singing birds, while the spirits of commoners would pass into weasels and beetles. Transmigration in its highest form, perfected by the Hindus, held that those who had done evil would migrate downward into the bodies of lower animals, while those who had been virtuous would ascend to higher and higher forms until they reached freedom.

The philosophy of a future life was perhaps developed from the notion of the dead inhabiting the grave or residing near it and still requiring food. The Algonquins made offerings of food to a dead ancestory; the Hurons were certain that the dead came to eat the leftovers after the villagers had finished a meal. In the Congo the natives made a channel into the grave down to the mouth of the corpse, and every month they poured food and drink through it. The Turanians of Northern Asia put food and napkins on the grave, saying: "Rise at night and eat your fill. You have napkins to wipe your mouths." In Ovid's time the *manes* were fed on fruits, grains of salt, and corn soaked in wine. There was also an old English begging rhyme:

> *Soul, soul, for a soul a cake,*
> *Pray you, Mistress, a soul a cake.*

A less material interpretation of the land of the dead pictured it under the earth. Wainamoinen, the Finnish hero, visited the land of the dead under the earth, as did Dionysius to bring back Semele, and Orpheus to regain Eurydice. In Christian mythology Christ descended into Hades to release Adam and Eve and the prophets.

A more cheerful picture was that of the earthly paradise. In Mexican Tlocan crops of maize, pumpkins, and tomatoes never failed. The Australians said the soul went to the land of the setting sun, an island northwest of Tonga. The Greeks spoke of the Island of the Blest. Procopius identified this with a Frankish legend in which the island was Brittany. Frankish fishermen had the task of transporting souls. The ones chosen for each night remained at home until there came a knock on the door and the voice of someone unseen called to them. "Then, without delay, rising from their beds, compelled by an unknown power, they go down to the beach and there they see boats, not their own but others, lying ready but empty of men. Going on board and taking the oars, they find that by the burden of the multitude of souls embarked, the vessel lies low in the water, the gunwale within a finger's breadth of it. In an hour they are at the opposite shore, though in their own boats they would hardly make the voyage in a night and a day. When they reach the island, the vessel becomes empty till it is so light that only the keel touches the water. They see no man on the voyage, no man at the landing, but a voice is heard that proclaims the name, rank, and parentage of each newly arrived passenger, if women, those of their husbands."

The next world might be a continuance or reflection of this one, or a place of retribution in which punishments and rewards were meted out. Among Indians and savages it was generally thought to be the first. More highly complicated religions such as Buddhist, Moslem, and Christian were examples of belief in the second. Tylor felt that as savagery gave way to barbarism, the doctrine of the hovering ghost or transmigration gave way to more philosophical concepts and life after death ceased to require local geography. The idea of continuance having given rise to rewards and punishments, belief in ghosts gradually degenerated into folklore and superstition.

"The ideas of souls, demons, deities, and any other classes of spiritual beings are of a similar nature throughout, the concept of souls being the original one of the series." Ancestor-worship being the earliest form of worship, there was a progression from simple propitiation of the dead to their deification. The Zulus, the Veddas of Ceylon, the Japanese, the Chinese, the Romans all worshipped their ancestors. Christian saints were an example of deification of the dead. To sum up, the dead received worship from the larger half of mankind. It seemed likely that this shed light on primitive times.

The theory that souls could exist independently of the dead was used by Tylor to explain other branches of religion. The morbid state of psychological possession was accounted for by the notion of an alien spirit that had taken up residence in the body. "This is the savage theory of possession and obsession which has been for ages and still remains the dominant theory of disease and inspiration among lower races."

The New Zealand exorcist, finding the path by which a disease spirit came from below to feed on the vitals of a sick relative, would persuade it by a charm to get onto a flax stalk and creep back home. The Dakotas of North America were accustomed to recite charms to the sound of a gourd rattle, sucking at the seat of the pain to get the spirit out. Such ceremonies were common to Patagonia, West Africa, Ceylon, and the Fiji Islands. A South Sea islander would have understood the Delphic oracle. The Catholic ceremony of exorcism was a survival.

Tylor proposed to narrow down the use of the word *fetishes* to the use of inanimate objects in religious ceremonies. They could be thought to have a live spirit embodied in them. Medicine men sometimes extracted diseases from their patients in the form of a thorn, a stone, or a morsel of bone, the spirit of the disease being embodied in the object. In Thuringia a string of rowan berries touched by a sick person imparted the disease to someone else. In modern European folklore a person afflicted with warts touched an ash tree, saying: "Ash tree, ash tree, pray buy this wart of me."

The Polynesians preserved the bones of dead relatives because they contained the spirits of the dead. The Mandans talked to the skulls of departed kinfolk. Relics of saints were a survival of fetish-worship.

Brazilians set up their maracas (rattles) and burned incense before them. North American Indians had *medicine* fetishes: skin or claws of animals or birds, stone knives and pipes. These suggested a transition phase to idolatry. The stick or stone would gradually be painted to look anthropomorphic. Idolatry, for Tylor, belonged neither to the highest nor to the lowest culture. The Jews forbade it, the Christians revived it. Also, it appeared, some idols were originally portraits of spirits and acquired the property of fetishes. The beating of saints by Catholic peasants indicated fetish psychology.

In his anxiety to fit everything into the scheme of animism, Tylor tended to underemphasize the materialistic and practical element of the savage mind. The fetish can be regarded as a mere implement of magic and hardly needs a resident spirit to explain it. Tylor was honest enough to admit this. On the whole, he felt that magic was more closely related to science than to the development of truly religious feeling.

The worship of the totem as a sacred thing, either to be eaten ceremonially or never to be eaten, was also a stumbling-block. Tylor again admitted that religious feeling might arise because of a feeling of awe toward the animal itself.

Although Tylor's scheme did not quite succeed in encompassing all the complicated aspects of religious and magical phenomena, it was an impressive and well-reasoned analysis of primitive psychology and far more general in application than anything that had been suggested before. When he came to interpret mythology, however, his theory required stretching, even though it had been developed mainly as a reaction against the prevailing attitude toward the myth. Before discussing his work in this field, it is necessary to pay a visit to the rival camp.

Chapter 9

DAWN'S ROSY FINGERS

Concerning Sir Edward Burnett Tylor (Part III)

■ Ever since men passed beyond the stage of communication by emotional grunts or yells, ever since language gained the power of narrating an event or painting a word picture, men have told one another stories. And, strangely enough, the very oldest literatures were not simple, down-to-earth chronicles of everyday events but a tissue of magic and marvels. In them, gods and heroes perform impossible and wonderful feats; beasts, birds, trees, stones, and even the abstract forces of nature become actors in fantastic dramas. For centuries, passed down from generation to generation, shaped and reshaped by countless retellings, the myths lived in the mouths of the people.

In the 1820's Schoolcraft was amazed to discover a rich oral literature among the simple savages of North America. He was, as we have seen, acute enough to realize that they were the key to vast areas of primitive thinking.

What did they mean? How did they grow? Why did they fall into certain patterns?

German philologists of the early nineteenth century who had concerned themselves with the origin of the Teutonic languages had discovered their affinities with Greek, Latin, and Sanskrit. They posited an ancient Aryan race speaking an ancestral Eurasian tongue. From language it was an easy step to the study of folk sayings and myths. In 1835 Jacob Grimm published his *Deutsche*

Mythologie. Pursuing Germanic myths from Holland to the Scandinavian countries, the Balkans, and even as far as England, he made it clear how far such myths traveled, influencing one another and playing an important role in cultural diffusion. He also pioneered in collecting superstitions, magic, folk customs, accounts of werewolves, pixies, and brownies, proverbs, riddles, and traditional games. Thus a library of material was made available for further study.

In 1846 a German philologist named Friedrich Max Mueller went to teach at Oxford, where he spent the remainder of his life. He was a handsome, courtly, ruddy-faced man with an erect, military carriage. He used to point his cane as if it were a spear, to emphasize some point in a discussion when walking with his friends. He was also a scholar of international repute, deeply versed in Oriental as well as classical and Teutonic cultures. Once when a poor but learned Indian student, stranded in England, came to him for help and addressed him in Sanskrit, Max Mueller was able to answer him fluently, to the Hindu's amazement and delight.

Max Mueller investigated myths from the point of view of language and evolved a theory that he published in his *Comparative Mythology* (1856). "Why do men study ancient history?" he inquired. "Why do the puerile and often repulsive legends of savage tribes rivet their attention and engage their thoughts?" In order to know what man is, he answered himself, we must know what he has been. Nevertheless, the Greek myths were absurd and irrational and seemed at variance with the rather advanced barbarism of the heroic period. To explain so horrible a myth as that of Chronos swallowing his children, was it necessary to imagine a period of temporary insanity through which the human race had passed?

Max Mueller felt that philology could provide a rational explanation, and he developed his "disease of language" theory. In ancient times, when Greek was not yet Greek, men spoke the hypothetical Aryan tongue. The primitives who used this language were the myth-makers. It will be seen at once that Max Mueller failed to include in his scheme the myths of primitives from other parts of the world.

He began with a discussion of ancient word meanings. *Daughter* derived from an old Sanskrit word meaning "to milk." This indicated that the little daughter of the nomadic Aryan herder was a milkmaid. *Peculiar*, meaning originally "private," came from Latin *peculum*, derived from *pecus*, "cattle"; cattle had been the private property of the ancient Aryans. Gender in ancient Aryan gave all words a sexual nature. *Morning, evening, spring, winter, sun*, and *moon* were all distinguished as male or female by virtue of grammar. It was hard for primitives to think of anything abstract. The verb *I shall* in Gothic meant originally "I must," "I owe," with the sense "I have killed," "I am guilty." In the myth-making ages, every word, whether noun or verb, kept its original social and material meaning as well as a growing abstract grammatical meaning. Words were heavy and unwieldy; they said more than they ought to say. When a man spoke of the sun following the dawn, the ancient barbarian, a poet in spite of himself, could only speak and think of the sun as loving and embracing the dawn. Similarly, sunrise was night giving birth to a child. The sentence "The heroic maid Kyrene, who lived in Thessaly, is loved by Apollo and carried off to Libya" simply meant that the town of Kyrene sent a colony to Libya under the auspices of Apollo.

Myths having been germinated, the original literal meanings tended to be forgotten. *Endymion* was supposed to have an ancient meaning of "setting sun." This meaning was lost when, in primitive poetic language, people said "Selene kisses Endymion into sleep" instead of, literally, "It is night." In the resulting confusion Endymion was pictured as a young man, and was finally given parentage and a geographical location, imaginary or real. In this way myths came to be assigned to actual historical persons.

"In these legends the Greek language supplies almost all that is necessary to render these strange stories intelligible and rational. . . . The dawn is really one of the richest sources of Aryan mythology. Winter and spring are merely reflections of night and day." *Dyotana*, the Sanskrit word for dawn, reminded Max Mueller of Daphne, young and beautiful as she flies from the brilliant rays of the ardent Apollo. In Greek, *Daphne* no longer meant dawn, but had become the word for laurel, hence the metamorphosis of the myth.

"Mythology," Max Mueller announced, "is only a dialect, an ancient form of language."

What started out as philology, as Mueller extended his theory, became an expression of nineteenth-century romanticism. The romantic movement in poetry had discovered the beauties of nature. It was easy for Max Mueller, steeped in the literary graces of his period, to discover that his early Aryans were inveterate nature poets. His argument was ingenious, but born and nurtured entirely in the library without benefit of contact with actual primitives. He was guilty of starting a fad. Almost everything could be interpreted as a solar myth, and was by his followers.

Edward Tylor's first mention of mythology, in his earliest book, *Anahuac*, was a discussion of the legend of Quetzalcoatl, whom he accepted as a deified historical personage. In his second book he accepted a sun-myth explanation of Quetzalcoatl, but in the third edition of the work he changed his mind and suggested that only parts of the myth were solar. In the same book he developed two categories of his own, *myths of historical tradition* and *myths of observation.*

An example of a historical myth was the North American story of the great elk beside whom others seemed like ants. Its legs were so high that eight feet of snow did not embarrass it, its skin was proof against all sorts of weapons, and out of its shoulder came an arm which it used like that of a man. This, he felt, was a dim traditional memory of the mammoth.

A myth of observation also dealt with the mammoth. The Siberians found the remains of these beasts imbedded in the faces of cliffs or riverbanks at some depth below the surface. They decided the creature was some huge burrowing animal that lived underground. They always found it dead; it was therefore unable to endure air or light, and when it broke out into the air it died immediately. This was finally elaborated to the point where it was reported that the earth had been seen to heave and sink in marshes as the animals traveled underground. In Chinese books it was called *Fen-shu* or "digging rat."

When Tylor came to write *Primitive Culture* and had developed fully his theory of animism, he showed himself highly critical of the Max Mueller school of myth-interpretation. "Rash inferences on the strength of mere resemblances from episodes of nature must be regarded with utter mistrust, for the student who has no more stringent criticism than this for his myths of sun, sky, and dawn will find them wherever it pleases him to seek them." He then solemnly analyzed the "Song of Sixpence." "Obviously the four-and-twenty

77

blackbirds are the four-and-twenty hours and the pie that holds them is the underlying earth covered with the overarching sky; how true a touch of nature it is when the pie is opened, that is, when day breaks, the birds begin to sing. The king is the sun, and his counting out his money is pouring out the sunshine, the golden shower of Danaë, the queen is the moon and her transparent honey the moonlight; the maid is the rosy-fingered dawn who rises before the sun, her master, and hangs out the clouds, his clothes, across the sky; the particular blackbird who so tragically ends the tale, by snipping off her nose, is the hour of sunrise."

Although he was skeptical of the solar-myth theory, Tylor was never very successful at bridging the gap between his animism and the fantastic world of myth. If the gods were derived from ancestors, as a result of dream experience, it was hard to see any connection between personified nature as it appeared in mythology and the doctrine of the soul as the germinal point of religious experience. Tylor suggested that "to the lower tribes of man, sun and stars, trees and rivers, wind and clouds become personal, animate creatures leading lives conforming to human or animal analogies, and performing their special functions in the universe with the aid of limbs like beasts." This is something very like Comte's fetishism. Tylor went on determinedly: "The basis in which such ideas as these are built is not to be narrowed down to poetic fantasy and transformed metaphor. They rest upon a broad philosophy of nature, early and crude indeed, but thoughtful, consistent, and quite really and seriously meant." The philosophy was, of course, animism. Tylor would not grant that early man was an unconscious poet, but was ready to make him a primitive philosopher. He and Max Mueller were not of the same literary school.

Social anthropology is not without its subjective element. It reflects the tastes, ethics, and cultural backgrounds of its theorists.

To Tylor, the marriage of ethics and religion was a later development. "In general the animistic doctrine of the lower races is not yet an ethical institution, so savage dualism is not yet a theory of abstract moral principles, but a theory of pleasure or pain, profit or loss, affecting the individual man, his family, at the utmost stretch, his people." A savage would argue that if someone took away his wife, it would be bad, but if he took someone else's it would be good.

In Tylor's time men were sure that such a stage had been left far behind. The passage of some decades has only emphasized how much of this point of view is still with us.

An example of the primitive beginnings of dualism was to be found in the Tuscarora myth of two brothers, one white, the other dark, who fought each other with a stag horn and wild rose berries respectively. The one armed with the berries was wounded. As he ran away, the drops of his blood made flints. The white brother was the sun; the myth in its entirety was a conflict between day and night. The sun, Iouskeha, had the attributes of good, made kettles boil and corn grow, and helped the hunter. Taouskaron, the dark brother, was associated with the moon, their mother. The moon was considered to be evil.

"The conception of the light god as the good deity in contrast to the rival god of evil is one plainly suggested by nature, and naturally recurring in the religions of the world."

In attempting to study polytheism, Tylor piled up categories of nature-worship, sun gods, moon goddesses, thunder gods, earthquake gods, hurricane gods. He felt that it was a transitional stage to monotheism. "To mark off the doctrines of the lower races, closer definition is required, assigning distinctive attributes of deity to none save the Almighty Creator. It may be declared, in this strict sense, no savage tribe of monotheists has ever been known. . . . The doctrine they do widely hold and which opens to them a course tending in one or other of these directions [monotheism or pantheism] is polytheism culminating in the rule of one supreme deity."

Tylor examined alleged monotheism in savage races skeptically. The Jesuit missionaries of Canada infused their own theology into the idea of the Great Manitou; their testimony was suspect. Allah had been lent to various races. The Caribs talked of Louquo, who died, came to life again after three days, and went to heaven. On the whole, Tylor thought that barbaric religions raised some member of the pantheon to supremacy. It might be an ancestor or a nature spirit. Pachacamac was an earth spirit taken over by the Incas and integrated into their sun-worship. The Australian Baime he considered to be a thunder god equivalent to the Scandinavian Thor. The North American Oki was a sky demon. There were such superior gods as the Greenlanders' Torngarsuk, consulted in spirit by the angekok concerning sickness, the weather, and sport, beneficent in nature, but scarcely worshipped. The Canadian Indians were said to have an Andougni, a creator for whom they had no form of prayer. Tescatlipoca, sometimes called the supreme deity of Mexico, was a sun god. Tylor found traces of ancestor-worship in the case of the Zulus, who merged the first man, the Old-Old-One, Unkulunkulu, into the idea of creator and thunderer.

The coalescence of a polytheistic nature pantheon into monotheism, a more abstract idea, took place almost philosophically in Tylor's scheme. By this time he was unwilling to accept the older explanation of a ruling god derived from an actual king or culture hero.

Animism, which was founded on the doctrine of souls and extended to a doctrine of spiritual beings animating the universe, became in Tylor's view a kind of unconscious philosophy of man and nature.

In the quarterly *Mind* for April 1877, Tylor reviewed the first volume of Herbert Spencer's *Principles of Sociology*. In his review he implied that Spencer was a convert to animism. An oddly querulous controversy followed. In the April issue of *The Academy*, Spencer published a letter announcing that he had elaborated the doctrine of animism in 1870, a year before Tylor had first publicly stated his views.

Tylor immediately pointed out that he had first published a sketch of his theory in a paper, *The Religion of Savages*, in 1866. Spencer, with his back to the wall, feebly suggested that he had developed the idea of a second self or soul as far back as 1854 in a paper on *Manners and Fashion*. Tylor replied frostily that he resented Spencer's attempt to read the theory of animism back into his earlier publication. Spencer backed down and suggested they had both invented the theory.

For once Tylor's Olympian dignity was ruffled. He said he found it odd that Spencer had used terms that he, Tylor, had invented.

Spencer remains on the outskirts of anthropology. According to R. R. Marett, "He has never been recognized as belonging to the true tradition of British anthropology simply because he uses his vast collection of facts to establish rather than to test his preformed opinions." It was Huxley who remarked: "Oh, you know Spencer's idea of a tragedy is a deduction killed by a fact."

In 1883 Tylor was invited to deliver lectures on anthropology at Oxford University; the following year the first readership in the science was created to be held by him. A few years later when the religious requirements were relaxed (formerly all appointees had had to be Church of England) he was appointed Professor of Anthropology, a position he held until 1909.

Although Tylor was cautiously interested in Morgan's doctrines, he made no contribution to the study of marriage until late in life. Then he again showed his interest in method. His paper *A Method of Investigating the Development of Institutions Applied to the Law of Marriage and Descent* was published in the *Royal Anthropological Society Journal* in 1888. "Strict method," he wrote, "has as yet only been introduced over a part of the anthropological field. . . . It is my aim to show that the development of institutions may be investigated on a basis of tabulation and classification." Tylor started from the odd taboo that forbade a husband to look at or speak to his wife's relatives, especially his mother-in-law. This had puzzled Tylor as far back as his first anthropological work. He found sixty-six cases of peoples who subscribed to this taboo. Against it he set the custom of a husband's residing with his wife's family after marriage. He found a correlation greater than the laws of chance between the two customs. This seemed to show that there was a connection between ceremonial avoidance of and residence with the wife's family.

He then checked the number of cases in which a husband was named after his first child against those in which there was ceremonial avoidance. There was a correlation of twenty-two instead of the probable eleven of chance.

He then instanced a custom of the Cree Indians by which the husband, who took up residence with his wife's family, was treated as a stranger until the birth of his first child, at which time he took the child's name and was recognized as a member of the family.

The last custom seemed to be the explanation of the other three elements in the situation, found sometimes singly and sometimes together. But what connection did it have with patriarchal or matriarchal social systems?

There was another odd marriage custom, that of *couvade*. It was a situation in which the husband as well as the wife went to bed at the time of the wife's confinement. Sometimes he was treated as an invalid. It occurred in many parts of the world. To explain it, Max Mueller had put forward a naïve theory. The father, he pointed out, was a nuisance about the house at the time of parturition. Something he might do or not do could be associated with ill health of the baby or injury to it. Mueller believed the father might take to his hammock *to keep out of mischief*. If the child turned out to be healthy, this practice would be said to be good for the baby. Thus other husbands would be intimidated into maintaining the superstition.

Tylor in his first book had tried a semi-animistic, semi-magical explanation. The savage did not separate subjective associations from objective fact. Therefore, couvade might be a parallel to the notion that a husband must not eat the flesh of a sea cow lest his child develop the round eyes of that animal. The inference was that the husband took to his bed to give aid and comfort to his wife by paralleling her condition and taking good care of himself.

Now Tylor tried correlating couvade with matriarchal society. Bachofen had explained the custom as a development at the turning-point when matriarchy was giving way to patriarchy. Maternity had to be lent to the father to make him acceptable. Thus the fiction that he was a second mother had to be devised to create a position for him in the social system. Checking the known cases of couvade against the known matriarchal and patriarchal organizations, Tylor proved that it was correlated only with the former system. He took these statistics to indicate that there was truth in Bachofen's conjecture. Couvade could therefore be related to ceremonial avoidance and all the other customs that treated the father as a stranger gradually being accepted into his wife's family.

Tylor finally tackled the problem of exogamy. He showed by the same statistical system that cross-cousin marriage—a system resulting from two marriage classes; one could marry a father's sister's son or daughter because they were of the other class but not a father's brother's son or daughter because they were of the same class—was correlated with exogamy. Actually, one was a statement of the other.

"I hardly know whether I feel more glad or sorry that my old friend McLennan to the day of his death never knew that Morgan and he who believed themselves adversaries, were all the while allies, pushing forward the same doctrine from different sides."

Finally he dealt a blow to the theory of marriage by capture by pointing out that in what were considered to be the most primitive cases of exogamy the husband went to live with the bride's family.

In other words, the husband was stolen and not the bride. He suggested as a more practical explanation of exogamy the political value of joining together small, isolated, unprotected tribes by ties of marriage. This indeed accorded well with what Morgan had stated concerning the tenacity of kinship bonds in the Iroquois federation.

Tylor's statistical method, according to R. H. Lowie (*History of Ethnological Theory*), raises him above other important figures of the nineteenth century. There were some drawbacks—for example, the difficulty of allowing for the influence of one culture on another—but his method pointed toward a more exact approach than was to be employed for decades.

Anthropology, Tylor felt, could be a mirror in which to view contemporary society. A comparison of customs which revealed their origin could point out the dead wood of survivals. A custom or belief that had lost its original meaning or purpose was often quite harmful when retained in a world that had outgrown it. Old habits of mind were an obstacle in the path of new scientific truth and a barrier between peoples. Anthropology, by revealing the impulses behind folkways, provided a critical apparatus for testing the validity of contemporary behavior. His summation is valid today. "To the promotors of what is sound and reformers of what is faulty in modern culture, ethnography has a double help to give. To impress men's minds with the doctrine of development will lead them in all honor to their ancestors, to continue it more vigorously because light has increased in the world."

Tylor died in 1917, internationally honored, having seen the science of anthropology, which he did so much to found, grow in his lifetime to a serious professional study respected in all parts of the world.

Chapter 10

A LIVING STONE AGE PEOPLE

Concerning Lorimer Fison, A. W. Howitt,
Sir Baldwin Spencer, F. J. Gillen

■ Australia, the last great continent to be settled by the white race, owed its first colony to the American Revolution. When the United States became independent, Britain, deprived of a place to which she could transport her criminals, was forced to find a new dumping-ground. Port Jackson, near Botany Bay, was founded in 1788 to meet this need. Many of the criminals transported to Australia were made lawbreakers by poverty resulting from the enclosure movement, which benefited the gentry but deprived the peasantry of the common land. At this time the British penal system was particularly savage, for it made petty theft a transportation offense.

Not until the middle of the nineteenth century did the English settlers begin to explore the interior of the continent, a rocky, desert country through which traveling was extremely difficult. One man who tried it on foot encountered dreadful heat that "blistered the skin off the feet of his dogs, split lead pencils, and drew screws out of wooden boxes."

The penal code of the colony was no milder than that of England. A not uncommon punishment was three hundred lashes, which meant, of course, that the victim's back was flayed, generally resulting in death.

The new settlers encountered natives, black-skinned, wavy-haired, and bearded, naked except for an opossum-fur string wound around their waists. They were armed with that curious weapon the boomerang and launched spears from spear-throwers, but, unless provoked, were generally peaceable and friendly.

In Australia, frontiersmen were called bushrangers. They were the equivalent of the rangers of the old American west, and among them arose the inevitable outlaws and bad men. It is not surprising that such rugged colonial types, brutalized by legal savagery, were not inclined to be tolerant of a dark-skinned race of beings whom they soon branded as "treacherous" and scarcely more human than dogs. In Tasmania, where thousands were hunted down like beasts and shot, by 1835 only 203 aboriginals were left, the pitiful remnant of thousands. The last pure-blooded Tasmanian died in 1861. On the continent they did not fare much better. Sheepherders, in order to clear the grazing-grounds more rapidly, offered them, in apparent friendliness, cakes of flour dosed with arsenic, and thus poisoned off black humanity like ground squirrels. Other ingenious native-exterminators poisoned the waterholes.

Despite the rapid decline of the blacks, immigration was slow until the discovery of gold in New South Wales in 1852 by an Englishman who had failed to find it in California.

Later in the same year newcomers were arriving in Victoria at the rate of seven thousand every week. Melbourne became a boomtown, with a mushroom growth of shacks and tents; ships moored close to shore turned themselves into lodginghouses. Robbery, murder, banditry flourished, all the lawlessness with which we of the United States are familiar from the history of our own west. Fortunes were made by lucky strikes, and countless unsuccessful prospectors died from dysentery, yellow fever, or the hardships of the bush. Nevertheless, in 1853 the mines produced twelve million pounds' worth of gold.

Two men who were to found the science of anthropology in Australia were drawn to the new continent by the gold fever.

There was a certain repetition of a pattern. Again the expansion of European industrial civilization resulted in the conquest of a primitive race that the whites first treated with contempt but finally took the trouble to study. Above all, it was the work of the American Lewis Morgan which stimulated the Australian pioneer anthropologists.

One of these, Lorimer Fison, was the son of a Suffolk land-owner. He was born in 1832, had a Spartan upbringing, and was trained to respect and emulate men of great intellectual attainments. Nevertheless, he did not finish his course at Cambridge and suffered from a sense of inferiority all his life because he did not possess a university degree. In 1856 he sailed to Australia as a prospector. Apparently he was not one of the lucky few, for he left the gold diggings and entered the University of Melbourne five years later. Again he failed to be graduated. Instead, at the death of his father, whom he worshipped, he underwent a sudden conversion, became a Wesleyan missionary, and went to work among the natives of the Fiji Islands.

It was there that Morgan's questionnaire of 1858 reached him. Fascinated and excited, he contributed kinship tables of the Fijian and Tongan islanders. His material arrived late, but was included in an appendix to Morgan's book.

This was the beginning of a long and warm correspondence. Fison became a loyal defender of the Morgan hypothesis. His pet hate was McLennan. "I must express my indignation at McLennan's contemptuous words and his impertinent disposal of your hypothesis." Lubbock's *Origin of Civilization* also displeased him. He thought that it could have been compiled by anyone with sufficient means to hire research workers. It was based on secondhand, mostly incorrect facts.

Fison was a big, hearty man with a sense of humor, greatly loved by his native parishioners. He was also rather temperamental, for he wrote Morgan that at forty-six his lungs were irreparably injured and he was a "totally broken man." As he lived to the ripe and active old age of seventy-five, this seems a slight exaggeration. In 1871 he returned to New South Wales and started investigating the marriage-and-kinship system of the native tribe called the Kamileroi. Some of his letters were published in the *Australian*, where they were read by Alfred L. Howitt, police magistrate of a district of Gippsland.

Howitt was the son of two English writers. As a boy, he had traveled with his parents in Germany. Later he studied at the University of London. In 1852 his entire family sailed for Australia, lured by the gold strike. A few years later his father and brother returned to England, but Howitt stayed, first as a cattle-drover, later to become a seasoned explorer.

This was the period (1861) of the ill-fated Burke expedition. Robert O'Hara Burke set out with camels to cross the continent for the first time from north to south. There were desertions and mismanagement. Burke was not an experienced bushranger and did not know how to live off the country. He and three other survivors, after crossing the continent, lost their way on the return trip and ran out of supplies.

When they had not been heard from for weeks, Howitt was chosen to head a rescue expedition. With horses and camels he crossed stony tablelands, almost devoid of vegetation, and scrub-covered ranges with here and there a tree whose outlines were lost in the maze of distance. He encountered natives who fled from him and with whom his own black bearers could not communicate. At last, by signs, a group of natives succeeded in indicating that King, the last survivor, was in their camp. He wore only a few rags of clothing and at first was scarcely able to talk to Howitt. Burke and his men had wandered for twenty-one days practically without water until all but King had died of starvation after subsisting on roots and seeds. With King's aid Howitt finally located the body of Burke lying in a small hollow among the dried stems of some plants. "The bones were entire with the exception of one hand and the feet. . . . I found the revolver which Burke held in his hand when he expired, partly covered over with leaves and earth and corroded with rust."

It was during such journeys into the heart of the strange, arid continent that Howitt came to know and like the natives who had made it their home and who were able, by simple but stubborn adaptation, to survive when the clumsy white man with his camels, portable stoves, and tents left his bones to whiten in the bush.

When Howitt became a magistrate, he took a serious interest in his charges, the Kurnai tribe, won their confidence, and was adopted into the tribe.

Small, hawk-faced, nervous, and alert, Howitt sought out the six-foot, two-hundred-and-twenty-four-pound Fison and found in him a kindred soul. Together they planned a book that should preserve all they had learned of the life and culture of the vanishing blacks. They were keenly aware that priceless anthropological data were being rapidly lost. Howitt complained to Morgan: "As to the whole field of inquiry in Australia—I am quite disheartened. There is no chance of getting it done unless individuals, like myself, who are on good terms with some tribe, will take it in hand. That which I have tried to do for the Kurnai tribe I could not do for any other until I became fully acquainted with its members. . . . One man's life would not suffice and by that time it would be too late." And Fison raged against the laxness and lack of interest of his informants when he could not obtain firsthand data.

Although he was a clergyman, Fison possessed the true scientific spirit. When Morgan wondered if the primitive promiscuity theory might not be detrimental to religion, Fison replied: "I have only to say that the religion to which any fact whatever can be detrimental can not be true." He had established that each half of the Kamileroi tribe was divided into four marriage classes or clans, and he was looking for evidence of the "reformatory movement" by which primitive group marriage could evolve into monogamy.

Meanwhile, by letter Fison became almost fanatically attached to Morgan (who perhaps replaced his father in his hero-worshipping soul). He wrote: "I owe you far more than I can ever repay. It was you who first set me to work on a subject which has given me the keenest delight for years. . . . I am proud to look upon myself as a member of your gens."

In the Fiji Islands he had come across a shocking and painful native custom. A stick was thrust up the male urinal canal to the scrotum, and the penis below it was slit. After the wound healed, normal urination was not possible, but it apparently did not interfere with reproduction. The vaginal parts of women were scraped with a sharp bamboo sliver. The natives ascribed this to some medicinal intention, but Fison thought it was expiation for pair marriage, a theory put forward by Lubbock. The communal law by which all women were common to all men of their marriage class was broken by monogamy. Hence the sex organ of each sex was tortured to atone for the offense against the group.

The Kamileroi and the Kurnai, by Fison and Howitt, published in Sydney in 1880, still remains a basic work on Australian aboriginals. It was warmly received by Tylor in England and Adolph Bastian (of whom we shall hear more subsequently) in Germany. The Lubbock-McLennan camp remained hostile.

Totemism, in contrast to Lubbock's theory that it could have arisen from a habit of naming individuals after animals, was always a group phenomenon. Fison wrote Morgan: "The totem is not always an animal. But I think you will see that it has a more intimate connection with the gens than that of a mere symbol." When savages were obliged by dire necessity to eat their own totem, they apologized to it and told it lies. The totemic animal "is bone of their bone and flesh of their flesh." They did not precisely worship it, but felt more a sense of piety as toward kinsfolk. It was because the Greeks were matriarchal, Fison pointed out, that the Furies were able to absolve Orestes of the murder of Clytemnestra: she was his mother, but she was not of his totem.

Howitt's material was less theoretical. He had learned the Kurnai tongue, and his official position gave him much influence over them. In thirty-two years his native wards had diminished in numbers from 1,500 to about 140. The warriors had been slaughtered, and alcoholism, venereal disease, and tuberculosis had done the rest. Howitt bewailed the rapidity with which they lost their culture—as soon as the white men destroyed the equilibrium between them and their environment, they were doomed. Already the initiation ceremony, performed when the boys reached puberty, was beginning to die, for it had been forbidden by the missionaries. He succeeded in getting some of his native friends to re-enact the ritual.

The boys sat in a row, a girl beside each one. The boys were decorated with feathers, pipe clay, and red ocher. Dingo tails and skins of kangaroo rats were worn on their heads. The older women beat the ground with opossum-skin rugs. The men came from the forest in line, keeping in step and chanting. They were smeared with charcoal, their heads feathered and painted. They were naked from the waist down, the upper half of the body was wound with bark, and a bushy tuft of grass transfixed the pierced nose. As they advanced they beat the ground with a strip of bark. The girls and boys tilted their heads sharply from one side to the other in unison and in time to the rhythm of the men who danced before them.

Later the boys were laid on their backs on canopies of boughs and thus spent the night. The men who were guarding them kept them in the forest for several months, during which they were not allowed to eat female animals or porcupines. For the first time Howitt described the function of the bull-roarer, that oval slat of wood, pierced and tied to a string, which, when swung rapidly about the head, could be made to hum, roar, and shriek. The boys hid their heads under opossum rugs when it was used. They were told that women and children were to be kept in awe of the sound and must never know the secret of how it was produced. The boys were finally given a secret name that could never be mentioned, and were then considered to be men.

Patiently Howitt accumulated the details of Kurnai daily life. The men fished, hunted, fought, and sat about. The women fished, gathered vegetables, fruit, and seeds, cooked, wove bags, and made nets.

When an animal was caught, certain parts were always allotted to specific members of the family group. A sloth, for instance, was divided as follows: the father and mother got the right leg and gave the right arm away; the left arm and leg went to the wife's father and mother, the left foot to the brother; the head, backbone, and liver were eaten by the man himself and his wife; the ears were given to the wife, who gave the right one to her sister. There were also traditional spots in relation to the fire where each member of the family was supposed to sleep.

The Kurnai believed in ghosts, some of which were dangerous. They were afraid to name the dead for fear they might be listening. Death was not normal, but was caused by magic and could be averted by countercharms. They often carried a round black pebble with them. When this was buried with the excreta of an enemy, it was supposed to cause the enemy's death. If the hair of an enemy was tied to the end of a throwing-stick with feathers of the eagle hawk and roasted before the fire with some kangaroo fat, it would cause the person to whom it belonged to pine away and die.

When death took place, a hut was built over the corpse, which was rolled in an opossum rug and bark and tied tightly. As many mourners as could get into the hut and lay their heads on the package containing the body did so, moaning: "Why did you go? Why did you leave us?" They cut themselves until they bled. Finally the corpse was unrolled, the hair was plucked out, and the mourners anointed themselves with the "oil" from the corpse. The relatives wrapped it up again and carried it about with them for years until it would no longer hold together, whereupon they casually left it in a hollow tree.

A still more bizarre custom was that of cutting off one of the hands of the departed. This was hung around the neck on a fur string. At the approach of an enemy, it was supposed to give the alert by pinching the wearer. The latter then took it off and dangled it by the string, and the hand was supposed to rotate until it pointed in the direction from which the danger was approaching.

The Kurnai, unlike the Kamileroi, were patriarchal: all the men belonged to one totem, the women to another. They had no hereditary chiefs, but the old men were looked up to, and experienced warriors wielded a certain influence. The men habitually wore no clothes, but sometimes hung a ceremonial tassel over the penis. The women wore an opossum-fur string around the waist until they were married, then wore nothing.

Fison, during the latter part of his life, gave up active anthropology and took to editing and writing. Howitt was appointed superintendent of mines, a position he held until he resigned in 1901 to write his final classic monograph, *The Native Tribes of Southeastern Australia,* published in 1904. Both Fison and Howitt died in 1907. Highly respected by other anthropologists in their later years, they had become firm friends of James G. Frazer and had inspired the investigations of Baldwin Spencer and F. J. Gillen among the Arunta of central Australia.

Baldwin Spencer (1860–1929) was trained in biology and zoology at Oxford, where he came under the influence of Tylor and assisted him in arranging the famous Pitt Rivers museum. When he was called to the chair of zoology at the University of Melbourne he began to make trips into the interior to study the local fauna. Oddly enough, it was a marsupial mole that set off a chain of events which turned him into an anthropologist. His discovery of this animal so impressed Australian biologists that they felt more investigation should be carried on in central Australia. The result was the Horn expedition, which set off in May 1894, complete with camels.

Spencer wrote feelingly of the bad temper and unattractive habits of the camels. For the first time he was able to examine a water frog. This was a species of tree frog which, when the dry season came on, filled itself with water and hibernated in the mud. One of his black boys dug down a foot into a clay pan after locating certain almost invisible tracks. Encased in the dry clay was a dirty yellow frog, inflated to the size of a small orange. Within its bladder it had stored away about two spoonfuls of pure water, which was quite drinkable. The natives made use of these frogs when there was no other source of water.

At an isolated telegraph station, called Charlotte Waters, Spencer encountered a genial Irishman, F. J. Gillen, who both ran the station and held the position of Sub-protector of the Aborigines. Although not a scientist, Gillen had been making notes on the Arunta tribe and encouraging them to keep to their old customs. Spencer was deeply impressed by this golden opportunity to learn the intimate details of native life. Gillen invited him to share his studies. When the expedition was over, Spencer returned to Charlotte Waters to spend a month with his new friend. The month changed him from a zoologist to an anthropologist. The Arunta loved and trusted Gillen and had adopted him into their tribe. Spencer was also adopted as Gillen's younger tribal brother. Spencer wrote James Frazer, with whom he corresponded regularly: "We have fortunately been just in time to record details of this tribe for it is astonishing how rapidly customs die the moment the white man comes on the scene. Unless we can in some way set to work seriously we shall soon be too late to do much for Australia, for, despite the work of men like Howitt and Fison, we know as yet very little. I need hardly say that to these two Gillen and myself are much indebted."

Spencer and Gillen formed a lasting friendship not unlike that between Fison and Howitt, and spent months with the Arunta. The two traveled across Australia together and produced two books that still constitute a landmark in field observation, *The Native Tribes of Central Australia* (1899) and *The Northern Tribes of Central Australia* (1904).

Gillen died in 1911, but Spencer continued their work. Aside from his scientific interests, he loved pictures and helped found an art gallery in Melbourne. Indeed, his eye for scenery is exemplified in the many fine descriptions of the Australian bush with which his books are filled. He was extremely tactful in handling the natives. When trouble arose from their habit of stealing glass insulators from the telegraph line in order to chip them into implements, Spencer solved the situation by supplying them with plenty of broken bottles. He patiently worked with natives with whom he was able to converse only in pidgin English. Day in and day out he could be seen sitting under a scanty tree, in the blazing heat, carefully laying out matches with different-colored heads which he used to diagram totem and kinship relationships as he gradually extracted them from grimy and evil-smelling elders of the tribe.

He published two popular books, *Across Australia* (1912) and *Wanderings in Wild Australia* (1928). In 1919, when he was made Chief Protector of the Aborigines, he resigned his professorship. In 1929, at the age of sixty-nine, when his health was no longer good, a curious romantic desire to follow in the footsteps of Darwin impelled him to set out on a last expedition to Tierra del Fuego. The Fuegians proved to be a vanishing race. Their customs had almost disappeared. Disappointed and forlorn, attended by a devoted secretary, he was still trying to gather stories of the past from an old woman reputed to be a witch when he died of a heart attack in a snowbound hut on Hoste Island, a spot that had been visited decades before by Darwin in the *Beagle*.

Central Australia, the home of the Arunta and the Urubunna, was a combination of desert or steppe and low mountain ranges. Of the desert Spencer wrote: "Nothing can be more dreary than this country; there is simply a succession of sandhills covered with tussocks of porcupine grass, the leaves of which resemble knitting needles radiating from a huge pincushion or, where the sandhills die down, there is a flat stretch of plain hard country with some belts of desert oaks or, more often, dreary mulga scrub."

Water, that rare and precious liquid—around it all of life in central Australia revolved.

"It is difficult to realize without having seen it the contrast between the steppe lands of Australia in the dry and rainy season. In the former, the scene is one of desolation, the sun shines down hotly on stony plains or yellow sandy ground. . . . A desert oak or an acacia tree now and then affords a scanty shade. . . . When such a flood does occur the ordinary river beds are not deep enough to hold it. . . . What has been for many months dry and parched land is suddenly transformed into a vast sheet of water. It is only a matter of a short time; the rainfall ceases and rapidly the water sinks. . . . The sun once more shines hotly and in the damp ground seeds which have lain dormant for months germinate and, as if by magic, the once arid land becomes covered with luxuriant herbage." Plants and animals were forced to grow and reproduce with great rapidity in the brief period of the rains, for soon the blazing sun parched the face of the land once more.

Although at night the temperature fell several degrees below freezing, the natives who wrung a difficult living from this country went completely naked except for a ceremonial pubic tassel worn by the men on formal occasions. They were not Negroes, although dark-skinned, for their hair and beards were wavy or frizzy. Their huts were simply lean-tos of shrubs. They used spears, boomerangs, and wooden shields. They hunted emus, kangaroos, and wallabys and knocked down rock pigeons with the boomerang. A few vegetables were roasted in hot ashes. Seeds of the acacia were roasted, ground on a grinding-stone, made into mush by adding water, and eaten raw or baked. Meat was cooked by placing it in a pit with hot coals. A sharp flint was fixed at the end of a man's spear-thrower. This he carried always with him and used as a knife. For lashings of their tools and weapons they used the strong tendons of the kangaroo's hind leg.

The men were great trackers who could distinguish between the barefoot tracks of individuals and recognize those of their friends. They could count up to five, using their fingers, but any greater number was *oknira*—meaning much. Time they reckoned by sleeps or moons. They knew how to use the digging-stick, which they employed to obtain wild yams.

The indispensable property of the women was the *pitchi*, a trough hollowed out of soft bean-tree wood which they carried slung across the hips or on the head. They carried everything in it, including their babies. It also served as a mixing-bowl. String was made by spinning the fur of opossums, using a weighted spindle. The women wore nothing but strings of bean-tree seeds. Carrying pitchis on their heads gave the girls a graceful walk, but the struggle with a harsh and hostile environment made them shriveled hags by the time they were thirty.

The central Australians were not warlike and did very little fighting. Spencer and Gillen, who were of the Morgan school, thought they found evidence of group marriage in the past. Although there was actually monogamy, the patriarchal Urubunna had only two totemic marriage classes. The kinship terminology network was similar to that which Morgan had discovered among the North American Indians. The Arunta further complicated their lives by having four marriage classes in each of the two moieties, or halves, of the tribe. The individuals of one class in one moiety were restricted to marriage with individuals of specific class in the other moiety. This system, which was matriarchal, resembled that of Fison's Kamileroi. Fison maintained that upon a couple who transgressed this law so much scorn and social pressure was brought to bear that such unions soon broke up.

In the women's puberty ceremony, during which the hymen was perforated with a stone knife, men of forbidden classes had access to the girl. In accordance with the "thousand miles of wives" theory, all women of a marrying class were technically wives of all men in the class into which they might marry. This was not, however, put into practice. The anthropologists did discover that before certain ceremonies women had ritual intercourse with men who were normally taboo to them.

Most interesting, and carefully investigated by Spencer and Gillen, was the totemic philosophy that was the key to most of the natives' activities, intertwined as it was with mythology, magic, social organization, and ritual.

In the dim past, which they called the *Alcheringa*, their ancestors had been closely associated with animals and plants, so closely that they were identified with them. These ancestors carried *churingas* about with them which were identified with specific totems. Churingas were ovoid stones or pieces of wood shaped like bull-roarers (some were used in the same way) which bore sacred symbolic markings. Various totems were connected with localized areas and landmarks at which churingas were deposited to show where ancestors had camped or died. It was thought that when a woman conceived a child near one of these totem spots, the spirit of an ancestor entered into her, and the child belonged to that totem.

Churingas were not supposed to be seen by women or uninitiated men. After the child entered the woman, it was customary for the relatives to visit the spot to look for the churinga the spirit had dropped. In cases where it could not be found, they made a wooden one from the tree nearest the spot and carved the proper totemic markings on it. It was then put in a little cave sacred to the totemic group. Churingas, which were cherished for generations, seemed to be thought of as carrying the spirits of ancestors. They were used in all ceremonies, and their guardian was called an *alatunja*.

At puberty, boys were circumcised and then had to submit to suburethral incision. A spear decorated with eagles' feathers was

95

set up. The novices lay in a row upon the ground while the men chanted and sang. The boys then, one by one, embraced the spear for ten minutes as a precaution against the pain of the operation. Then a man lay down upon his stomach, another lay on top of him, and the boy was placed upon the living altar. The operator grasped the penis, stretching the urethra, and another man laid it open from below with a stone knife. The boy then allowed the blood to drip into a special shield. While recovering, he was not allowed to eat opossum, snake, lizard, or echidna meat, which would retard his recovery. The natives had no explanation for the origin of this rite, which was widely practiced in Australia. It was notable that the Arunta did not believe that children were the result of sexual intercourse.

Various myths were told which seemed to have vaguely historical connotations. They were connected with totem ceremonies.

Totemic rituals were performed at great fiestas called *corroborees*. The Engwara ceremony went on from September to January. The natives made a low mound two feet wide and a foot high by digging up the sandy soil. This was ornamented by a row of small gumtree boughs. A spear eight feet high was wound with grass stalks and fur waist girdles and topped with a bunch of emu and eagle feathers. One of the men cut his arm and allowed half a pint of blood to drain into a shield. Blood was smeared on the pole, and to it was stuck white down and red died with ocher. Six churingas ornamented with down were hung on the pole. (The eagle down that was used to decorate both objects and the bodies of performers was always stuck on with blood, sometimes taken from the penis.)

When the spear, or *nurtunja*, was prepared, six men walked behind the bearer, lifting their knees until they touched their stomachs, and escorted it to the ceremonial ground. The man who had decorated it called the men who had not been present to come up, slapping his hand in front of his mouth to create a vibratory effect. The men came up on the run. They danced in front of the nurtunja-bearers for half a minute. The latter rose and, moving with the high knee action, slowly bent the nurtunja over the group, then resumed their former position. Two or three men laid their hands on the shoulders of the nurtunja-bearers, and it was over.

Afterward pieces of the nurtunja were pressed to the stomach of each of the older men present. They were supposed to have become so agitated by witnessing the sacred ceremony that their bowels got tied up in knots which had to be loosened by the application of the sacred objects.

As the fiesta continued, countless ceremonies were performed connected with various totems, and in each case the performers were elaborately decorated with down and churingas. Often towering nurtunjas were constructed for rituals that lasted only a few minutes. Sometimes the performers were so encased in weird trappings that they almost lost human form.

Churingas.

One of the most dramatic performances was the eagle-hawk ceremony. The hair of each of the two men was bunched up and, together with a conical crown of cassia twigs, was bound around and around with fur string. On top of this were fixed three three-foot churingas topped with black eagle-hawk feathers. On the front of the headdress and in a broad band around the waist and a band over each shoulder like a harness was stuck a solid area of pink down edged with white. In his mouth one man carried a small wad of grass bound with fur string. Both sat on their haunches on the convex sides of small shields facing each other eight feet apart. They squatted and moved their arms up and down like wings. Then they jumped off the shields, bodies bent, sweaty black skins glistening under their brilliant patterns of red and white down, and circled facing each other, bending and flapping their wings, looking for an opening. They stopped, side-stepped, moved in, and began fighting with their heads and trying to snatch the grass bundle that represented a piece of meat over which two hawks were struggling. This went on for some time. Then two men stepped out of the audience (which, of course, consisted entirely of initiated men) and took away the churingas, which were of great weight and must have caused a strain on the head in the great heat of the afternoon sun. They went on jumping, flapping, advancing, and retreating like fighting birds until finally the attacker snatched away the piece of meat and the ceremony was over.

Each night, to prepare the ground for the following day's ceremony, they "sang the ground"—that is, danced over it in a file, singing to consecrate it.

The Arunta believed that in the Alcheringa, or olden times, men were created by the Ungambikula, two beings who came down from the western sky with big stone knives. On earth they found the Inapertwa, creatures who had no distinct limbs or organs of sight, hearing, or smell. They did not eat, and looked something like human beings doubled up in a congealed round mass. With their stone knives the Ungambikula shaped them into human beings.

A medicine man was created by the spirits. When he slept near a certain cave, a spirit pierced his tongue with a lance. A second lance, driven through his head, killed him. The spirit dragged him into a cave, took out his entrails, and magically replaced them. He came to life totally insane, then recovered, having had placed in his body certain quartz stones, which he could project at his patients to cure them. He could also cause death by magic. He had to be careful not to eat fat or warm meat, inhale the odor of burning bones, or listen to barking dogs for fear he might lose his stones. It was a fact that a native who thought he had been wounded by a weapon that had been "sung over" inevitably died unless saved by a medicine man.

Australian love life was bound up with magic. When dancing, a man desirous of charming a woman attached to his girdle a shell ornament that had been "sung over." The shell attracted lightning. The woman, seeing the flashes of lightning, all at once felt her entrails shaken and immediately eloped with him.

Women, on the other hand, were sexually dangerous. If they wished to harm a man, they could sing over a spear of grass and point it at him. Thereupon his penis would swell up and become very painful. Still worse, they could sing over a finger and insert it into their vaginas. Any man who made love to them would thereafter lose his sex organs.

Particularly noteworthy in Spencer's and Gillen's study was the fact that education among such primitives as the Arunta was by ritual. In preparation for ceremonies, their semi-historical meaning was impressed upon the young people. Thus an interlocking tradition of magic, mythology, social organization, art, philosophy, and ethics was transmitted dramatically, and each generation absorbed it painlessly in the form of exciting entertainment.

The books of Fison and Howitt and Spencer and Gillen broke ground in many ways. They remain classics of field observation. They were the first unbiased, closely observed, general treatises on a particular culture made by men with a scientific point of view who had attained some familiarity with native languages and had gained the confidence of their informants. As such, they were a storehouse of facts, "a full and detailed description of a people living in the Stone Age, without metals, without clothes, without domestic animals (except the dog) and not only without agriculture but without even the conception that seeds will grow if you plant them in the ground. . . . Thus their material condition was the simplest and the lowest consistent with the existence of human life on the earth," as Frazer put it. And yet the social system and totemic mythology of these people was highly complex. Frazer's final judgment was: "Books like mine, merely speculation, will be superseded sooner or later (the sooner the better for the sake of the truth) by better induction based on fuller knowledge; books like yours containing records of observation will never be superseded."

The Australian material focused anthropological attention upon totemism as a central problem in primitive culture. The facts were used by most theorists of the period and for decades afterward by later scholars. The Australian pioneers also awakened other scientists to the need for preserving data on the fast-vanishing primitives of other areas. The next part of the world to be investigated was the Torres Strait, and for this purpose the first purely anthropological expedition was organized by Alfred Cort Haddon.

Chapter 11

A VANISHING EDEN

Concerning Alfred Cort Haddon

■ On April 22, 1898, a vessel anchored in the coral-reef-lined Torres Straits between the southern coast of New Guinea and Cape York, the northernmost tip of Australia. Aboard her was a group of scientists led by Alfred C. Haddon (1855-1940), a zoologist who ten years before, while studying the coral reefs, had begun to take an interest in the natives of the islands off New Guinea.

Anthropology had come of age. For the first time in the history of the science a *team* of experts was setting out to study various aspects of a culture.

The port at which they disembarked was an assemblage of corrugated-iron and wooden buildings garishly broiling under a fierce tropical sun, unrelieved by the green of vegetation. The settlement was decorated by mountains of empty sardine tins, kerosene cans, and empty bottles. The town's chief commerce was some trade in pearl shells, *bêche de mer* (a large, leathery sea slug, related to the starfish, which, when boiled, smoked, and dried and shriveled into hard rolls, was sold to the Chinese), and copra, the dried meat of the coconut.

The company of scientists boarded a ketch for Murray Island, their destination, leaving the baggage and the rest of the expedition to follow. On the trip they encountered storms and heavy seas, the native pilot deserted them, they anchored, dragged their anchor, and were nearly wrecked on a coral reef during the night, but they finally arrived safely.

Murray Island was a small volcanic area surrounded by coral reefs and enriched by floating pumice. Where the lava had streamed down from the ancient crater, the soil was fertile and covered with lush vegetables, green with banana fronds, and feathery coco palms. The whole island was shaped like a *dugong*, or sea cow, which the natives were convinced it had at one time been.

The group of islands in the Torres Straits (named for a Spanish explorer) had been claimed for Great Britain in 1771 by Captain James Cook, who reported: "We saw several naked people, all or most of them women, down upon a beach picking up Shells, etc. They had not a single rag of cloathing upon them and both these and those we saw yesterday were in every respect the same sort of people we have seen everywhere upon the coast. 2 or 3 of the men we saw yesterday had on pretty large breast plates, which we supposed were made of pearl Oyster Shells; this was a thing as well as bows and arrows we had not seen before."

Captain Bligh of the legendary *Bounty*, when put off his ship in the launch, sailed through the strait and named Wednesday Island. A series of skirmishes during the early nineteenth century in which landing-parties were killed gave the natives a bad name, although it was never clear who was the aggressor. Permanent settlement took place on Cape York, on the mainland of Australia, in 1862. Missionary work in the area began in the seventies.

When the expedition arrived, traditions were vanishing fast. Already, thanks to misguided missionary effort, the islanders were wearing cotton clothes instead of going naked as their forefathers had, and their ancient ceremonies were remembered only by the old men. They were now subjects of the Crown. The British legal system was imposed by the magistrate. Punishment for most offenses consisted of enforced work on roads or husking coconuts to obtain copra.

Haddon was greeted by Ani, chief of the island, whom he had known on his previous trip. The island's only permanent white resident was the schoolmaster-magistrate. Haddon engaged two boys and took up quarters in an abandoned mission. He invited all the natives he had known previously to view the slides he had made from photographs taken ten years before. There were yells of laughter and delight as the islanders recognized themselves, and tears when they saw portraits of relatives who had died. When the party was over, the scientists were brought presents of bananas and coconuts.

The dark-skinned, fuzzy-haired Papuans were somewhat similar in appearance to the Australians, but their cultures were strikingly different. White men considered them lazy. Haddon observed: "They have no need for money. Their wants are few and easily supplied. Surely they have to be commended for not wearing out their lives to obtain what is really of no use to them. The truth is we call them lazy because they won't work for the white man more than they care to. Why should they?"

Alfred Haddon was another scientist who had been attracted to anthropology almost against his will. The son of a nonconformist London printer, he was put into his father's business, where he designed letterheads and visiting-cards. He had always sketched and studied natural science as a hobby, but he considered the printing business silly and boring. To compensate, he filled his room with specimens and dissected dead turtles, drowned kittens, and dead hens. Frustration brought about sick headaches, but for twelve years he was obliged to relegate his real interest to his spare time. Everyone whom he consulted told him there was no way of making a living in science.

Nevertheless, in 1874 an aunt took pity on him and arranged an introduction to Professor Foster, a Cambridge zoologist. Foster also was pessimistic about the financial rewards of science, but Haddon's father had at last decided that the young man was no asset to the business. Haddon went to Cambridge, where he achieved a brilliant record as a biology student. He met Thomas Henry Huxley, who became through most of his career a friend and adviser. Haddon specialized in marine biology, married, and obtained a position in the Royal College of Dublin. After teaching successfully for several years, he decided he ought to become acquainted in their native habitat with the sea creatures about which he lectured.

On the advice of Huxley, he chose the Torres Straits. He was given a grant of three hundred pounds to map the reefs of the strait and study its fauna. Gradually the human fauna weaned him away from the polyps and echinoderms, for he realized that the latter would endure, while the Papuans were fast vanishing.

He spent his evenings "yarning" with the natives, persuading them to describe their lives before the white men had come. For three fathoms of calico he obtained a decorated skull with artificial eyes used in divination. He bought tobacco pipes, bows and arrows, spears. Here, as everywhere else, the natives and their culture were dying out, blighted by the touch of the European. Visiting a small islet, he found that all the inhabitants had died except three men and two boys; "the old men were sitting listlessly, caring for nothing and waiting to join the majority. I felt quite sad for them."

The young scientist was becoming emotionally involved with a simple people who, in the lush climate of the islands, had achieved a primitive Eden gay with ritual dancing, painted masks, and percussive music. The Eden was no more, the lithe bodies were covered with ill-fitting calico, and the dances were almost forgotten, but there was still time to record something of a significant culture.

Masked dancers from the Torres Straits (from a native drawing).

The germ of a new kind of expedition was already in his mind when he wrote in his journal: "A proper anthropologist requires wider knowledge and more versatile talents than I can lay claim to. He should be a linguist, an artist, a musician, and have an extensive knowledge of natural and mechanical science."

When he returned home, he published some papers on the culture of his island friends. James Frazer wrote an encouraging letter, urging him to prepare a book. For a time he was torn between zoology and anthropology. Huxley warned him anxiously: "Don't burn your ships." There were scarcely any paying posts open to exponents of the young science.

The pull of the islands was strong. The kind of work he wished to undertake required another expedition. He began contacting the experts he considered necessary to the project. W. H. R. Rivers (whose anthropological works will be discussed later) was lecturer in psychology in St. John's College, and one of his students was William McDougall. Failing to enlist Rivers, Haddon signed up McDougall. When the master learned that his best pupil was going, he held out no longer. S. S. Meyers was the expert on music, Sidney H. Ray the authority on Melanesian and Papuan languages, Anthony Wilkin was the photographer, C. G. Seligman studied pathology and native medicine.

The natives cheerfully submitted to the various tests Rivers administered. They were told that white men had heard that natives could see and hear better than European people, and the results would be written in a great book that everyone would read. Rivers investigated sense perception, memory, reading, writing, and drawing ability. He found their vision better than that of Europeans. They had no words for measures of weight, but were better than the whites at judging it. Their hearing was about the same as the Europeans', but because most of the natives were divers it might have been impaired. They seemed slightly less sensitive to pain than the whites. Under Rivers's prompting they produced naïve and remarkably effective drawings of spirits and gods.

Haddon was endeavoring to re-create the old ceremonies. Most of the natives knew some English. The scientists conversed with them in a mixture of pidgin English and native terms.

Only the old men could help him. He kept handy a drum and such weapons as spears and clubs, and every now and then these would be snatched up as his informants broke into song and dance. There was, of course, some resistance to disclosing secret ritual. His method was to check one informant against another. When he obtained bits of detail from one patriarch, this would, in turn, prompt another to reveal further material. As a relaxation he showed them lantern slides and played European music on his phonograph. Pidgin English had its drawbacks. One day one of his boys told him: "Milk no good. He full plenty big black pigeon." It turned out that the milk was full of ants; *pigeon* was used to mean any animal not possessing four legs.

The Samoan missionary on the island disapproved, for he considered old ritual evil and pagan, but Haddon made progress—

"the old men doing everything half seriously and at the same time laughing as if they were truant schoolboys at some forbidden pleasure."

The rain-making ceremony was re-enacted for his benefit. Four large plaited coconut leaves were set up in the forest to represent rain clouds, a blackened patch on each to stand for the blackness of the cloud. The four screens enclosed a small space in which a hole was dug in the ground. The *doim* or idol, a stone roughly chipped to human form, was decorated with certain leaves and packed in a banana leaf with various minced herbs and red seeds. The leaf was filled with water and placed in the hole. The magicians waved torches, shook bamboo clappers, and chanted:

> *Clouds close together.*
> *Black clouds close together.*
> *Rain to fall heavily.*
> *Black clouds gathered together.*
> *Ends of clouds gathered together.*
> *Streaks of clouds gathered together.*
> *Waterspouts rising from the sea*
> *To darken like night.*
> *Coconut leaves hang down.*
> *Heavy rain with mist.*
> *Ends of black clouds meeting.*
> *Ends of black clouds meeting.*
> *And covering each other.*
> *Ends of waterspouts meeting.*

Belief in the traditional magic was not altogether dead. A shower took place after the ceremony, which the islanders were convinced had produced it. The owner of the *doim* had sold the idol to Haddon, only to repent bitterly afterward when he decided that it had not lost its power.

Before the coming of the whites, the women of Murray Island wore a bark or split-leaf skirt, the men went naked. They did not practice circumcision, and indeed the standard of manly beauty (displayed in the naked dances) required that the foreskin should completely cover the end of the penis.

Houses were simply long gables set on the ground. They were formed of bamboo rafters tied to a central ridgepole and thatched with grass. The natives caught fish by driving them into plaited baskets, and employed suckerfish to capture turtles. The suckerfish were attached to lines. When one was tossed into the sea, it made for any large object such as a turtle and attached itself by means of the sucker on its head. The natives were than able to tie a line to the turtle and drag it ashore.

There was a wealth of mythology. Some of it Haddon took down directly, some he obtained from John Bruce, a government magistrate who had spent years on the island and had made copious notes on native customs. The story of the Murray Island Adam and Eve went as follows: "In the beginning there were only two people. Pop appeared first and had the island to himself. After a time he noticed that birds were of two sorts and he caught a copulating pair of turtles. He decided he must have a mate, took some white mud and made it into a female dugong but added two legs. When the sun set, he lay down to sleep beside the mud figure. In the morning he awoke at sunrise, took the figure, held it up to his face and coughed into its mouth. The image then began to get warm. He held it close to himself and after a while said, 'I think your name is Kod.' They went outside the hut and climbed to the top of a large coral tree and, as they saw the sun rise, they began to sing. When the song was finished, they went down from the tree, went into the hut and made love. While they were making love they blew feathers from their mouths and sang. They moved to a place called Arp where they fell ill. From there they walked to another place called Tomog. After a time the two people lay down and died."

Haddon and Rivers spent their leisure learning complicated string games, a sort of glorified cat's-cradle pastime, in which string patterns were made to represent objects and even episodes with movement, such as a man having a fight with an enemy and returning with his opponent's head. The anthropologists worked out methods for recording these games. One would read the directions while another would try to reproduce the pattern without mistakes.

Another native diversion was top-spinning. Colored wooden tops were decorated with designs and spun in competitions. Experts could keep them going for half an hour.

Haddon was particularly interested in recapturing the Malu or initiation ceremony, in which, as in Australia, the bull-roarer was used, that curious instrument which women and children were never supposed to see. There were no masks left, but Haddon persuaded the islanders to re-create them, using cardboard instead of tortoise shell. The boys to be initiated sat in a taboo area in a semicircle near a band of drummers. The drums were beaten. A group of men waved sticks. Then the *zogotes,* or sacred performers, marched in from the forest. The first wore a mask representing a gigantic human face with great staring eyes topped with feathers and with a beard of human jawbones. On the back of the head was a turtle shell from which hung a string. The second zogote, unmasked, held the string. The third wore a mask of a hammerhead shark with a human face and small arms and legs protruding from it.

The zogotes danced in front of the boys and chanted. The boys were told the secret name of the god, which must never be revealed to the uninitiated. A later part of the Malu ceremony consisted of frightening the boys. The latter were covered with coconut leaves while the zogotes rasped clamshells and whirled bull-roarers.

The scientists spent from April to November on Murray Island, with trips to other islets in the group. After this they passed some months in Borneo and returned to England the following April.

Their rich haul of artifacts of native culture was so extensive that there was no place to display it in Cambridge. Some of the cases remained unpacked for twenty years.

Haddon was anxious to return with a second expedition, but could not raise the money. The first had cost one thousand pounds. All his life he struggled with financial problems. With Frazer's aid he was appointed to a part-time lectureship at Cambridge, but the stipend was so small that he had to continue teaching in Dublin and lecturing on the side to support his family, which now included two children. "Who cares for anthropology?" he asked bitterly. "There's no money in it." It is no wonder that his politics were socialist. Not until 1904 was a separate anthropology department created in Cambridge which provided him with a full-time lectureship that he held until his death.

Eventually Haddon became the grand old man of anthropology in Cambridge, the father of the science in that university, as Tylor had been at Oxford some decades before. Tall, loose-knit, restless, with rough-hewn features, a craggy nose, a trooper's mustache, and a shock of black hair which turned snow white in his old age, he exuded vitality. He was simple, direct, and outspoken. "I don't dine," he said, "I feed." His house was a museum of drums, spears, skulls, bows and arrows, baskets, shields, masks. His motto was "You can travel anywhere with a smile and a piece of string." When he had to make friends with a strange group of primitives, he began showing his repertoire of string games to the children, and this disarming approach soon put him at ease with the adults.

A scar design, a turtle drawn by a native, and a comb.

While in America to lecture at the Field Museum in Chicago, he managed to visit the Blackfeet Indians of Montana, sat naked in a sweat bath with the performers, and took part in a medicine-pipe dance.

Although lecturing did not come easily to him, for he was a hesitant, jerky speaker, he was a great teacher whose energy and enthusiasm fired all who came in contact with him. Once, when talking about his beloved islanders to a class containing some girl students, he ran over his time. Just as he was pointing out that, in the Straits, women were accustomed to propose to the men, the women students began slipping out at the back of the hall. He called after them: "There's no hurry, girls. There won't be a boat for some weeks."

He wrote a number of books that were quite widely read. A popular work on the Torres Straits, *Head Hunters, Black and*

White, was published in 1901; *Evolution in Art* (1895) was his chief contribution to theory, and in 1910 he produced a *History of Anthropology*, the first of its kind. In 1914 he made another trip to the Straits and gathered material for a monograph on native canoes. His material on string games was eventually put into written form by his daughter.

Ironically enough, Cambridge did not create a full professorship in anthropology until 1933, when Haddon was nearing eighty and ineligible. He died in 1940.

His monument, the report on the Torres Straits Expedition, was not completed until thirty-five years after the scientists had returned. It comprised six volumes of from three to four hundred quarto pages, each with many photographs and line cuts. The first volume covered geography, history, and general ethnology; the second, psychology in terms of measurement of reaction and sensation; the third, language; the fourth, arts, crafts, music, dance ceremonies, dress; the fifth and sixth, sociology, magic, religion, morals, and totemism of the western and eastern islands, respectively. The whole was a great step forward in organization and method, a model for future studies.

Haddon was a well-balanced scholar who combined a theorist's grasp of the broad outlines of cultural phenomena with the tireless energy of a field worker. While anthropologists of his type were scouring remote parts of the world for precious, fast-disappearing data, the purely speculative minds were making use of this material to attack the problems already raised by the founders of the science. The origin and development of religion were by now the subject of brisk controversy between two camps.

Chapter 12

WHO WROTE DEUTERONOMY?

Concerning William Robertson Smith

■ So far, except for Sir John Lubbock's brush with a conservative British electorate over his book on prehistoric man, anthropology had met with no serious opposition. Unlike some of the pioneers of medicine who were subjected to persecution, anthropologists had been able to go on quietly examining the early history of man's institutions. After the first lost battles with Darwinism a kind of truce was made between theologians and scientists. The former managed to adjust to new points of view by symbolical interpretations of the Scriptures. The anthropologists' investigations of primitive behavior and myth were rather remote from anything in the average man's daily life. And as long as issues are not clearly drawn, a remarkable amount of self-deception can go on, and contradictory concepts can exist side by side.

When a combative Scotch anthropologist applied the tools of comparative study to the Bible itself, however, he ran head first into the entrenched folkways of his own culture and became, in a mild way, a martyr to his science.

William Robertson Smith (1846–1894) was the son of a clergyman who was also a classical scholar. Brought up in rural surroundings, Smith studied at the University of Aberdeen and went on to the University of Edinburgh to specialize in Hebrew. The early death of a younger brother had stirred his religious emotions. During his undergraduate years, when he was a member of the Edinburgh Theological Society, he seemed merely a pious young student, not likely to trouble the fiercely conservative Presbyterian Church, which controlled the universities of Scotland. Such matters as infant damnation were burning questions in the intellectual circles in which he moved. He took part in minor doctrinal controversies and gained practice as a debater which was to prove useful later on. In 1870, when he was called to the professorship of Hebrew in the University of Aberdeen, he was ordained a minister of the Free Church, a prerequisite for holding any university position. The young teacher's speech of acceptance was a little out of the ordinary, for he proclaimed himself in favor of the so-called "higher criticism" of the Bible.

Higher criticism meant simply using to examine the sources of the texts, dates of composition, and authenticity of various parts of the Bible the same scholarly apparatus that was currently employed in discussing other documents of ancient literature. This scientific attitude toward literary texts, born of philology, was particularly well entrenched in Germany, and it was in Germany that the most important contributions to such biblical study were being made. Young Robertson Smith and his father had traveled in Germany during one of his vacations. The tenor of his remarks shows that he was well acquainted with what was going on across the channel. In part, he said: "The higher criticism does not mean negative criticism. It means the fair and honest looking at the Bible as a historical record and the effort everywhere to reach the real meaning and historical setting not of individual passages of Scripture but of Scripture records as a whole. . . . We must let the Bible speak for itself. . . . The process can be dangerous to faith only when it is begun without faith—when we forget that the Bible history is no profane history but the story of God's saving self-manifestation."

Smith's conviction that there was no danger to orthodox faith in the higher criticism seems, in perspective, a trifle naïve. If it could be shown that certain passages were interpolations of a much later date than the body of the work (as was shown), and if it could be proved that whole books attributed to certain historical characters could not have been written by them, doubt would certainly be cast on the nature of divine authority and the revealed truth of much of the Scriptures. For, once absolute literal belief in the divine inspiration of every word had to be abandoned, the foot of rationalization was in the door. None of this was evident to Robertson Smith. His was the eternally human desire to have his cake and eat it too.

As it happened, there was little historical criticism of the Bible in Scotland at the time. The heads of the church were engaged in fierce battles over ecclesiastical government and their relation to English Presbyterianism. They did not notice the danger signals in the young professor's address.

While in Edinburgh, as a member of the Evening Club he had come in contact with the scientific elite of the city, which included Robert Louis Stevenson's father and Carlyle's brother. The most important contact for Smith was J. F. McLennan, who, as we have seen, proposed the theory of primitive marriage-by-capture. With the latter he formed a friendship that lasted during the whole of McLennan's life. It was evidently this contact which turned his thought toward anthropology. He read *Primitive Marriage*, and must have discussed it with the author, for he adopted McLennan's views wholeheartedly. In a letter to McLennan in 1871 he was already discussing sorcery in the Bible.

Thus the torch of inquiry was handed on. If it was possible to trace the stories and chronicles of the Bible to concrete sources, and to be precise about dates of composition, was it not possible to go a step further and investigate the meaning of puzzling ceremonies and rituals of the Hebrews in terms of other related peoples?

As luck would have it, Robertson Smith was invited by the *Encyclopaedia Britannica*, then preparing its ninth edition, to write the article on the Bible. Once more he revealed the trend of his thinking. "The Bible may be viewed either from a purely theological viewpoint, as is done from the dogmatic system, or from the standpoint of literary and historical criticism. The two views are not naturally exclusive though theology has sometimes formulated the divine authority of the Scriptures in such a way that it excludes all human spontaneity on the part of the writers and forbids the application to the Bible of any of the ordinary laws of criticism and exegesis." Smith made it plain he had no use for the dogmatic system. He applied the laws of criticism in detail.

This time the fat was in the fire. He was attacked by reviewers, and in an anonymous pamphlet he was accused of heresy. He was described as being as wicked as the Dutch and German critics who got their inspiration directly from the Devil. His college committee asked him to write a letter reconsidering his position and reaffirming his faith. He indignantly declined.

The college committee, after some hesitation—for Robertson Smith was a man with a distinguished scholarly reputation and of unimpeachably virtuous life—announced that his article was "of a dangerous and unsettling tendency" because his critical position "had frequently been associated with denial of [divine] inspiration." Some of the members dissented from this hedging, guilt-by-association charge, but the newspapers gleefully fanned the flames of controversy. The matter was sent up to a higher court, the Presbytery of Aberdeen. Robertson Smith was called in and questioned. He fought back, stoutly maintaining that he was as orthodox in belief as the next. The case went to a still higher court, the Assembly of the Free Church. The biblical critic was once more accused of a "tendency" and suspended from his chair pending investigation. Smith's obstinate Scotch blood was up. He answered his accusers roundly, saying that historical criticism had nothing to do with his faith and scoring his judges for never examining his article in detail. "It can not be proposed to stifle historical criticism!" he cried angrily.

Two years had been consumed in this theological argument. The liberals within the church were fighting for Robertson Smith, the governing hierarchy was against him. Of course, from the perspective of history, the arguments of the conservatives seemed logical enough. It was Robertson Smith who was defending—in utter sincerity—a false position, divorcing his intellectual activities from his beliefs. But he was not alone in his time. Such outstanding scientists as Lord Kelvin and Clerk Maxwell cultivated a similar state of mind.

The Assembly finally revised the charges, omitting some counts, and sent the case back to the lower ecclesiastical courts.

Fortunately, Robertson Smith does not seem to have been dependent on his professorship for a living. He was happily continuing his anthropological work during the periods when his case was inactive. He visited Italy and Egypt, for his studies in comparative religion had led him to other Semitic cultures, and he was learning Arabic. He talked to grooms, street beggars, donkey boys, and gradually acquired fluency in the language. He sailed up the Nile, visiting the monuments of ancient Egypt, looking busily, as he wrote McLennan, for traces of matriarchy among the Egyptians and totemism among the Bedouin.

When the traveler returned to face his obstinate accusers once more, he discovered that he had been offered the chair of Hebrew at Harvard. He refused it, for his reinstatement as professor in the University of Aberdeen was to him a matter of principle. He felt that he was fighting for the cause of intellectual freedom. At last his case came to a vote. On May 27, 1880, thousands of spectators crowded the halls of the Assembly to hear the verdict. There were many women present, and the galleries were crowded with hissing and cheering students. The heresies of Professor Robertson Smith had become a *cause célèbre*. Smith got a prolonged ovation when he appeared. His chief opponent, Principal Rainy, was hissed. A prayer for guidance put an end to the disturbance. Two motions were made: one that he be deprived of his chair at Aberdeen, the other that he be mildly censured and warned to exercise caution in future public utterances. Amid great suspense, a vote was taken.

Ladies whispered behind their veils, while students muttered and scuffed their feet. Suddenly from the platform a staid professor began to wave his hat. The ladies waved their scraps of lace hand-kerchiefs. Then the whole assemblage burst into loud cheers. The mild censure had won, and Robertson Smith was considered to be vindicated. Scientists all over the world sent congratulations.

But the little Scot was not to be muzzled. McLennan had just published a paper on totemism, which he considered a form of primitive animal worship. Influenced by his master, Robertson Smith published in the *Journal of Philology* of June 1 (just three days after his case ended) an article on "Animal Worship and Animal Tribes among the Arabs and in the Old Testament." In it he pointed out that a number of tribal names among the Arabs were those of animals, such as dog, lizard, panther. He found a quote from Ezekiel which referred to a chamber in which the elders worshipped and on whose walls were pictures of quadrupeds and creeping things. Then, too, the Arabs of the Sinai Peninsula refused to eat the flesh of the rock badger, calling it their brother. There was enough evidence, he thought, to suggest that the ancient Hebrew gods were personifications not of astronomical bodies, but rather of animals. It was a short article, but it contained the germ of his later work. It also brought the fire of his enemies upon him once again. A member of the Presbytery immediately petitioned that he be suspended from his post because of his "unscriptural and pernicious views" as set forth in the article. Said his opponent, one Professor Macauley: "The views expressed are so gross and so fitted to pollute the moral sentiments of the community that they can not be considered except within the closed doors of any court of this church."

The old routine was re-enacted. Robertson Smith's publications were again reviewed, and a new committee of the Assembly announced that his writing "tended to create the impression that Scripture does not present a reliable statement of truth and that God is not the author of it."

Perhaps nowhere but in the theological backwaters of Scotland would such an issue have been so bitterly debated in 1880. The teaching profession, however, is frequently the target of those who wish to enforce a dogmatic point of view or wish to stamp out dissent from officially accepted ideologies. Oddly enough, Robertson Smith, still loudly protesting his orthodoxy, was unable to perceive his own anthropological situation, violating, as he was, the taboos of his particular cultural group.

Once more the issue came to a vote. The five-year struggle was at an end. Smith's liberal friends could defend him no longer. In May 1881 the Assembly voted, 178 strong, to deprive him of his post in the University of Aberdeen.

It was a hollow victory for his opponents. A group of Smith's partisans held a rump meeting and voted to censure the heads of their church. Smith himself was immediately offered an editorship of the *Encyclopaedia Britannica*. He moved to Edinburgh and rejoined his friends of the Evening Club.

In 1882 the reader in Arabic in Cambridge was tossed over a cliff by the Arabs of the Sinai Peninsula. Robertson Smith, a more cautious traveler, profited, for he was appointed to the position the following year. He grew friendly with young James Frazer, who became his disciple. Frazer was already collecting material on magic and religion, all of which he made available to Robertson Smith. The latter, in 1888, was invited to give a series of lectures in Aberdeen on comparative religion. From these lectures in 1889 came his famous work, *The Religion of the Semites*.

The central idea was developed from the small monograph on animal worship. Smith noted that there was a great solidarity between a tribal god and its worshippers. Ancient Semitic communities were small and indulged in many feuds. The enemies of the tribesmen were enemies of the god. It also seemed that the tribesmen were related to the god. One tribe, for instance, called its members "the sons and daughters of Chemash," the divinity they worshipped. This might have been taken as a proof of ancestor-worship, but Smith does not seem to have been influenced by Tylor, and nowhere cites his work. McLennan was his master, and McLennan was concerned with totemism. Consequently, Smith picks up hints of animal affinities. There were myths of men transposed into animals. A clan of Israelites was said to have given birth to lizards. Another group could turn themselves into werewolves. On the Sinai Peninsula, panthers had once been men.

Working from another angle, he found that many early Semitic gods, called *Baals*, were associated with springs, streams, pools, or green oases. There was an association with the fertility-bestowing power of water. These fertility Baals were the divinities of an agricultural society.

An agricultural society had to struggle with the untamed wilderness, with the hostile animals it contained. In Semitic tradition there was a special type of non-material being called a *djinn*. Djinns did not have the specific personalities of gods, but appeared sometimes as men, sometimes as animals. They were often hostile, but could be controlled by magic. In investigating tree cults he found that the Arabs called sacred trees *manahil*, places where angels or djinns descended and were heard singing and dancing.

It seemed to Smith that djinns were spirits of the wild, a midway stage between an animal and a totem. The early agriculturalists in their battle with the wilderness imperfectly understood the nature of animals and clothed them with the marvelous. Because of the life-giving power of water, which was also marvelous, there might be an association of djinn with specific locality. The ancient god "was not an omnipotent and omnipresent being but was himself linked to the physical world by a series of affinities connecting him not merely with man but with beasts, trees, inanimate things."

The spirits of the wild were metamorphosed into the chauvinistic clan-god by means of sacrifice, according to Robertson Smith.

This custom he found associated with totemism. The latter was connected with uncleanness, and uncleanness was the same thing as sacredness or taboo in the South Seas. The fish in the sacred pools of the Semites were taboo. Swine were unclean among all the

Hebrew tribes. The Syrians considered doves unclean. Now, totemism, as observed among primitive peoples, always involved a close network of kinship, a blood brotherhood within the tribe. If certain animals were not eaten, this fact pointed to a totemistic taboo: they could not be eaten because they were ancestors or relatives, members of the tribe. But in certain cases the totem *was* eaten.

Looking about for an analogy among the Semites, he found that the Saracens, who never ate camel meat normally, consumed it in a special ritual feast. The early agriculturist, in order to overcome his fear of animals and wild spirits, had to make an alliance with them. This alliance was to develop into the totemic system; the animal became a blood brother, a friend and protector, bound to his human relatives by the responsibilities of tribal kinship.

The alliance was symbolized by the rite of *communion* or ritual partaking of the flesh of a victim whose flesh was also the flesh of the tribe. Hence the eating of the totem or animal blood brother took place *only* at certain special community festivals. The modern conception of unclean animals, which were never eaten, was simply a half-understood survival of totemism.

Robertson Smith cited the Todas of India, who worshipped their cattle, but never ate them except when once a year they killed a bull calf for a sacrificial meal. They also killed one of their beasts at funerals, caressing it beforehand and bewailing it afterward as though it were a relative.

The evidence from the Book of Ezekiel indicated that the Israelites, in a period of disorganization, had regressed to totemism, including worship of swine, dogs, and mice.

Priests clad in animal skins were also a relic of totemism, for dressing in the skin of an animal was an effort to claim kinship with it.

All through the Bible ran the theme of the burnt offering. In this case, a part of the sacrificial victim was burned, sublimating its substance so that the god could partake of it as smoke while the human worshippers ate the rest of the meat.

The eating of salt together, which made enmity impossible— an Arab custom—was one more proof of the sacredness and brotherhood of the communal meal.

Thus, to Smith, all sacrifice was originally a ritual of communion. Animals were not a later substitute for human beings, but rather the two were interchangeable, for both were members of the totemic clan. Sacrifice as an expiation or an attempt to bribe the god was a later rationalization. This, of course, led up to Christian communion. Although Smith did not carry it that far, one of his disciples did.

Robertson Smith, the staunch Presbyterian, had to admit that his ancient Semites were frivolous people whose religion had little place for sin. "The habitual temper of the worshippers is one of joyous confidence in their god, untroubled by a habitual sense of human guilt, and resting on the firm conviction that they and the deity they adore are good friends. . . . The basis of this confidence lies of course in the view that the gods are part and parcel of the same natural community as their worshippers."

Smith's book was stimulating and ingenious. The weakness of part of his case lay in the fact that many of the data subsequently compiled on totemism indicated that the totemic animal was not a god and was never actually worshipped.

Nevertheless, the book had its effect on anthropological thinking. James Frazer called it "a striking and powerful book." In retrospect, Malinowski praised Robertson Smith as "a great Scottish scholar . . . the first modern anthropologist to establish the sociological point of view in the treatment of religion." As we shall see later, he also greatly influenced Freud.

In other words, up to his time religion had been treated as a kind of detachable philosophic structure. It was he who first tried to examine it as a functioning part of its specific social context. Modern anthropology has more and more tried to look at cultures as a whole. Smith was therefore a pioneer who not only broke through the taboo against the anthropological study of the Bible as a part of comparative religion, but also pointed the way toward contemporary scientific attitudes.

A slight, nervous man who remained a bachelor, he drank claret, rolled cigarettes incessantly, and collected engravings. In his forties the family scourge, tuberculosis, attacked his spine. He endured a painful spinal operation and, after a period of invalidism, died in March 1894.

To the end of his life he never abandoned an innocent mystical faith in the divine inspiration of the Bible, which was never allowed to affect his critical scholarship. There is, however, a faint air of bewilderment in the statement he made to a friend at the close of his life: "I begin to think I can never have been a theologian."

Chapter 13

THE PRIEST WHO SLAYS THE SLAYER

Concerning Sir James Frazer

■ Today at Christmastime mistletoe is sold in florists' shops. Traditionally, of course, a girl who is caught under the mistletoe is fair game to be kissed. This custom is a part of the folk history of the plant.

When mistletoe was cut on All Hallows' Day and used with a certain charm, it was a sure protection against witchery. In Brittany it was hung in stables to protect cattle. In Sweden it possessed the power to reveal the existence of gold. In a Scandinavian myth it killed the god Baldur. Such magical properties show that its folk history began long before the Christian festival and connects it with ancient pagan rites.

Mistletoe's tendency to turn yellow when cut and hung to dry gave it the name "the golden bough," in turn the title of one of the most famous books in the history of anthropology. Before Robertson Smith died, he read the proofs of this book. From McLennan to Robertson Smith to its author, James George Frazer, there is an unbroken chain of Scotch ethnological scholarship.

Frazer, who has been called the last of the British classical evolutionists, is one of the monumental figures not only of anthropology, but also of nineteenth-century literature. Above all, he is the representative of his science who has most appealed to the general public. The list of scientists and literary critics influenced by him is extraordinary: Spencer and Gillen, A. C. Haddon, W. R. R. Rivers, A. E. Crawley, R. R. Marett in his own country; Freud in Vienna; K. T. Preuss and Wilhelm Wundt in Germany; Durkheim in France; Malinowski in Poland; in the literary field, Gilbert Murray, Jane Harrison, Andrew Lang; even Anatole France, Henri Bergson, and Arnold Toynbee have been affected by his work.

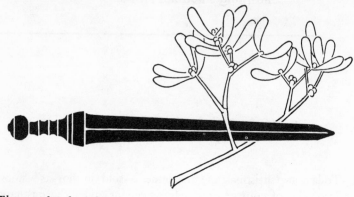

The sword and mistletoe.

The details of his life are unspectacular. Born in 1854 into a family of solid, pious Glasgow merchants, he was destined for the bar. Young Frazer leaned toward Oxford, but his Presbyterian father ruled that the atmosphere of that university was too high-church. He finally obtained a scholarship to Cambridge in 1873. Six years later he was granted a fellowship to Trinity College of that university, a fellowship which he held for life. The lure of the classics had already obliterated whatever interest he may have had in a legal career. He set about editing and translating the second-century Greek traveler Pausanius. A friend gave him a copy of Edward Tylor's *Primitive Culture,* and from then on his career took a new direction. If any further incentive was needed, it came in the eighties when he met Robertson Smith, then editing the *Encyclopaedia Britannica.* The friendship was mutually stimulating. Frazer regarded Smith as the greatest man he had ever known. Smith invited Frazer to write the articles on *totem* and *taboo* for the *Britannica.* In 1887 Frazer sent a pamphlet containing a questionnaire on manners, customs, and beliefs of primitive and semi-primitive peoples to missionaries and administrators all over the world. It was the material gleaned from this survey (which reminds us of Morgan) to which he gave Robertson Smith access.

Most of Frazer's life seems to have been spent in a library. Although he traveled in Italy, Greece, and the Holy Land in the nineties, and mused poetically on the classic past in various historic spots, his real adventures took place among myth and folklore. He was an encyclopedic collector of data, surpassing even Tylor. After his dozens of volumes were published, there was still material for four volumes of notebooks (he had a trunkful of these, filled with extracts in all languages in his small, precise handwriting), and when he died at eighty-seven he left stacks of unpublished data which he had not had time to use.

Although he was a speculative scholar who never set foot in the field, sometimes when he talked with government administrators or missionaries home from distant parts of the world, these travelers, astonished by his insight, would exclaim: "Why, you know my blacks better than I know them after twenty years' residence among them!" Yet when the American psychologist William James asked Frazer to tell him about primitives he had met, Frazer's shocked response was: "But God forbid!"

Frazer was a small, slender man with a neatly trimmed, pointed beard. His chief diversion was walking, and even in his old age he would sometimes cover thirty miles a day.

His poetic gifts, revealed in many lyrically exalted (if slightly purple) passages in his important books, reflect his classical scholarship. As Malinowski points out, he grew up in an age of unspecialized learning and read widely enough to be able to discuss physics with Clerk Maxwell and biology with Huxley. He could write essays in the style of Addison, read his Homer in the Greek, his Bible in Aramaic. In his work he was able to use French, German, Italian, Spanish, and Dutch.

There was, however, a core of narrowness in the distinguished little Scotch gentleman who was knighted in 1914, showered with decorations and honorary degrees, and presented with the freedom of the City of Glasgow in 1932. Freud, whom he influenced, he would never read, prudishly rejecting psychoanalysis without trying to understand it. He was not interested in the ideas of other anthropologists, and could not stand personal contradiction. Nor could he bear controversy. When Andrew Lang ridiculed *The Golden Bough* in a review, labeling it the "vegetable" school of anthropology, Frazer was so upset that he could not work for months. After that he took care never to read unfavorable reviews of his books.

In 1895 he married Mrs. Lilly Grove, a Frenchwoman of literary tastes. She took charge of his career, managed his correspondence, shielded him from the world. One has the impression that Frazer, whose first important book brought him fame in his thirties, slipped into the role of grand old man rather easily, while his wife occupied herself with playing midwife to genius.

It is to his credit that he was a warm and generous friend. Even Westermarck, with whose ideas he had no sympathy, records that Frazer came to lunch, when the young scholar was residing in a cottage in a grove of beeches, and playfully appointed his host "King of the Wood."

He was at his best in correspondence with field workers. His eager interest in and encouragement of Spencer and the practical help he extended to A. C. Haddon have already been noted. Malinowski, too, admits that Frazer's letters and queries were a great stimulus while he was working in Melanesia.

Oddly enough, he was a poor teacher and an indifferent lecturer. Apparently his was a personality that could not respond to the give and take of the classroom. Fundamentally, he was an artist rather than an analytical thinker.

Witness the opening page of *The Golden Bough*: "Who does not know Turner's picture of the Golden Bough? The scene, suffused with the golden glow of imagination in which the divine mind of Turner steeped and transfigured even the fairest natural landscape, is a dreamlike vision of the little woodland lake of Nemi—'Diana's mirror'—as it was called by the ancients." The same stately periods continue to unroll as he pursues his theme throughout the folklore of the world.

In this grove of Aricia, near Lake Nemi in Italy, a man with a drawn sword, in Roman times, constantly circled a tree. The man was a priest and nominally a king—

> *The priest who slays the slayer*
> *And shall himself be slain. . . .*

He had killed his predecessor and would eventually be killed by the one who would succeed him.

How did this strange custom arise?

According to the legend, only a runaway slave was supposed to break, if he could, a branch from the tree. This branch was identified with the Golden Bough that Aeneas, at the bidding of the soothsayer, plucked before he descended into the underworld. The slave, when he had plucked the bough, was entitled to fight the priest and succeed to the title and office of king if he killed him. Various other classical figures—Diana, the Greek hero Hippolytus who rejected Aphrodite's advances, and the hero's son Virbius— were vaguely connected with religious rites practiced at or near this spot.

This tangle of mythology obscured more than it explained.

According to Frazer, the sacred tree, the plucking of the bough, and the killing of the king could be analyzed in terms of magic and folklore. The search for the real meaning of the king of the wood became in Frazer's hands a kind of mystery story.

Kings or king-priests were often charged with the responsibility of ensuring good crops for their subjects. This involved magic. There were two kinds. A Dyak medicine man of Borneo pretended to die and get well, a process supposed to cure his patient. The Bataks performed make-believe pantomime with a doll to help a woman in childbirth. These were cases of *imitative magic*. Securing hair, nail parings, spittle, teeth, the navel cord, foreskin, or anything connected with a person's body, and using it in a charm to injure or control its owner was an operation exemplifying *contagious magic*. The Malay practice of putting nail parings in a wax image and holding it over a fire for seven nights while repeating:

> It is not the wax I am holding,
> It is the liver, heart, and spleen
> of so-and-so that I scorch

combined both principles.

Particularly quaint was the Ruthenian thieves' custom of playing on a flute made from the leg bone of a corpse in the hope that those inhabiting the house to be robbed would sleep like the dead.

Taboo was a negative application of magic, and magic in general was a pseudo-science, an erroneous notion of the laws of nature, a mistaken conclusion resulting from the "association of ideas."

The magician was a clever semi-impostor. He gradually, by

means of his pretensions, replaced the more primitive council of old men. Eventually he developed into king and priest.

Frazer defined religion as a conciliation of powers superior to man who were believed to control and direct nature and men's lives. He thought that belief came first, followed by ritual. The sorcerer *controlled* unseen powers, the priest *propitiated* them.

Thus religion was everywhere preceded by an age of magic. When the spell-weaving primitive finally became disillusioned as a result of too many failures of his spells, his attitude toward nature and the unseen powers changed to one of awe, and he commenced to worship.

Specifically, one of the magician's most important tasks was rain-making. There were many instances of kings with this talent and, in general, the power of increasing fertility.

The king of the wood of Nemi was evidently a nature king allied to such rain kings.

Frazer then attacked the problem of the tree. Trees were worshipped all over the world. The Bulgarians sometimes threatened trees with an ax if they refused to bear. The Maypole in German countries was often a fir tree and a survival of fertility worship. The enduring green of the fir symbolized continuity of vegetable life. There was a connection between human fertility and vegetable fertility. After a Baganda woman of Africa had borne twins, she lay down upon her back in the grass with a plantain flower between her legs. Her husband then came and knocked away the flower with his penis. This was supposed to improve the plantain yield. Diana, associated with the forest, was a fertility goddess. Frazer believed that Virbius, king of the wood, was Diana's male partner. The sacred tree was an oak—a tree associated with Jupiter. Therefore the priest at Nemi probably also embodied the old Aryan oak god.

By such examples Frazer established that the powers of nature were tied up with the king. His person was extraordinarily sacred, and many actions were taboo. The touch of iron, that anti-magical metal, might be dangerous. His name might not be spoken, for, on the principle of contagious magic, it might harm him.

The death of a king was a crisis. If he died naturally, it was the result of sorcery or else he was deserting his people. If his bodily powers began to fail, such failure became a symbol of failing fertility in general.

Frazer sought for historical evidence of kings being killed in their prime to prevent a failure of fertility. In his first edition he instanced a custom in Babylon of dethroning the real ruler for a day and killing his substitute. This seemed to him evidence of the sacrifice of a ruler. In folk festivals he found other examples of the mock king for a day. In other areas there was a wealth of folklore data dealing with the dramatic or symbolic destruction of a vegetable spirit. The Whitsuntide mummers of Bavaria killed a "maybearer" by cutting off an artificial head and neck, a part of his costume. In Saxony they "killed" a wild man and brought him to life again in a spring festival. In Bohemia they killed a "king." With this was associated the carrying-out of death in spring and the funeral of the carnival. All activity of this sort was symbolic of the death and reincarnation of the fertility spirit. The killing of the king of the wood at Nemi in Italy seemed to Frazer another example of the death of the fertility spirit.

"Primitive man believed that in order to produce the great phenomena of nature on which his life depended he had only to imitate them, and that immediately by a secret sympathy or mystic influence the little drama which he acted in the forest glade or mountain dell, on the desert plain or wind-swept shore, would be taken up and repeated by mightier actors on a vaster stage. He fancied that by masquerading in leaves and flowers he helped the bare earth to clothe herself in verdure and that by playing the death and burial of winter he drove that gloomy season away, and made smooth the path for the footsteps of returning spring."

Much of this material and its interpretation Frazer borrowed from Wilhelm Mannhardt, who from 1865 to the 1880's diligently collected European folklore dealing with water, corn, and tree spirits and cults of the wood and field. The concept of the killing of the god of course also owed something to Robertson Smith's theory of sacrifice.

Frazer continued his thesis with an examination of the Babylonian god Tammuz, the Greek Attis, and the Egyptian Osiris, whose mythology he also identified with the killing of the nature spirit. He rose to new poetic heights when he discussed the death of Adonis: "Every year, in the belief of his worshippers, Adonis was wounded to death on the mountains, and every year the face of nature itself was dyed with his sacred blood. So year by year, the Syrian damsels lamented his untimely fate, while the red anemone, his flower, bloomed among the cedars of Lebanon, and the river ran red to the sea, fringing the winding shores of the blue Mediterranean, whenever the wind set inshore, with a sinuous band of crimson."

He even suggested that the Catholic celebration of the death and resurrection of Christ had been grafted onto Adonis-worship, and that the Greek artists' picture of the sorrowful goddess with her dying lover in her arms was the model for the Christian *Pietà*.

When Frazer had outlined his explanation of the killing of the priest-king and the significance of the sacred tree, the problem of the Golden Bough still remained. Why must it be cut before the priest could be killed?

In search of new clues, he attacked the myth of Baldur, the Scandinavian fertility god. The divinity, so the story ran, dreamed of his own death. Alarmed by this prophecy, the goddess Frigga persuaded all animate and inanimate things to consider the person of Baldur taboo—all things, alas, except an insignificant plant, the mistletoe, which she overlooked. Loki, the troublemaker, plucked the mistletoe and gave it to the blind god Hother to throw at Baldur in sport. Baldur was killed and his body burned on a funeral pyre.

This myth could be divided into two elements. One was the burning of the god. There were folklore data from all over on midsummer fires, St. John's fires, customs of leaping over these fires for luck, and other customs in which wicked giants, puppets, or animals were burned. The latter suggested some sort of living sacrifice. Mannhardt thought that such fires were an imitation of sunlight, a magic ceremony to attract sunlight to crops. In any case, these fires seemed to have a fertility significance.

Mistletoe, as we pointed out at the beginning of this chapter, had a magical history. It was cut by the Druids for use in religious ceremonies. In folk belief it was considered to be the seat of life of the oak. This idea of a separable soul or vital principle was found in much European folklore. Therefore, Baldur's life was probably originally thought of as residing in the mistletoe. Neither he nor the priest of Nemi could be killed until the bough containing the vital spark was cut. Frazer interpreted the myth of Baldur as a later rationalization devised to cover a fertility drama of death and resurrection.

Frazer summed up his impressive study of magic and religion by stating that magic came first in men's minds, then religion, then science, each giving way slowly and incompletely to the other. *The Golden Bough*, first published in two volumes, was expanded to twelve as Frazer inserted more digressions and illustrative material, and then, many years later, was abridged into one. Although its central ideas were accepted by a majority of scholars in the field at the time when it was published, some critical voices were raised against it, as we shall presently see.

Applying the same type of evidence to the Old Testament, Frazer produced a two-volume study, *Folklore in the Old Testament*, in 1918, wishing, as he said, to follow in the footsteps of his "revered friend and master," Robertson Smith. His treatment of the story of the creation and the fall is a good example of his approach. He pointed out certain inconsistencies in the story of the creation. In the first version the animals were created, then man and woman; in the second, man appears first, then the animals, then woman is made from man's rib. The first account had less priestly editing and was closer to folklore. The creation of man from clay was an idea common to Babylonia, Egypt, and Greece, as well as Israel. Frazer had visited the Valley of Phocis in Greece, where Prometheus had originally created man. "It was a hot summer day in late autumn—the first of November—and after the long rainless summer of Greece, the little glen was quite dry, but at the bottom I found a reddish crumbling earth, perhaps a relic of the clay out of which Prometheus modelled our first parents. The place was solitary and deserted; only the line of mouldering towers and battlements on the hill above spoke of the busy life that had passed away." Creation from clay was a myth also found in Tahiti, New Zealand, Australia, and among North American Indians. In many cases the clay was described as red. The Hebrew word for man, *adam*, was similar to that for the ground, *adamah*, and the word for red was *adom*.

Next to the tree of knowledge in the Garden of Eden stood the tree of life, which was almost ignored until the tragic end of the story of the fall. It was only as an afterthought that the Lord drove the sinful couple out of the garden to prevent their eating of the fruit and becoming immortal.

Frazer suggested that the original form of the story had been distorted in the Old Testament. Instead of a choice between the tree of knowledge and the tree of life, perhaps the basis of the legend was the apposition of a tree of life and a tree of death.

Frazer looked for folklore parallels.

In the Babylonian epic of Gilgamesh, the serpent stole the magic plant that conferred immortality, whereupon the hero sat down and wept. Many primitive peoples considered the snake to be immortal because it shed its skin.

There were two familiar elements in folklore—the perverted message and the cast skin. In African legends, hares and dogs were messengers bearing the gift of immortality, but they distorted the message and destroyed the gift. The Zulus said that God sent two lizards with messages concerning immortality. The first bestowed it; the second, an afterthought, canceled it. Unfortunately, the second messenger was faster than the first, so man remained mortal. The Zulus have hated lizards ever since. An East African story related that one day God came down to earth and addressed all living things, saying: "Who wishes not to die?" All were asleep except the serpent, and that is why the serpent does not die unless killed, but renews its youth by casting its skin. In Celebes a lizard played the same role. On an island west of Samoa a creator god was putting the finishing touches to his work when he became hungry and ate some bananas. This was a pity, for if he had eaten crabs, which cast their shell, men and animals would have been immortal.

A composite myth in East Africa stated that God sent a bird to tell men they would not die, but instead would shed their skins and renew their youth. The bird met a snake making a meal on some carrion. The bird longed for a bite of the loathsome food. "Give me some meat and blood," it said, "and I will tell you God's message." The snake grumpily told the bird to go away, but the greedy fowl persisted and finally got its way. While it feasted shamefully, the snake received the gift. Vice was punished, however, for the traitor bird was visited by God with a perpetual stomach ache, and that is why it sits wailing in the tops of trees to this day.

This, to Frazer, was the germ of the creation story. The addition of the eating of the apple and the subtraction of the serpent's deceitful acquisition of immortality was due to Semitic editing.

By the time Frazer had worked his way through the Old Testament in this style, the familiar stories had acquired some rather startling variations and interpretations. But it was over thirty years since Robertson Smith's martyrdom. The pace of cultural evolution had been rapid. The work was everywhere received tranquilly. The reviewer in the publication *Theology* wrote: "A very remarkable book, showing amazing industry and varied learning, dealing with the interpretation of the Bible."

Frazer had published an important book on totemism in 1910, which will be discussed elsewhere, and in the second edition of *The Golden Bough* he made great use of Spencer's and Gillen's *The Native Tribes of Central Australia,* a book which he had edited and polished, and for which, with Tylor's aid, he had secured a publisher.

In 1935 he published *The Fear of the Dead in Primitive Religion.* Four volumes of anthropological notebooks were also published under the title *Anthologica Anthropologica* in the late thirties.

A short essay, "The Task of Psyche" (1909), in which he set out to show the constructive value of superstition in the evolution of culture, reveals the quaintly conservative character of his social thinking. One virtue of superstition was the fact that "it has strengthened the respect for private property and has thereby contributed to the security of its enjoyment." In Polynesia, "Taboo was the bulwark of the landowners; it was that alone which elevated them by a sort of divine right to a position of affluence and luxury among the vulgar: it was that alone which insured their safety and protected them from the encroachments of poor and envious neighbors." When it came to sexual customs, "Among the African Basonga, when a man got a virgin with child, the guilty couple used to be dragged to the River Ntatswe; stones were tied to their ankles and legs and, along with a sacrificial sheep, they were thrown into the water and drowned." The Bataks of central Sumatra condemned an adulteress to be killed and eaten; sometimes they began nibbling on choice morsels before she was dead! Frazer regarded these playful customs with an indulgent eye because "superstition has strengthened the respect for marriage and has thereby contributed to a stricter observance of the rules of sexual morality."

As the decades have gone by, Frazer's central theses and theories have commanded less and less respect, but his magnificent array of material, his stimulating digressions, and his vivid presentations of folk custom and ritual are still full of vitality.

Bronislaw Malinowski, who liked and respected Frazer, never- theless found him a contradictory figure: "His inability to convince seems to contradict his power to convert and inspire." Yet there is no doubt that Frazer was a great figure who made ethnology read like a dramatic narrative, a man whose prestige was so great that he even made governments conscious of the need for trained anthropologists to advise them on their colonial policies.

Because he belongs to a school that stresses the facts of distribution of institutions, Robert Lowie, the American diffusionist, accuses Frazer of "false intellectualistic psychologizing." It is true that Frazer himself is often guilty, like his own magic-making primitive, of drawing conclusions from a mere association of ideas. His essential greatness derives from the fact that he was an artist and a myth-maker. Like that dream-poet of our own era, Freud, he reared an intellectual structure of elegance and symmetry which captured the imagination of his time.

When a scientist grows too literary, however, corrective criticism is necessary. It was, oddly enough, another Scotch poet who couched his lance against the dragons of Frazer's lyrical fantasy.

PART *Two*

The Critical Reaction

Chapter 14

THE IRONIC GADFLY

Concerning Andrew Lang

■ Andrew Lang, the blithe iconoclast who was to challenge both Tylor's animism and Frazer's vegetation hypothesis, was a relative outsider, unawed by reputations or anthropological tradition. A handsome man who looked like Robert Louis Stevenson (to whom he was remotely related) and even wore a replica of Stevenson's piratical mustache, he was born on the Scotch border in 1844. His temperament was conditioned by a youth spent among the pixies and bogles of Celtic tradition, for he imbibed folklore from an old nurse. When he was a boy, his favorite reading was fairy tales, *The Arabian Nights*, *A Midsummer Night's Dream*. In later life, folklore and fairy tales continued to be among his chief interests.

As an undergraduate at St. Andrew's College in Glasgow, he tried, by following old alchemy books and medieval formulas, to raise the Devil in one of its haunted towers. The Devil did not appear, but Lang was to raise him in other ways. Indeed, the devil of contradiction was already inspiring him. While a member of the college literary society, as he later confessed, just to liven things up he read a paper in which the national hero, Wallace, was painted as a villain. Things did grow lively, so lively that he had to withdraw from the club.

While a fellow at Oxford in 1870 he read Tylor's *Primitive Culture*. By this time he was an accomplished essayist and a poet in the Rossetti-William Morris tradition. He did not at first venture into the field of anthropology, but began his literary career by reviewing and publishing books of verse. He soon blossomed into the "divine amateur," as W. E. Henley called him, and his editorials for the London *Daily News* in the eighties had a cult of admirers of which the young Bernard Shaw was a member.

Today he is remembered for the red, blue, and other variously colored fairy-tale books that he edited for children. Poet, literary editor, literary historian, novelist, journalist, translator, he brought to anthropology an engaging wit and a keen sense of satire against which his victims had no weapons.

Early in his career he joined forces with Tylor to annihilate Max Mueller. In *Custom and Myth,* which he dedicated to Tylor in 1888, the essay "Cupid, Psyche and the Sun Frog" illustrates his method of attack. The germ of the story was an episode in which a woman married to a more-than-mortal husband lost him when she broke a mystic prohibition against looking at him or speaking his name. Sometimes they were reunited; sometimes they lost each other forever. The oldest version was found in the Rig Veda, in which the fairy Urvasi becomes the mistress of Pururavas, a mortal. After the prohibition is broken, she leaves him "like the first of the dawns," with some suggestion of a reconciliation. In another Veda she says: "Embrace me three times a day but never against my will and never let me see you without your royal garments for *this is the custom of women.*" By a trick the immortal kinsmen of the fairy make Pururavas spring up from the bed, and in a flash of lightning she sees him naked. She vanishes. He seeks her and finds her among her friends, who have all taken the shape of birds. He is finally made immortal and allowed to dwell among them.

Max Mueller, of course, interpreted this as an expression of the dawn and evening twilight. *Urvasi* must have meant "dawn" and *Pururavas* "sun." *Uru* actually meant "pervading," which Mueller connected with dawn.

Unfortunately, another philologist, Kuhn, interpreted the man's name to mean "fire"; hence the story was a fire myth. Still another scholar, Roth, said the woman's name meant "lewd" and the man's name "roarer" or the "bull," and found a crudely copulatory significance for the myth.

Lang insisted that the phrase "for this is the custom of women" was the key to the story. This he saw as the relic of a taboo that forbade women to look at their husbands naked, the myth being a later rationalization. Among certain African primitives, men could not see their wives naked for three years after marriage. Yoruba women of West Africa could not speak to their husbands. A Breton folk tale told how the son of a Boulogne pilot married the daughter of the King of Naz. In that land a man could not look upon his wife's face until she had borne him a child. The husband broke the taboo at night, dropped candle wax, and waked the bride. The King learned of the offense and turned him into a monster. The veiling of the bride was the custom of women in that land: "*C'est usage du pays.*" This, Lang felt, was a triumph of comparative folklore over philology.

In another form of the myth, the bride was not a fairy but an animal, and the husband had to promise not to perform some act which recalled associations of her animal existence.

In a Sanskrit tale, a king married a frog princess. Only a corruption of language could account for such a ridiculous notion, said Max Mueller. The girl's name was *Bheki*, the "frog." She agreed to marry the king on condition that he never show her a drop of water. One day she asked for water. He forgot his promise, brought it, and she disappeared. According to Max Mueller, this meant that the sun would die at the sight of water, from which it rose in the morning, by setting. But why should the sun be identified with Bheki, the frog? Max Mueller blandly said that frogs must have been associated with the sun.

"But when," asked Lang, "did a Sanskrit people ever live by a great sea?" And there was no proof that the word for "frog" ever meant "sun."

On the other hand, it was a fact that totemistic peoples considered themselves to be descended from animals. A tribe in northwest America actually said it was descended from a frog. In an Ojibway parallel a man was married to a beautiful beaver girl. She asked him to build a bridge over a swollen stream, for she must not touch water. He failed to bridge one trickle of water, her foot got wet, and she changed back to a beaver forever.

Such comparative study of taboos, Lang insisted, revealed more about the origin of myths than dubious and fanciful etymologies. "As for the frog," he concluded, "we may hope that he has sunk forever beneath the western wave."

Although he admired Tylor, he did not hesitate to attack Tylor's evolutionary scheme of the origin of religion, based on animism, in two books, *The Making of Religion* (1900) and *Magic and Religion* (1901). Tylor, of course, believed that a single high god gradually evolved from a multitude of nature spirits, which in turn were derived from the idea of ghosts. The basic idea of a supreme being with moral characteristics could just as easily have degenerated, said Lang, in some cultures to inferior nature beings or even magic.

"Anthropology has mainly kept her eyes fixed on the impure stream, the lusts, mummeries, conjurings, and frauds of priesthoods, while relatively or altogether neglecting . . . what is honest and of good report." He felt sure Tylor was guilty of willful blindness in refusing to admit there was monotheism among primitive peoples. "Anything you please you may find among your useful savages. . . . You have but to skim a few books of travel, pencil in hand, and pick out what suits your case."

There was justice in the accusation, but Lang then proceeded to do some skimming himself. He maintained that he found traces of a supreme being in Fison's and Howitt's reports on the Australians. In a book that Tylor had never read, Lang triumphantly dug up mention of Powhatan's great god, Ahone, who governed the world and did not require sacrifice. The natives of central Africa and the Zunis of America had a creator god. The fact that these divinities were not upholders of moral principles merely showed that they had degenerated. Tylor felt that most cases of supreme gods among simple peoples were the result of missionary influence. Lang replied by attacking Tylor's sources. While Lang's sources were also dubious, he did succeed in showing that high gods might be present alongside a host of other animistic deities. He divided mythology into the silly or obscene and the noble and moral; the first tendency was merely false and tended to die out; the second had the right to be called religion. Thus Lang the anti-rationalist dealt out praise and blame to cultural institutions as if he were reviewing for the London *Daily News*.

Actually, he did not succeed in proving that many gods represented a degeneration from a higher and purer monotheism. His hypothesis was an acknowledged echo of Bishop Whately and was colored by his personal taste.

He was equally hard on Frazer's analysis of magic and religion.

He accused the latter of mixing the gods of all nations with a great multitude of cattle, cats, horses, bulls, goats, cocks, and equating the whole with the vegetation spirit.

He then attacked Frazer's examples of the killing of kings. The latter, he said, had only one dubious example: that of Babylonia, where a divine king was said to have abdicated for a day while a substitute slave was killed in his stead. The source was doubtful, the interpretation farfetched. As for the may kings or the bean kings in folklore, what connection had they with the Babylonian instance except by inference? The destruction of the effigy of Haman by the Jews and the burning of Guy Fawkes by the British merely proved that both these individuals were unpopular. Cases of regicide in central Africa were not evidence, for it could not be shown that such kings were gods. Frazer had connected sexual orgies or periods of license with mock executions. Lang mockingly cited the central Australians who practiced sexual promiscuity for ritual reasons. "These," he said, "have no native strong drink and can not get intoxicated, but what they can they do, in the way of license, like the more civilized races and necessarily *not* for agricultural reasons as they have no agriculture. . . . O vegetation, what crimes are committed in thy name!"

If magic gave way to religion because those who practiced it became disillusioned with their lack of success, the Dieri of Australia were indeed stupid, for in a parched, rainless area they went on with futile rain charms that accomplished nothing. On the other hand, Frazer discovered traces of real religion in southeast Australia, where there was great fertility. If there was greater fertility, Lang rejoined scornfully, and magic seemed to work, there was no explanation for the development of religion.

So Lang poked holes in elaborate theoretical structures and ironically pointed out the weak chain of association upon which they were built.

His constructive contribution came from the bogles and second sight of his Scotch childhood. Why, Lang wanted to know, did Tylor disdain as mere delusions the psychic phenomena experienced by savages? Perhaps the hallucinations of shamans were true revelations. "We hold that very probably there exist human faculties of unknown scope: that these conceivably were more powerful and prevalent among our very remote ancestors who founded religion; that they still may exist in savage as in civilized races, and that they may have confirmed if they did not originate, the doctrine of separable souls. If they *do* exist, the circumstance is important, in view of the fact that modern ideas rest on a denial of their existence."

Lang cited episodes of what we should now call extrasensory perception. A Zulu, by eating some medicine, was enabled to tell how many elephants had been killed by an absent hunting-party. Then there were clairvoyance, and crystal-reading, and the strange behavior of inanimate objects at seances. Perhaps savages endowed objects with life not because of animistic philosophizing, but because there really were spirits in them! The Scots mystic was actually trying to bring the supernatural back into theories of religion by way of the Ouija board.

While few anthropologists would follow him into table-tapping, nevertheless the experimenters at Duke University in recent years have attempted to prove that there are uncharted areas among the human faculties which science has not succeeded in pigeonholing.

In *The Secret of the Totem* (1905) and *Methods in the Study of Totemism* (1911) Lang made a contribution in another area. Although only a fraction of his varied output was concerned with anthropology, the science profited from his irreverent skepticism. He died in 1912. Despite his fame as a man of letters, he secretly fancied himself as a scientist. In a moment of confidence he once said to R. R. Marett: "If I could have made a living at it, I would have been a great anthropologist."

Chapter 15

AND WHETHER PIGS HAVE
SOULS . . .

Concerning R. R. Marett, A. E. Crawley

■ In *A Passage to India* E. M. Forster depicts the difficulties of a missionary who admits "that the mercy of God, being infinite, may well embrace all mammals. And the wasps? He became uneasy during the descent to wasps, and was apt to change the conversation. And oranges, cactuses, crystals, and mud? And the bacteria inside Mr. Sorley? No, no, this is going too far. . . ." The dilemma facing the missionary was not unlike that of the anthropologist bravely trying to fit the theological vagaries of the primitives into a logical formula satisfactory to the European mind. Magic, the concept of the soul, the origin of the idea of divinity continued to be controversial matters. There was no agreement on a definition of religion. It was becoming clear that all-embracing schemes might be esthetically pleasing, but that human behavior was not neatly symmetrical. From the nineties on, a critical spirit grew which was to destroy the comfortable utopias of the pioneers.

Tylor's successor at Oxford was a rather dashing Jerseyman, Robert Ranulph Marett (1866–1943). Marett was also a classicist and began his career as a student of philosophy and ethics. A competition for a prize essay encouraged him to write about the ethics of savage races. Impressed by the "old light" of Tylor and the "new light" of Frazer, he continued reading in anthropology during the nineties, more or less as a hobby. In 1899 a friend urged him to read a paper before a meeting of the British Association for the Advancement of Science. It promised to be a dull meeting, and Marett was told to contribute "something startling." His wife had been helping him collect some notes on primitive religion. Marett looked them over. He was acquainted with Lang's critique of animism, but his own approach was from a different angle. He worked his material into an essay on "preanimistic religion." After delivering it he found himself, as he says, "notorious." He had made a contribution to the theory of the origin of religion with which his name was to become identified.

In 1909 he developed his thesis in a book, *The Threshold of Religion*. It seemed to him that earlier writers had conceived of the savage "exactly as if he were an Oxford professor who sat down and mused on the nature of things and then got up and fitted his actions to his conclusions." Tylor had pictured his primitive meditating on the nature of dreams. To Lang's savage, religion was revealed in hallucinatory phenomena. For Marett the beginnings of religion must have been vaguer and less intellectual. Was not a feeling of *awe* or *wonder* at the bottom of all religious emotion? From this simple reaction more formalized activities might develop.

The Madagascans used the word *god* for anything they did not understand. When they first saw a book, they called it *god* because it could miraculously speak to those who could read. Similarly, the Cree Indians, when they caught a strange-looking fish, returned it to the water and spent five days appeasing it.

Marett assumed that there was an instinctive fear and horror of dead bodies and blood which accounted for cults of the dead and for the role that blood played in ritual. This instinctive sense of fear or awe, which caused a shudder to run through the body or the pulse to quicken, was the basic emotion. Marett's theory of religion was thus physiological and emotional.

Marett went on to criticize Frazer's definition of magic as a kind of incorrect science. The basis of magic, too, was emotional. Violent passions such as anger or love could be expressed toward a substitute. The lover who kissed his mistress's portrait and the angry man who kicked a door because someone had annoyed him were performing actions that could easily become magic as soon as they were carried out with a practical purpose.

Such an action acquired a new meaning when one took into account the power of suggestion among primitives. If an angry man cursed an enemy to his face and wished he might fall sick, suggestion, operating on the primitive mind and emotions, could be so strong that the victim would actually fall sick. In this way simple peoples had come to believe that emotional wishes could be projected. There were many cases of savages who had died because they considered themselves bewitched. Once emotional projection of the will combined with suggestion was established as a practical process, the basis for magical practice was laid down. Magic was therefore *not* inefficient science, but simply *magic*—a mysterious intensification and projection of the will which had a supernatural color.

Marett felt that there was a kind of generalized supernatural power behind all magical and religious activities. It was best described by the Melanesian word *mana* reported in Bishop R. H. Codrington's studies of Melanesia. Mana was an electrical god-stuff that could be identified with a symbol, an instrument, or a man. It was either magical or divine. The concept of mana tended to disprove Frazer's effort to put magic before religion and to see the shift from sorcerer to priest as late in human history. It was more likely that the idea of mana could be applied to both.

Taboo was not a negative magic, but simply fear of mana. A king was an extraordinary person, hence full of mana, hence taboo. The many taboos associated with women arose *not* from fear of contagion, of acquiring their weakness, but from the strangeness of women, from awe at the mysterious menstrual and reproductive process.

Marett found the theological distinctions made by the Melanesians significant. A yam had no *tarunga* or soul; a pig and a man had a tarunga; but when a pig died, it had no *tindalo* or ghost. Only a great man's tindalo had true mana and was worshipped.

From this a minimum definition of religion could be derived. It was a supernatural power, differing at times in intensity, or voltage, but never in essence. This, Marett thought, was more accurate than Tylor's definition, which involved spirits and did not cover impersonal religions such as Buddhism.

Marett suggested that mana in almost anything could give whatever it occupied the aspect of divinity. The bull-roarer, for instance, used especially in puberty ceremonies in Australia and

Melanesia, was often called the voice of the thunder god. It seemed as though the object might have gradually become personified until an actual god developed from it.

Marett represented a generation that was bringing fresh concepts into anthropology. Psychology, also a new science, was beginning to influence related fields. Marett considered the work of Galton and McDougall an important antidote to academic theorizing.

His doctrine of preanimism brought him wide recognition. Among those who accepted it were Wilhelm Wundt and K. T. Preuss in Germany, A. C. Haddon, and William James in America.

Despite his criticism of animism, Marett admired Tylor intensely and edited the commemorative essays presented to him in 1907. Although Tylor had held his readership in Oxford for years, no diploma was given in anthropology; consequently, he had very few students. He lectured conscientiously, nevertheless, and Lady Tylor never failed to be present. It was said that someone passing by in the corridor heard his voice boom in the empty lecture hall: "And now, my dear Anna, we observe . . ."

Marett, a lively lecturer and a virtuoso on the bull-roarer, which he used to keep his students awake, took over the readership in Oxford in 1910. A worthy successor to Tylor, he helped found a school of anthropology which granted degrees to students.

The discussion of religion continued in the first decades of the twentieth century. Another psychologically minded student was A. E. Crawley, the headmaster of a public school and an expert athlete, who wrote books on skating and tennis. In *The Tree of Life* (1905) he re-analyzed Spencer's and Gillen's work on the Arunta of central Australia. Even among these simple savages most elements of religion were present. They had wandering spirits similar to souls, elements of propitiation in their magical dramas, and moral elements in their initiatory ceremonies. Magic and religion were intertwined; there was no point in trying to separate them. Everything important in life was holy or taboo: puberty, courtship, marriage, death, burial, hunting, war, seed time, and harvest. And this sense of holiness was religious, whether it was ascribed to gods, magic, or taboo. Religion was not a separate department of life, but was woven through the whole texture of social existence.

This religious "vitalism" was something like Marett's mana, but lacked the tone of supernaturalism. It was a "will to life" which Crawley used to show that Christianity preserved the original characteristics of religion. Thus the central Australians were witnesses to the validity of the Church of England, and a new age of faith could dawn.

Crawley's thinking in a book entitled *The Idea of the Soul* (1907) put him squarely in the camp of the rationalists. Tylor's animism was inadequate, because dreams appeared perfectly real to the dreamer. They had no reason to give rise to the idea of a non-material separable soul. Lang's hallucinations were too abnormal to serve as a universal basis for the concept of the soul. On the other hand, he was not convinced by Marett's mana. Savages exhibited no awe before the dead—they even ate them. The central Australians often drank blood from a living person; to them it was no more impressive than milk. On the whole, the *mana* concept could not lead to the soul, for it was a psychological axiom that the mind did not work from the abstract to the concrete.

The theory that primitive man imagined everything to be alive was a fallacy, Crawley stated. Savages were essentially practical people, not philosophers. The idea of the soul could be shown to be the natural by-product of elementary mental processes.

Much confusion about primitive notions was semantic. Savage languages had no words for abstractions. Investigators who were equally imprecise got the impression that the soul was called "breath" or "shadow." Then, too, simple languages had peculiar ways of expressing relationships. The most important problem was to distinguish the outside world from the speaker. Hence there was the concept "my father" and "your father" denoted by specific words, but no abstract word for "father." Crawley took time out to annihilate Morgan's kinship terms on this basis. When the savage talked of a he-rock or a he-tree, he was not attributing life or sex, but simply distinguishing between the otherness of the object and the I-ness of the speaker. "I am I, he is rock" did not impute an abstract element of life in either the I-I or the he-rock.

The savage did not analyze what he believed. Psychologists had proved that his perception and visual memory, sharpened by the practical requirements of his life, were very keen. The memory image was a universal phenomenon that presented a double or copy of everything in the outside world. It was patently non-material and also detachable from its source. There was no doubt that it was *not* the thing itself. Likewise, it was no abstract concept, but a simple psychological fact. Was this not obviously the origin of the idea of the soul? No associative jump was necessary to give life to inanimate objects—anything that could create a mental image *might* have a soul.

The soul of a live man was alive and healthy; the soul of a dead man would be something strange, being a composite of the memory image of the person alive and as a corpse.

The Egyptian Ka was the exact picture of a man as he might have been called up in the minds of those who knew him. In the Hervey Islands of the South Pacific, fat men had fat souls, thin men thin souls. Sorcerers used fiber loops to capture them, large for the fat souls, small for the thin ones. The Bavili spoke of the voices of dead people living after them in the heads of some of their relatives. The Andamanese thought of a reflection in a mirror as the soul, and feared cameras, lest the white man, by capturing the reflection, take their souls away in his black box. Some primitives thought the mirage was the soul of water. The Fijians pointed out a deep hole in the ground in the bottom of which could be seen "the souls of men and women, beasts and plants, of sticks and stones, and of all the broken utensils of this frail world, swimming or rather tumbling along, one over the other, pell-mell into the regions of immortality."

An Egyptian Ka visiting the mummy.

Souls were often conceived of as miniature, and Crawley accounted for this easily. The memory image might be that of a person at a distance, made smaller by perspective.

The permanence of the soul depended upon the strength of the memory left behind, and this in turn depended upon the intensity of the affection the dead man aroused or the impact of his personality. Thus a remarkable character or a hero would develop into a revered "ancestor" to be worshipped.

Early religion was therefore simply the primitive trying to come to grips with his perceptions of the world, his sense images.

Crawley was insisting that all of primitive man's feeling about the world was of one piece, that he did not distinguish between things natural and what we should call supernatural.

The argument over the origin of religion began to die out during the next ten years as the mainstream of anthropology veered away from the evolutionary point of view. In order to polish off the controversy and to indicate the modern attitude, we shall skip forward to a book, *Primitive Religion*, written in 1924 by the American Robert Lowie. Lowie represents the diffusionist school, which emphasized the distribution of institutions, a school to be discussed more fully later on.

Lowie was most sympathetic to Marett's point of view. His own phrase for religion was "a sense of the Extraordinary, Mysterious, or Supernatural." He analyzed four cultures to show how this element appeared in different forms. He concluded that the great variety in organization found in primitive religions and the shifting emotional emphasis placed upon magic, spirits, visions, or gods tended to disprove any simple recipe for deriving all of these from a single origin. He distrusted all historical reconstructions and insisted that the prime task was to study the distribution of institutions until enough was known of the relationships between cultures to start theorizing on a sound basis.

As an example, he cited the idea that disease is something lodged in the patient's body which has to be removed by spells and incantations. This notion could be found all over North America from Mexico to Alaska. From there it could be traced to Siberia. It was present among the Eskimos of Greenland. Tylor had shown that it occurred in Europe, South Africa, Australia, and Malaya.

Such distribution indicated that the idea was of great antiquity; since it had spread over the whole American area and underlay more recent ideas, it must have been carried into the New World by very early immigrants. Hence it was not too much to assume that it was a genuine survival from the Old Stone Age.

This is the cautious, step-by-step point of view that is employed by most recent scholarship.

There will be occasion to return again to the study of religion, but the problem of its origin still remains unsolved. In the opinion of some, it never can be solved. Although the scholars of the turn of the century failed in this attempt, they collected such a wealth of material and examined so many other institutions that the science of anthropology began to branch in all directions. We shall have to backtrack in order to catch up with the investigations in these other areas.

Chapter 16

BOA CONSTRICTOR DIGESTING AN ELEPHANT

Concerning Anthropology and Primitive Art

■ Saint-Exupéry's charming book about the little prince begins with the following anecdote: "After some work with a colored pencil, I succeeded in making my first drawing. My Drawing Number One. It looked like this:

I showed my masterpiece to the grownups and asked them whether the drawing frightened them.

"But they answered: 'Frightened? Why should anyone be frightened by a hat?'

"My drawing was not a picture of a hat. It was a picture of a boa constrictor digesting an elephant."

In simple form Saint-Exupéry sketched the relationship between the artist and the naïve critic.

Art among primitive people did not catch the attention of anthropologists until some decades of work on other human institutions had been done. This was partly because of nineteenth-century critical attitudes. It was a period, particularly in Anglo-

American society, in which naturalism was the official art style. Scientists, as a rule, are not deeply versed in the arts. It is not surprising, therefore, that the early anthropologists, imbued with the current belief that the highest art was a copy of nature, tended to disregard primitive art as crude and unimportant.

Actually, primitive peoples practice not one but many kinds of art. Fantastically accurate and lifelike paintings of wild horses and bison, destined to be accepted as the work of Stone Age man, had already been discovered in 1878 in certain caves in Spain. African and South Sea idols are carved in the general shape of men and animals, but distorted and exaggerated by the imagination of the artist. Masks were encountered on all continents in weird and terrifying shapes. The sacred sticks of the central Australians called *churingas* were covered with odd circles and dots. The North American Indians used crude sketches of men and animals to convey messages. Lastly, practically every primitive culture had decorative patterns of some sort with which they adorned houses, tools and utensils, or their own bodies.

To return to the boa-constrictor-digesting-an-elephant of Saint-Exupéry—most art, except the most photographically naturalistic, is symbolic. That is, certain shapes, lines, or spaces, or color relationships, or any combination of these are meant to convey some sort of meaning. On the one hand, there is the artist's intention; on the other, varying degrees of emotional reaction and acceptance. The early anthropologist first looked at the simpler patterns used by the primitives: meanders, lozenges, chevrons, scrolls, spirals, and (despite the fact that primitives are ignorant of geometry) pronounced them geometrical designs and nothing more. To him a hat was a hat. He had no way of knowing whether the primitive thought he was portraying a boa constrictor digesting an elephant. The evolutionary impulse, however, impelled scholars at the end of the century to look for a chain of development in style and form and to speculate concerning origins.

A German art historian, Gottfried Semper, had suggested in 1879 that the Greek key or meander was fundamentally a textile weave. There was no doubt that it was a very old invention, for it had been found to have been scratched upon a mammoth tusk fifteen thousand years ago.

In America in the 1880's an ethnologist named W. H. Holmes also took an interest in pattern, but his area of investigation was the ceramic art of the ancient Pueblo Indians of the southwest. Holmes believed that because this art had grown up before the acquisition of writing or the potter's wheel, it would shed light on the earliest steps in the development of form and decoration. His research led him back to basket-making.

"There are no savages on earth so rude that they have no form of basketry," said Otis Mason, another student of primitive handicrafts. Basket-making was possible before the use of fire, and a variety of materials such as grass, skin, roots, leaves, strips of wood, and twigs were used. Most savages can count up to ten. By skipping several strands of the warp an angular pattern was automatically produced. If the warp and the woof were of different colors, an alternating pattern resulted. By counting stitches more elaborately it was possible to create lines, triangles, checkers, meanders, lozenges, frets, squares, zigzags, chevrons, polygons of all sorts, and stepped curves or scrolls.

Subsequent studies by Gene Weltfish have shown how many such patterns are created by the basket-making technique of the Indians of California.

Holmes, however, was interested in the pottery. It was a fact that designs *painted* on baskets followed the patterns created by the stitches. In addition, the impress of all the familiar types of basket stitch had been found on ancient pottery. Fragments of such pottery had been found which had been made *in* a basket. Modern Pueblo and Papuan women when making pottery by the coil method often started their bottom coil within a symmetrical basket as a kind of mold. The coil method of making pottery even had similarities to the coil-stitched basket. Thus the evidence seemed to indicate that the art of coil-molded pottery had been derived from basketry. Basketry was not the only influence. Pottery that imitated shells, hammered stone pots, and square bark vessels was found. All in all, it seemed that the higher art of pottery was influenced by both the shape and the decorative treatment of more primitive types of vessels.

In Pueblo ceramic-decoration the link with basketry was plain, for the same geometric elements were present on both utensils. Scrolls, circles, spirals, which were stepped in basketry, became smooth and flowing on the pots. Straight lines became curved to adapt to a rounded surface. This was proof that the nature of the material affected the design. Otis Mason later pointed out that there are no sharp, square corners in Middle and South American sculpture. Such sculpture was created by the pecking method; the tool used was an implement of harder stone, pointed at the end, by means of which it was possible to peck out the design in relief. With such equipment sharp angles could not be achieved and the work took on the flowing, rounded character best exemplified in the Mayan monuments.

Holmes, in 1886, summed up his theory in the phrase "Geometrical ornament is the offspring of technique." This general principle is now quite widely accepted.

Holmes's work was stimulating in so far as it suggested how some designs might have arisen. But did they mean anything? Was the hat no more than a hat?

It was a fact that primitive peoples did name their designs. Frank Hamilton Cushing, studying Zuni pottery at about the same time as Holmes, noted that among the Zunis the scroll was a symbol for the wind. Certain bushes, blown around and around their stems by the wind, described scrolls in the desert sand. This scroll, Cushing thought, was thus associated with the wind, and the design element, also *by association*, came to be known as a wind symbol.

The evolution-minded scientist would have liked to trace a progression from technically produced geometric forms to crude representation of natural objects to full-blown naturalism. Otis Mason, following Holmes's lead, arranged Pueblo designs in a sequence. He suggested that first came technically inspired geometrical ornaments, then totemic emblems, magical figures, drawn with some realism. The latter he likened to metaphors in speech. In the third stage the pictorial elements became more formalized. "The hieroglyphic art became still more abbreviated, syncopated, until the relics of former ideograms became mere letters in an alphabet on the way to a higher language." Under the spell of the evolutionary scheme, he was thus placing representational art as a step in the development of language.

While American scholars were studying technique, Hjalmar Stolpe, a Swedish anthropologist, made a trip through Europe in 1881, visiting ethnological museums in leading cities. He was armed with sheets of Japanese paper and black wax.

Stolpe was fascinated by primitive ornament. Wherever he went, he sought out primitive utensils and, with his black wax, took rubbings of the patterns on them. At this time museums had scarcely begun to arrange their collections. He sometimes had to persuade authorities to open packing-cases to give him access to the objects in which he was interested. Stolpe was concerned with the meaning and origin of the designs. His approach was the exact opposite of that of Holmes, for he was not satisfied that geometric ornament was what it seemed.

Stolpe accumulated three thousand rubbings.

From 1883 to 1885 he was ethnologist on board the frigate *Vanadis*, which sailed around the world, stopping at Brazil, Chile, India, Japan, and Tahiti. Stolpe continued to visit museums and added to his collection of rubbings. In Tahiti he had a brief glimpse of a primitive people in their natural habitat. It was this visit which led him to take a particular interest in the art of the Polynesian islands.

The wooden handles of basalt adzes and large paddle-shaped wooden implements were covered with a carved network of rectangles divided by tiny solid triangles in what was known as the shark-tooth pattern, so-called because the carving was done with

Polynesian patterns placed in sequence.

a shark tooth. This design looked geometrical. In certain instances, however, it was bordered by squatting figures with hands and legs joined. The figures were equipped with pointed breasts, proving them female, and their position reminded him of the erotic hupa-

hupa dance. On the knobs of some of the paddles he found the joined rows of bodies without heads. From these rows of zigzags to the network pattern was, in Stolpe's opinion, an easy last step in the transition from naturalistic form to mere pattern.

A missionary told him that the adzes were sacred objects used by priests, and Stolpe decided that the figures represented a goddess. The adzes were therefore ceremonial objects used only in ancestor-worship.

Stolpe did not pursue any firsthand investigations to document this part of his theory, but the series of "degradations" of naturalistic form which he traced had a profound effect on ethnological thinking.

In an essay written in 1890 he stated the principle that geometric form could be derived from progressive modifications of natural objects.

Alfred C. Haddon, whom we have already encountered as the leader of the Torres Strait expedition, in 1895 developed this point of view still further in terms of Papuan art of the South Seas, by arranging a series of arrows, some decorated with realistic crocodiles, some in a transition stage, and some showing a conventional pattern of chevrons, dots, and bands. He also showed the development of a scroll design from interlocking heads and beaks of frigate birds. Both the crocodile and the frigate bird had totemistic significance. This, of course, was an added indication of the religious significance of ornament.

Haddon was inclined to think ornament had various origins. He was willing to accept Holmes's view in some cases where it seemed clear that basketry motifs—lashings, plaitings, and stitching—gave rise to design elements. He was convinced, however, that naturalism was characteristic of the highest stage of civilization. He also believed that the artistic impulse could be religious, informative (pictographs leading to language), a sign of wealth, or lead to art for art's sake.

On the whole, he believed that the bulk of art proceeded from representation or copying of the natural object. The transformation of the copy into design often took place as an adaptation to the shape or area of the object to be decorated. In many cases he felt that the crudeness of the representation was merely lack of ability. Savages, like children, could not draw and were satisfied with a rough map of a real object.

So far anthropological discussion of art had pretty much ignored the fact that art affords enjoyment. It seemed hard for scholars to realize that, even though their standards were different from those of Europe, primitive peoples were not without the concept of beauty. In 1927, however, Franz Boas published his book *Primitive Art*, a work written from a far more sophisticated point of view than that of his predecessors. To Boas it was significant that great productivity in art was coupled with a high level of technique. California Indian basketry, Northwest Indian woodwork and painting, and Pueblo pottery all displayed a skill that even civilized technicians were bound to respect. In all such work the devices of symmetry, repetition, regularity, and balance could be found.

The latter were *formal* elements imposed either by the materials used or by physiological impulses in the body of the artist. Art, Boas decided, in its simplest form was not necessarily created with some intellectual purpose in mind, but was rather the product of skill and emotions aroused by skill.

In other words, he maintained that *pattern* had a logic of its own quite different from copying nature. The repeats and balance of pattern led the eye and the unconscious nervous system into a kind of dance. Indeed, as Gene Weltfish in her book *The Origin of Art* (1953) has pointed out, the activity of weaving *is* a dance of the hands. This physiological or, as Boas called it, *kinesthetic* enjoyment of design was a fundamental emotional response to art which could be independent of any symbolic or intellectual content.

Boas found that the same group of people was able to copy nature and also to construct formal design. The Kwakiutls of Canada carved a naturalistic head for use in a decapitation ceremony. This head bore no resemblance to the highly formalized decorative art with which they adorned totem poles, house fronts, and utensils and painted their bodies. The Eskimos carved naturalistic groups depicting seal-hunting on ivory, but at the same time used conventional designs in bone-carving and in tattooing. This, he felt, showed that one type of art did not develop from another.

He went on to consider the meanings assigned to patterns by their creators. His thesis was that all symbolical or intellectual meanings were a matter of association. In this he was not far from Frank Cushing and the wind scroll. Boas went on to document his case. He cited the fact that the Bakaïri Indians of the Amazon basin, according to Max Schmidt, who studied them in 1905, called a series of zigzags bats, a pattern of diamond fish scales. Among the North American Indians, diamonds were wasp nests, zigzags bats. But to the natives of New Ireland in the Pacific a chevron could mean a palm leaf, an arm ring, a worm, a bird's foot, crustacean tracks, or a fishbone. In California basket patterns, diamonds were butterflies and narrow triangles were sharp arrowheads. On the other hand, the Arapaho said a diamond was a person, a turtle, the navel, a mountain, a lake, a star, an eye. In the case of northwest Indian art, "the symbols lend themselves," he wrote, "to various explanations which are presumably selected in accordance with the totemic affiliations of the owner."

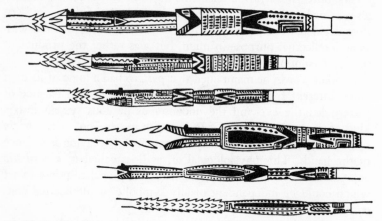

Haddon's crocodile arrows.

He might also have added that the designs on the sacred churingas of the central Australians made use of repeated curves that could mean either a man sitting squeezing dirt out of a grub or the ribs of a lizard, while dots could mean tracks or eggs.

Following out the contention that pattern came first and meaning was a later added rationalization, Boas took up Stolpe's wooden-handled adzes and Haddon's crocodile arrows. What proof was there that the natural form came first and was then "degraded" into a pattern? It was easy to arrange objects to fit a theory, but there was no way of demonstrating conclusively which arrow was the beginning of the series. If a style of pattern had developed from technique, was it not just as logical that an animal form being absorbed into it would be more or less conventionalized to fit? He was inclined to reverse Stolpe's theory. A scaly pattern may have suggested the crocodile, and the growth of totemism may have led to the animal's inclusion in the decorative scheme. A pattern of diamonds would be called fish scales because someone happened to notice the resemblance.

He traced the decorative element ⌂ through various adjoining areas in North America, in which its shape and meaning changed. At first it was called a hill or a tent. When it reached the Pueblo area, the rounded style current there transformed it into

the familiar ⌂ which was given the symbolic meaning of rain clouds and lightning.

To return to the image with which this chapter commenced, Saint-Exupéry drew what looked, to the unsophisticated eye, like a hat but was really meant to portray a boa constrictor digesting an elephant. To Boas the hat was a doodle that was finally assigned the meaning of hat, boa-constrictor-digesting-an-elephant, or, perhaps, a loaf of bread, each time with some modification of its shape.

Boas suggested that the form of utensils flowed from the specific motor habits of the group, and that these, in turn, were of course conditioned by environment. For instance, in islands where stones were absent, the natives made chisels and blades of shell. The particular style developed by any group was, of course, influenced by the complexities of its history and environment. He concluded: "I doubt very much that it will ever be possible to give a satisfactory explanation of the origin of these styles, just as little as we can discover all the psychological and historical connections that determine the development of language, social structure, mythology or religion."

Boas illustrated by modern emblems the associative process by which conventional form acquires symbolic meaning. The cross has a history of religious passion. The American flag arouses patriotic emotion. Military insignia carry the meaning of rank and authority. The tremendous emotional significance of the swastika in our time (distinct from its ancient symbolisms, which were many) does not have to be underlined.

Even primitive peoples are capable of associating abstractions with arbitrary symbols. The Arapaho place a long stripe on the front of their moccasins to signify the long path to their destination, a short stripe on the heel to symbolize the place from which they have come.

Boas also attacked the notion that a conventionalized form was a "degradation" of a more realistic element resulting from inaccurate copying (a theory put forth by Henry Balfour of the Pitt Rivers Museum, and accepted by Haddon). Savages do not *copy* other designs or nature when they work. They have absorbed the tribal style and work in it automatically. When they introduce something new, it is generally a conscious minor modification. Native artists, when questioned, say that such novelties come to them in dreams. In other words, they invent them.

Boas maintained that "neither the primitive man nor the child believes that the design or figure he produces is actually an accurate picture of the object he represents." Both child and savage have a tendency to exaggerate or distort elements that have caught their interest or seem important in a natural object. The child puts a huge nose or an enlarged hat on a figure. The primitive enlarges the sex organs, attenuates the body, breaks it up, or creates female forms with huge buttocks.

Pictographs, drawn to record events or for magical and religious purposes, Boas set aside as essentially inartistic because they showed no formal patterns, were lacking in technique, and arose from a direct impulse to communicate. In other words, the development of language was distinct from art.

Sir Herbert Read has combined the perspective of a modern art critic with a considerable knowledge of ethnological theory in his book *Art and Society* (1937). In the first place, he insisted on a distinct aesthetic impulse, apart from such other practical motivations as religion, display, and communication. This impulse has always been present, among primitives perhaps unconsciously and operating with or through the more practical impulses.

Indeed, most children in our own mechanized civilization are instinctive artists who delight in pattern and color until at a certain age they become inhibited by the stereotypes of their society.

In this connection, it is significant that when F. J. Gillen asked the Australian Arunta what certain rock-paintings meant—a dingo, an emu seen from below, outlines of lizards from above, a snake coming out of a hole, a hand, a Thurberlike profile of a face —he was told they were just play. This appears to be an indication of art for art's sake among primitive people. Yet drawings of the same type, when found on ceremonial objects, were given very specific meanings.

Read also pointed out that where savage art is well developed, artists are recognized as professionals and skill is handed down in families. That some painters or carvers are considered to be better than others proves that even primitives have conscious critical standards. This is a valid correction of the anthropologist's tendency to view art as an anonymous product of a group.

Read, influenced by Freud, suggested that artists are those individuals who have a more direct and uninhibited access to the unconscious, which is thought of as containing a timeless emotional heritage (from the Jungian point of view, some kind of group subconscious). This might account for the enduring and transcendent appeal of successful art.

Read defined the different types of art which he believed arose from different impulses. Brushing aside the formal element and its possible technical origin (he seemed to be ignorant of Boas's work), he listed:

1. *Purely abstract design*
2. *Geometrized or distorted representations of natural phenomena*
3. *Vitalized or "enhanced" representations of natural phenomena similar to those of the Old Stone Age*

The first category included shapes, such as those used on the Australian churingas, to which were added concrete mythological interpretations; the second included New Guinea formalized designs in which animals and human beings became symbols; the third was the fairly naturalistic but "vitalized" Cro-Magnon and ancient Bushman rock-painting, which Read found a more individual expression, and which he liked best.

Read maintained that Bushman and Cro-Magnon art was *magical*. It resulted from a direct connection with reality without the intervention of idols or gods. Thanks to a close and emotional connection with nature, the artist of this type was able to give life and style to his work.

Symbolic art such as the New Guinea carving or African sculpture was *animistic*, symbolizing the spirituality behind existence. It therefore did not need to adhere to outward form, but constructed a summary or distorted version of the object. "Symbolism, far from encouraging a higher aesthetic standard . . . being satisfied with the most summary representation of the object, im-

Three types of art: abstract, geometric naturalism, enhanced naturalism.

age, or idea, tends actually to discourage any elaboration in the interests of purely aesthetic qualities." This was also Boas's point of view toward religious art.

The abstract but symbolic Australian churinga designs he put even farther down on his list.

Behind a cloud of psychological distinctions, Read was not far from Haddon or the nineteenth-century admirer of naturalism.

Pictographs he ignored completely.

It is possible to divide the major types of art in a way that holds good for both the primitive and the contemporary practitioner, making use of a number of points elaborated by the writers who have just been discussed.

If we use the term *abstract art* to cover all types of pattern dependent upon formal elements—that is: repeat, balance, regularity, and symmetry, everything based upon conscious *arrangement*—then abstract art, which may have arisen from technique, could develop in two ways: arbitrary meaning could be added to the pattern, such as diamonds symbolizing butterflies, or natural form could be absorbed into the pattern as in New Guinea art. In general, mythological or religious meanings are added to what was fundamentally a kinesthetic pleasure in pattern.

Representational art, which copies nature or modifies it, seems to have had a separate origin. Read suggested that it could arise among savages as it develops among young children. The child first makes random scratches, then at a later age rhythmic doodles, then sees resemblances to persons or things in the doodles and accentuates the resemblances. This explanation was essentially the same as that put forward by E. B. Tylor and accepted by Alfred Haddon. A stone might be picked up which resembled a human face. It would be pecked or hammered to increase the resemblance. This process, Tylor said, could have magical significance, because in magical practice a copy or picture was used to affect the real person or animal. It has also been suggested that the animals painted in the Spanish caverns and those similar to them drawn by the Bushmen in South Africa were copies of the living creatures used in ceremonies to insure luck in hunting. Gene Weltfish, who was influenced by Boas, has suggested that the ancient chipped-stone hand ax, a pear-shaped lump of stone which fitted easily into the palm, would have afforded a tactile pleasure that might have led the Stone Age artisan to chip and polish it into the broad-buttocked, ovoid female figures, such as the Venus of Willendorf, which are the earliest sculpture known.

In whatever manner representation first arose, it is clear that such art can develop in two directions. For magical purposes the Cro-Magnon and Bushman hunter and the Eskimo drew fairly naturalistic and "vitalized" copies of the animals with which he was deeply concerned. Sometimes he included human beings engaged in important social activities. The other direction of representation is toward *expressionism,* which is generally religious or totemic. Exaggerated treatments of men and animals result in totem-pole art, Negro sculpture, Easter Island sculpture, the sculpture of San Agustín, Colombia. There is, of course, a point at which this type of symbolic art crosses the borderline into pattern-containing-elements-from-nature. In general, however, the distinguishing characteristic of representational art is the fact that its elements are individual and not repeated motifs. Each Old Stone Age bison is an individual act of creation; each African idol, though its style may be traditional, is a distinct, self-contained entity.

Finally, there is *pictographic art*, which always stems from a language impulse and never follows a formal pattern. At times it may be crudely naturalistic, as in North American pictographs or the figures on a shaman's shirt. Again, it may take the form of abstract symbols or rudimentary markings such as the decorations on Australian churingas, some Indian pictographs, and Negrito bamboo-carvings used in treating disease. The last three examples all possess religious significance.

Perhaps the most stimulating conclusion which emerges from the study of primitive art so far is the fact that all the types of art practiced today have their origin in the early history of society and that no one style can claim priority, higher rank aesthetically, or a monopoly of religious origin.

For instance, abstract patterned art hangs upon the walls of our advanced museums, and has influenced architecture and design throughout the civilized world. In its purest form it is exemplified by the painting of Mondriaan.

Naturalistic art we have always with us. It is promoted by the academies of the world and is one of the chief mainstays of the advertising industry. Paintings by Stevan Dohanos and Norman Rockwell appeal to millions on the covers of the *Saturday Evening Post*.

Its offspring, expressionistic art, has been developed by Picasso (in certain periods), Rouault, George Grosz, Max Beckman. Its practitioners have made primitive African sculpture and the art of the South Seas popular in sophisticated circles today.

Surrealism must also be regarded as an offspring of representation, exemplifying a revolution against the common-sense perception of the natural world and a self-conscious attempt to return to primitive magic.

Even pictographic art cannot be handed over to philology. Among the Chinese, writing has always been considered an aesthetic act. Today the doodles of the Australians and the North American Indians have begotten a new progeny in the mysterious signs and symbols that appear in the canvases of Miró, Paul Klee, and Adolph Gottlieb, and Japanese artists are exhibiting paintings admittedly developed from the style of their own calligraphy.

Chapter 17

A FINNISH MONOGAMIST

Concerning Edward Westermarck

■ The first uncompromisingly tough-minded scientist to attack the problems of anthropology and specifically those of the origin of marriage, Edward Westermarck (1862–1939) spent much of his youth in bed breathing turpentine and aniseed, fighting attacks of asthma. Fortunately, his father, who was bursar of the University of Finland, was well off and able to give him every comfort. During the summers when he was well, he enjoyed boating and fishing on the island of Gullo, off the coast of Finland. There he listened to folk tales told by the fishermen. In Helsingfors he was surrounded by university intellectuals.

Despite his asthmatic condition, he got through school, acquiring a considerable liking for botany. Just after matriculating at the university in 1880, he had a particularly bad attack. His doctors believed it would probably lead to tuberculosis, and he was not expected to live. A summer in a Norwegian sanatorium improved his condition so that he was able to continue his university career.

It seems evident there must have been a large psychosomatic element in Westermarck's asthma, for he conquered it by the most drastic measures. On various trips to Norway he took to mountain-climbing and finally attempted the fourth-highest peak in the country. On the climb he hurt his knee, was caught in a terrific snowstorm, but struggled on the next day to reach the summit. It was a symbolic conquest of his disease. None the worse for the experience, he decided he had acquired the stamina he would need to visit distant lands and study the primitive peoples who were beginning to interest him.

Westermarck was something of a student radical. He studied psychology, decided that German philosophy was "a systematic misuse of terminology created expressly for this purpose," and developed an admiration for English scientific empiricism, which he found clear and realistic. At this time he also became an agnostic. Revealed religion did not rest on a factual basis. "The first object of science is to search for truth," he wrote, "that of religion to give happiness. I can not find happiness in a faith that is founded only on the deceptive will to believe." Nurtured on Herbert Spencer, Darwin, and Darwin's German disciple Ernst Henry Haeckel, all of Westermarck's thinking was influenced by the doctrine of natural selection. He had at first accepted Morgan's primitive-promiscuity hypothesis, but, on further reflection, decided that arguments based on survivals were not convincing, especially when the facts of biology were not being taken into account. He wrote matter-of-factly: "I saw clearly that I should have to write a book on the history of marriage. I had been led to this decision, not by any specific inclination and least of all by any personal interest in the subject, but by pure accident."

This decision was made in 1886. The following year a small legacy gave him freedom to travel. He had already sent out a questionnaire to missionaries and administrators of colonies. Armed with this material, he set out for London to work in the British Museum and to see something of England, a country that was eventually to become his second home.

When he returned to Finland a year later to publish the first chapters of his book as a doctor's thesis, he was elected president of the Students' Union. His connection with this organization reveals a side of his character at variance with the impersonal scientific temper. Finland, conquered by Alexander I of Russia in 1809, was still fiercely jealous of her autonomy and resentful of domination by her giant neighbor. The student groups were a hotbed of patriotism, an emotion that Westermarck shared to an intense degree.

Back in England again, he made the acquaintance of Tylor, who took an interest in his work and recommended him to the publisher Macmillan. His book was accepted, and an introduction was contributed by Alfred Wallace, co-propounder with Darwin of the evolutionary theory. Westermarck, citizen of a small country, felt the need to write in a language with a wider currency than Finnish. Swedish, used fluently by cultured Finns, was still not a major tongue. German he disliked. He chose English. His editor polished the book, chapter by chapter, growing more and more excited as he read on. The proofs were then sent to Wallace for criticism by letter, and, finally, the youthful Westermarck was almost struck dumb with delight when the old gentleman was so impressed that he came to call.

When the book was about to appear, Westermarck took a vacation in the Shetland Islands. At first he was almost afraid to admit that he was a Finn, for the Shetland Islanders, of Scandinavian stock, traditionally considered all Finns to be wizards. There were tales current of great sea monsters called *finns* which chased boats at sea and every ninth night came ashore in the form of seals, cast their skins, and danced in the shape of men on the sands. The expert on marriage gained the confidence of the islanders by joining them on fishing-trips. While he was enjoying this outdoor life, the reviews of his book, *The History of Human Marriage*, reached him. Tylor, always open-minded, praised it. Robertson Smith, defending McLennan, damned it. Westermarck's attack on the primitive-promiscuity doctrine was revolutionary, but by 1892 the critical tide had begun to turn, and scientists all over the world studied his ideas with respect as editions of the book appeared in all major languages. He had piled up such a catalogue of documentation that the public conceived of him as a bearded patriarch who had spent a lifetime on the work. Sometimes the thirty-year-old scholar was asked if his father had written the book.

The final sentence of the book stated: "The history of human marriage is the history of a relation in which women have been gradually triumphing over the passions, prejudices, and the selfish interests of men." On the strength of it, Westermarck was invited to become vice-president of two feminist societies that were not on speaking terms with each other. As it happened, however, the sentence had been written by his editor, who thought an inspiring punch line was needed. In the second edition Westermarck changed it, for he decided that the status of women did *not* improve in proportion as civilization advanced.

Westermarck approached marriage from the biological point of view. Abandoning the primitive horde, he examined the behavior of the lower animals for signs of virtuous family life. Certain male fish took part in nest-building. Male birds even shared in the task of raising the young, and some birds paired for life. Among monogamous mammals he included whales, seals, hippopotamuses, and squirrels.

He believed that the orangutan, the gorilla, and the chimpanzee also paired, the latter building a nest for the female in a forked branch.

All existing savages, whether polygamous, polyandrous, or monogamous, had a family group of father, mother, and offspring, the group being supported by the male.

He did not think that marriage had been correctly defined. He described it as a more or less durable connection between male and female lasting beyond the act of propagation till after the birth of offspring.

The early evolutionists, in their enthusiasm for an ascending series, had pretty much equated marriage with sexual intercourse gradually restricted by legal forms. Westermarck, by viewing it as a relationship among male, female, and offspring, almost by definition gave it a monogamous basis.

Human young were helpless and unspecialized, and their infancy was prolonged. This was the fundamental necessity for a marriage lasting a considerable period of time.

What evidence was there for this view of marriage?

Among many simple peoples, such as the Ainus of Japan, the Siamese, and the Aleuts, a woman was not considered permanently married until she had had a child. Also, many tribes permitted sexual freedom among young people, but obliged a man to marry a girl made pregnant by him. He found cases where a woman had a right to kill her child if the father refused to marry her.

He was convinced that the earliest stage of society was not a horde, but a series of isolated families like the gorillas'. The Fuegians, the Veddas, and the West Australians were still in this condition. Schoolcraft had reported that the Snake Indians originally came together only to hunt salmon. Later, when they obtained horses from the whites, they co-operated to hunt buffalo. It was conceivable that social organization originated in such associations for food-gathering. "Neither do I see any reason to believe that there *ever* was a time when the family was quite absorbed into the tribe."

Neither J. F. McLennan, Lewis Morgan, nor John Lubbock had ever found any documented case of primitive promiscuity without marriage. Listing the matriarchal and patriarchal peoples, Westermarck did not see any evidence of a transition from one to the other. Although there were peoples who did not understand the physiological mechanics of parenthood, none failed to connect the father with the child. Matriarchal descent may have arisen from the fact that the child was more often with the mother and more intimately associated with her.

As sexual jealousy occurred among primitives, and even among animals, this would be a force in support of exclusive pairing. Finally, he had a Darwinian argument. Prostitutes tended to be sterile. Therefore, continual promiscuity would have militated against the propagation of the race. On the basis of natural selection, those practicing pair marriage would be more likely to leave descendants. Thus biology saw to it that conjugal virtue paid off.

Among primitive peoples, whose economic development was rudimentary, marriage was early and celibacy practically unheard of. It was only in more complex civilizations that economic obstacles postponed the age of marriage and a greater critical sense made individuals more highly selective of their marital partners.

Inspired by Darwin, Westermarck insisted that ornaments, elaborate hairdressing, tattooing, and self-mutilation were all techniques of sexual attraction rather than totemic in origin. Among most natives it was the males who practiced such arts as a form of courtship.

Casting Victorian prudery to the winds, he faced the question of modesty without flinching. Many naked peoples showed no sense of shame. Some wore clothes, but did not cover the sexual organs. Some tribes, on the other hand, covered their women's bodies as a means of sex titillation. The Admiralty Islanders of the Pacific wore nothing but a white shell covering the end of the penis, evidently using it to draw attention to that organ. Circumcision and elongation of the clitoris belonged in the same category. Thus the whole idea of modesty was relative and a matter of local convention. The Admiralty Islander felt naked without his shell. A Chinese woman would not show her feet, while the women of

Sumatra did not expose their knees. Alaskan women wore a huge ornament in the lower part of the mouth and felt indecent without it. A Mohammedan was shocked at the décolleté European dress. The evidence all tended to show that shame was a convention and that dress arose either for warmth or to enhance sexual charm.

Male animals tended to pair with any available female, but men, as civilization evolved, developed aesthetic and emotional standards of selectivity when it came to their sexual partners. One of the strongest restrictions involving selectivity was the prohibition of incest. How did this prohibition arise?

Other scholars, including Morgan, had credited savages with the nineteenth-century scientific notion that incest must be prevented to avoid degeneracy in the offspring.

It was true that the objection to incest was widespread, but there was no agreement on the exact degree of kinship to be avoided.

In the Finnish epic, the Kalevala, Kullero committed incest with his sister and exclaimed afterward:

> *Woe is me, my life hard-fated*
> *I have slain my virgin sister;*
> *Woe to thee, my ancient father!*
> *Woe to thee, my gray-haired mother!*
> *Wherefore was I born and nurtured,*
> *Why this hopeless child's existence?*

The tragedy of Oedipus centered around the same crime, committed with his mother.

Among the Veddas of Ceylon, however, marriage with a younger sister was right and proper, but union with an elder sister or aunt was incestuous and revolting. In the royal families of Siam, Burma, and Polynesia, and among the ancient Incas, marriage with sisters or half-sisters was customary. On the other hand, the Australians, with a rudimentary material culture, had one of the most elaborate systems of prohibition, far more strict than in western civilization, extending even to third cousins.

The fact that incest could and did take place between near relatives who did not know they were related could and did show that there was no mystical aversion.

Westermarck utilized his favorite explanation, natural selection. Figures tended to prove, he believed, that inbred marriages were less fertile than those between unrelated pairs. The stock of those who married close relatives would tend to die out.

Then Westermarck took time to examine marriage by purchase. This transaction was not a case of buying the bride by the pound, but rather a propitiatory offering to please her parents and prove that the groom was economically reliable. This then tended to degenerate into an exchange of presents, as in China. The marriage portion in Europe, which the groom received with the bride, was a symbolic return of the purchase money.

In summation, Westermarck believed that in primitive times marriage lasted until the birth of offspring or somewhat longer, and was monogamous. It was possible to conclude from figures that difficult economic conditions resulted in more male than female births. Polyandry might result, as among the Todas. Polygamy could be assigned to several causes. Men, for magical or religious reasons, were forbidden intercourse with their wives during periods of menstruation, pregnancy, and, in some cases, nursing. This would lead them to take an additional mate. In Indochina and among the Eskimos, if a woman was barren, a man was entitled to take a second wife. Among the American Indians, Zulus, and Aleuts, numerous wives were an indication of wealth.

Despite some authorities who saw no reason for monogamy to continue as the dominant form, Westermarck, its prophet, believed that if the current trend toward high selectivity continued, it would become even more strict. The monogamous horizon was not unclouded, however. He concluded, regretfully, that there was no reason to believe that divorce would be less frequent in the future.

Even before the study of marriage was finished, Westermarck had embarked on his second major project, a book on the development of morals. Meanwhile, having received a travel grant from the University of Finland, where he taught philosophy on and off for the next few years, he took a trip through Europe. While in Capri he had a narrow escape. He met a young American woman painter who, "after some slight demonstration of affection," forthrightly asked him to marry her. The historian of marriage was not prepared for this type of research. He rapidly drew out a picture of his two nephews, remarked: "Aren't they dear children? They are mine," and fled.

Westermarck indulged his hobby of climbing by ascending

Mount Etna. While he was in Italy, Lombroso, the famous Italian criminologist, took him on a tour of a prison, explaining that the criminal type always had projecting big toes. He removed the shoes of two prisoners to demonstrate, but both proved to be exceptions. Westermarck was itching to display his own projecting big toes, but concluded that they, too, would be classed as exceptions.

Westermarck continued to work in the British Museum during the late nineties, dividing his time between London and Helsingfors, teaching and working on his study of morals. At a congress of psychologists he met Henry Sidgwick, author of a book, *Methods of Ethics.* He thanked the latter for what he had learned from his book. Sidgwick admitted he was preparing a new edition, and politely asked for criticism. Westermarck, the *enfant terrible,* blandly remarked that he disagreed with him on only one point: "I do not believe there is anything objectively right or wrong." Sidgwick stared at him in horror. "No, that I can not alter!" he cried, and made his escape.

Westermarck had begun to take an interest in Arab culture. He set out for Morocco, working his way down through Spain. "The splendid ornamentation in the Alhambra," he pointed out, "is in a great measure founded on designs which are at the present day still used in Morocco as amulets against the evil eye; conventionalized images of eyes or eyebrows and various combinations of the number five, representing the five fingers of the hand, with which the evil influence emanating from the eye is thrown back or the eye itself is, in a symbolic manner, put out."

Traveling in Morocco in 1897 was still not safe for Christians. Mohammedans hissed Westermarck behind his back. Sometimes he was not allowed to enter cafés. Short, stout, genial, and determined, with a scrubby mustache that accentuated a certain resemblance to Theodore Roosevelt, Westermarck went his way undismayed by almost unbearable heat and the spiders, beetles, flies, and scorpions that swarmed into his tent. When he was robbed of all his money, clothes, and papers, he wrote: "What did small discomforts matter? . . . I had got an idea of Oriental life and had been brought into contact with a people who had kept their ancient belief in magic powers and mystic spirits. . . ."

His chief objective was the study of Arab morals and customs. Like Robertson Smith, he wore native dress when he attended local festivals—yellow leather slippers, a white turban around his head, a long cloak over his clothes. He was able to overawe superstitious bandit chieftains by exhibitions of magic. He had a bottle containing metholated spirits in which floated a small red-and-black devil. Westermarck let his Arab visitor hold the bottle, saying that he could tell if the devil was afraid of him. If the man's hand was warm enough, the devil danced up and down in terror. Such devices were useful because the prejudice against Christians was deep-seated. They were said to grow from seeds in the ground and to have horns on their foreheads. An Arab proverb, "to have a heart like a Christian," meant to be hard and cruel. Other magic tricks Westermarck used to maintain his prestige were an inflatable rubber bladder to make plates jump and a Pharaoh's Serpent, a chemical pellet that grew, when lighted, into a wormlike shape.

He also experienced, at first hand, a type of primitive hospitality he had described in his book, the courteous offer of wives, which he parried neatly by insisting that he had a dozen back home, all he could afford.

Arabs never under any circumstances showed any interest in their wives in public. Once he told a group of friends that in Europe husbands and wives went out together, the woman taking her husband's arm. His female hearers cast down their eyes and blushed, the men tittered with embarrassment. Westermarck realized that this was probably the most indecent thing he had said in his whole life.

He alternated his Moroccan residence with periods of teaching philosophy in Helsingfors and sociology at the University of London. The first part of his book *The Origin and Development of Moral Ideas* was published in 1906, the rest in 1908. Marett and Havelock Ellis praised it highly. He was now free to finish his studies on religion and magic of the Moors. *Marriage Ceremonies in Morocco* was published in 1914.

The First World War found him living in a cottage in a beech grove not far from London. The position of a patriotic Finn was difficult. He hated Russia, England's ally, and longed for that nation's defeat, but he loved England. The Russian spy service was taking an interest in him because he belonged to an organization for the liberation of Finland. Young Finns were training in England to fight for the freedom of their country. Westermarck was asked to head a movement for the cause, which included German members. He considered his position carefully and decided that his obligations and loyalty to England could not allow him to accept, as he would be placed in the position of being, indirectly, a spy for Germany.

While German air raids took place, he worked on a new two-volume edition of the history of marriage. The British police investigated him to learn whether he harbored a radio. His difficulties were not severe, however, and with the Russian revolution at the end of the war, his beloved Finland got her freedom. After the war he helped draw up a report for the League of Nations on the problem of the island of Aaland. Sweden claimed it, but the Finnish population wanted to remain a part of Finland. It was a plebiscite which actually settled the question in favor of Finland, but the report was considered a model of its kind, for it laid down guarantees that preserved the interests of the Swedish minority.

Westermarck finally bought a house in Morocco, where he finished his two-volume work *Ritual and Belief in Morocco* in 1926. He died in 1939.

Although he married, nowhere in his autobiography did he mention his wife's name. It was doubtless with a double meaning that he wrote: "It has been said that marriage has many thorns, but celibacy no roses. For my part I would say that marriage has brought me many roses and bachelorhood no thorns."

Chapter 18

MARRIAGE, MORALS, AND
GORILLAS
Concerning Edward Westermarck,
A. E. Crawley, Robert Briffault

■ A. E. Crawley, in *The Mystic Rose* (1902), agreed that Westermarck's biological emphasis on monogamy was useful, but he felt that the latter knew nothing about the primitive mind. Following Frazer's *Golden Bough*, he insisted that to primitive man the objects of his imagination were just as real as scientifically demonstrable facts. Religion entered into all departments of thought. Consequently, all sex relations were surrounded by religious meaning. Even the crudest form of marriage known, that of the Australian Arunta, was not without ritual.

Most important, and running through the ritual of tribes all over the world, was the idea of *danger in sex*.

In the Marquesas Islands of the Pacific, canoes were taboo to women. African Kaffirs did not let women tend their cattle. Moslems repeated religious formulas before the sex act. In Costa Rica a woman pregnant for the first time infected the neighborhood, and deaths were laid to her charge. To the Maoris of New Zealand, menstruating women were taboo. And not only women and sex were full of peril; there was a wealth of animistic evidence to show that from the point of view of the native the whole world was full of dangerous influences. Maoris, before entering a strange country, performed a ceremony to protect themselves. In German folklore there was a custom of blowing three times into a new spoon before eating with it.

Whatever was strange, unaccustomed, inexplicable to the pre-scientific primitive mind was also fearful and a source of danger. Women were a strange people by virtue of menstruation and the phenomenon of birth, and thus sex differentiation gave rise to various taboos. In many cases a man could not touch anything belonging to a woman and vice versa. Often the two sexes did not eat together.

To savages functional crises were strange and hence dangerous. The sex act plus the strangeness of a new relationship, intimacy with an alien and dubious being, a female, made marriage doubly perilous. There was also the notion that the dangerous qualities of a taboo individual were contagious and transmissible. A kind of spiritual smallpox threatened on every side. Indeed, the hazards discovered by Crawley were so great that it was remarkable that propagation of the human race had gone on so long.

Contagion was associated with contact. Intimacy, either friendly or erotic, was related to physical contact and expressed through it. Animosity was expressed through avoidance of such contact—with the sick, with strangers, with enemies. The tactile sensitivity of human membranes had psychic significance. "These ideas of contact are primitive in each sense of the word, at whatever stage of culture they appear. They seem to go back in origin and character to the highly developed sensitivity of all animal and even organized life forms, at once a biological monitor and a safeguard for the whole organism in relation to its environment." In human beings the feelings about contact were largely subconscious and, without being verbalized, had entered into magical and religious practice.

The central Australians had a myth of an old man who plucked from his body boils, each of which turned into a stone. They were still to be seen and were called *stone sores*. Men who wished to do harm to others hit one of these stones with a spear and then threw the spear in the direction of the victim. The Maoris believed that anything which came in contact with a sacred object became sacred. There were many examples of contagious magic, with particular emphasis on the potency of sexual elements. Some savages believed that the penis of a great warrior possessed virtue; the victor who killed him wore it on his person. The prepuce removed at circumcision was worn as an amulet to gain potency. Human semen was used as a medicine by the Australians. Pliny mentioned menstrual blood placed on doorposts to dissolve harmful spells.

Likewise, such organs of the body as were specialized channels of contact with the outer world required extra precautions to safeguard them. Nutritive, sexual, and excretory functions put the individual in a defenseless state. Consequently, such functions were invested with religious rites.

Tattooing, scarifying, circumcising were connected with the idea of securing the safety of the whole organ by sacrificing a bit of it to the deity. This would consecrate the rest of the organ, making it less "impure." The Yorubas interpreted circumcision as a sacrifice to the erotic deity Elegba. (This view, of course, contradicted Westermarck entirely.)

Plugs, sticks, or other ornaments inserted in the body could act as a kind of lightning rod to divert evil influences from the body itself.

Among the Arunta of central Australia it was thought that during sexual connection women could injure the male organ by magic. Some tribes insisted that women, at puberty, had intercourse with demons or gods. Menstrual bleeding was considered by some tribes to result from the bite of a supernatural bird. The Abyssinians blamed it on a snake.

Crawley wrote: "The usual working motive in sexual taboo is that the properties of one sex can be transmitted to the other by all methods of contact. . . . Two remarkable facts have emerged— first that it is dangerous, and later wrong, for men to have anything to do with women; intercourse commensual and sexual being especially dangerous because especially intimate; and secondly that sexual intercourse, even when lawful morally and legally, is dangerous first, and later, sinful. To primitive thought all intercourse has one connotation of material danger, which later split into ideas of sins, such as incest and fornication, for any intercourse is the breaking of a personal taboo, and the material results of such breaking develop into moral sin."

This was an interesting and ingenious explanation of the subconscious basis for celibate religious groups and for the virtues attributed by some religions to virginity.

When this terrible impasse in matters of sex had been reached, some recipe had to be found to allow primitive men to marry or even to touch a member of the opposite sex.

By taking the proper precautions the dangers could be annulled, explained Crawley. The system of precautions was essentially a kind of cross-inoculation. Each of two separate individuals took, actually or symbolically, something of the other individual into contact with his or her body. Thus they became one, no longer strange to each other, no longer able or willing to hurt each other.

Hair, garments, blood, names could be used as inoculation. Smoking together, eating food together, especially salt, was a sign of blood brotherhood, as Robertson Smith had pointed out in his theory of the sacred meal. Exchanging of names was a common form of brotherhood. The Dyaks of Borneo and the Madagascans drank each other's blood. The Timorese saluted by touching noses and drawing a deep breath. From this it was only a step to the modern handshake, which also showed that hands were empty of weapons. The Timorese also exchanged wives when making a pact of friendship, for wives were a part of themselves.

Mutual inoculation ran through kinship bonds, Freemasonry, clubs of all kinds. Dionysiac festivals and Saturnalias, which allowed the breaking of taboos by sexual promiscuity, were a symbol of the desire for unity. Eating a portion of the dead, which, as we have seen, was practiced among the Melanesians, was probably an inoculation against the dangers that might arise from their spirits. All through social life the technique of cross-inoculation to avoid the perils of the alien was employed. In modern marriage it had survived in the exchange of wedding rings.

Among primitives, the bride and groom often had to avoid each other until the actual ceremony, the ritual neutralizing of sexual danger, had taken place. In modern life there was the superstition that the groom must not see the bride on the day of the wedding before the ceremony. The Christian service spoke of "one flesh," the Hebrew stated: "so ought men to love their wives as their own bodies." Marriage was always a magical affair affecting the relationship between two *individuals*.

From the psychological point of view, Crawley thus reinforced Westermarck. Cases in which the bride had the hymen perforated and submitted to ritual intercourse with certain priests or elders were not a survival of group marriage, but a matter of neutralizing the sexual danger to the husband. Struggles of the bride's relatives against the bridegroom were not a survival of marriage by capture, but a symbolic struggle against the female sex; violence neutralized the taboo by breaking it forcibly. Crawley saw no evidence that the matriarchal system preceded the patriarchal. The taboo against speaking to the mother-in-law (which Tylor suggested was a matter of the husband treated as a stranger at the point of transition from one system to the other) Crawley said arose because the mother-in-law was a dangerously sexed female in an equivocal relationship: she was the groom's mother, yet not his mother.

For the *couvade*, the custom of the husband taking to his bed while his wife gave birth (which, as we have seen, was variously explained), Crawley found a new interpretation. On the basis of misdirection, evil influences could be averted from the person upon whom they were intended to light. The father was simply pretending to be the mother in order to draw away the dangers surrounding birth (like a partridge that pretends to have a broken wing).

Exogamy did not arise from any instinctive horror of incest. Crawley quarreled with Westermarck's statistics, rejecting the notion that inbreeding could cause sterility. Since an instinct was physiological and could not be inherited, there could be no transmission of an acquired aversion to incest. Exogamy had to be a formal elaboration of the sexual taboos just discussed.

Puberty rites were, of course, precautions against the first contact with sex, and it was noticeable that in some cases the initiate must have intercourse immediately after initiation.

Marriage, in all of Crawley's thinking, was no more than a ceremony. He was not concerned with its duration or its social function.

Although Westermarck's rebuttal, plus Crawley's psychological attack, was a serious setback to believers in the priority of matriarchy and primitive promiscuity, still Morgan's thinking showed remarkable vitality. His scheme had had great attraction for Marxists ever since Friedrich Engels had used it as a basis for his book on the origin of the family. It was heartening to be able to look back to a primitive utopia, an Eden lacking private property while based on matrilineal clan organization. From this could be elaborated a new story of the Fall, with the roles reversed and, instead of the snake, the ancient patriarch clutching his herds selfishly, degrading women, and destroying the democratic clan system in order to pass on his ill-gotten sheep to his son. Modern Soviet Russian anthropology has installed Morgan as one of its chief authorities.

It is not surprising, therefore, that the most elaborate restatement of Morgan's position in recent decades came from the left. Robert Briffault (1876–1942), the son of a French diplomat married to an Englishwoman, had a cosmopolitan education culminating in a degree in medicine from the University of London. For a time he practiced in New Zealand. After serving in the First World War, he retired from practice and produced a huge three-volume work, *The Mothers* (1927), his chief contribution to anthropology. Aggressive and controversial, after writing other books on history and social theory, he turned novelist with the rather lurid three-volume *Europa* (1935–7), which was a scathing dramatization of the decadence of the European bourgeoisie. A somewhat melodramatic performance, the book achieved a certain *succès de scandale*. Although a Communist Party member in 1930, Briffault later broke with the orthodox line. A restless spirit, he felt himself one of a lost generation that could not accept the conventional intellectual currents of his day, but he also could not find a place for himself among the masses. During the Second World War he was in Paris, and during the German occupation he spent some time in a Nazi prison for publishing works of English history through the underground press. After seventeen years in France he returned to England a month before his death.

Briffault's work in anthropology reflects the wave of social thinking which affected the intellectual climate of the twenties and thirties. His chief target was Westermarck. Zoological field study had made strides since the latter's time, for back in the nineties much of his evidence had been rather shaky, being based on the observations of hunters and travelers.

Briffault assembled evidence to show that the idyllic monogamy of the brutes was a myth; most of them came together briefly in the period of rut. The bull moose, cited as a faithful lover, spent a short time with one cow and then went bellowing in search of another. As for those loyal spouses, the higher apes, careful observation showed that most of them were polygamous, a dominant male monopolizing the females and keeping the younger suitors at bay. The chimpanzee, so tenderly building a nest in a tree for his mate, was a fiction.

"In bands of gorillas the sexes keep separate, the females and young forming one group, the males keeping to themselves." Alas for the morals of baboons; their sex life was continual and indiscriminate, the females never refusing!

Among animals that congregated in groups, leadership rested mainly with an old female. To Briffault the essential family unit among animals consisted of the mother and her offspring. She chose the nest or burrow, suckled the young, and fed them or taught them to find food. The male's association was intermittent or nonexistent.

The maternal instinct in lower animals was purely physical; only when the sex glands were active did they take an interest in their young. When disturbed, they sometimes ate them, particularly females of the cat family. The males very often ate the young if not driven off by the females.

He took a dim view of the basis of sex attraction, which in animals was highly sadistic. From carnivores to camels, they delighted in inflicting pain during sex activities. Even the kiss, with all its romantic associations, originated in biting. And "the desire expressed by lovers to 'eat' the object of their affections contains more sinister biological reminiscences than they are aware."

There was no doubt that maternal love was an older drive than sexual tenderness. In complicated animals such as apes it was quite well developed in proportion to a longer period of infancy and helplessness. Savages, too, in general were notable for the intensity of their affection for children. In most cases they would never strike a child, and missionaries were attacked by screaming mothers when they corrected children in their schools.

All this pointed to the close union of mother and child, while the male remained more or less unattached—a roving hunter who did not even sleep at home. In this stage of society, women were highly self-sufficient. They carried on digging-stick agriculture, food-preparation, and all of the home manufactures such as house-building, basketry, ceramics.

With the mother established as the dominant member of the family relation, how did the clan system with its rules of exogamy arise?

Prohibition of incest for eugenic reasons was beyond the native mind. Statistics did not show that it caused weakening of the stock (or sterility, as Westermarck believed). The idea that sexual attraction between housemates was low did not have any factual basis. The savage, unaffected by instinct or moral sense, would ravish any woman if not deterred by magical fears. To Briffault the only practical bar to incest would be the efforts of the mothers to protect the immature younger sisters from the activities of their brothers. (The older sister was safe, she was already married.) Also, the subconscious jealousy of the mothers, deeply attached to their sons, would impel them to preserve the chastity of their daughters.

Matrilocal residence, a state of affairs in which the husband went to live with the wife's family, was Briffault's chief proof of the priority of the matriarchy. It harked back to the female animal's choice of the nest. Mother-in-law-avoidance indicated that the husband had to bow down before a powerful person, his chief. She was taboo because a matriarchal ruler. The fact that such a taboo could sometimes be lifted by payment was proof that the wife's mother had to be propitiated.

What was marriage actually? Among the early theorists there was a tendency to confuse it with either sexual intercourse or sexual affection. Monogamists such as Westermarck still seemed to think of it in ideal Victorian terms—as a romantic pairing for life, preceded by continence.

Among the Australians, however, pair marriage took place at about thirty, which was *old* for such peoples, and it was preceded by considerable promiscuity. The Veddas of Ceylon, those shining examples of low-culture monogamy, could and did send their wives home whenever they felt like it, sometimes after a day or two, whereupon they took another wife. Since their girls were married at puberty, ten or eleven, their prenuptial chastity resulted from an absence of a prenuptial period. In general, divorce was easy and widespread among primitives, and marriage so unstable as to be not far removed from a real free-for-all.

As for the emotional and social side of the matter, it did not seem to Briffault that marriage arose either from tender and undying love or as a sex regulation. An Australian, asked why he wanted a wife, replied: so that she might fetch wood and water. The Papuans of the South Seas were indifferent to the sex conduct of their wives provided they were not deprived of their labor.

Since neither love, sex, nor morals brought the primitive male and female together for an enduring relationship, it followed that marriage was an *economic* arrangement. "In the matrilocal form of marriage, the husband is expected to contribute by the product of his hunting and by personal service to the economic needs of his wife's family. All matrilocal marriage is by service and the evidence is, I believe, conclusive that this has everywhere been the most ancient form of individual marriage." In other words, as the nest-building female developed the domestic arts and agriculture, the hunting male found it worth while to exchange his booty for the comforts of a home. The lady's kinfolk took advantage of his weakness and saw to it that a permanent economic arrangement arose.

Symbolic marriage by capture, which McLennan had made so much of, Briffault saw as the transitional stage when the male began to be dominant and broke the traditional matrilocal custom. The resentment of the bride's kin at loss of services finally became a theatrical performance, and their mock anger could be bought off. Hence marriage by purchase reimbursed the bride's kin for both the husband and the bride's former contribution to the household economy in the matrilocal arrangement.

Briffault believed that, with the domestication of animals by men and the pastoral stage that followed, men became the property-holders. Likewise, plow agriculture, based on domestic cattle, put agriculture into the hands of the men. Thus the male-dominated patriarchal system arose. Women, often stronger in character than men under the old system, and well treated, lost their economic advantage and were relegated to an inferior position. In Oriental countries women had one valuable commodity left: their sex. From this arose polygamy, and marriage took on a predominantly sexual aspect.

In Europe, where agriculture and industry developed without a true pastoral stage, women retained their connection with the soil longer and became heiresses. Then the object of marriage was to gain access to their property, and monogamy resulted. "No other culture," Briffault announced, "has been monogamous."

The maternal instinct could be credited with the tightly woven communal relationships of the clan, which were the basis of society. This sense of solidarity "has become lost with the rise of competitive interests; but originally the emergence of social humanity out of animality would have been impossible had the members of the primitive social groups been actuated by the individualism which governs the behavior of modern man."

Briffault disagreed with Westermarck on modesty, as he did on almost every other point. "Taboos of bodily modesty have their origin in superstitious ideas which, far from being associated with any feeling of sinfulness, are on the contrary connected with anxiety lest the sexual organs should be exposed to injury through magical influences and more particularly through that of the evil eye." But the patriarchal villain took advantage of this anxiety and decreed the covering of women's sex organs to indicate his monopoly of those parts. The overemphasis on the sinfulness of sex was a pure Christian attitude, unknown in other societies.

His final attack on Westermarck cut both ways. "Those anthropologists who are concerned with upholding the patriarchal theory of social origins show an anxiety to trace sexual prohibitions and restrictions arising from social and magical principles to biological or natural 'instinct.' . . . In endeavoring to trace germs of patriarchal institutions in an imaginary natural history of gorillas, they likewise seek to detect among the anthropoids the rudiments of Christian morality." If the agnostic Westermarck was still subconsciously in the grip of Christian morality, Briffault the Marxist was no less a special pleader for his own particular philosophy.

Although he still clung to evolution in a straight line, his emphasis on the economic factor in marriage had its value, and he was wise enough to give up the kinship-terminology argument and the dubious notion of group marriage.

A temperate and factually argued statement of the views of the school opposing Briffault's reasoning is found in R. H. Lowie's *Primitive Society*, published in 1925. Like Lowie's book on religion, it is also a general criticism of the nineteenth-century evolutionary point of view.

Primitive promiscuity "or sexual communism exists nowhere at the present time, and the arguments for its former existence must be rejected as unsatisfactory." Lowie accepted the economic factor in marriage and agreed with Briffault that there was much primitive divorce and concubinage. "One fact stands out beyond all others that everywhere the husband, the wife, and immature children constitute a unit apart from the remainder of the community."

Westermarck was right, though, as Lowie put it, mostly for the wrong reasons.

There was no very solid evidence for the theory that the matriarchal system was transformed into the patriarchal during the pastoral stage. "The Navaho of northern Arizona profited by the introduction of sheep into the Southwest some time in the seventeenth century so as to develop into a prosperous pastoral people, yet in spite of their thriving flocks, tended by the men, they have remained obstinately matrilineal." The Hidatsa, too, although their society changed in many ways with the introduction of the horse, remained matrilineal.

Tylor had tried to correlate elements in the two social systems. Cases of the dominant authority of the maternal uncle occurring in a patriarchal tribe might mean the tribe had originally been matriarchal. But, on the other hand, plenty of matriarchal tribes did *not* grant the maternal uncle authority over the family.

Evidence drawn from the distribution of the two institutions was the most striking objection to the theory that all of humanity had passed from one stage to the other. Northwest Indian tribes were predominantly patriarchal, but where their territories overlapped those of groups with the opposite system they adopted it. The small Gros Ventre tribe, at one time a clanless group, was dominated by the Blackfeet, and developed patriarchal clans.

In Siberia the most primitive tribes, the Chuckchis and Koryaks, were clanless. But the more civilized Yakuts were exogamous and patrilineal. On the whole, in this area there was no trace of matriarchy, and patrilineal clans seemed to have developed from none at all. In general it seemed that there was no fixed succession, and from no clans at all either patriarchal or matriarchal systems might develop. "If the highest civilizations emphasize the paternal side of the family, so do many of the lowest."

The Todas' curious type of polyandry, in which a group of brothers married one woman, had been interpreted in various ways: as a survival of group marriage, or as a step on the road to monogamy. To Lowie it indicated that the type of marriage had something to do with the proportion between the two sexes. The Todas formerly practiced female infanticide, which, of course, caused a shortage of women. The pressure of British rule in India put a stop to this practice, and the proportion of women rose. Thereupon a group of brothers married *two* women!

The modern view of the marriage problem is the same as the modern view of religion—it cannot be proved, from a mixture of data on contemporary savages and retrospective conjecture, that all of mankind in the distant past traveled any single road of development.

Chapter 19

FROM CORROBOREE TO
MARTHA GRAHAM
Concerning Anthropology and the Dance

■ Among the simpler peoples of the earth whose decorative or pictorial art is only rudimentary, the dance is well developed. Religion, as we have seen, runs through all the departments of savage life. So do dancing and music. They are the constant handmaids of ritual, and ritual regulates the behavior of those living close to nature.

Life itself is rhythmical: breathing, the heartbeat, walking, the flapping of a bird's wing or the slow undulation of a snake or worm; among the mammalian forms even the act of procreation and the pangs accompanying birth are rhythmical. Marching or work is made easier by marking and intensifying a strong rhythm; apparently a tendency to enjoy actions performed in unison to a regular beat is deeply rooted in human nature.

Music and dance are probably the oldest of the arts and are certainly those which contribute most to the social organization of man. In spite of this fact, anthropology has, so far, scarcely begun to study them. For this oversight there are several reasons. Few anthropologists have been dancers or musicians. Likewise, until recent times a patronizing attitude toward the art forms of alien peoples has hindered investigation in this field.

Music and dance are also very intimately related among primitives. For this reason there has been some speculation as to which came first. The psychologist Wilhelm Wundt wrote, in *Volkers-psychologie* (*The Elements of Folk Psychology*), published in 1912: "Not epic song but the dance, accompanied by a monotonous and meaningless song, constitutes everywhere the most primitive and, in spite of that primitiveness, the most highly developed art form." Richard Wagner, too, as far back as 1877, said that music arose from the dance. In 1894 Richard Wallaschek, at the suggestion of his friend Westermarck, collected some papers he had published and worked them into a book entitled *Primitive Music*. In this work he carried the discussion further. Both Herbert Spencer and Charles

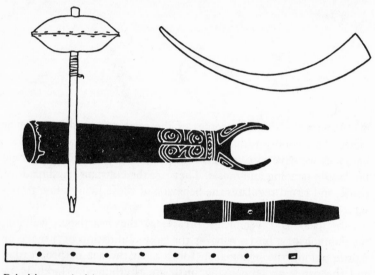

Primitive musical instruments. TOP: *Hupa Indian rattle, African horn.*
MIDDLE: *Fly River drum, Northwest Indian whistle.*
BOTTOM: *California Indian whistle.*

Darwin had commented on music. Darwin, who had no ear for music and thought it useless, suggested that, like the warbling of birds which danced and sang before their mates, the music of aboriginals was merely an example of sexual display. Spencer held that music was derived from the cadences of emotional speech, in which there was change of pitch and volume. In other words, song was a kind of heightened recitative.

In his book Wallaschek compiled a long list of music and dancing from the simpler cultures and concluded that both Spencer and Darwin were wrong. Rhythm, regular and pronounced, was the constant characteristic of all primitive music, and as dancing was essentially rhythm expressed in motion, he suggested that musical rhythm and the dance arose together, while melody was a later elaboration.

Wallaschek seemed rather surprised that savages were indifferent to European music when it was played to them. He felt that primitive people were unable to produce works of art in this field because "primitive man lacks the power of elaborating the outcome of his fancy. The circle of his ideas is too limited."

The descriptions of dancing which he collected largely from travelers' and missionaries' accounts suffered from hostility and lack of comprehension. His informants used phrases such as "monotonous and harsh chants," "mere jumping in a circle," "immodest and lewd," or "jerking their posteriors in an absurd manner" to describe what they heard and saw. If it wasn't a waltz, it wasn't dancing, and as the tunes couldn't be whistled, they were of no consequence.

A more sophisticated book written by Ernst Grosse, *Der Anfang der Kunst* (*The Beginning of Art*), appeared a year later. Like Wallaschek, Grosse disagreed with Spencer and Darwin and believed that the germ of both music and dancing was rhythm. He pointed out that much primitive song consisted of two or three adjacent notes producing a monotonous repetition totally unlike the wide variations of pitch and volume in emotional speech.

Several of those isolated cultures which have been used so often to illustrate theories concerning the origin of religion and marriage also illustrate his main thesis. He wrote: "the dances of the hunting peoples can be divided, according to their character, into two groups, mimetic and gymnastic."

The Andaman Islanders were Negritos, whose home islands were near Sumatra in the Bay of Bengal. They were seldom more than five feet tall, and before they encountered the white man their society was so simply organized that they did not even have a word for "chief." Their religion was dominated by shamans or witch doctors. They lived in rude thatched huts. Their graphic art was undeveloped and mostly decorative.

An Oxford-trained professor, Alfred Reginald Radcliffe-Brown, observing them in 1909, made a study of their dancing which is one of the first sensitive accounts of its kind and deserves to be a model for future investigators. He wrote: "Ask an Andaman Islander why he dances, he gives an answer that amounts to saying he does so because he enjoys it. . . . The Andaman Islanders dance after a successful day of hunting; they do not dance if their day has been one of disappointment."

Radcliffe-Brown commented on the lack of previous study of the dance. He ventured to speculate on the origin of the dance form that he observed among the Andaman Islanders. Pleasurable mental exercise finds its expression in muscular activity. A child or man jumps and shouts for joy. Society turns the jumps into a dance, the shouts into a song. Dancing is thus related to the play instinct. As Andaman dancing was accompanied by group clapping, singing, and rhythmical activity, a common action in which all joined, this suggested a social origin of the dance. These islanders had but one dance form, a gymnastic one without mimicry. Its aim seemed to be to bring as many muscles as possible into play. The body was bent at the hips and knees, the arms were held level with the shoulders, the elbows were crooked, the head was thrown slightly back. Thus an equal tension was created between opposing groups of muscles—"the whole body of the dancer is full of active forces balanced one against the other, resulting in a condition of flexibility and alertness without strain." Every adult member of the community took part in the dance, the women acting as a chorus. Those barred by age or sickness were spectators. The movements, reinforced by clapping, singing, and the sounding-board, forced the members of the group to join in a restrained action that was in itself a source of emotional release. The resulting harmony of motion produced an aesthetic enjoyment and also a feeling of good-fellowship and social unity. This was important, for the well-being of Andaman society depended on social harmony.

A war dance naturally aroused warlike emotions and also stimulated unity. Isolated communities of the Andamanese often came together for a day or two and, by dancing, restored tribal ties. When they made peace with an enemy, they danced a peace dance. The participants in all important affairs painted their almost naked bodies with linear designs and dots of red paint and white clay. Thus decorative art was joined with dancing.

The dancing of this people had absolutely no sexual connotation. It took place, normally, after the evening meal. The center of the village was swept clean. Fires and little heaps of resin were lighted. Near one end of the ground the sounding-board was set up. This was a concave piece of board shaped like a shield, painted with designs of white clay; it was sharpened at one end and driven into the ground with a stone propped under the concave side. The leader of the dance beat on it with his foot while he sang. The women sat in a row and took up the chorus after the leader sang a song through. They clapped their hands on the hollow caused by their crossed thighs, in time to the sounding-board. The soloist was replaced when he grew tired, and the dance often continued without a pause for five or six hours. The step was a hop with the right foot, a backward scrape with the left, and another hop with the right, done to two beats of the song. The simple two- or three-note songs composed by the leaders, dealt with familiar activities. A canoe-building song went: "Knots are very hard to cut with an adze. They blunt the edge of the adze. How hard I am working cutting these knots."

In Queensland the corroboree or gymnastic dance of the Australian aboriginals was somewhat similar. To quote Ernst Grosse's informant: "The women have arranged themselves in a horseshoe-shaped group. They are entirely naked. Each holds on her knees a neatly-folded tightly-stretched opossum skin which at other times serves as a robe. Between them and the fire stands the director. He strikes his two sticks abruptly together; the dancers [about thirty, decorated with white clay] have arranged themselves with the rapidity of lightning and advance: then they halt. . . . He begins by beating time with his two sticks: the dancers fall into movement; the women sing and beat on the opossum hides and the corroborry begins. It is astonishing how accurately the time is kept. The tunes and movements are all in unison. The dancers move as smoothly as the best trained ballet troop. They assume all possible positions, sometimes springing aside, sometimes advancing, sometimes retiring one or two steps; they stretch and bend themselves, swing their arms, stamp their feet. Nor is the director idle. While he is beating time with his sticks, he continually executes a particular nasal song, louder or more softly by turns as he makes a step forward or backward. He does not stand in the same place for an instant; now he turns toward the dancers, now toward the women who lift up their voices with all their might; the motions gradually become more rapid and vigorous; the dancers shake themselves, spring into the air to an incredible height and finally utter a shrill cry as if from one mouth. An instant later they have all vanished into the bushes as suddenly as they came."

The whole performance was repeated several times. This gymnastic dance, sometimes involving as many as four hundred people, was not the Australian's only form of expression. As we have seen from Spencer's and Gillen's account of the Arunta, their totemic dances were often mimetic and dealt with animals on which they were dependent for food. Their imitation of kangaroos was particularly vivid.

The Veddas of the island of Ceylon, a diminutive Stone Age people of Caucasian extraction, still lived in caves when Professor Seligman (one of Alfred Haddon's team on the Torres Straits expedition) studied them in 1911. Their economy consisted of growing yams and hunting. Their religion was also shamanistic; they believed in *yaku* or spirits who were sometimes dangerous but could be made helpful by the proper ceremonies. They had no gymnastic dances in which all participated. Instead, their dances were mimetic, performed by a shaman and two or three assistants. In one dance the shaman became possessed by a yaka named Kande, an ancestral hero and a great deer-hunter. In another ceremony to insure good hunting they danced a dance that invoked an arrow yaka. It differed considerably from the dances just described, for it was essentially a trance dance. They moved spasmodically around an arrow set in the ground, jerking backward with each step and making trembling movements, and executing half-turns. After every half-turn they beat hard on their bodies, which served as drums because they had no musical instruments. Their heads, flung up and down after every turn, tossed their tangled mops of hair wildly, and they gasped out a monotonous song to which they kept time. One after another, howling between gasps and trembling more violently, they worked themselves into a seizure in which they were possessed by the yaka, and all finally fell to the ground. Women did not participate in such ceremonies. The Veddas' dancing, on the whole, was not athletic but magical and religious.

Their melodies, like those of the Andamanese, consisted of two or three adjacent notes. C. S. Myers (of the Torres Straits expedition), in a 1913 article on the beginnings of music, compared Vedda songs to those of the Murray Islanders of the Straits. The islanders used fourths and fifths and sometimes octaves, but more often their melodies progressed downward note by note. Myers noted that most primitives seemed to have absolute pitch. He felt that the Vedda songs were more primitive, the use of fourths, fifths, and octaves by the Murray Islanders a later development, while the splitting up of the octave into equal parts might be the result of the invention of musical instruments that could produce all eight notes mechanically. The Murray Islanders had got only as far as drums.

To digress for a moment into the field of musical instruments, from the cultures just discussed several examples can be arranged in an interesting series. The Veddas, who had no instruments, slapped their own bellies. The Andamanese women slapped the hollows of their thighs. The Australian women went one step further, stretching an opossum skin across the thighs to create a temporary drum. The next step would probably be a permanent drum like that of the Bushmen, the rommelpot, which consisted of a skin stretched over a clay pot. On the other hand, the sounding-board of the Andamanese, which could easily have developed from a wooden shield, leads to another type of drum, the hollow log that can be slapped or pounded.

Prehistoric bone whistles do not disprove the priority of drums in the development of music, for drums made of wood or skin would not have survived.

A third example of a musical instrument that seems to have developed as a temporary expedient from another artifact is the musical bow. Henry Balfour, who as curator of the Pitt Rivers Museum at Oxford made that institution a treasure house of ethnological lore, wrote *The Natural History of the Musical Bow* in 1899. He described a Southwest African form in which a cord was tied around a hunting-bow somewhat off center, forming a sort of violin bridge between bow and bowstring. The player held the bow in his teeth and tapped the bowstring on either side of the bridge with a stick. He varied the pitch somewhat by putting his finger on the cord. This instrument must have arisen quite independently from percussion devices that accompany dancing, for the sound was so weak that scarcely anyone but the performer, who half felt it through his teeth, could hear it. A half-gourd tied to the wood of the bow and pressed against the chest acted as a sounding-chamber for greater resonance. Another development was the addition of one or more strings by widening the bow into a slat and cutting a series of pegs at one end. This instrument looked like an ancestor of the harp. Either something like it or the whistle with multiple stops might, if Myers was right, have led to the invention of the full octave and melody for its own sake.

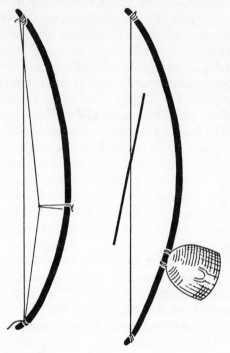

Two types of music bow.

To return to the dance proper, an examination of the dance as described in modern anthropological literature leads to an expansion of Ernst Grosse's classification as follows: (1) gymnastic or social dancing, an expression of group euphoria; (2) trance dancing, associated with possession and religious ritual; (3) mimetic or theatrical dancing.

In addition to the Andaman Islands and Australia, the first type can be found in various other areas. In Samoa, according to Margaret Mead, children were trained to dance from an early age. Dances had a leader, and those not dancing marked the rhythm by clapping or beating on the floor with their knuckles. There was the dreamy, graceful dance of the princesses, the boisterous dance of the boys, and the jokers' dance with horseplay and burlesque and animal mimicry. When visitors arrived, guests and hosts alternated in dances given in the large guesthouses. Dancing was definitely a social affair, and the performers were encouraged to express originality, a quality frowned on in other departments of life.

In Africa, E. E. Evans-Pritchard (a disciple of Radcliffe-Brown) described the *bhere buda* or beer dance of the Azande, a Negro tribe in Egyptian Sudan. Although this was a festival in which beer was supplied by a family in mourning, the dance itself was a social affair, drawing family groups from as far as several hours away. The music was supplied by a wood slit drum played by the leader, who was a professional composer. A small chorus occupied the center of the circle, and around it a line of men danced clockwise and then counterclockwise. The women, hugging one another, danced in an outer circle. Wrote Evans-Pritchard: "The African . . . not only makes movements with his feet to the music but holds out his arms and moves his hands up and down, shakes his head backward, leans from side to side, shifts and lowers his shoulders, and exercises his abdominal muscles. All the muscles of the body seem to be in action and the skin looks as though it accommodated a multitude of snakes."

Bronislaw Malinowski has described the *milamila*, a yearly harvest festival, at which time the spirits of the dead returned from the lower world to the Trobriand Islands. Dances were performed by the men, painted and sometimes decorated with flowerlike cockatoo headdresses. In one type of dance the drums and singer stood in the middle and the performers circled counterclockwise. There was a slow beat for one type of performance and a quick one for another. In the latter, women could occasionally participate, and the men wore women's palm skirts. In another group of dances, three men imitated animals. The Trobriand Islanders danced only at the milamila. After two weeks of festivity, at dawn the drums took up a special beat and with a particular dance step the spirits were sped out of the village back to the lower world and the milamila was at an end.

In America the Eskimos of Baffin Land, whom Franz Boas studied, held their social gatherings in the singing-house. The men were ranged in an inner circle outside of which the women stood but did not dance. The soloist and singer had a drum made of deerskin stretched over a bone hoop with a handle. He sang and danced his own compositions, which dealt with his feelings or with events or satirized individuals. The women joined in the chorus. The men spectators stood silent. Although this was a type of festivity similar to those just described, here there was less participation of the whole group. The Eskimos of Alaska, however, had social dances in which all took part.

These few examples indicate something of the distribution of primitive social dancing and strengthen Radcliffe-Brown's statement of its importance as a group expression.

Trance dancing, in contrast to the above, since it is magical or religious in character, as in the case of the Veddas, is associated with the shaman or medicine man. The Kwakiutl Indians of northwestern America, according to Boas, had several types of dancing. The Killer Whale Society, for example, danced a killer-whale pantomime. Among the Veddas the shamans monopolized the performance, but among the Kwakiutls, Boas wrote, "Although there are expert performers, everyone is obliged to take part . . . so that the separation between performer and audience that we find in modern society does not occur." The trance element was similar in both groups. "The vibration of the hands is produced by a very rapid stretching and bending of the straight fingers at their base, where they join the metacarpals. The thumb is held quiet. The body vibration can be produced only when the body becomes fixed in certain positions producing a strong counter tension to the desired gesture. All of these vibrations acquire a definite ecstatic quality in order to be executed. When inquiring of an Indian how it is done technically, he can only say 'when my excitement reaches a certain point, and my knee is bent so, then I begin to vibrate.' " This technique was not used in war or ghost dances; it was highly stylized and was intended to summon up supernatural powers. Ruth Benedict has pointed out that in certain cannibal dances the Kwakiutl performer was supposed to go out of his mind and bite the spectators. There was no stamping but rather a great feeling of lightness about such dancing.

Among the Alaskan Eskimos, who were studied by E. W. Hawkins, when a shaman impersonated an animal he was possessed by the beast's spirit, and such shamans were noted for the wild and ecstatic quality of their dancing, in which they ran in dizzy circles.

If the gymnastic dance is an expression of emotion, in trance dancing the reverse is the case; dance motion is deliberately used to work up an emotional or psychological state. The Veddas flung the head up and down, which caused pressure on the ganglia in the back of the neck. Such special movements affecting the nervous system seem to be common. The Woloffs of west Africa, according to Geoffrey Gorer, practiced witch-hunting. When the female *M'deup* or witch-finder heard a particular type of tom-tom she was forced to dance uncontrollably with much undulation of the head and torso. This, too, applied pressure to the neck ganglia. The arms were jerked forcibly backward so that the elbows nearly met. Finally she fell to the ground in a cataleptic state, her eyes rolled back. When she awoke she named the witch.

In the famous Vodoun, or Voodoo, ceremonies, Haitians of Yoruba and Dahomey stock of west Africa performed dances in connection with spirit cults. Wrote Geoffrey Gorer: "Suddenly, while the dance is in progress, one of the participants staggers and lurches from side to side. He has been mounted by his *'loa.'* His eyes take on a fixed look or perhaps the lids close. In this trance condition he may continue to dance, the other performers moving aside to give him right of way. If he becomes violent, the other dancers remove themselves from the court altogether, leaving it to the possessed person, for in his head the spirit resides. The Vodoun priest or assistant must control the spirit or it will do damage to the mounted person or to others." Haitian dancing is also characterized by undulations of the neck and shoulders.

The third type of dance, mimicry, may combine with either of the other two. Its development is particularly complicated, for it contains the germ of the theater. That it is an ancient art is proved by a number of prehistoric rock-paintings that depict dancing in animal masks.

Among the modern primitives, we have already noted that there is mimicry in Samoa, mostly for comic effect. There are many cases of a specialized group or society that creates elaborate costumes and masks, such as the Dukduk society we shall describe later in the Pacific, or the Killer Whale Society mentioned by Boas. Curiously costumed Australian totemic mimicry has been recorded by Spencer and Gillen. The Veddas used mimicry in crude form in the deer dance. The ceremonial dance of the Alaskan Eskimo, says E. W. Hawkins, "is a rhythmic pantomime—the story in gesture and song of the lives of various animals from whom they believe their ancient clans have sprung. These are performances by trained actors who hold their positions from year to year according to artistic merit." This, of course, again points to the close connection between totemism and animal mimicry.

Among most of the totemistic North American Indian tribes there are dance societies (identical with the men's clubs to be discussed in the next chapter), many of which take their names from animals. The plains Indians nearly all danced buffalo dances. Volume XI of *Anthropological Papers of the American Museum of Natural History* contains a number of descriptions of these dances. The Sioux regalia consisted of headdresses made from horned buffalo heads, dried and used as masks. Little feathers or shells were added, a buffalo tail hung down behind. Forty-four dancers and singers took part. They hooked one another and imitated the buffalo. The Ojibway said their buffalo dance was intended to heal the sick and increase the buffalo in time of scarcity. The Mandans wore masks similar to those of the Sioux.

The Fox Indian buffalo dance, according to Truman Michelson, was a great totemic festival. One of the tribe described it as follows: "This is the reason a woman follows a man in the dance, it is because the old male buffaloes are the leaders. It seems as if the leader is in full control, verily he leads as he goes about. . . . The buffaloes are imitated in a way as they move along. This is why they dance in a circle when they imitate what they do, when they imitate their actions. It is as if the buffalo were doing it." A part of the accompanying song went:

> *He feeds you,*
> *He feeds you,*
> *A buffalo.*

These examples show how prevalent hunting or animal pantomime is in mimetic dancing. It is quite probable that animal-miming is the earliest type of theatrical performance. It has a magical connection with the food supply of the simplest peoples and parallels the earliest known type of pictorial art, the cave-painting, which many scholars believe to have been practiced for magical or religious reasons.

Sir William Ridgeway, the Cambridge classicist and archeologist, in *The Origin of Tragedy* (1912), cited mimetic dancing in support of his theory of the origin of Greek tragedy, which was opposed to that of the followers of James Frazer. Frazer had influenced literary critics, and in the early decades of the twentieth century his theories were used to explain the origin of literary forms. Gilbert Murray and Jane Harrison thought they found evidence of the death and resurrection of the vegetation spirit in early Greek religion. On this basis, the death of a hero in the Greek plays was a modification of the ritual death of the nature god, Dionysius. Ridgeway, who fought this theory stoutly, insisted that tragedy arose from dancing and games at the tomb of a specific dead hero, and he compiled a list of primitive dances connected with ancestor-worship to prove, by inference, how they might lead to tragedy.

Such theories brought together elements separated by a great gulf in time and development. It is a far cry from the Trobriand milamila to Oedipus Rex. There is no doubt, however, that the rudimentary elements of drama in primitive mimetic dancing would repay further study.

Probably because of the intolerance and prudery of some missionaries, native dancing has gained the reputation of being intimately connected with sexual orgies. James Frazer recorded a number of fertility rites that involved dancing. In certain islands off New Guinea "the mystic union of the sun and the earth is dramatically presented in public, amid song and dance, by the real union of the sexes." This, of course, is a magical ritual. According to Spencer and Gillen, the central Australians, by using a certain charm, could cause women to fall in love with them while they danced. The Trobriand Islanders indulged in love affairs during the milamila, but this was merely an adjunct of the social occasion. The Samoan dance, in exceptional situations, led to sex indulgence, but this was not its primary function. The Azande beer dance "to both sexes is a means of display which becomes intensified at puberty. . . . Boys and girls come to flirt and flirtation leads to sexual connection but society insists that neither the one nor the other shall be indulged in blatantly. At the same time society permits these sexual incidents so long as they occur with discretion and moderate concealment."

Apparently sex and dancing can be associated in two different ways. As in the case of the Azande social dance mentioned above or the milamila, sex activity results from the flirtatious contact between young people. And, indeed, something similar occurs in social dancing in contemporary civilized society. On the other hand, sex and dancing may occur together for some religious reason.

Aside from the conscious desire to promote fertility, there are also dances followed by exchange of wives. The Alaskan Eskimo women's dance called "The Asking" has a ritual or mythological origin. It has an audience of men. After the dance, which is not particularly lascivious, the men invite the participants to spend the night with them. This is evidently a survival of a ritual exchange of wives. The latter practice occurs among the northern Australians and has been described by William Lloyd Warner. The men sit in a half-circle around the fire, the women dance on the other side facing them. As they dance, the men occasionally arise and hand the women presents of food or objects of value. The husbands have previously agreed who shall exchange with whom. If a wife is reluctant, her husband explains that she must not refuse or Father Snake will make them both sick. Indeed, the old men of the tribe say the ceremony makes everybody "clean." When it is over, the husband rubs his sweat on the legs and arms of his wife's partner so that he will not become "sick."

In Dahomey, in west Africa, according to Melville Herskovits, there is an elaborate mythology with cult worship of certain sky gods. The initiation ceremony for one of these cults lasts for several days. The drums must be consecrated with chicken blood, and initiates undergo secret preparations in a cult house under the guidance of priestesses. The final emergence from the cult house is the rite of Legba. Legba is the son of the sky goddess, Mawu. He is associated with fate and is a divine trickster and, like other tricksters in primitive mythologies, a bawdy character. His representative is a girl in a straw hat and a purple raffia skirt, intentionally comic in appearance. Herskovits writes: "The large drum sounded, the Legba danced toward the drums. When she reached the drummer, she put her hand under the raffia skirt (which it was explained represented pubic hair) and brought out a wooden phallus the color of Negro skin. This was apparently attached in such a way that it would remain in the horizontal position of the erect male organ and, as she danced, now beyond the drums toward a large tree where many women were sitting, she made motions of masturbation, first running her curved right hand backwards over the phallus, then her left in which she carried a small white cloth which may have been a handkerchief. As she approached the women they ran from her shrieking with laughter, and they were made the butt of many jokes by the spectators. . . . When she reached the tree where the women were seated, some of the younger ones held their ground and, much to the shrieking amusement of the other spectators, Legba approached one of them, placed the wooden phallus against her side and proceeded with a highly realistic miming of sexual intercourse. . . ."

Many primitive groups do not consider sex indecent or in a special category apart from other natural functions. Apparently the Legba rite, apart from its mythological origin, was bawdy comedy not unlike some passages in the plays of Aristophanes.

In recent years the interest in the dancing of native peoples has grown with the rise of the modern-dance movement. Obviously when ethereal and romantic ballet was the standard of reference, other types of movement had no aesthetic meaning for the European observer. Isadora Duncan stepped into a new dance world, followed by Ruth St. Denis and Ted Shawn, who began to draw their inspiration from exotic themes. La Meri, in turn, specialized in "ethnic" dancing. Such modern artists as Martha Graham and Mary Wigman widened the dance horizon still more. Both Katherine Dunham and Pearl Primus have taken an avowedly ethnological interest in African and Caribbean dancing, and in several brilliant group recitals Asadata Dafora brought African dancing to the modern stage. Finally even Hollywood, in a few films with African background, has capitalized on the excitement of primitive rhythms.

In still another way, primitive dance, in a somewhat modified form, has influenced contemporary civilization. The spread of slavery through the Caribbean, parts of South America, and the southern United States arbitrarily diffused peoples of west African stock, who brought with them their innate sense of rhythm and survivals of their ancient ritual. As a result, American jazz owes much to the civilization of Africa. In the last decades Afro-Cuban music and dancing has become internationally popular. From Brazil comes the samba and from the Caribbean islands the mambo, the cha-cha-cha, and the meringue, all examples of acculturation, a fusion of Spanish and African melody and rhythm.

Indeed, in an era when mass communications have put such a distance between audience and entertainers and reduced the masses to passive spectators, modern man begins to look back nostalgically upon a more integrated society. The vital communal spirit permeating the village group as it claps and sings, and dances to a rhythm that grows from its way of life, brown limbs flashing in subtle and expressive gesture, is something which civilized man would gladly regain if he could.

Chapter 20

PRIMITIVE CLUBMEN

Concerning Heinrich Schurtz, Hutton Webster, Arnold Van Gennep

■ In the Bismarck Archipelago of the South Seas, six times a year at the advent of the new moon, an impressive ceremony takes place. In the gray of the dawn the inhabitants of the village assemble on the beach. When the first streaks of pale pink appear on the horizon, a faint sound of singing and the beat of drums is heard. As the light grows brighter, six canoes lashed together and surmounted by a platform move slowly in from the sea. While drumming and singing grow louder, two awesome figures, whom the magic of the Dukduk society has conjured up from the deep, become visible. The spirits wear masks made of woven fiber, supported on a framework of wicker, ornamented with shells and painted designs in the form of a face. The masks are conical, in some cases towering upward to a height of five feet. The bodies of these beings, who seem to have no arms or hands, are covered to the ankles with a cloak of hibiscus or palm leaves. The makers of the masks have received the inspiration for the decoration from a drug-induced dream. Afterward the mask has been buried for a time at the foot of the tree in which artistic inspiration dwells. It has also been put in contact with Tubuan, the mother of masks. As the floating stage approaches, the apparitions on it dance violently, uttering shrill cries like the yelpings of a puppy. The villagers receive them fearfully. When the canoes touch the beach, the masked spirits jump onto shore. The natives fall back respectfully so as to avoid touching them. If one is touched even by accident, he may tomahawk the unfortunate savage on the spot.

After the Dukduks have landed, the old men of the village conduct them to a secret house that has been built for them in the woods. For three weeks these awful visitors remain in the village, and at intervals the young men of the tribe are lined up and beaten by them with sticks until the blood flows, a ceremony which the youths must endure without protest. Meanwhile, piles of food have been collected and are offered to the Dukduks, who carry them off. Unlike the usual puberty initiations, the ceremonial beating which the young men endure sometimes continues with the visits of the Dukduks for as long as twenty years.

Dukduk dancers.

We have already seen that mimetic dances are often performed by a special men's society. The Dukduk organization, widespread in the South Seas, is an example of this institution, which occurs in various forms all over the world. Not only do natives form men's clubs, but they even possess clubhouses in which, in many cases, they spend a great part of their time, and from which women are usually barred.

Ethnologists, hypnotized by the institution of marriage, at first tended to see in it the key to the development of society. A German historian, Heinrich Schurtz (1863–1903), in 1900, while working on a history of prehistoric culture, became convinced that these men's organizations were equally important in the growth of social organization. Schurtz, well acquainted with the work of both Morgan and Westermarck, was not wholly convinced by either. His study of men's clubs, *Altersklasse und Männerbunde* (1902), set forth a new point of view. Not marriage but the *difference* between the sexes was the key to the evolution of social relationships. Schurtz used a highly subjective brand of psychology as a basis for his theory. With truly Strindbergian insistence, he maintained that men and women were basically antagonistic to each other. Women, conservative and concerned only with the family and the kinship unit, were really selfishly anti-social; they tried to keep men isolated in the little world of marriage. But, men, who did not like women anyway, always tended to escape into hunting and warlike activities. In them was an inbred gregariousness, a desire for brotherhood with their peers. Because their sex love was more profound than men's, women were able to overcome their dislike of the loathsome male creatures. But men, once sexually gratified, were anxious to rid themselves of the stifling bonds flung about them by their sex partners.

Schurtz's psychological notions were evidently influenced by a dislike of the rampant feminist movement of the period, to which he alluded, and also he seems to have envisioned something similar to Crawley's physiological-repulsion idea. He found, besides, another source of antagonism: that between the adult male and the ripening youth (almost anticipating Freud), that between father and son.

Two forces were thus set up which drove the mature males into self-defensive groups, into withdrawal from women and efforts to present a solid front toward encroaching youth. The men's groups therefore excluded boys until they were adult and tended to lose the married men, whose family responsibilities kept them from the gay camaraderie of the bachelors bent on promiscuous sex experience.

The examples of the men's houses which could be found all through the Pacific and also in Africa and Asia were the chief bulwarks of Schurtz's theories. In these institutions the young unmarried warriors ate and slept and received guests. In some cases the married men were excluded, in others they returned at times for a respite from their circumscribed existence. The men's clubs were sometimes boathouses for the war canoes and repositories for the skulls taken as trophies in war. From this they easily developed into cult houses dealing with ancestor-worship, adorned with dancing-masks, weapons, and musical instruments. Their exteriors were often handsomely decorated. At times they could become centers of wood-carving, leatherwork, and weapon-making. In this way they might have been the origin of bazaars and artisans' guilds. The parallel with army barracks was also strong.

In many cases the young men who occupied these men's houses used them as houses of assignation for the promiscuous erotic activity that was permitted before marriage. Sometimes certain girls lived with the men, ministering to their sexual needs. Pre-marital erotic freedom always accompanied men's societies. Sometimes a captive woman was used as a communal prostitute. It was when pre-marital promiscuity was abolished by society, Schurtz felt, that commercial prostitution began.

As hunting societies these groups sometimes had political power. Such power was even stronger when, with the accumulation of mythology and ritual, they developed into secret societies such as the Dukduks.

To sum up, in Schurtz's view, men's societies were the basis of non-kinship groupings that made possible the higher organization of civilized society.

Without having read Schurtz's book, an American anthropologist, Hutton Webster (1875–   ), published only a year later a similar study, *Primitive Secret Societies*. Webster, less ambitious than his predecessor, was chiefly concerned with the origin of men's clubs and their development out of groups responsible for the puberty initiation rites. Webster felt that the older men selfishly bolstered their own prestige by using terrifying ceremonies when initiating boys into adulthood. Circumcision, subincision, knocking out of teeth, whirling of bull-roarers, and dancing in awe-inspiring masks were the techniques used. At the same time, moral instruction and traditional lore were taught. Even dramatic performances were carried out to impress the boys with the importance of the event. The Fijians would line up the initiates in front of the temple, where the chief sat at the entrance regarding them with a fixed stare. Between him and them lay a row of dead men, covered with blood, their bodies apparently cut open and their entrails protruding. The boys, led by a priest, were obliged to step over them, one by one, trembling with fear, until they stood in a row before the high priest, "their souls drying up" before his awful stare. Suddenly he let out a great yell, and the dead men leaped to their feet and ran down to the river to wash off the blood and filth with which they were smeared.

Hutton Webster believed that men's societies arose from the clan system. Originally they were groups that carried out the initiation rites. When clans came together in larger units, one clan totem would dominate and then become a god into whose cult all the youths of the tribe would be inducted. Then the group of initiates would become exclusive, narrow into an aristocracy or priesthood. Membership would become a matter of payment, and the character of the organization would change to that of a secret society, often with a series of degrees of status within it. Sometimes such societies were benevolent; some practiced medicine, as did the False Faces of the Iroquois, or concerned themselves with ancestor-worship, as did those of the Hopi. In other cases an element of blackmail entered in. The Dukduks were run by the old men, and thus the elders made sure they acquired plenty of gifts of food. As the nature of the societies changed and they lost their masculine exclusiveness, Webster felt, they decayed. Among numerous North American tribes women were admitted. At their lowest ebb, as in the case of some African Yoruba cults, they could turn into ritual murder associations.

Men's clubs were strongest and most vital in societies where there was no true political chief or civil government. With the rise of government they lost their importance.

Both Schurtz and Webster were criticized by a gallicized Dutch scholar, Arnold Van Gennep. The latter, born in Holland in 1873, was educated in France and became professor of ethnography at the University of Neuchâtel, Switzerland. He wrote *Tabou et totémisme à Madagascar* (*Taboo and Totemism in Madagascar*) in 1904, and two years later he wrote on the myths of Australia. He also studied Arab ethnology and wrote both a popular and a scientific book about Algeria. The title of his most famous work, published in 1909, became a famous phrase: *Les Rites de passage.* The image *"rites de passage"* or "ceremonies of transition" was a poetic one, and its creator developed it with elegance and style. A disciple of Marett (who developed the preanimist theory), Van Gennep maintained that all magical ceremonies were based on the conception of moving from one state, or condition, or place, to another. Society was like a house with many rooms. Getting from one room to another was a "passage." A man from one room who

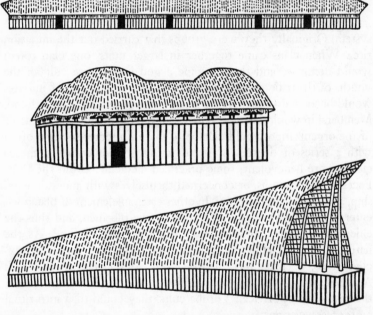

Men's houses. Top to bottom: Torres Straits, Cameroons, New Guinea.

did not have the right by birth or group membership to enter the other found himself in a precarious state. Crawley (who influenced Van Gennep) had shown how aliens were feared and hated. Some method had to be devised to get an individual safely through the doorway and into the other room.

A stranger, entering the territory of the Masai in South Africa, was met by an official of the chief and a goat. The stranger held one ear of the goat and swore that he was not a black magician. The official held the other ear of the goat and swore that he would not harm the stranger and would give him food. Then the goat was sacrificed with much ceremony. The official and the stranger finally took hold of the end of a piece of the goat's skin, which was then cut in half, each retaining a fragment. The stranger was now a blood brother of the chief and able to travel in his territory.

This process could be broken into three parts. The first was a process of separation, in which the newcomer swore to be peaceable. This got him out of his alien state. Now there intervened an intermediate period, the sill of the door, a kind of no-man's-land between the two rooms. Here the individual had to be purified—the ceremony of sacrificing the goat. The third step was the rite of union or acceptance, a blood-brotherhood ceremony—often a matter of eating together, which was the same as Robertson Smith's sacred meal.

Van Gennep found his three steps everywhere: at birth, at puberty, at marriage, at the woman's menstrual period, and in funeral ritual. "For groups as for individuals, to live is to ceaselessly disintegrate and again take shape, to change condition and fortune, to die and to be reborn. It is to act and to pause, to await and to repose, to begin to act again but differently, and always there are new thresholds to cross, thresholds of summer and winter, of season or year, of the month or of night, thresholds of birth, of adolescence or of maturity, thresholds of old age, thresholds of death, and thresholds of another life—for those who believe in it."

Van Gennep's disagreement with Schurtz and Webster arose from the fact that physical puberty seldom or never coincided exactly with the initiatory rite. Facts showed that initiation occurred at all ages. (There were distinct puberty rites which were *not* initiation rites.) What the other two scholars had been confused by was initiation into the clan, a *"rite de passage,"* a separation of the individual from other clan groups and the rest of mankind, a purification period and an acceptance into a new status (hence the death-and-resurrection idea, which had nothing to do with sexual maturity). Cutting or scarifying of the body, the knocking out of teeth, subincision or circumcision had nothing to do with sex, but was merely a way of distinguishing members of a special group. This contradicted both Westermarck's and Crawley's explanations of these customs, for the former considered them sexual ornament, the latter magical averting of danger.

Van Gennep believed that Schurtz's and Webster's notion that men's societies were age groupings, set off by puberty initiation, was inaccurate.

Although his criticisms were theoretical, a broader accumulation of data tended to back them up. Subsequent investigators, such as R. H. Lowie, give Schurtz and Webster great credit for first stressing the importance of men's clubs, but Lowie's evidence from North America tends to destroy the idea that the clubs were fundamentally based on age groupings. Among the North American Indians, married and unmarried men were not separated into exclusive clubs. Then, too, the same society found in several tribes could be composed, in one, of young men, in another, of old men. Likewise, the existence of many women's clubs refuted Schurtz's sex psychology.

The fact that emerged is that the club instinct is deeply rooted in mankind, plays a different role from kinship groups, and is just as important in the more complex development of society as the institution of marriage.

Chapter 21

MAPPING THE MIND OF MAN

Concerning Anthropology

and Experimental Psychology

■ If the latter part of the nineteenth century was the era of Darwinism, the twentieth century is likely to appear in retrospect the era of psychology. Psychology and anthropology are intimately connected, for the latter study follows the course of the shifting intellectual currents of the last hundred years.

That particular eddy which deals with the mind of man had considerable trouble detaching itself from the vague and mystical speculations of philosophy. The science we know of as psychology got off to a series of false starts. There were quasi-charlatans such as Franz Gall, who, although he did some good anatomical work, began measuring skulls and launched the popular, if unfounded, art of bump-reading or phrenology. This was all the rage in the early decades of the nineteenth century, as was mesmerism. Anton Mesmer had hit upon the significant phenomenon of hypnosis, but he turned it into a semi-mystical parlor game and a source of literary shudders for gothic horror novelists.

In England, until Darwin's time, the prevailing psychology was associationist. John Stuart Mill's father, James, a liberal ex-clergyman, was influenced by the ideas of the eighteenth-century philosopher David Hartley and developed them into a system. He started with pleasure and pain. These were caused by sensation. By repetition the mind put two and two together and finally formed conscious ideas from associated sensations. When the mind became aware of other people as causes of pleasure and pain, social feelings were connected with them. Thus pleasure and pain were the motives of all actions. His thinking reflected the opinions of British industrialism of his time. Virtues were simply the means of securing pleasures and avoiding pains. Free trade and high profits would create the ideal society. Social good would result from the automatic working of self-interest. "The great difficulty here," said his biographer Alexander Bain doubtfully, "is to account for seeking other men's pleasures or to trace to self-seeking causes our Disinterested Benevolence."

The explorers of the mind who followed him were divided into the sense-measurers, or early experimentalists, and the mind doctors.

One of the earliest German measurers was Gustav Theodor Fechner (1801–1887). His character can be understood only in the light of the schizoid nineteenth century, which in Germany gave rise to the romantic movement. Philosophers brooded over all that was poetic, mysterious, and unknown in the universe. Opposed to their romantic excesses was a patient scholarship, and unending ability to collect detail, channeled by the industrial revolution. What resulted was a quite practical interest in mathematical sciences which could improve technical devices and produce more profits for the emerging capitalist system.

Fechner, a true child of his century, first planned to be a writer. Changing his mind, he studied medicine at Leipzig and from it went on to physics. He began some experiments to test his own perception of color images. Shortly after his marriage it became clear that all was not well with him. Fechner had a bony face and a strong jaw. Dreamy eyes looked out from under a wide forehead. Behind that forehead there was a violent conflict between his affinity for exact science and a romantic desire to find a view of life which should satisfy his spiritual and aesthetic cravings. The conflict set his mind reeling. A series of literary essays reflects his state of confusion. In some he cleverly satirized the scientific thinking of the period; in others, such as the half-playful "Comparative Anatomy of the Angels," he indulged in eccentric fantasy. The angels, it seemed, changed their colors and expanded and contracted in accordance with the state of their feelings. Their language was light and their tones were colors. The earth itself was a living angel, using the sense organs of men to perceive sensation.

His eyes were strained by staring into lights during his experiments, and it seemed as if he were about to go blind. He was obliged to spend months in a darkened room. Sometimes he could neither eat nor sleep. Anxiously nursed by his wife, he went on spinning visionary images of the universe and the human soul. When he ventured out of his darkened room he wore a mask over his face. His thoughts grew more disordered until he reached the crisis of his breakdown, and was bedridden for a time. Then he rose up with the conviction that he had looked death in the face and was now reborn. He also believed that he had acquired extraordinary powers and was called by God to do great things. He gave up physics entirely for the study of psychology and philosophy. In 1850 he began testing the theory that the increase in the subjective intensity of sensation is proportional to the increase in the strength of the external stimulus. He began to weigh the sense of touch to determine the lightest pressures that could be felt, and finally achieved a mathematical formula for the relation between stimulus and sensation.

This was "applying mathematics to the soul" in an attempt to marry mysticism and science. Fechner went on measuring and spinning cosmic and often beautiful images of eternal unity, and, oddly enough, out of this curious conflict came experimental psychology. His follower at Leipzig, Wilhelm Wundt, was a black-bearded, square-faced man with tiny oval spectacles, the typical kindly German professor of pre-World War I tradition. In 1879 he set up the first laboratory of experimental psychology. Wundt's mind was shaped in the post-Darwin era. He had worked with the physicist Helmholtz and had no use for metaphysical speculation. The soul was a rational entity, the problem was to analyze it. In his time the mind was a structure like a house. A picture of it could be built up by measuring and describing its component parts, sensation and the mechanism of perception. The bricks of sensation (both factual and hallucinatory), the role of pleasure and pain in mortaring them together—all this could be dealt with by the science of psychophysics. The picture was not unlike the associationist one, but the method was to be soundly quantitative. He accepted the idea already current in anthropology that savages and children did not distinguish between the real and the imaginary.

Wundt fought the application of psychology to education, thinking his science should be kept "pure," but he had no hesitation about plunging into the territory of anthropology. In fact, he tried to capture most of this field for his own science. In *Volker-psychologie* (*Elements of Folk Psychology*) (1912) he maintained that the study of diffusion rightly belonged to ethnography, but that the ideas of the primitives, which took in most of their institutions, "those mental products which are created by a community of human life," were the province of the psychologist. In this three-volume work he synthesized practically all of the material that has been discussed in the foregoing chapters. This was the first real union of psychology and anthropology, but Wundt's creative addition was small.

Proof that the savage thought in pictures was derived from language. The west was "sun-sit-place." A palace was "house-be-long-king." Language on the primitive level was arranged in conceptual order. As this kind of thinking was always attached to specific objects, there were no abstract concepts. The native's thinking was strictly associative. One set of ideas was derived from the objects of daily life: he knew how to build canoes, to make a bow and arrow, to hunt animals. The other set of concepts were feeling-perceptions, emotions projected toward the environment. These were reinforced by hallucinatory images and gave rise to myth. For instance, the savage might feel fear of the dark and, from this emotion, shape a malignant spirit. Wundt concluded: "The intelligence of primitive man is indeed restricted to a narrow sphere of activity. Within his sphere, however, his intelligence is not noticeably inferior to that of civilized man. His morality is dependent upon the environment in which he lives."

While German psychology was attempting to create an experimental science of the mind, the English branch of the study was also making progress. The man who changed it most was Francis Galton, a gentleman-amateur cousin of Charles Darwin, who came of an aristocratic family that had gone into industry. His father was a wealthy businessman who made science a hobby. The boy studied medicine, but not too seriously—his sensitive stomach was upset by the operating-room. When his father died and he became financially independent, he decided to travel. He disappeared into the heart of Africa and was not heard from for two years. He was taking notes on marriage customs among the natives, making the acquaintance of the Bushman, whom he respected highly, shooting a lion or two, and having a fine time. The trip was his introduction to anthropology. He brought out a book, *An Explorer in Tropical South Africa,* in 1853. A few years later his cousin Charles published his epoch-making *Origin of Species.* It was exciting enough reading to make a scientist of Francis Galton.

Another force pushing him in the same direction was a local battle among the anthropologists. In 1837 the Quakers had formed the "Aborigines' Protective Association" to improve the condition of Britain's native colonials. Such liberal activities were a typical product of the romantic movement that colored half the century. The spirit of William Godwin and Frances Wright, filled with visions of the soul of humanity uplifted and old injustices redressed in the coming brotherhood of man, was Dr. Jekyll to the Mr. Hyde of a flinty-faced industrialism that starved its workers and wrecked the health of children in its factories.

This duality, which we have already noted in Germany, was present even among the meek and philanthropic Quakers. A part of the society viewed the natives as inferior beings: nothing could be done with them except to give them Bibles and the afterworld, if they would accept it. The liberal group felt that all men were equal and wanted to study the blacks scientifically. In the fifties a schism resulted, and the society split into two groups; the Anthropological Society was formed by the conservatives, and the Ethnological Society by the liberals. Galton, who by virtue of his travels was an expert on Africa, plunged into the heart of the controversy on the liberal side, armed with Darwinist arguments. The controversy directed him toward a study of the differences between groups of men. He too became a measurer and began his work by comparing the mental attainments of various religious groups. In a study of famous Britishers, *Hereditary Genius* (1869), he tried to find out if specific talents were a variation transmitted in certain families. Darwin had brought the concept of variation to the fore. Perhaps it was the explanation of different types of human character. At one point he attempted a beauty map of the British Isles. He carried a chart and hastily recorded on it the score of all the girls he saw. Aberdeen ranked lowest aesthetically, London highest.

The liberal Galton saw about him the industrial poor, ill-fed and physically inferior. He wished to find ways of improving the human race. What was the role of environment, what part did heredity play? First he had to have more precise data. The subjective method of the beauty map was insufficient.

In 1884, five years after Wundt had set up the first psychological laboratory, Galton created an anthropometric laboratory to measure physical and psychological characteristics. During the six years it continued, data were collected on nearly ten thousand subjects —including Prime Minister Gladstone, who was vain enough to volunteer. By now Galton felt the need of precision methods for studying the senses. He developed practical devices to measure smell, sight, hearing, and touch which are still a part of laboratory equipment today.

But Galton did not stop at the senses. He studied the nature of images, dreams, fantasies, and the association of ideas. Types of mental imagery, some of which had never been noted before, he collected by means of questionnaires sent to the universities of Great Britain and the United States. In 1883 he wrote *Inquiries into Human Faculty* an early classic of psychology. He was knighted in 1909.

One of Galton's innovations was a word-association test. He prepared a list of words, and his subjects responded within a limited time either with words or descriptions of images. This pioneer device was taken over by Wundt, who refined it into the single-word-response method that is used today. James M. Cattel, an American pupil of Wundt's, adopted it, added other techniques, and invented the first of the intelligence and personality tests that have now become standard equipment in all areas of applied psychology. The impact of Galton's work was felt in anthropology in the 1890's. It will be remembered that C. S. Myers, the psychologist of the Torres Straits expedition, set out to measure the sense perceptions of the natives; for this study he used the techniques devised by Galton.

If German psychology pioneered in bringing physics into psychology and the English school was chiefly Darwinian, France had the honor of making great strides in the investigation of mental illness.

The most dramatic figure in this field was Dr. Jean Martin Charcot, who was once described as looking like Dante in a frock coat. His exciting lectures in the 1880's so captured the interest of the public that they became a fad. Because he experimented with hypnosis, to his audience he seemed a kind of magician, a romantic actor in a starring role. He had been investigating the mental illness called hysteria, which produced various inexplicable symptoms ranging from irrational aversions and obsessions to actual paralysis. Hysteria (from the Greek word that meant "womb") was supposed to be a disease of the female organism. But Charcot found male patients with the same symptoms. By the use of hypnotism Charcot effected startling, if not always permanent, improvement.

A pupil of his, a young Jewish doctor from Vienna named Sigmund Freud, discussed with him the nervous difficulties of a woman patient. Freud expressed surprise when Charcot brought up the fact that she and her husband were sexually maladjusted. "But in such cases it's always a genital matter—always, always, always!" Charcot exclaimed, leaping up and down with excitement. Freud, impressed, thought to himself: "If he knows that, why does he never say so?"

In Charcot's time nobody said so.

Black-bearded, slightly stooping, slender, sensitive, with dark poet's eyes, Freud continued to study the aberrations of the soul. Following Charcot, he used hypnosis, but was dissatisfied because the results were too often temporary. Another doctor, Berheim of Nancy, had found he could abolish symptoms without hypnosis simply by employing suggestion. This method had its drawbacks. When the patient did not react favorably, the doctor shouted at him: "What are you doing, countersuggesting?"

A Viennese colleague of Freud's, Dr. Joseph Breuer, told him of a curious case he had been treating. A girl who suffered from a variety of symptoms, even to the point of forgetting her native language and speaking only in English, did not react to any conventional form of treatment. Breuer tried letting her talk herself out, freely relating her emotional impressions and associations. Most of her problems seemed to go back to her relationship with her father. Freud was fascinated, and himself tried the free-association method. He began to get astonishing results. There were undreamed-of levels below the conscious mind. As he amassed data showing the relationship between neurosis and disordered sex lives, a new world opened up in psychology.

But it was not a world that Freud's contemporaries wished to acknowledge. They considered it indecent.

From the point of view of A. E. Crawley (who was almost a precursor of Freud), western civilization had developed religious sanctions from the primitive notion of the dangers and evils of sex, and the Victorian era had gone so far as to pretend that it did not exist. A kind of mass neurosis had developed around this highly important human activity. A society that modestly draped the legs of pianos was to learn from Freud that the innocence of childhood and the purity of women, two of its favorite illusions, were pure myth.

This concept was as shocking as Darwin's assault upon the Garden of Eden.

As Freud continued his work, Breuer became frightened and ceased to collaborate with him. He was, after all, a family man with a big practice. When Freud published *The Interpretation of Dreams* in 1900, both laymen and his colleagues of the medical profession were horrified.

Although he suffered from isolation, Freud had the courage of his facts, and he continued to document the statement: "In a normal sex life no neurosis is possible." If nice people would not admit they ever thought about sex, it simply meant there were mental devices by which they were able to deceive themselves. Their dreams, when properly interpreted, betrayed them, as did slips of the tongue and significant lapses of memory.

Gradually Freud worked out the doctrine that bears the name *psychoanalysis.* The sexuality of the child was at first auto-erotic, then it turned upon the parent of the opposite sex. Small boys, noticing that girls have no penis, developed the fear of castration or loss of the organ. Girls, realizing that they lacked the male genitalia, developed penis envy.

The boy tended to become jealous of his larger and stronger father and wished to replace him in the mother's affections. Thus ambivalent emotions arose in the family; the child both loved and hated its parent. The love of the son for the mother, which resulted in subconscious guilt feelings, Freud named the *Oedipus complex.* The mechanisms of *displacement* and *substitution* made it possible for these socially unacceptable urges to be disguised or associated with other aims. When repressed too harshly, they sometimes led to neurosis in which elaborate symbolisms hid their true nature and compulsive behavior sometimes resulted. In normal development the sexual energy was directed toward a heterosexual partner or sublimated into creative ends.

Freud's conception of eros was far wider and more philosophical than his antagonists cared to admit. In retrospect, it is possible to see how his own temperament shaped his doctrine. His father, though no sterner than most patriarchs of the period, was nevertheless associated in his mind with restraint and denial. His mother was easygoing and indulgent. His own ambivalence is illustrated by the statement: "An intimate friend and a hated enemy have always been indispensable to my emotional life; I have always been able to create them anew, and not infrequently my childish ideal has been so closely approached that friend and enemy have coincided in the same person." Freud was something of a patriarch himself. He felt that women should be subordinate to men, and himself married one who was his intellectual inferior but who cared for his physical comfort like a mother. He seems to have been a somewhat remote husband. Toward his own children he was aloof and not particularly outgoing. When he became head of an international movement, he was uncompromising toward heretics and bitter toward those, such as Adler and Jung, who broke away.

For all his intellectual daring, Freud was socially the most conventional of men. When he was traveling without his wife during a lecture tour in America, he complained to Jung that he could not sleep. He continually dreamed of prostitutes. "Well," said Jung, shrugging, "why don't you do something about it?" "But," cried the pioneer of sexual study, horrified, "I'm a married man!"

Freud's interest in anthropology came about when he was close to a break with Jung, whom he had made his first lieutenant. Jung, something of a Protestant clergyman by nature, had always tried to minimize sex and believed in what he called a *racial unconscious*. Freud at this time had no use for so mystical a concept. Because he disagreed with Jung on the history of religion, he began to think of investigating the subject. Cases of certain children reported by the analyst Ferenczi had disclosed totemistic fantasies. This prompted Freud to read Frazer's *Totemism and Exogamy*.

He was struck by numerous aspects of primitive life which fitted into his psychoanalytic doctrines. Since it looked as though the history of the prehistoric mind would help to clarify contemporary aberrations, he undertook to bring psychology and anthropology together. It was the first time a psychologist had attempted to compare what he had learned from contemporary case work with what was known of the mental habits of savages in the hope that each would throw light upon the other.

Chapter 22

THE RIDDLE OF TOTEMISM

Concerning Andrew Lang, Sir James Frazer,

Sigmund Freud, Franz Boas

■ To call a man a rat, a dog, or a swine is a nasty insult. On the other hand, we have such metaphors as brave as a lion, proud as a peacock, busy as a bee, to work like a horse.

Civilized man can never quite deny his animal biology, but he is often vehement in proving the great distance between him and his dumb relatives. Among the primitives, affinities between men and animals are greater, living as they do close to them in their wild state and dependent upon them for food and various materials essential to their economy.

In fact, natives often seem convinced that they are sons of crocodiles, emus, kangaroos, or even grubs.

The institution of totemism puzzled and fascinated scholars from the time they became aware of its wide diffusion and its curious significance in native life. The word *totem* was first noted by an Englishman who came in contact with American Indians in 1791. Schoolcraft, as we have seen, observed that it signified an animal clan badge and had great importance in Indian life.

It was J. F. McLennan who first called attention to its connection with exogamy in an article in *Chambers's Encyclopaedia* in 1867. Two years later he expanded his study into a series of three articles. He discussed the diffusion of totemism in North America and Australia and decided it was a religious stage through which all mankind had passed. Discovering traces of animal worship in classical antiquity, he concluded that totems were animal gods who later took on human form. With remarkable restraint he presented no theory of the origin of totemism.

His pupil, Robertson Smith, next traced a connection with the sacrificial meal of the Semites. Frazer at first decided, on the basis of folklore, that the totem animal was the soul box of the primitive and that the initiation ritual was performed in order to transfer a man's soul to his totem for safekeeping.

Andrew Lang, in *The Secret of the Totem* (1905), attacked the question from another angle. Names, as Frazer had shown, have magical power. Once groups found themselves with animal names (having forgotten how they had originally acquired them), the processes of magic began to operate, and they imagined supernatural relationships between them and their namesakes. From this the various taboos arose. Myths to explain totem relationships indicated that the origin of the connection had been forgotten. Lang was of the opinion that animal names might have been acquired accidentally, possibly as nicknames or disrespectful epithets just as the English used to call the French "frogs."

In 1910, Frazer, as we earlier noted, brought out his four-volume study *Totemism and Exogamy*, in which he reviewed all that was known of the institution and came up with a new theory. Investigators had found that some natives of the South Seas and Australia did not understand the process of impregnation and the relationship of the father. Sex to them was merely a pleasant pastime. The growth of the child within the mother was a miracle to be explained only by magic. Spencer and Gillen had described the belief of the Arunta that a woman lingering near a certain object or animal would be entered by the spirit of that object or animal. Her child would therefore be the descendant of the totem that had magically impregnated her. This was a possible explanation of the basic relationship between the man and the totem with which he claimed kinship. W. H. R. Rivers reported that the Melanesians of the Banks Islands (where no totemism existed) believed that if a woman found an animal, an insect, or a plant in her loincloth it would cause her to conceive. She was supposed to care for this creature or plant carefully, and any child born soon afterward was never allowed to eat it. This was an example of the beginning of the totemic idea. Exogamy was a later institution grafted upon totemism, and to explain the former Rivers accepted Morgan's ideas.

Sigmund Freud read Frazer, Lang, and Crawley. Robertson Smith particularly fascinated him. Reading the latter's book *The Religion of the Semites* was "like floating in a gondola." As his studies progressed, he immersed himself in Spencer and Gillen and finally made the acquaintance of Wundt's *Elements of Folk Psychology*.

The question of incest was naturally a subject on which psychoanalysis had much to say. Fear of incest was easy to understand from the point of view that the most basic human urge was to commit it. (There was sound sense in laws prohibiting incest if the first sex urges were directed toward the parent.)

Mother-in-law avoidance could be explained in the same way. The image of the mother-in-law reminded the native of his repressed desire for his own mother. Then, too, a woman dissatisfied with her husband often fell in love with a son-in-law. Thus there could be an uneasy ambivalent relationship on both sides which was solved by a formal rule of avoidance.

But what about the whole system of taboos: ruler taboos, sex taboos, totem taboos? This was complicated and confusing. Was there an underlying unity behind the system?

Wundt, following Robertson Smith and Marett, had suggested that *taboo* originally meant both "holy" and "unclean" during a preanimist stage. With the development of actual gods the idea separated into two distinct feelings of *awe* and *aversion*.

But, said Freud, let us compare the behavior of savages with that of modern compulsion neurotics—individuals who for no logical reason are obliged to wash their hands many times a day, or to set their pillows in a certain order before they can sleep, or who cannot refrain from avoiding cracks in the sidewalk when walking down the street. Primitive magical practice was similar to these compulsions. It looked as though taboo were almost a disease.

A Maori chief, for instance, would not blow on the fire with his mouth because his sacred breath would infect the fire and from it the contagion would travel to the meat in the pot, causing the death of the man who ate it. In the same way: "My patient demanded that a utensil which her husband had purchased and brought home should be removed lest it make the place where she lived impossible. For she had heard the object was bought in a store which was situated, let us say on 'Stag' street. But the word 'stag' was the name of a friend now in a distant city, whom she

had known in her youth and whom she now found 'impossible.'"
The name and the object were as taboo as the friend.

Both compulsive neurotics and savages carried out rituals and
had recourse to purification in connection with taboo. One phobia,
the fear of touching, was the result of a childhood prohibition
against playing with the genitals. The inner urge, being blocked,
appeared later in life as a negative compulsion.

It seemed possible to study taboo from this point of view. Apparently taboos repressed deep desires. They also represented an
ambivalent attitude; the individual would like to commit the act,
but was restrained by magical fears. Two taboos, the type surrounding the ruler and that concerning the dead, were fairly
typical.

Rulers must be guarded and guarded against. The king was
magically important for the welfare of his people. For this reason
he had to be protected, yet if he failed his people he might be suddenly killed. There was true ambivalence here: the ruler was loved
as a protector, yet hated and envied for his importance—just as in
classical psychoanalytical doctrine the father was both loved and
hated by the son.

In the case of the dead there were extreme taboos against
touching, even extending to people in mourning or to mentioning
the name of the deceased. A parallel was a patient of Freud's who
would not sign his name lest it come into somebody's hands.
Finally the taboo was extended to his handwriting and he gave up
writing altogether.

The fear of the dead often seemed to result from the idea that
their spirits were malicious demons. Why? If they were friendly
in life, why not after death?

If there was normally ambivalence toward the nearest and dear-
est, then it often happened that the survivors had entertained death
wishes toward the deceased, with accompanying feelings of guilt.
Both the modern neurotic and the savage denied these hostile
impulses toward his loved ones and, to salve his guilt feelings,
projected them into the object. This reversal made the victim
hostile and the individual innocent. In extreme form, this process
led to paranoia, in which the whole world was felt to be hostile.

Freud held that the savage was more ambivalent than civilized
man. Therefore the institution of taboo had great social importance. It was the earliest form of conscience, or inner check on

emotional wishes. In civilized man, conditioned by education in a formalized society, the taboo-conscience recurred only in individual compulsion neuroses.

The formalization of taboo into folk custom was brought about by the collected emotions of the group. If an individual broke the taboo and carried out a suppressed wish of the group, the sense of temptation grew stronger and a need was felt to punish the criminal in order to hold the rest in check. This was particularly the case in sex taboos, as sex urges were anti-social and did not unite the group as did food-gathering or defense.

A study of neurotics threw light on the nature of primitive magic. The neurotic was convinced of the *omnipotence of thought*. He placed an irrational value on his own and other people's mental impulses and wishes with respect to their material effectiveness. The neurotic, who believed his enemies were injuring him in mysterious ways, was on a par with the savage who believed that death was caused by magic.

Freud envisioned a historical sequence in which the preanimistic magical stage corresponded to the autoeroticism of the child. Later the belief in the power of external gods corresponded to the mature sexual stage of an external love partner.

Primitive thought, from this point of view, did not differ in essence from that of civilized man. More elaborate societies made use of these fundamental psychological traits and channelized them.

Freud was now ready to examine totemism and exogamy. The following were for him the essential elements of totemism: the belief that a group was descended from an animal, the fact that the group was forbidden to kill or eat it and, if the totem was killed accidentally or ritually, the necessity of mourning for it; finally, the prohibition against sexual intercourse with members of the same totem.

Disagreeing with Frazer, Freud decided that totemism and exogamy arose together. Again his thinking started with modern psychoanalytical practice. The child, like the savage, did not draw a sharp dividing-line between himself and animals. Animal phobias, when treated, turned to be substitution. The child suffering from an Oedipus complex and fear of castration, instead of admitting to himself that he feared his father, substituted an animal. One case of this kind (reported by Sandor Ferenczi), in which the child's ambivalence was displaced, took on a totemistic color. The boy, when visiting a farm, tried to urinate into a chicken coop, and a chicken pecked at his penis. The next year when he came back to the farm he pretended he was a chicken, cackled, crowed, and sang chicken songs. At the same time he gloated over the idea of killing chickens and mixed it up with making his relatives into a pie. When a chicken was actually killed for dinner it was the occasion for quite a totemic festival. He danced around the dead bird for hours and also kissed and caressed it. Along with this went much curiosity about the sex habits of chickens.

The savage who behaved in a somewhat similar way toward his totemic animal also called it his ancestor or *father*.

Freud cited Robertson Smith to show that the totem was killed only sacrificially in order to serve as a meal to cement the brotherhood of the clan. From this he argued: "Psychoanalysis has revealed to us that the totem animal is really a substitute for the father, and this really explains the contradiction that it is usually forbidden to kill the totem animal and that the killing of it results in a holiday and that the animal is killed and yet mourned."

At this point gorillas once more entered the picture. Freud picked up a suggestion of Darwin's that a dominant old male jealously guarded his harem of females and drove off the young males, who had to seek mates outside the group.

Accepting the dominant-old-male idea, Freud maintained that one day a group of rebellious brothers, no longer able to endure their sex deprivation, got together, killed their patriarchal father, and ate him!

Having both envied and feared this violent old male, they (in accordance with cannibalistic magic) now acquired a part of his strength and an identification with him which was to survive in the sacrificial meal. They also acquired a heavy load of guilt.

The guilt was the explanation of exogamy. Instead of gaily ravishing the now unprotected women, they punished themselves by giving them up and seeking their sex gratification elsewhere. Their guilt pursued them even further; they persuaded themselves they had killed not their father but an animal, and, united by their deed, they became a brother clan with a totem. Around this totem all the taboos arising from their father ambivalence were woven.

When the domestication of animals had weakened totemistic psychology, the longing for the father image reasserted itself and the totem was reconverted into an anthropomorphic god. To Freud, gods were always father images, and Frazer's examples of the castration of Attis and the killing of nature gods fitted perfectly into the psychoanalytical doctrine of the fundamental hostility toward father and ruler.

Freud felt that psychoanalytical theory went a long way toward explaining the origins of society. The modern neurotic had guilt feelings about what he would *like* to do. The savage's guilt feelings probably concerned what he actually did. His guilts became the taboos and finally the laws on which society was based.

Although the critics of psychoanalysis treated the whole book as a personal fantasy its author, Freud had made more of an effort to analyze primitive thinking than anyone before him. Wundtian psychology, preoccupied with its measurement of sensation and image, never quite knew what to do with human emotions. It never seemed able to go on to human relationships and the higher activities of the mind. Behind psychoanalysis could be discerned the old pleasure-pain formula of James Mill. Freud was endeavoring to study the complicated associational structures that were erected upon it.

It took time for Freud's views to make an impression on professional anthropologists. A. L. Kroeber, of the University of California, considered them critically when *Totem and Taboo* was translated into English and published in the United States in 1920. The explanation of the origin of totemism did not convince him. He listed the doubtful steps in the argument. Robertson Smith's sacrificial meal applied only to some Mediterranean tribes. There were no statistics to show how often the ambivalence of the father-son relationship was displaced by substituting an animal. Some proof was needed to establish this as a typical psychological mechanism. The killing of the father was pure conjecture. If the band of brothers then renounced the women of the family and sought other mates, this would tend to disperse them rather than hold them together.

Freud's analysis of magic and neuroticism Kroeber found impressive. He was willing to believe that primitives, through taboo and ritual, had channeled tendencies that in modern life led to neurosis. Native groups were apt to have fewer neurotics than civilized cultures. Among the Siberians, for example, homosexuals became shamans, which gave them a traditional place in society.

They were subject to less painful tensions than in the civilized world. Kroeber concluded that to ethnology "Freud brings a keen insight, a fecund imagination, and above all a point of view which can henceforth never be ignored without stultification."

The subsequent history of anthropology would demonstrate that the Freudian influence had only begun.

A devastatingly different opinion on totemism was voiced by Franz Boas in 1916. His questioning mind never slipped into the traditional attitude toward any problem. In the first place, he disclaimed the intention of setting up "an American theory" as some of his disciples had tried to do. It seemed to him that the concept of totemism had crystallized too early on the basis of insufficient data. Said Boas: "I do not believe that ethnic phenomena are simply the expressions of . . . psychological laws. On the contrary, it seems to my mind that the actual processes are immensely diversified and that similar types of ethnic thought may develop in quite different ways."

The contents of totemism in different regions of the world showed striking differences. Therefore, it did not seem to him that all totemic cultures could be derived from the same psychological or historical source.

The concept of totemism which Frazer, Freud, and others had worked with "is an artificial unit, not a natural one." What they had chiefly pounced upon, the identification of men with animals, was a single, non-characteristic element. To Boas it was a separate philosophical problem, that of man's place in nature.

Exogamy he found to be fairly universal. Among peoples broken up into small family groups that lived apart (such as the Eskimos) and practiced avoidance of incest, the marriage system could easily be kept track of. When people lived together in large cohesive tribal groups, it might be harder to distinguish tribal relationships. A badge might be necessary to mark off the marriage clan. This badge could be an animal. Distinctive dress, special ritual, or names would do as well.

This was as far as Boas would go. His multiple-origin point of view rather cut the ground from under the other theorists except for Andrew Lang, who thought totemic names had arisen from accidental epithets.

Perhaps the last word belongs to Kroeber. "Ethnology, like every other branch of science, is work not a game where lucky guesses score. . . . Our business is first to understand as thoroughly as possible the nature of existing phenomena as they exist at present in the hope that such an understanding may gradually lead to a partial reconstruction of origins—without undue guessing."

PART *Three*

Diffusion and Sociology

Chapter 23

BEHOLD MY LONESOME PATH

Concerning Franz Boas (Part I)

■ Early in July 1883 the schooner *Germania* beat up into Cumberland Sound. The Cumberland Peninsula is situated on the west coast of Baffin Island, a part of Canada's Northwest Territory. In 1847 Sir John Franklin, a famous English explorer seeking a northwest passage, had lost his life when his ships were icebound for two years. Since his time there had been little exploration of the far north, although a few whaling-stations were maintained.

The *Germania* found the going rough. A heavy icepack off the point of the Cumberland Peninsula closed in on her like a vise. Scarcely a spot of water was to be seen among the far-reaching floes and icebergs. For three weeks the ship was immobilized. Finally the pack loosened, and on a light easterly wind she sailed into Kikkerton Harbor at the foot of the peninsula.

On board the *Germania* an intense young man with an eagle's profile, a crest of bushy black hair, and a fierce mustache paced up and down, impatiently waiting to set foot on the Arctic. Presently kayaks swarmed out to the ship. At first the *Germania*'s passenger was shocked. "I was really astonished at the figures I saw. The little bandy-legged fellows who ran laughing and chewing over the deck of the vessel, with their long black hair, flat faces and dripping eyes made an extremely repulsive impression." The women were without exception dreadfully ugly, though fairly clean, for they had had a feast of purification before coming to greet the white men.

The German physicist-geographer Franz Boas was meeting primitives for the first time. At this time no one would have guessed that he was to become the greatest American anthropologist of his period and, in the opinion of some, the greatest in the world.

Boas, whom we have mentioned before in connection with primitive art and totemism, was the son of a solid German-Jewish merchant of Minden. He had been educated in the universities of Heidelberg, Bonn, and Kiel. His doctoral thesis was entitled *Contributions to the Understanding of the Color of Water*. His training in physics and psychology had made him a measurer of the school of Fechner and Wundt, but he had also studied physical and cultural geography. One of the theses he defended on his examination was the contention that contemporary German operetta was artistically deplorable. He was a lover of Beethoven and Mozart, and all his life he enjoyed playing the piano for relaxation.

He was also a fiery and independent character. There is a story that, when he was a member of a student corps at Heidelberg, he happened to hear some anti-Semitic remarks in a café. He challenged the other student and went through with the *Schläger* duel. In later life he liked to pretend the dueling scars on his face were the marks of polar bears' claws.

The theories of Friedrich Ratzel were typical of the German approach to cultural geography in the eighties. Ratzel, also a Heidelberg graduate, began his career as a zoologist and a traveling journalist. The latter part of his life was spent as a high-school teacher in Leipzig, where he taught geography. He developed the doctrine that environment was the force which automatically shaped culture. The first volume of his *Anthropogeographie* (*Anthropological Geography*) had come out in 1882. Ratzel taught that man was a passive creature rigidly ruled by climate and geography. The abundance or scarcity of natural resources, the proximity of rivers or harbors dictated the forms of society. Island peoples, for instance, where there was poverty of fauna, suffered from overpopulation that resulted either in advanced forms of agriculture, cannibalism, or infanticide. His point of view was dogmatic and, rejecting psychology, completely mechanical.

Young Boas, who had come to the Arctic to make maps and to observe the effects of climate upon the inhabitants, found that the living, breathing natives were something different from imaginary puppets set going by the immutable laws of climate.

The Eskimos of Cumberland Sound were neater than those of the interior, who had never seen a white man. In summer they lived in tents made of split and semi-transparent skins. The odor within was repellent. "And when I drew the curtain and looked around on the piles of meat, the filthy cooking vessels and the heaps of reindeer skins in the background, I ran out and away as quickly as I could." After a few trips in the cold and wet the anthropologist-to-be changed his point of view. "It was not long before I found myself sharing the deerskin bedplace of the natives and cooking with them in the same pot."

Boas was held up in Kikkerton for some months. Farther north there was a German meteorological station whose personnel was to be taken home by the *Germania*. She could not beat up the sound against the head winds. On a trip north in a kayak to notify the scientists that their relief had come, Boas began to experience the hazards of Arctic travel. The kayak was nearly crushed by the ice. Back at Kikkerton he had the friendship and advice of a Scotch whaling-agent, Mr. Mutch, who helped him in his long and tedious conversations with the natives until he was able to speak their language. Boas, a brilliant linguist, soon was able to speak the language of the Inuits fluently. He had hoped to begin traveling by dogsled, but an epidemic had killed off all the available dogs. For a time he had to content himself with surveying the near-by fiords. On one trip in the frail native vessels, he and his companions were isolated in the sound. "The snow squalls which blew down the deep mountains made the sea foam, and very nearly upset the boat. The water froze on the boat as it dashed over it, so that the little vessel was soon almost imbedded in heavy ice and only by the hardest work could we keep her afloat." It took them four days to get back to Kikkerton. By this time a warm Eskimo tent seemed like home, and he was glad enough to have the lady of the house dry and clean his clothes. The men wore sealskin jackets, small hoods, and breeches ornamented with fur. The long hair fluttering about their heads gave them a wild look, but their quiet eyes and childish sense of pleasure contradicted it. They were eager for tobacco, which they smoked in small clay pipes. In this area they had become dependent on guns, which they got from the white whalers, and were beginning to use civilized provisions such as bread.

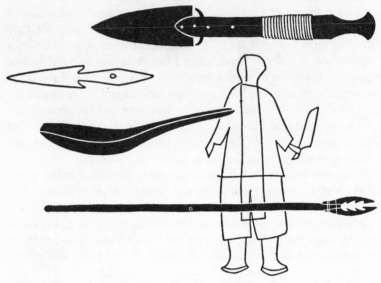

FROM TOP TO BOTTOM: *cutting knife, harpoon head, ice scoop, fish spear. The figure is based upon an Eskimo drawing.*

Some natives returning from one of their summer journeys to the north in an old whaleboat arrived "loaded to the gunwale with skins, men, women, and children, singing, laughing and chattering, dogs howling. A pot of food stood in the center of the boat which they kept dipping into. Only the helmsman was earnest and serious." If they had time when a seal raised his head, they stopped and took a shot at it. From them Boas purchased skins for his winter clothes. Mr. Mutch was finally able to lend him dogs and equipment, and he got an Eskimo guide from one of the whalers. This man proved good and trustworthy and accompanied Boas on all of his trips in return for a gun and ammunition.

By October the Eskimos were able to go sealing on the ice. They traveled with their guns to the edges of the newly formed floes, shot the seals, and made sure of them with their harpoons. They were obliged to pay strict attention to every change of wind because if the wind set offshore they were likely to go adrift.

Boas was spending every night with his Eskimo friends, "who told me about the configuration of the land, sang old songs after the old, monotonous tunes, and I saw them playing the old games with which they shorten the dark winter nights."

One young man "had been hunting on a projecting point of ice and even before he was aware of his danger the whole point had broken off and he was rapidly drifting out to sea. There was nothing for him to do but to yield to his fate and see whether the gale would exhaust itself soon, and whether by chance the floe that carried him might be blown back to land. Fortunately he had just killed a seal. He flensed it and made a little shelter of the fresh hide. His lance had to serve as a tent pole. He protected his tent cover against the wind by piling snow all over it. He made a receptacle for the blubber out of a piece of skin and thus improvised a little lamp. Fortunately, too, he carried his fire drill and a little of the moss that was used for wicks so that he was able to start a fire in his shelter. . . ." Meanwhile, the courageous seal-hunter composed a song to cheer himself up. When he got back to shore after drifting for three days, he sang it for his friends, and it became very popular. It began and ended as follows:

> *Aya!*
> *It's glorious on the ice!*
> *Behold my lonesome path*
> *All snow and slush and ice!*
> *This is nice!*
> *Aya!*
> *Oh when I reach the land*
> *It will be nice,*
> *When will this roaming end?*
> *When will I be home?*
> *Then it's nice!*

Undaunted by the prospect of such hardships, Boas continued his preparations and, on December 11, started on a trip north. Winter had begun to set in, the new ice floes had hardened, and the temperature had dropped to forty below zero. He was accompanied by a servant he had brought from Germany and the Eskimo guide. On the fourteenth a heavy fall of snow covered the ice to a depth of two feet. The party could scarcely travel. One of the guns snapped in the cold. They ran out of ammunition and were unable to kill seals for meat. The lack of food began to be alarming. Boas decided to make for the nearest settlement. By now the thermometer had dropped still lower, to fifty-five degrees below.

On December 21, taking advantage of the bright moonlight, they started off over the snow in the direction the guide maintained would bring them to a settlement. All went well at first, but by the end of the day a thick fog had come up. Boas wrote: "The compass was of no use to us and, as I did not know the position of the settlement I had to follow the native who pretended to know his place exactly. . . . It is very difficult to recognize any part of this country and now in the deep and dark night, in the thick fog, it proved impossible. A number of grounded icebergs we took for islands. . . . All night we kept roaming over a small space comparatively free from snow, to keep ourselves warm!"

The unfortunate servant froze his feet. The little expedition was now really in danger. Finally the fog lifted, the moon rose, and they reached the settlement just in time. They got back to Kikkerton by Christmas, but the German servant was incapacitated and was unable to travel with Boas during the rest of his stay.

About this time an epidemic of diphtheria ran through the Eskimo settlement at Kikkerton. The shaman decided to use Boas as a scapegoat (perhaps to disguise his failure as a medicine man) and announced that the foreigner had brought the disease upon them. He told his followers to have nothing to do with the anthropologist.

Boas took stern measures. The native encampment had been without tobacco and bread because very few whalers had been visiting the area. Boas told them they would get no more white man's goods from him if they boycotted him. They soon disregarded the shaman and gave him some sealskins as a peace offering.

In January he prepared to travel northwest across the Cumberland Peninsula to Davis Strait. In this little-explored region, which he intended to map, he expected to find Eskimos uncorrupted by contact with the whites. When he arrived at the strait the men of the settlement were out hunting, but the women and children, who had vaguely heard of white men, swarmed out of their huts in great excitement. Discovering that he was really a foreigner, they were so delighted that they burst into a wild dance and sang a song about summer, a production of one of their most popular composers.

Boas developed a keen interest in Eskimo music and poetry. When they gathered at night, the women sat in a circle and one male soloist after another tried to outdo his competitors. As the singers stripped off their jackets, seized the hand drum, swung their bodies and chanted, the women joined in with the chorus of *"Ayaya!"*

The explorer was able to buy more dogs and, after returning for provisions to Kikkerton, came back in May with two sledges loaded with ninety-five pounds of bread, thirty-six of mutton, twelve of butter, and plenty of tobacco and ammunition for trading.

He spent the summer with the natives of Davis Strait, living in a skin tent, learning their customs. By now he was fully acclimated and remarkably happy. On one of his last surveying expeditions he was caught in a snowstorm, and a five-day fog had brought him almost to the point of eating his dogs when the fog lifted and he was able to get back to the village. Such adventures had now become routine. In return for his welcome provisions he learned the secrets of the shamans.

They described how, when winter storms raged and the ice broke with loud cracks and reports and the cakes piled up in the freezing gale, the natives huddled in their huts in fear of the spirits of the dead who banged wildly on the outside of the snow dwellings. Anyone these spirits caught outside was sure to die. Another demon, Krikoin, pursued the dogs, which died in convulsions when they saw his face. Kallofalling was a terrible entity who, in winter, dragged brave hunters down under the water and concealed them in the hood of his duckskin dress. Worst of all was Sedna, mistress of the underworld.

The angekok sat in mystic gloom at the back of the hut. Presently he began to scream and throw his arms about. At last his guardian spirit was induced to respond. While the angekok lay in a trance, the spirit promised help. Meanwhile, two of the most powerful wizards of the community coiled a rope on the floor of the hut to represent a seal hole. One held a seal spear, the other a harpoon rope. The angekok at the back of the hut now began to lure Sedna with his song. Up she came through the hard earth. They could hear her heavy breathing, the sound of the wind and the sea. As she came nearer and nearer, the sound grew louder. At last she broke through, but the harpoon was ready. They struck without mercy. Back went Sedna into the ground. The two wizards clung to the rope, but after a struggle she tore loose, and they proudly exhibited a bloodstained harpoon. The village knew the wounded Sedna was angry, and all during the festival on the following day everyone wore amulets on top of their hoods to protect them.

A kayak.

The snow was melting, there was plenty of water, and the eiderducks were raising their young when a whaler from St. John's came up the strait and picked up Boas, who, with his precious hoard of notes, was now ready to leave the Arctic.

He returned home by way of the United States in 1884. He had managed to finance his trip by means of articles for the *Frankfurter Zeitung,* and now he also took time to write travel articles for *Popular Science Monthly* and the *American Anthropologist.* It is significant that he was already able to write in excellent English, which he also spoke. While in New York he began to make scientific contacts and to learn something of the country that was to play such an important role in his career.

Boas had been captivated by the far north. Ratzel's geographic determinism by now seemed totally unreal. The living culture of native peoples was an organic thing not to be understood by mechanical laws. Boas had made his surveys, discovered two lakes, and corrected the maps, but he now knew that the passion of his life would be the study of the inexhaustibly absorbing and intricate structure of human culture.

"After long and intimate intercourse with the Eskimo, it was with feelings of sorrow and regret that I parted from my Arctic friends. I had seen that they enjoyed life, as we do, that nature is also beautiful to them; that feelings of friendship also root in the

Eskimo heart; that, although the character of their life is so rude as compared to civilized life, the Eskimo is a man as we are; his feelings, his virtues and his shortcomings are based on human nature like ours."

These words sound like an echo of Schoolcraft, who had made the same discovery nearly half a century before.

Chapter 24

WHITE MAN'S BURDEN

Concerning Diffusion, Race, Colonialism

■ On his return to Germany, Boas became a docent at the University of Berlin. He was also made assistant to Adolph Bastian in the Imperial Ethnological Museum, the contents of which were, with the appointment of Bastian as director in 1886, being moved to a new building.

Until now we have been following the course of the British and American school of ethnology. In Germany, during the latter part of the nineteenth century, the science was developing along a different path.

How did it differ? Chiefly in terms of the mentality of the scientists. In the English-speaking countries Darwin was the influence that shaped the form of ethnological thought, while a hard-headed dependence on facts determined its content. The German point of view was conditioned by philosophy and geography. Germany, the country of Kant, Hegel, and Schelling, produced philosophical scientists; in every department, scholars tried to erect large schemes that should contain all of subjective and objective reality.

On the other hand, Germany, coming late into the sphere of world exploration, was intensely aware of geography and sustained many active geographical societies and publications. To understand the temper of German ethnology when Boas began his studies, once more it is necessary to go back to the mid-nine-teenth century.

The influence of that great cosmopolitan, the scientist-traveler Baron Alexander von Humboldt, in the area of geography can not be disregarded. Humboldt, half French, half German, was a spirit-ual child of the French Revolution. A romantic interest in the world of nature eulogized by Rousseau, a friendship with a writer who had sailed around the world with Captain Cook, plus the scientific curiosity resulting from his own training in geology, inspired him to visit exotic and little-known areas of the earth. He traversed the mountains and the rivers of South America, explored the headwaters of the Orinoco, lived among forest Indians, studied the ruins and records of the Aztecs of Mexico, and brought back collections of flora and fauna which stimulated European interest in the natural sciences. In his later years he worked on a huge book, *Cosmos,* which was to synthesize all he had learned of natural science and geography. In it his comparisons between Asiatic, Polynesian, and American cultures touched on the problems of ethnology. The book was still uncompleted when he died in 1845.

We have already had a glimpse of that pioneer theorist of mar-riage Johan Bachofen, who wrote in the fifties. Like Humboldt, he exemplified the typically romantic and philosophical point of view of German anthropology. Ratzel, the determinist and geog-rapher, was also a philosopher on the grand scale. The three im-portant names in Germany contemporary with that of E. B. Tylor in England were Gustav Klemm, Theodor Waitz, and Adolph Bastian (whom we have already mentioned as director of the Berlin Anthropological Museum).

Klemm (1802–1867) is chiefly remembered for first defining the classic three stages of civilization: the period of roaming hunters, that of pastoral life, that of agriculture and permanent settlement. His *Allgemeine Culturgeschichte der Menschheit* (*General Culture-History of Mankind*) appeared in ten volumes between 1843 and 1852.

Waitz (1821–1865) is a more interesting figure and, as he slightly predated Bastian, will be considered first. The first volume of his *Anthropologie der Natürvolker* was published in 1859, the same year as *The Origin of Species.* Under the title *An Introduction to Anthropology,* four years later it was brought out in English by the London Anthropological Society as the most important European work on the subject. In it Waitz collected all the data he could find on primitive people in contemporary travelers' accounts. His facts are now dated, but his rational attitude toward the races of mankind is distinctive.

The trend toward travel and geographical exploration had practical reasons behind it. Europe was intent on colonizing the technically backward areas of the earth. Spain and Portugal had taken over South America and Mexico. Portugal had secured parts of Africa. England had all of India, Australia, New Zealand, and parts of the Orient. The United States had successfully displaced the Indians. Out of the Portuguese colonization of Africa had come Negro slavery. The white races of Europe had dominated all other peoples with less advanced technical civilizations. Along with the missionary and the tax-collector had come the geographer and the ethnologist.

Many of the scientists whom we have earlier discussed were champions of the primitive peoples and fully aware of their sufferings when exploited by their conquerors. Not all ethnological thinking was humanitarian, however. If you have enslaved someone, it is easy to convince yourself that it was his own fault. In anthropological terms this is the doctrine of superior and inferior races.

This doctrine survives in parts of the United States today, is still a political issue, and has a curious history. One of its earliest proponents was Comte Joseph Arthur de Gobineau, an impoverished French aristocrat who, failing to make a living writing fiction, entered the diplomatic service and served in Persia and Scandinavia. Born in 1816, Gobineau never recovered from the French Revolution. He hated the democracy of his time, which he referred to as "the dirty shirts." Embittered, egotistic, and obsessed, he wrote a fantastic book to prove that he was descended from the Vikings and ultimately from the Norse god Odin.

In 1853–5 he published his two-volume work *Essai sur l'inégalité des races* (*Essay on the Inequality of Races*). A textbook for discrimination, it elaborated the thesis that the white race was supreme; next came the yellow race, whose characteristic was mediocrity; then, at the bottom, the Negro race, the slave of blind appetite. He made use of the Bible, relating the three divisions of mankind to Shem, Ham, and Japheth. Wherever the black or yellow race mixed with the white, decay and eventually nineteenth-century democracy resulted. The godlike Aryans included the Hellenic Greeks and, of course, the Germanic peoples, and were also to be found in India and Persia. Because racial purity had not been maintained in Europe, by Gobineau's time culture had already gone into a two-hundred-year decline.

Gobineau's book was received in France with distaste, but was accepted with enthusiasm by many Germans. Gobineau societies were formed, and there is some evidence that Friedrich Nietzsche derived his concept of the superman from Gobineau's ideas.

Across the Atlantic, Louis Agassiz, who had a genius for being on the wrong side of the fence, was arguing for "The Diversity of Origin of the Human Race" in an article published in the *Christian Examiner* in 1850. He, too, made use of the Bible. Genesis, he said, made no mention of inhabitants in the Arctic Zone, Japan, New Holland, or America. The first human pair "to which the white race is distinctly referred" were Adam and Eve. As the Bible mentioned the creation of only a single pair of Aryans, the races of a different skin color must have arisen independently. It could not be denied that there were physical differences between races, for these differences existed as far back as the time of the Egyptians, as was proved by the records on their monuments. These differences had always existed and were not modifications caused by climate. How the other races arose he did not explain—perhaps by spontaneous generation.

At any rate, because the non-Aryans were not mentioned in Genesis, "it seems to us to be mock philosophy and mock philanthropy to assume that all races have the same abilities and enjoy the same powers, and show the same natural dispositions." To Agassiz the anti-evolutionist, the Mongolians were "obsequious" and the Negroes "submissive"; their apathy was so great that they had not progressed materially since the time of the Pharaohs. Ancient Egypt seemed to be as far back in time as Agassiz was able to imagine.

To Waitz's credit, he opposed on logical grounds all such apologies for white supremacy. He felt that the religion, customs, and legends of the primitives had been so little studied that there was no sound basis on which to compare them with the achievements of the civilized races. Indeed, the so-called civilized races did not seem morally superior to the primitives. The Portuguese tortured the inhabitants of the Congo, the Russians destroyed the

Aleuts in Siberia, the American colonists exterminated the Indians, and Waitz thought the behavior of the Southern slaveholders in the United States far from ideal.

He made other comparisons. It was true that some savages bought their wives, but was the marriage market in high European society essentially different? If primitives were superstitious, were there not plenty of survivals of the self-same superstitions in Europe? Then there was the argument that Negroes did not possess the ability to progress materially and culturally. This was supposed to be an unvarying racial characteristic. But everything depended on the time span in which a people was studied. In the Middle Ages the Arabs would have been considered an inherently progressive people, for they were the leaders of Europe in mathematics and philosophy. In Waitz's time, however, they had retrogressed into a thievish, lazy condition and their countries were backwaters of culture.

Waitz held that the differences in psychic life of various peoples were merely the result of a *fluctuating* difference in culture. Climate could be an important modifying element. A hot area was not inducive to energetic labor; even the whites succumbed to the effects of the heat. Migrations of peoples and wars resulted in interchange of culture and changes in its level. From this it will be seen that Waitz had an almost modern feeling for multiplicity of causation affecting culture.

He had little patience with his contemporary Klemm, who paralleled Gobineau by dividing mankind into "active" and "passive" races. Needless to say, white Europeans were classed among the active races. For North American racists Waitz had outright contempt. Agassiz had decided that the higher races would eventually replace the lower ones. Wrote Waitz acidly: "This extinction of the lower races is predetermined by nature, and it would appear that we must not merely acknowledge the right of the white American to destroy the red man, but perhaps praise him that he has constituted himself the instrument of Progress in carrying out and promoting this law of destruction."

It is well to remember that Waitz was the founder of a tradition of racial tolerance in Germany. We shall have occasion to return to the racial problem in tracing the latter part of Boas's life. Before doing so, something must be told of the man who helped shape his anthropological career, Adolph Bastian.

Chapter 25

THE TIRELESS TRAVELER

Concerning Adolph Bastian

■ Adolph Bastian, Boas's employer and director of the Berlin Ethnological Museum, combined philosophy and geography in an extraordinary way. He was perhaps the most determined literary traveler on record. In the northern wastes of Siberia, the coral-reefed Pacific, the jungles of Burma and Siam, the desert coast of South America, in China, Japan, the Celebes, Java, Sumatra, Adolph Bastian, notebook in hand, was everywhere at home. The world was indeed his country. Yet, while constantly exploring it, he found time to turn out more than ten thousand printed pages.

Bastian (1826–1905) was the son of a prosperous and rather well-known Bremen merchant. In the nineteenth century Bremen was already an important harbor, and it is probable that even during his childhood foreign visitors frequented the home of his family, for his father had far-flung mercantile connections. In 1865, he tells us, he had a brother working in the house of Büsing, Schroeder & Company in Singapore.

Bastian's education was varied. He studied law at the University of Heidelberg, biology at the universities of Jena and Würtzburg, and received the degree of doctor of medicine from the University of Prague. In 1851, as soon as he finished his medical education, he obtained a position as a ship's doctor on a schooner bound for Sydney, Australia. From then on he was a citizen of the earth.

During the next seven years he traversed five continents, and

June 1857 found him in Capetown, South Africa. His subsequent trip to the west coast of that continent is described in his first book, *Ein Besuch nach San Salvador* (*A Visit to San Salvador*), which was published in 1859 (the same date as *The Origin of Species*).

Bastian, who was probably acquainted with the early writings of Waitz, explained in the introduction to his book that he wished to correct his impressions by comparing them with what he knew of customs all over the world. The subtitle, *A Contribution to Psychology and Mythology*, showed that he had already begun the study that was to be the primary interest of his career.

The book set the pattern for the travel works that were to follow. They were constructed rather like club sandwiches: a slice of narrative and firsthand description, then a slice of comparative customs which displayed his vast erudition, then another slice of travel, then perhaps a slice of philosophizing. He was also addicted to long and theoretical prefaces in which he set forth his views on anthropology again and again.

Bastian, who always got on well with the English—he considered them good administrators—sailed from Capetown on the frigate of the admiral of the British fleet. Twenty-one guns greeted them as they put into the port of Loango in Portuguese West Africa. Bastian was preparing to visit the interior of the Congo.

The twenty-nine-year-old traveler quickly adopted the local form of transportation: a hammock slung on a pole carried by two bearers. In this conveyance he proceeded up the coast to Quinsembo, surrounded by noisy, naked black children begging for alms.

The King of Quinsembo lived some distance from the coast and never came near the sea, for it was believed that if he looked upon it he would die and his kingdom would be destroyed. This was a taboo established by the King's fetish (Bastian used the Portuguese word *fetish* for what we should now call cult worship). When Bastian, borne in his hammock, paid a visit to the King, he found himself in a small plaza surrounded by mud huts, one of which was the King's palace. The whitewashed walls were decorated with allegorical figures of warriors and canoes. A large tamarind tree stood in the center of the plaza, and a wooden phallic statue leaned against it. With great difficulty the King's armchair was brought out of his hut, which threatened to topple in the process. The monarch wore a red uniform and tight, uncomfortable white trousers, which he seemed unused to. When he was seated, a feathered three-cornered hat was ceremoniously placed on his head.

When their sovereign was enthroned, his subjects clapped. Bastian spoke to him in the local pidgin English (the ethnologist seemed to speak and write all European languages without effort), announcing that he had come "to look at the King's face and hope his belly was well." Presents of rum and calico were given, the subjects clapped loudly at the beginning and end of every sentence, and, when the audience was over, Bastian was carried off at a dead run in his wildly swinging hammock.

For his trip into the Congo Bastian required eight bearers for his hammock, twelve for his baggage, and a headman to interpret and manage the expedition. For the latter post he engaged a former factory worker who had been dismissed for stealing. The Europeans said Bastian was insane to choose a desperate character who would surely cut his throat. The anthropologist's formula for handling the ex-criminal was to trust him completely, now and then demonstrating his white superiority, but respecting the native's prejudices. In the end the trip cost half what he had expected. This method of treating natives worked everywhere. Bastian found the headman intelligent, and he stuck to the motto that he would rather have a clever rascal than an honorable idiot.

The journey was not easy, for the rainy season was about to begin. Passing the village of Impambu, where he was greeted by yellow-and-red-painted fetish-worshippers with tigerskins around their loins, he made some progress up the river and at night hung his hammock between two trees. In the morning a thin rain awoke him. Presently a whirlwind struck, blowing hammock, bearers, and baggage into a heap. Then a tropical downpour soaked everything through. Some bearers became discouraged and deserted, but he replaced them with boys from Impambu.

Presently the group reached a fetish hut. The bearers refused to go near it. When Bastian got out of his hammock, they tried to prevent him from entering it. They made it plain that he was going to his death. The temple had three wood-framed doors and was covered with straw matting, the doorposts being painted with green-and-yellow figures. Inside it he found nothing but a heap of earth with three red-and-white-striped wooden forks stuck in it. In this area the cult of Dambu was dominant.

At the next village he fainted and realized he had come down with malaria. His bearers pointed out that he had touched the fetish temple. They expected to bury him by nightfall.

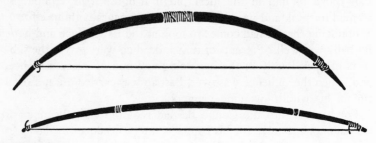

African bows.

Bastian had no intention of allowing himself to be buried. He spent three days getting over his attack of fever. He had an audience with the local king, who sang a song in his honor accompanied by a chorus of courtiers. In this area there had originally been a clan system which had given way to local kings with the power of life and death over their subjects, any one of whom they had the right to enslave. This was generally true of west Africa, and the habit of enslaving war prisoners had made it easy for the Portuguese to obtain human goods for the American market. In Havana, from where they were reshipped to the United States, they brought a thousand dollars apiece.

Bastian, a true German of his time, was keenly interested in colonization. His own country was anxious to obtain a foothold in Africa, and he pounced on the incapacity and brutality of the Portuguese with relish. He had seen the stone seat on the pier at Loanda where the Portuguese bishop used to sit and bless the slaves as they entered the holds of the slavers "and through his apostolic blessing guaranteed them the inexpressible bliss of a future life with which the short period of earthly tribulation could not be compared."

On and on, swaying in his hammock, Bastian traveled through the tropical rain. After traversing many hills and valleys he climbed to the isolated plateau that held the Portuguese capital.

San Salvador consisted of a group of huts built on a plain that was covered with grass as tall as a man and ringed with higher mountains fluted by deep ravines. On the whitewashed walls of the mud huts were colored murals of soldiers and rows of slaves. The grass was so high that it hid the huts, and the pattern of the streets was lost among tall palm trees and shade trees that spread over the courtyards. Now and then the green was broken by richly colored flower beds. Around the edge of the city were fields of maize and wheat. Among the palm trees, the broken arches and ruined chapels of several churches rose from the grass—all that remained of the unfulfilled imperial dreams of the Portuguese who had here baptized the first Christian King of the Congo in 1491.

Bastian was given several huts for his party and was immediately visited by Dom Antonio and Dom Domingo, sons of the king who had just died. The farce of Portuguese royalty was still kept up, and all of the reigning family had high-sounding Portuguese names in addition to their African ones. In the fifteenth century, when the invaders were creating black counts and marquises, the royal patent was indicated by branding the arms of Portugal on their shoulders with a red-hot iron.

The two princes informed Bastian that they were scholars and could read. One of them drew from a leather portfolio the tattered remnants of a book, which turned out to be some loose leaves from a Latin missal and a few holy pictures. Adjusting his spectacles, which had lost their lenses and kept slipping off his nose, Dom Domingo failed to read any of the Latin, but when Bastian gave him a Portuguese book he made out a couple of isolated words. In all the Congo this was the extent of the educational system set up by two hundred and fifty years of European rule.

Bastian was visited by the regent's son, with whom he got drunk, and had an audience with the crown prince, who wore a blue uniform and white trousers and sat under a red, yellow, and blue umbrella. On this occasion Bastian gave his royal friends a short talk on world trade, urging them to deal with the British and also not to forget the Germans.

On the way back to the coast the indomitable ethnologist had another attack of fever. While he was trying to recover from it in a native village, the wails of a newborn baby kept him awake and served as a point of departure for reflections on the custom of couvade, which he interpreted much as Crawley was to do half a century later. The motion of his hammock made him feel worse, and he could not endure rubber waterproof clothing on account of the heat. He envied his naked bearers, to whom the rain was nothing, but he was of the Victorian era and the idea of adopting the native lack of clothing was foreign to him. He suffered in respectability.

At the mines of Pembe he decided to travel with an armed caravan that was transporting copper to the coast. He set off with eighty soldiers and three hundred and fifty bearers carrying loads of copper ore in baskets on their heads. Each basket had a pole projecting in front, and when the bearer wanted to unload, he could incline his head and rest the pole on the ground. Unfortunately, the caravan was attacked by hostile natives. All was in confusion; poor Bastian had to leap from his hammock and run for his life. The party broke through the ambush, however, and pushed on. Back at Impambu, where he was tortured by mosquitoes so ferocious that neither he nor his bearers could sleep, the Negroes decided to pass the night dancing. To the accompaniment of a marimba, maraccas, and beaten pots, a solo dancer performed a kind of pantomime while a chorus sat in a circle, shouting and clapping. Each dance ended with cries of "Zimba, zimba!" Later the performance turned into "an obscene cancan," which, he had to admit, except for the lack of costume, "was not much worse than the scenes which formerly could be seen in certain public halls in Berlin."

Bastian's connection with the arts, however, was remote. Toward the end of his life a friend asked him when he had last been to a play. He said: "In eighteen fifty-nine." When had he been to an art exhibition? "Never," he replied.

The British and French had agreed to suppress the slave trade, but the Portuguese were still carrying it on. Americans, who also were technically debarred from dealing in human flesh, kept a Portuguese or Spanish flag aboard and gave their command over to one of the latter nationalities when they carried a cargo of slaves. The Negroes, Bastian concluded, were better off in their darkest ignorance, for Europe, self-appointed apostle of civilization to the world, had brought them only firearms, firewater, and slavery.

Bastian finished his book with a long appendix on comparative mythology. In 1860 he published his three-volume *Der Mensch in der Geschichte* (*Man in History*). It was a book which in a sense paralleled Edward Tylor's *Primitive Culture* and may have had some influence on it. Bastian, however, could never put his ideas in clear and logical order nor fully define his main theme. Like all German scientists of his period, he was trying to construct a cosmic view of existence. Impatient with subjective philosophy, he maintained that scholars must learn to understand the psychology of social groups.

Religion was the key to psychology. The soul always sought for unity and expressed itself in terms of its material environment. The savage, not distinguishing between the subjective and objective worlds, tried to find forms in the objective world corresponding to his subjective feelings.

The notion of omens was basic. If a man fell into the water and was saved by catching hold of an overhanging twig, the episode would make a great impression on him. It was a circumstance that ordinary cause and effect would not seem to explain. The man's feelings took on great significance; he projected them into the object that saved him. The twig acquired power and importance and mystical strangeness. In a similar way, a boy clung to a lucky marble with which he had won many games. This was the psychology of fetishism. Upon it mythology and divine hierarchies were built. The resulting religious structures were modified by contact between peoples. Reaction to a foreign culture was largely determined by the stage of development a folk had reached before the contact. Very early in its history a people could passively accept a higher culture. But a primitive group which was already worshipping a stone, for instance, and was then taught by another group to worship the stars, would for a long time connect its new worship with the old.

Bastian's book piled up all the phenomena of primitive religion on a comparative basis. In the last volume he attacked the psychology of government.

Behind all of Bastian's thinking is the idea of the basic unity of mankind, a similarity of custom and belief. He was himself, on a foundation of comparative mythology, trying to construct a view of the world which should rest on objective facts. Darwin's hypothesis was not an isolated phenomenon. The most inquiring minds of the period were all trying to organize the new data of science into a comprehensive scheme. Bastian, however (perhaps influenced by Buddhism), subscribed to an almost mystic belief in unity which sent him tirelessly scouring the surface of the earth for more and more ethnic facts, insatiably scrutinizing culture after culture for the fundamental mythological ideas that he felt were the key to society and the human mind.

Bastian did not, like the English thinkers, set himself specific limited goals. In proportion to the grandiosity of his aims, his writing grew diffuse and, as he neared the end of his life, obscure.

In 1861 he set off for eastern Asia, a journey that was to last four years and result in a six-volume account of travel experiences and the Buddhist religion. His adventure with the King of Burma is perhaps the most colorful episode in his life.

One afternoon in October his ship sailed into the Irrawaddy River and entered a busy harbor full of Burmese in tall pointed straw hats who sailed small fishing-boats or poled bamboo rafts. It proceeded upstream between carefully tilled fields, passing the silver tip of a pagoda that shimmered in the sun above a wood of dark-leaved trees. Another turn in the river and the magnificence of the colossal pagoda of Rangoon confronted Bastian, flanked by rows of huts which stretched along the river, making up the city.

England, always pushing into the Orient, had annexed Burma's coastal provinces, and, although hostilities between the two countries had ceased, the technicalities of peace had not been concluded. Burma was an absolute monarchy, a true Oriental despotism where the Buddhist religion was supreme and Europeans were not particularly welcome.

As the river was the highroad to Mandalay, Bastian got himself a Burmese houseboat complete with four rowers and a pilot. The boat had a mast with a matting sail; in front of it was his dining-room, enclosed by matting, and behind it his bedroom. He engaged a cook who also tutored him in the language and literature of the country. The Burmese were slender, tawny, attractive people who tattooed their skins. Good Buddhists, they would not shed blood, so newly caught fish were left to gasp and die in the sun; if they could not breathe air, it was not the fault of the fisherman. Burmese women, when they bathed, stepped out of their loincloths. Bastian remarked that the true tint of the skin could be seen on the hips and loins, which were as light as those of Europeans.

When he reached Mandalay and was preparing to continue on toward the north, he was suddenly visited by officials of the king who told him that his passport was no longer valid and he must leave his boat and take up residence on shore. This was a blow. Bastian wrote a letter to the King saying that he had many valuables on his boat and could not leave it. The officials wanted him, not his letter, but he put them off his boat forcibly. They returned shortly, summoning him to an audience with the King.

Rangoon pagoda with statue of Buddha.

When he reached the palace, he had to leave his shoes outside. He was conducted to a small audience hall with pillars decorated in red and gold. Stairs mounted to a balustrade at one end. The courtiers sat on the floor looking toward the stairs. The King came from a door behind them and sat on a divan placed on the top step. The courtiers put their hands together and threw themselves face down on the floor, where they remained on elbows and knees.

Bastian contented himself with nodding. Feet were supposed to be hidden from the King, on aesthetic grounds; Bastian, squatting, made efforts to fulfill the demands of etiquette. The King, in rich silks encrusted with gold ornaments, surrounded by his young children, stared at Bastian for a while and finally asked the purpose of his trip. There was a distinct atmosphere of intrigue and menace, and Bastian knew he had to be careful. He replied that, as a European, he wished to know foreign countries and study their religion. Burma was ideal for the study of Buddhism at its purest.

This pleased the King, who asked him how long he intended to stay. Bastian made the mistake of saying he wanted to travel in the north and visit ancient shrines. The King told him tartly that it was impossible to travel and study at the same time, and that he did not think Bastian was honest. Because of his recent troubles with the English he may well have suspected the German of being a spy. For a time they both sat silent and the tension mounted.

Finally the King said: "There is no better place than Burma for the study of Buddhism, in Burma no better place than Mandalay, in Mandalay no better place than my palace. There is plenty of room for you in the palace. I shall send for a teacher and books. Is your answer yes or no?"

Bastian knew very well that any utterance of the King's was a royal command to be obeyed without question. The answer had to be yes.

His friends among the merchants in Mandalay watched him disappear into the palace, sadly assuring him he would never come out again.

When Bastian was installed in the palace, a learned scholar came to teach him Buddhism. The King had commanded that he first study Burmese thoroughly, then the ancient Pali, finally the holy books. Bastian insisted on reversing the process. The poor professor was in a constant state of terror for fear the King would find out that his orders had not been obeyed.

He was again received by the King, this time in the great audience hall. Luckily, there were some packages of gifts heaped in front of him so that he was able to hide his feet politely.

The King preached on the importance of the Buddhist refusal to destroy life. Bastian asked if it was permitted to defend one's own life. The King said no, such a crude idea would lead to killing insects (fleas existed in the palace of the Gold-Footed One). After the King vainly tried to make Bastian reject the heresy of self-defense, he ordered some parrots brought in in a golden cage. As an example to the flea-killing heathen, he ceremoniously freed them to show his respect for life. Bastian reflected that they could quite easily be caught in the next room to be used for another parable.

Some weeks passed before the reason for Bastian's semi-imprisonment became clear. While in Mandalay he had taken some wax from a child's ear and improved the boy's hearing. The mother had visited a friend in the King's harem. Rumors concerning Bastian had raced through the harem and through the court. Now several courtiers came to him with ear ailments. All he did was syringe their ears with water, but they insisted they had benefited tremendously. Finally Bastian got tired of the stream of patients and prescribed mustard plasters. It had gradually dawned on him that the King, hearing that he was a foreign doctor, and having a good deal of respect for European medicine, had decided that a doctor was what he needed in his court.

Now began an oblique struggle between the stubborn German scientist and the Oriental potentate, who had never before in his life been opposed. Bastian was afraid that if he became established as a doctor he would never be allowed to leave. Conveniently, he had lost his medicine chest. The King summoned him to an audience and asked him to give the harem beauties medicine. Bastian insisted that he had none.

He was told that, medicine or no medicine, "the King commands."

Bastian refused.

Such a thing had never been heard of. The King's son stamped his foot, rustling his silks under his gold umbrella. An icy chill invaded the court atmosphere. This lasted for eight days. It was generally expected that he would mysteriously disappear. "Fear," wrote Bastian calmly, "is useless and in this case it would have been dangerous."

His teacher came to him, trembling with fear, and asked if he perhaps knew how to make gold. This might distract and appease the King.

One evening a detachment of troops marched into his quarters. The officers looked at him sternly as if they were about to arrest him. Bastian blandly asked them to be seated and questioned them about Buddhism. They stared at him, astonished. Without a word they marched out again.

The ladies of the harem, whom Bastian was treating, begged for more medicine. Bastian made this an excuse to go into the city. He was stopped at the gate by a sentry. Bastian made a disturbance, insisted on seeing the King's son, who had been avoiding him, and shouted that he was a guest, not a prisoner. The prince made excuses, but Bastian was still not allowed to leave the palace.

He realized that there were no Europeans he could appeal to, not even a consul. He was completely cut off from the outside world.

The scientist courageously sat it out, and suddenly the King's mood changed, the court smiled on Bastian, the courtiers came to sing, dance, and drink his tea and smoke his cigarettes again.

Bastian struck while the iron was hot and demanded permission to leave. He got it, a passport written on a long palm leaf that could be conveniently rolled up. It was signed with the King's seal.

The traveler drew a long breath and continued on his way.

When next we see him, he is penetrating the jungles of Siam, sitting on the back of an elephant. He hired four of the forest giants, with wild tribesmen called Karens as guides. By day they traveled through the teak forests; each night his forest people built him a little house of bamboo, in which his sleep was disturbed by the yells of monkeys.

In Bangkok he saw the installation of the sacred white elephant. Although the scientist was invited by the King to witness an elephant fight (elephants maddened by picador-like lance thrusts were made to tear down barricades), he had no difficulties with him such as he had had with the Burmese sovereign.

When Bastian returned to Germany, he was made assistant curator of the ethnological museum, and on subsequent travels he began to collect for that institution.

In the seventies the museum financed a South American trip. On a cold damp day in April he met his friends at the station without an overcoat. He had decided he did not need it because it would be warm where he was going. They insisted on sending it after him to the boat.

A glimpse of his travels in Latin America will round out the picture of this intrepid scientist-adventurer. With a Peruvian guide he was crossing the Sechura Desert, that eternally dry seacoast, on horseback at night. He had been riding all day, for settlements were few and far between, and in the desert the lack of water forced the traveler to push on as rapidly as possible. In the darkness, half dead from long hours in the saddle, he was overcome with strange fantasies. "I rode as if with a world of ghosts around me. In front of me mighty terraces rose one upon the other in giant steps and, as I approached, retreated, building themselves higher and higher. Giant pilasters grew from them which phantasmagorically leaned into vaulted pyramidal towers. They were not the pillars and cupolas that I, in a similar mood, had seen around me on a night ride in Syria but they were like a theater backdrop let down in the air with wings on both sides. It was as if, through long lack of sleep, the tired eye had partly lost its function and, on awaking from the half-dose and fixing itself more carefully to make things out, the failure of accommodation constructed this fantastic scene out of blurred impressions which moved the distant horizon closer without its ever being reached. In spite of the dream which overcame my senses, the instinct of self-preservation reminded me to pay attention to the road when sometimes the horses, which left pretty much to their own resources, seemed uncertain of the way, so now and then I shook the guide who promptly once more began to nod in his saddle again. The safest way to orient oneself in general was by the wind, which always blew in the same direction and, since we were travelling against it, into our faces."

They reached a village called Motufe, where Bastian hoped to get some much needed rest, but after an hour and a half of sleep his guide woke him again. A caravan was just starting out, and they would be safer riding with it, for there was talk of bandits. Aware of the perenially unsettled state of Peru, Bastian pulled himself together and once more got into the saddle. "The sandy character of the road continued but the landscape was now covered with bushes and, on the side toward the sea, the plain ended, changing into the hilly projection of the cape. In the distance, signs of the town of Lambayeque appeared, and suddenly from the side of the road two shots rang out. The caravan was thrown into great confusion, the better mounted rushed off in full gallop toward the city, doubtless with the intention of getting help, to put the best construction on it, the others, with mules, pack animals, women and children, crowded together and did not know whether to go backwards or forwards. A couple of muleteers stood their ground for better or for worse, as they happened to be armed, and thereupon my guide got his double-barreled gun ready. On my side there were a couple of revolver shots, then the bandits decided, when, at close range, they discovered they had to do with foreigners and could make out the weapons, that they had better leave the train unmolested and, after circling a couple of times, disappeared into the bushes from whence they had sprung."

Bastian, among his other activities, found time to help establish the *Zeitschrift für Ethnologie* (*Ethnological Review*) and the *Gesellschaft für Anthropologie Ethnologie und Urgeschichte* (Society for Anthropology, Ethnology, and Prehistory) and to be president of the Geographical Society and a docent in the University of Berlin. In 1886, when the new ethnological museum building was opened, he was the logical man to become its director. The collections in the old Royal Museum had occupied a couple of badly lighted rooms in the rear building. They were arranged geographically, but tribes and peoples were not identified. Bastian filled the whole first floor of the new museum with carefully documented exhibits, a large part of which he himself had collected. He built it into one of the best institutions of its kind in the world, rivaling the Pitt Rivers Museum at Oxford and the Smithsonian Institution in Washington.

Bastian's views on the colonial problem reflected the international aspirations of his country. England had sealed off the east, but Germany could be her friendly rival in the splitting up of Africa. Europe had a historic task to perform: it must not only fulfill the promise of its own culture, but must also link the whole globe in a widespread net of commerce and industry. England and Germany, however, must remain comrades, for theirs was the responsibility of guiding the cultural destinies of the world!

Continuing his field trips, he ranged through Turkistan, India, Java and Bali. In the nineties he came back from Malaysia a living corpse, but his iron constitution pulled him through. In his seventy-seventh year, in 1903, he set off with a German writer, Berthold Mehrer, on his ninth journey, which included Malaysia, Jamaica, and Trinidad. The flesh at last failed the indomitable spirit in Port au Spain. After six days of illness he died there. There was only his friend Mehrer to accompany him to the grave, sitting on the mule-drawn wagon that carried the coffin. The German consul turned up late, apologizing for having missed the lonely ceremony.

Bastian, for all the prolix abstraction of his style and the lack of order in his thinking, was a man of remarkable insights. He is considered the father of German ethnology. Tylor knew him, respected him, and wrote that whenever he checked on Bastian's facts they generally proved to be reliable. His theory of elementary ideas and the essential unity of mankind paralleled that of the Darwinists.

These elementary ideas seemed to arise spontaneously everywhere; they could be borrowed and modified, but they were limited—were, in fact, "of an appalling monotony." The invention of the fire drill, stone scrapers and axes, forms such as exogamy, the concept of personified nature and of the soul—such basic human achievements were universal. It was impossible to discover their origin because the modern mind also was dominated by the basic concepts. They were metaphysical entities akin to Platonic ideas. Bastian stated that the problem of ethnology was to study the process by which these ideas were modified and developed into higher cultural forms in various specific areas. This doctrine of "geological provinces" is the germ of much ethnological thinking today, in which they are called "cultural areas." According to Bastian, each geographical area produced a specific physical and emotional form, shaped by environment. Contacts and interchanges between cultures then modified the forms of thought which had been molded by environment. Diffusionism, or the geographical approach, was a needed correction to the kind of theory which made it seem (by assembling facts out of context) that man had simply climbed up the cultural ladder by taking thought. It pointed to careful comparative studies of cultures as a whole. Civilization was, therefore, the product of an infinite number of mixtures, exchanges, and modifications; some variations survived and some died out. It was a conception that could include Darwin's hypothesis, and it paralleled Tylor's more precisely formulated scheme of religious development.

Bastian ranks as one of the truly great figures in the story of ethnology because his insights foreshadowed methods of study which are still valid.

Chapter 26

THE HIGHER TOLERANCE
Concerning Franz Boas (Part II)

■ During 1886, Franz Boas's apprentice year as Bastian's employee in the heavy-columned baroque building on Königgratzer Street in Berlin, he learned a good deal of the master's methods of organizing exhibits. But the young ethnologist had been smitten with a love of the far north which was never to leave him. After such an adventure it was hard to settle down. Bastian himself was a modest, kindly man without pomposity, but German intellectual circles were formal and full of petty protocol. Boas, from his earliest years, was a rebel. He was also a tough-minded materialist. The strain of mysticism in Bastian must have been uncongenial to the younger man.

On the other hand, Bastian could not fail to sympathize with the attraction that field work had for his restless subordinate. That winter a party of Bella Coola Indians from British Columbia was brought to Berlin and "exhibited." It was enough to touch off Boas's enthusiasm. He studied all the material dealing with these Indians in the museum and wrote an article on them.

Finally the pull of the north became too strong to resist. He presented a plan to Bastian, who was always anxious to get new material for exhibition. Boas was to obtain enough specimens to cover the cost of his trip to Canada, for which the museum would pay.

He spent some months in Canada and returned, in 1887, by way of New York. It was a turning-point in his life. He got a new job, a new country, and a wife.

He walked into the office of the publication *Science* intending to arrange for the publication of some articles and stayed to become an editor. The salary was small, but he augmented it by producing numerous articles. It enabled him to marry Mary Krackowiser, whom he had met once before in Germany. Her family, revolutionaries in 1848, had emigrated to America to escape imprisonment.

Circumstances had all worked together for Boas. It seemed to him that the new world offered a congenial atmosphere for an individualist like himself. There was another good reason for emigrating to America. Boas had become profoundly interested in that group of Indians which lived on the northwest coast of Canada and included the Kwakiutl, a society remarkable for its artistic and literary achievements. This area of culture was to be the object of Boas's major concentration for the rest of his life. Since his work lay in North America, he decided to become an American citizen.

In 1888 Boas published his classic treatise on the Central Arctic Eskimo, embodying all his researches during his trip to the Cumberland peninsula. The same year, after another trip north, he went to Cleveland to attend a meeting of the American Association for the Advancement of Science, and on the train he shared a seat with a scholarly gentleman with whom he began a conversation. As the train reached the Cleveland station, his seatmate offered him a teaching post in Clark University at Worcester, Massachusetts.

His traveling companion was G. Stanley Hall, founder of the *American Journal of Psychology*, one of the first American scholars to take an interest in the new doctrine of psychoanalysis. Hall had been given the task of organizing the new university at Worcester and was to be its first president.

Boas taught at Worcester for four years. All his life, however, he was impatient of administrative restrictions when he felt they were getting in the way of science. Boas granted to A. F. Chamberlain the first Ph.D. in Anthropology ever given in America. Chamberlain replaced Boas in Clark University when the latter disagreed with its head and left in 1892.

That same year he worked for the Chicago Exposition and became a curator of the Field Museum, which grew out of it. Here the combative Boas led a revolt of the staff against the trustees and once again parted company with his means of livelihood. Fortunately, he had friends in scientific circles. James Cattel, the psychologist, saw to it that he was appointed lecturer in physical anthropology in Columbia University, and his former employer in the Chicago Exposition helped him to the post of assistant curator in the Museum of Natural History of New York City. He became professor of anthropology in 1899 and curator of ethnology in 1901. During this time he had organized the Jesup expedition to the northwest. Boas and Livingston Farrand of Columbia University co-operated with several Canadian scientists, who worked under the auspices of the British Association for the Advancement of Science. The ethnologists rode through the glacial valleys of coastal Canada, taking physical measurements of the Bella Coolas, the Kwakiutl, the Cholcotin, and the Salish Indians. Boas also investigated the art of the Haidas and studied the mythology of all these groups.

Boas had written to the Russian Academy of Sciences, suggesting that the Russians work in the neighboring areas in Siberia to establish, if possible, correlations between the American Indians and their Asian neighbors. The Russian Academy replied that two exiled revolutionists, during their enforced stay in Siberia, had been studying the native tribes. When their work was published, the Czar's government finally released them. One of these men, Waldemar Bogoras, remained in his native country and became a famous Bolshevik. The other, Waldemar Jochelson, emigrated to America and ended his career in New York. The results of this international approach to anthropology helped document the route that ancient man must have taken across the Bering Strait and the Aleutian Islands into North America.

As a museum curator Boas profited from his work with Bastian. The traditional arrangement had been evolutionary. Weapons, utensils, and house models from all over the world were placed in a series in order of their complexity. Boas, as in the Northwest Coast hall, displayed all the specimens from allied tribes within one area to demonstrate regional unity, a concept that reinforced the culture-area approach.

Boas as a teacher was remarkable for his indifference to conventional academic standards. If he thought a man was capable, he granted him a degree. One student, A. L. Kroeber, described a pleasant hour of discussion around a table with Farrand, Cattel, Nicholas Murray Butler, and Boas, at the end of which Boas told him there was a lot of reading he needed to do and passed him. Boas was more concerned with the study of method than with imparting information.

During his career he investigated ten languages thoroughly and made partial studies of thirteen others. His first seminars took place around the family dining-table at his home. An archeologist, a teacher or two, and a stray drunk made up the group. The latter soon left, for after an evening of Chinook or Eskimo he found it necessary to make for the nearest bar and absorb several quarts of beer.

Boas was especially fond of his girl students at Barnard. When a friend spoke disdainfully of some ludicrous example of their stupidity, he said: "Well, they're young." "Yes, they're *young*, all right," was the sarcastic reply. Boas smiled and murmured: "*Aber das ist kein fehler*." ("But that's no defect.")

In 1905 he departed from the museum following a dispute over a question of jurisdiction. From then on he devoted himself to teaching and research. He had a low opinion of archeology at the turn of the century. "If a man finds a pot, he is an archeologist; if two, he is a great archeologist; if three, he is a renowned archeologist," he used to say. Nevertheless, in 1910 he founded the International School of American Archeology and Ethnology in Mexico and went south himself to help work out the three major sequences of culture in the Valley of Mexico. When he stopped off at the small village of Teul, he set about collecting remnants of the almost forgotten language of the region. To reach the Indians from the back-country districts, he took the place of the milkseller in the market at dawn.

His Spanish was good enough for him to lecture at the University of Mexico while he continued archeological investigations. On Sundays he and his assistant met in the outskirts of the city and tramped about, visiting the ruins in the suburbs. The assistant, being young, grew restive after some weeks of this rigid regimen. When he was invited to a Sunday picnic, he said to his taskmaster: "Dr. Boas, if you don't especially need me, I'd like to take tomorrow off." The intransigeant Boas looked at him sternly. "Dr. Mason," he said, "it isn't a question of whether I need you, but whether you need me."

When the First World War broke out, he had been in America for twenty-eight years. He had kept in touch with his old universities and had written occasionally for German publications. His emotional ties were with Germany, not with the Allies, but his position was strictly intellectual and pacifist. In 1917, when a blind hysterical patriotism resulted in a committee to investigate the loyalty of the Columbia faculty, he read a paper to his students defining his position. "I dare say if all nations cultivated the ideals of equal rights of all members of mankind by emotional means such as are now used to develop passionate patriotism, much of the mutual hatred, distrust, and disrespect would disappear." Boas, who was familiar with widely different types of cultures, respected them all. Like Bastian, he was impressed by the essential unity of man, and his ethnological experience had made him a stanch internationalist. He thought the patriotic emotion instilled into the young the world over was one of the most serious faults of the educational system. But he was wise enough, and well enough versed in the strength of emotional habits, to remark dispassionately: "Patriots are morally wrong just as little as the persecutors of witchcraft, who merely followed out their honest convictions and, much as we may like to convert them, there is no justice in impugning their moral character."

Although Boas stuck to his point of view, no effort was made to attack him as a teacher. His international ideals and his scientifically reasoned humanitarian point of view were already fully developed.

Boas's importance in the history of cultural anthropology (aside from his contributions to the physical branch of the science) is attested by the brilliance of his students, who never became a school (he would have been the last man to wish it) but who were formed by his habits of mind. Alexander Goldenweiser, Ruth Benedict, A. L. Kroeber, Margaret Mead, Edward Sapir, Robert Lowie, and Melville Herskovits are a few of the well-known names. Clark Wissler, Herbert Spinden, and Elsie Clews Parsons were also associated with his circle.

Aside from his exhaustive studies of the Eskimos and the Kwakiutl, his creative skepticism went far toward bringing a strict scientific spirit into a study that had been perilously infiltrated by literary dilettantism. Boas would never accept a theory, no matter how attractive and plausible, if any guesswork was necessary to sustain it. He insisted on rigid self-discipline, on the necessity of limiting research to problems that could be solved by observed facts. He raised field work to a more scientific level, taking down biographies of natives and recording their literature and beliefs by means of phonetic texts. Above all, he tried to penetrate the folkways of his primitives by putting aside all cultural bias. Previously, the European investigator had cultivated a condescending view-

Kwakiutl totem pole.

point toward his humble informant's culture; the civilized way of life was the standard of reference. Boas tried to see the Northwest Coast Indian culture as simply another form of human achievement, valid in its own way. The word *functionalist* has been used to mean the study of interrelations of all of the institutions of a group. Boas was putting this method into practice decades before it acquired a name.

Although he respected the fecundating influence of such great pioneer theorists as Tylor, Morgan, and Bastian and acknowledged a sense of continuity in tradition, he felt skeptical about the possibility of discovering general ethnological laws. "I am far from claiming that no general laws relating to the growth of culture exist, whatever they may be, they are in every particular case overlaid by a mass of accidents that were probably much more potent in the actual happenings than the general laws." Boas was really taking a position not far from that of the novelist.

It was this sense of the complexity of life which sustained his critical attitude and prevented him from accepting any of the popular oversimplifications of his time. Toward Freudian doctrines he had mixed feelings. On the one hand, he felt that the insistence of Freud on the importance of childhood experienced was valuable. It threw a new light on traits that had wrongly been considered a part of basic human nature. On the other hand, the approach to native psychology in the light of modern neuroses did not convince him. On the whole, he felt, the psychoanalyst was far too one-sided.

Toward the economic determinism of the Marxists he was equally skeptical. Hunting and fishing tribes with exactly the same economic forms differed radically in custom and belief. He felt that differences in energy or temperament could in turn affect the character of economic life. Society was the result of interacting forces. To select the economic one as the sole creative drive was, he felt, incorrect. Attitudes toward nature which shaped belief also affected economic behavior. As he saw it, invention, art, religion, and economic conditions influenced one another.

Boas did not, however, reject historical investigation when it was combined with the study of diffusion. We have seen his interpretation of designs in primitive art to which meanings were added by association. Toward myths he took a similar viewpoint. The basic element was not the *meaning* but the *plot*. The same plot, sufficiently detailed to indicate that it had not been invented more than once, could occur over wide areas with different meanings assigned to it. The story of a woman who gave birth to a litter of dogs, among the Eskimos, explained the origin of the Europeans (Eskimo humor, no doubt); in South Alaska it was the origin of the Milky Way, the rainbow, and thunderstorms. On Vancouver Island it explained some reefs in the sea; in the interior of British Columbia, the origin of a taboo; among the Blackfoot Indians, the origin of the Dog Society; among the Arapaho, why the dog is friend to man.

Some culture traits were probably ancient and universal, such as domestication of the dog, which must have taken place before the races of northeastern Asia and America separated. The dog was probably also taken along with early man to Australia. On the other hand, dissemination of tobacco and cassava could be traced; they reached Africa after the European discovery of America, but are now an intrinsic part of African culture.

Boas did not wholly accept Bastian's doctrine of elementary ideas. There were groups of ideas and activities which always existed interconnected, he felt, but their relationship was always in a state of flux. The anthropologist could investigate these relationships concretely from various points of view and build more general theories when the foundation was completely solid.

Boas's stamina and drive as a field worker were exceptional. When he was nearly seventy, he went on another trip to the Northwest Coast with two of his graduate students. The scientists found lodgings several miles from the encampment of Indians. Every day after breakfast he and the students walked to the Indian village, walked home for lunch, and then trudged off again for the afternoon session.

When Boas was obliged to undergo an operation for a cancer of the face in 1914 which resulted in a stiffening of the muscles and distortion of the cheek, A. S. Goldenweiser, visiting him in a New York hospital, found him practicing Kwakiutl phonetics, forcing his half-paralyzed mouth to obey him.

Between the two world wars the philosophy of racism, which had always found a foothold in the United States because of the two minorities, the Indians and the Negroes, received a new impetus from efforts to limit immigration. Popular authors and even Henry Fairfield Osborn, paleontologist and head of the Museum of Natural History, wrote articles in defense of Aryan supremacy, the Aryan now being christened "Nordic."

For the first time anthropology, which had remained a fairly obscure science, met the challenge and began to play a practical role in everyday life. Boas used his great erudition to combat what he considered dangerous and unscientific propaganda. When, with the rise of Hitler in the thirties, the doctrines of Aryan purity were used to justify persecution of a minority, he threw all of his weight into the struggle.

In 1931, when he received an honorary doctorate in medicine

from the University of Kiel, he spoke on "Race and Culture." In 1933 he published an open letter to Hindenburg protesting the elevation of Hitler to power. His paper *Aryans and Non-Aryans* was printed on thin paper and distributed by the underground. He resigned from his honorary membership in the Munich Academy of Science and publicly denounced a German anthropologist who sent him a communication that ended "Heil Hitler." In his eighties he accepted official positions in organizations that fought Nazism; he spoke over the radio and wrote ceaselessly, using all of his scholarship and prestige to denounce the degradation of the human spirit taking place in the land of his birth. Up to the end of his life he also championed academic freedom, civil liberties, and the defense of minority rights. On December 21, 1943, at a luncheon for Paul Rivet, head of the Musée de l'Homme of Paris, the talk ran on racism. Boas had just expressed himself strongly on the need for eternal vigilance against it when he fell over dead from a heart attack, fighting for the truth with his last breath.

Fearless and stubborn in the domain of scientific accuracy, Boas was nevertheless a sensitive and emotional man. The year before his death he was summering near Falls Village, Connecticut, where the Gordon String Quartet was giving a series of concerts. Boas asked to sit in on a rehearsal of one of his favorite Schubert quartets. When it was over, Jacques Gordon noticed that there were tears in his eyes. "Did we play *that* well?" Gordon inquired. "You played well," Boas said, then paused. "It just came over me that I shall never hear this music again."

Boas's closely reasoned critique of racism is an important contribution to the thinking of our time. He defined racism as the unproved assumption "that the aptitude of the European is the highest, his physical and mental type is also the highest, and every deviation from the white type necessarily represents a lower feature."

It was noticeable that most of the arguments for this point of view came from biologists or physical anthropologists. The great students of culture, Tylor, Bastian, Morgan, and Frazer, were so impressed by cultural likenesses that they never even thought in terms of race. Physical anthropologists such as Samuel Morton, a contemporary of Louis Agassiz, labeled the Indian "mentally slow, cruel and revengeful," the Negro "joyous and indolent." The notion that the European was the furthest removed from the animal, however, did not survive scrutiny. It could be granted that the European had the largest brain mass (modern scientists agree that the size of the brain is not correlated with intelligence), but the hairlessness of the Mongol was less animal than the European beard. The red lip, specifically human, was more developed in the Negro, and in some Negro tribes the length of limb was also further removed from the lower mammals.

Some of the psychological measurers had thought they could distinguish levels of racial intelligence by mechanical testing. The behaviorists and Freudians, however, were able to show how greatly basic aptitudes were modified by conditioning and experience.

What actually was race? Did the conception mean anything? It was commonly thought of as identical with nationality. But there were no pure nationalities. The French were a mixture of Teutonic, Mediterranean, and Celtic peoples; the Germans, of Teutonic, some Mediterranean, and some Slavic. The Spanish were a mixture of Basque, Teutonic, and Moor. Even the Jews, so often set apart racially, were a mixed people composed of blue-eyed Kurds, the tall-headed, narrow-nosed Armenian stock of Asia Minor, and Arabs with long, low heads and delicate features.

If, on the other hand, race was to be equated with physical type, even the three large divisions of Mongol, Negro, and Aryan varied tremendously: some people of African culture had yellowish skins, and some Indian Aryans were so dark-skinned that the average westerner classified them as colored. There were Chinese as white-skinned as Europeans.

Was a race, then, all those peoples speaking one language or one type of language? The history of language showed that speech was never a constant thing, but was continually modified by borrowing and assimilation. English was a mixture of Anglo-Saxon and Norman French. Investigation showed also that the major physical types now known must have been differentiated long before any of the families of speech now extant had acquired their specific character.

What, then, was race if physical type, intelligence, language, and culture could not be correlated?

The racist replied it was clear from history that peoples in certain areas were less gifted and less able to develop advanced civilizations than others. This, too, was a specious argument, based on a few hundred years of European domination. When a hundred thousand years or so of man's existence was taken into account, the picture was quite different. Between 2000 and 3000 B.C., when Egypt had a high artistic and technical civilization, the Europeans were a backward Stone Age people with no technology or architecture, obviously unable to progress. Ancient Peru had developed a great culture, the equal of the Babylonian or Sumerian civilizations. The fact that it was a few thousand years later in history had no meaning. In the course of a hundred thousand years, accidental or environmental features could account for time lags.

Negroes were often accused of being unable to assimilate the elements of a higher culture. But in the Middle Ages a high type of civilization developed in the Sudan, where the Mohammedans mingled with the Africans on an equal basis. When Negroes encountered the whites in the nineteenth century, after long isolation, they were weakened by European diseases, their economies were destroyed by an alien technical civilization, and discrimination prevented any racial mingling and assimilation of culture.

The Japanese, whose feudal society had long remained static, showed in recent decades that they were able to advance when they borrowed and adapted western science.

The concept of race with fixed characteristics was therefore a metaphysical idea born of emotional attitudes. In 1914, when Boas was lecturing in California, a student came up to him after a lecture to announce that the anthropologist had convinced him there was no such thing as racial integrity. As they were walking away from the lecture hall, the boy exclaimed passionately: "How I hate these Japanese! It makes my blood boil to see them on our farms, in our cities!"

About the same time Boas, on a train passing through Oregon, made the acquaintance of a fellow passenger. The latter said: "Would you believe it, there is not a single white man in the lumber industry." "What are they?" Boas asked. "They are all Swedes and Norwegians."

In 1897 he was traveling in British Columbia and camped near an isolated Indian home. The Indian, in the course of conversation, remarked: "The Jews are bad people. They cheat us Indians." "Have you ever seen a Jew?" Boas asked. "No, but that's what they say."

"The tendency to value our own form of civilization as higher, not as dearer to our hearts, than that of the whole rest of mankind is the same as that which prompts the actions of primitive man who considers every stranger his enemy, and who is not satisfied until the enemy is killed," wrote Boas.

Each group, religious, national, class, or cultural, was unfortunately prone to rationalize in this way. Racism, which arose as a defense of colonial conquest and in modern times became a political instrument, was worse than other such group concepts because, while other groupings were subject to change, the racist theory attempted to support discrimination biologically and to make it permanent.

Boas, contemplating modern society from the point of view of the primitive, had some sobering things to say about the concept of evolution. *Technical advance* from the simple to the complex could be shown. On the other hand, a man's participation in a variety of cultural activities was much greater among primitives. Some primitive languages were far more complex than modern ones, and the rhythms of primitive music were often so subtly intricate that a modern musician could scarcely grasp them.

Westermarck had tried to show the evolution of moral ideas. Said Boas: "There is no evolution of moral ideas. . . . The vices we know: lying, theft, murder, rape, are always discountenanced in the life of equals in a closed society." Complete absence of a moral attitude in dealing with outsiders, the double ethical standard that began with the feuds between clans, continued to the present. There was one ray of light—the fact that groups which found it convenient to live at peace and practice their internal standards of ethics toward one another were getting larger. Eventually, for purely practical reasons, the world might have to scrap anagonisms that led to war.

It looked as though the position of women had improved. The reduction of childbirth, made possible by the decrease in infant mortality, had freed modern woman for a more creative life, in contrast to that of the primitive woman tied to continual rearing of offspring.

Then, too, "the history of civilization demonstrates that the extent to which the status of a person is determined by birth, or by some later voluntary or enforced act has been losing force. . . . In this sense the freedom of the individual has been increasing."

All in all, the Victorian optimism concerning man's triumphant climb toward the angels had to be tempered with doubtful hope.

Boas held that anthropology could not become an exact enough science to predict the course of society, but it could serve as a valuable counselor and help free the modern mind from traditional fetters.

"The scientist who is searching for truth and adding by his work to the fund of knowledge *must be freed from all outer coercion* . . . and it is his duty to free himself as far as humanly possible of prejudice and bias."

Boas had tried to do this, and he wrote warningly: "It is somewhat difficult for us to recognize that the value which we attribute to our own civilization is due to the fact that we participate in this civilization and that it has been controlling all our actions from the time of our birth. . . . The general theory of valuation of human activities, as developed by anthropological research, teaches us a higher tolerance than the one we now profess."

Tylor, the pioneer, would have reached across a century to clasp his hand.

Chapter 27

POSEIDON'S CASTLE

Concerning Leo Frobenius

■ The story of Franz Boas has led us to German anthropology and the preoccupation with the spread of culture, that school of anthropology known as *diffusionism*. It must be pointed out, however, that E. B. Tylor had picked up a hint of this process from the accounts of the Conquest of Mexico.

When the Spaniards visited Moctezuma's court they found that one of the chief amusements of the courtiers was a game called Patolli, which the emperor himself used to watch. The board was marked on a palm mat, or *petate*. It consisted of a cross, the arms of which were divided into rows of squares on which counters were placed. The counters were moved up and down the arms of the cross, circumnavigating the board, and there were rules for taking them. The moves were controlled by throwing a group of lots. Sometimes these lots were merely two-sided. In this case, scoring was determined by a rough estimate of the laws of chance, all heads or all tails being the highest possible combinations. At other times the lots were four beans with various numbers of dots upon them, very much like the modern dice. The game was, of course, identical in principle with the modern Parcheesi.

Patolli was used as a gambling game by the wealthy Aztecs, who wagered gold and jewels with the same compulsiveness as the addicts at Monte Carlo. There was even a god of luck, Macuilxochtl, who was also the god of the tavern (appropriately enough, the name meant "five roses"). The Aztecs literally prayed for luck, burning copal before the elusive little deity.

After the conquest the Spaniards, with their usual summariness, burned the petate mats and abolished Patolli as conducive to idolatry.

In 1878 Tylor, who managed to anticipate almost every current of anthropology, wrote a paper pointing out the similarity between the Hindu game of Pachisi (our Parcheesi) and Patolli. In 1898, on the basis of an illustration in one of the Spanish chronicles, he elaborated the similarity. There was no doubt that Patolli had existed in America before the conquest. Did this mean that there had been a connection with Asia in the relatively recent past?

Other scholars argued that the game must have been invented independently on the two continents.

Thus a little game of chance touched off a new direction in ethnological thinking and a controversy that lasted for decades.

Classic evolutionary ethnology had been vertical scholarship, a historical survey moving from the remote past to the present. The question of diffusion initiated horizontal ethnology, the study of the spread of culture over the earth's surface.

What test can we use, what standards of similarity would prove the connection between a culture trait in one civilization and analagous traits in other civilizations, asked Tylor?

Let us divide the phenomenon into its elements. If there are a number of these, the chances are high that there is a connection. Pachisi and Patolli had in common divining by lot, the result based on the laws of chance. In both the process was used to wager; in both there was a counting-board, with rules for moving and taking the counters. Tylor was inclined to believe that Pachisi and Patolli were related.

It remained for the geographically minded Germans to formulate a diffusionist school.

Ratzel, the geographer, wrote on the spread of the African bow and arrow in 1887, and in 1891 he elaborated his ideas still further.

There were several forms of bow whose spread could be traced like that of a plant or animal. The bow was the signature of a folk group. As it was not generally an article of trade, it indicated the movement of peoples. The northern form of the bow was Asiatic, and this accorded with the Islamic Arab influence that penetrated downward into the continent. On the other hand, the west-coast bow was very similar to that used in New Guinea and to that of the Negritos of Luzon.

The new trend of thinking was in accord with the current of the times, strengthened by the growing belief that the interpretative methods of Morgan, Tylor, and Bastian had outlived their usefulness.

In 1895 the extraordinary prehistoric rock pictures of men and animals (first discovered in the caves of Spain in 1868) were finally recognized as authentic by the scientific world. A twenty-five-year-old German student of anthropology was fascinated by them. The official view, expressed by Bastian, was that if this was the work of Stone Age man, the people who made them had been limited to Europe and had been swept away by the Ice Age.

Leo Frobenius, the anthropology student (1873–1938), was the son of a retired Berlin army officer. For a time he worked on a farm. In the late eighties he apprenticed himself to an exporting firm in Bremen and began to study ethnology at night. The young man was highly imaginative, a sensitive art critic, and bursting with ideas. The ships that steamed in and out of the Bremen harbor stopped at African ports. Sometimes they brought back natives from that relatively unknown continent. Frobenius frequented the docks, talked to travelers, and read Bastian's books, and gradually the dark continent began to fascinate him. It became an obsession. He dreamed of finding there the answer to the great questions of cultural development.

It seemed to him that the culture of the Stone Age which had produced the famous rock pictures might well have spread all over the southern continent. Here, where no icecap had reached, what undreamed-of evidence of early civilization might still be found!

By 1893 he succeeded in getting a position as an assistant in science in the Bremen Municipal Museum of Commerce and Primitive Peoples. (The practical Germans combined ethnology with trade.) Here he studied with Heinrich Schurtz, who, as we have seen, wrote the definitive treatise on primitive men's clubs. Trained by Ratzel at Leipzig, Schurtz became an assistant at the Bremen Museum 1893 and stayed there the rest of his life. Although his own writing was evolutionist, he knew Ratzel's methods and formed a link between the two schools.

Frobenius, making use of all available published material and the collections of the museum, produced a preliminary study, *Afrikanische Kultur* (*African Culture*), in 1898. In it he followed the direction initiated by Ratzel. Wrote Frobenius: " 'The West Africans and the Papuan natives of New Guinea have inherited the same drum,' says one. 'No,' answers another and reddens with rage, 'they both invented them.' " Such controversies were fruitless without better methods of study. To Ratzel's mapping of the spread of different types of the bow Frobenius added shields, knives, throwing-weapons, axes, musical instruments, styles of hut. This was the "criterion of quantity."

His results strengthened the earlier surmise. The northern area and part of the Congo showed an Asiatic influence, while South Africa had a more indigenous style that was "a weaker repetition of the Asian melody." The west-coast culture was similar to the Negrito-Malayan.

Frobenius also suggested that by examining materials it would be possible to determine a point of origin. The lower Indian or Oceanian culture, being insular, used shells for axblades. In Africa the indigenous materials were antelope horn and elephant tusk. But in certain African axes made of iron the pattern of the shell blade was still discernible.

It was clear that the new method of comparison could also be applied to the study of culture sequences, an investigation that overlapped into archeology. (We have seen that Boas was led into the study of culture sequences in Mexico.)

Frobenius was indeed more of an archeologist in temperament than an anthropologist. The story of his adventures leads in and out of the two fields. While making his library study of African origins, he continued to haunt the Bremen docks. By now he was determined to get to Africa. Having no money for travel, he thought of interviewing whatever stray Africans he could find. In the popular mind Negroes were examples of "degenerate bestiality" and Africa had no history of ancient culture of any importance before the Islamic invasion. Frobenius, still thinking of the rock pictures, was convinced that this conception was absolutely wrong.

Through his exporting contacts he arranged to meet some Negroes from the Congo. To his dismay, the first specimen, John, was not from the Congo but from Nigeria. However, John said that there were five other Negroes on board his freighter. Frobenius ran to the ship and penetrated its oily, reeking forecastle. Here he was told that the others had gone ashore. Frobenius panted after his living exhibits and ran them down in a grimy public house. Here, amid the din of the eating-house, with sea chanties roared in his ears, he found James, a Roman Catholic, who spoke only French.

In response to his questions about African ruins or historical tradition, the badgered black could only respond helplessly: *"Tres vieux, tres vieux."*

The Negroes immediately demanded brandy, which Frobenius paid for. In the days that followed, the culture historian pursued his drunken quarry, paying for brandy and getting nowhere. Finally, when he was about to give up, John, the Nigerian from Lagos, said hopefully: "In my country is every old-time man big stone." Frobenius told him not to talk nonsense, but the boy repeated the phrase and added the names of several cities. Frobenius dismissed the whole affair. Years later, when he made his great discoveries, he realized that he had missed an important clue, the very signpost he had been looking for.

In the years that followed, Frobenius bombarded the old master Bastian with letters, proposals, and schemes for investigation, urging the need for exploration of the Yoruba territory. Some hints that interesting bronze sculptures were to be found at Benin had reached him, and he wanted to raise five thousand dollars for an expedition. Bastian replied with indulgent disbelief and treated the youthful enthusiast to a non-stop sentence on the unreliability of tradition. He agreed that investigation was a good thing, but saw no means of raising the money. Frobenius began to develop a sense of persecution. He was filled with the desperation of a man defending a lost cause.

In 1898 the British occupied the kingdom of Benin in Nigeria. It had been isolated from European contacts for several generations. Part of the plunder consisted of some unusual bronze sculpture, completely African in style. The character of the dress and weapons indicated, according to Professor von Luschan, Frobenius's employer, that they dated from the sixteenth or seventeenth century. No evidence of bronze-casting had been discovered previously in Africa outside the Islamic areas. Bastian's Berlin Museum paid over five thousand dollars to obtain some of these specimens.

Where did the tradition of bronze-casting come from? The sculptures were evidence that African history was more complicated than had been thought.

It is interesting to note how the story of diffusionism runs parallel with the German colonial interest in Africa, just as American penetration of the new world founded the study of the American native races and the British acquisition of Australia set off Australian ethnology.

Frobenius continued to collect historical traditions from African sailors. At last, in 1904, he extracted some funds from the Hamburg Museum for the collection of specimens and organized the First German Inner-African Exploration Expedition to the Congo. Because travel in Nigeria was more expensive, he had to postpone his visit to Ife, which legends identified as a center of ancient worship.

The pressure of his contract with the museum obliged him to collect as many specimens as he could lay hands on, as cheaply as possible. He brought back eight thousand, sufficiently impressing the authorities so that he was able to get off again next year. This time he had funds from both the Hamburg and Leipzig museums, and the connection between imperialism and anthropology was officially established, for the Imperial Colonial Office also contributed.

On this trip, into French Sudan, he resorted to truly drastic methods to fulfill his commitments. The king of the Mossi was a weak ruler, always in need of money but surrounded by fawning and conspiratorial nobles of whom he was afraid. The sovereign accepted money on condition that Frobenius would steal the ritual objects he wanted from a temple. When all of the palace was asleep, Frobenius and a couple of picked men, mounted on some of the royal stallions, galloped half the night and finally came to a large circular hut. Investigating by candlelight, he discovered scores of beautifully incised seven-foot ceremonial masks along the inner wall. He stole the best of them. At the last minute he came upon a four-foot opening in the cone-shaped adobe mound in the center of the hut. Climbing down a notched tree, he found a series of galleries dug in the earth, filled with bones and potsherds; the ground was dark with sacrificial blood (the blood of human victims, he was told). This catacomb was the tomb of the former king. Frobenius made a sketch, the first record of royal burial in that region, and made off with his purloined prizes.

It was not until 1910 that he had money enough for the trip to Nigeria. His adventures there were destined to increase his sense of persecution to near paranoia.

He seems to have been the victim of his own temperament and of the colonial situation. In 1910 another period of imperialist rivalry was in full swing. The early cycle, which included the Spanish and British discovery of the new world and the Portuguese penetration of Africa, had resulted in monopolist profits for the mother countries and the eventual revolt of the colonists. In the case of Portuguese Angola the project collapsed because of the decay of the mother country. There was a period around the 1860's, during which the British were apostles of free trade, when colonies were thought to be a liability. One of the fruits of the industrial revolution and the rise of capitalism, however, was the increase in funds for investment. Such funds had to be invested in new areas. In addition, there began to be a demand for such tropical products as rubber and coconuts. Conversely, the manufacturing countries needed new markets for their goods. The invention and development of railroads, steamboats, and the telegraph made communication with the far corners of the earth easy. Then, too, it was a period of intense national rivalry, each nation trying to acquire as much power and profit as possible.

Africa was the one great area that had not yet been divided up. A frantic chess game ensued in which Germans, French, Belgians, and Dutch raced to make treaties with uncomprehending savage kings and to plant flags in the blank spaces on the map. Along with the scramble went the pious rationalization that Europe had a duty to bring civilization to the heathen. But, as it happened, nearly every nation was ready to go to war to protect, in Kipling's words, the "new-caught sullen peoples" from its competitors' culture and ideology.

The colony of Nigeria, in particular, had been the prize won by the British in a race with the Germans and French only a couple of decades before. The English and Germans were still jockeying for position in central Africa.

All went well at Lagos. The British governor of southern Nigeria sent letters to Ibadan and Ife which were supposed to pave the way for government co-operation with Frobenius's investigations.

At Ibadan the weaknesses of his own character asserted themselves. He visited a temple of the god Chango and condescended to the priests, happy to display that his knowledge of their god's mythology was greater than their own. He also began to collect ethnological material, which consisted of religious objects. Frobenius had none of the true ethnologist's patience. He did not try to gain the confidence of the people, but merely extracted their possessions by a combination of browbeating and exploitation of greed. Indeed, he became irritated and petulant when the wealthier members of a group tried to prevent the sale of ritual objects by their pauper relatives.

Frobenius bought his way into the Ogboni League, a secret society that was suspected of ritual murder. He paid a Yoruban to go through the ceremony as his stand-in while he looked on. Initiation took place in the light of leaping bonfires while a crowd, naked to the waist, watched the initiate crawl on his face to the metal idol, which dripped with the blood of slaughtered ducks (a substitute for human blood), and pick up a bean with his lips. At the climax the group shouted "*Hecqua!*"

Later, when a dismembered corpse was found near the market place, he told the authorities what he knew of the secret society and apparently also blackmailed the members of the society to tell him more, playing one side against the other!

Frobenius was ecstatic over the magnificence of Africa's past and its ancient religions, and he ardently defended the Negroes as "culture-bearers." Yet he seems to have had nothing but contempt for the living members of the race. He particularly hated the semi-civilized, whom he called "trouser niggers." His book abounds in complaints against "humanitarianism," soft treatment of the natives brought about by the British missionaries.

Such a statement as "The godlike fortress of the sixteen-membered Ifa religion is enthroned, a solitary and sumptuous castle on a hill, rearing its front high above the lower levels of African spiritual abasement, and its shining light illuminates the spreading plains of the continent" is difficult to reconcile with his remarks on the fate of San Salvador, whose decay we have already seen in Bastian's description. "Discovered as a genuine African city toward the end of the fifteenth century," he wrote, "it had in the sixteenth century become the center of a Christian realm under the influence of Portugal and the church whose pomp was proverbial in Europe for a time and yet its dignitaries were only native negroes. Black bishops, robed in costly vestments, preached their sermons in a mighty cathedral. Dukes, Princes, and Noblemen habited in the fashion of that day, the short Spanish mantle on their shoulders and the sword upon their thighs, followed in the emperor's train. A century goes by . . . a second century goes by— naught but miserable ruins. And why? . . . Because the productive capacity of those races had been put too high . . . because the racial problem had been left unrecognized. The phlegmatic black had sucked up the strength and will power of the white man's race—the white man's racial energy had deliquesced into 'niggerdom.' "

This is indeed a far cry from "the higher tolerance." To add to his passionate confusion, when he requested that the British authorities furnish him with bearers to Ife, he was met with hostile indifference. The Resident was away. The order had only said "if possible." There was intrigue going on, but he could not put his finger on it. His man Bida, one of the few Negroes for whom he had a good word to say, finally got the bearers. After a few days' march they arrived at Ife, the holy city from which he expected so much. They passed through a ruined wall that had once surrounded it and reached the palace of the Oni, or local king.

"We stood before the portals of a castle in the middle of an enormous square. I sent my man, Bida, ahead to announce us and made my horse climb the high flight of steps and rode through the delicately carved doorway of the entrance, across the courtyard and through the dilapidated colonnades with my companions. It was like an enchanted castle. It was so large and noble in design, so superbly pure, despite its broken lines, its mouldering decay, and the sordid exterior it now presents. We did not meet a single soul. At last we came to where there were some people and there, clad in a gorgeous robe of bright green silk, a magnificent tiara on his brow and shaded by a huge silken canopy, the Oni, head of the Holy City of Ife's hierarchy, advanced to meet us with a great crowd."

The Oni, a wiry, wrinkled, evasive little man, had had no word of Frobenius's coming. He gave him a bungalow to live in, however, and made him formally welcome.

The hostile influences were still at work. One of the Oni's secretaries suspiciously asked Frobenius if he really had any right to travel in the Oni's kingdom. The secretary said he had a permit for two Frenchmen. Frobenius pointed out that he was German and refused to argue. Instead, he began his usual trade in ethnological specimens. Nothing very old or interesting turned up, and he

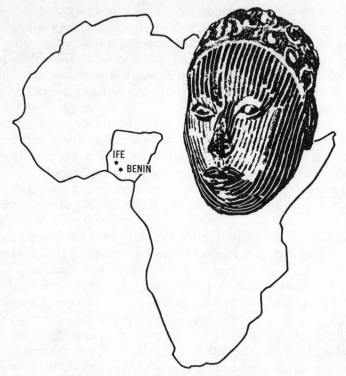

Map showing location of Benin and Ife. A head from Ife.

found that the press of people who crowded into the bungalow quite often stole back the specimens he had bought. The natives never took any of his European possessions, but this did not make him any happier.

The Oni ceremoniously conducted him to a park where there was a large head of a fish or crocodile carved out of quartz. When asked to display other ancient objects, the ruler smiled slyly and said there was nothing more—they had all been stolen by the

British. Frobenius argued and pleaded. Once more he was being persecuted. It seems never to have occurred to him that there was no good reason why the head of the Ife religion should be willing to hand over traditional religious objects to an importunate and impatient foreigner.

At any rate, the harried German ascribed it all to the meanness and craftiness of the African character. All the natives did was make empty promises. How they had degenerated since the old days!

After more audiences and polite evasions, the Oni with much mystery announced that he would show him the holy of holies. Frobenius, all on edge, was finally shown a crude modern wooden idol. He laughed loudly and told the Oni that it was a good joke but not what he wanted. In spite of all the obstacles, he never wavered in his faith that there was a continuity between the current religion and the ancient past and that the wily natives were hiding wonderful things from him. He clung to a story that the forebears of the natives had descended into the ground and turned into stone.

One day he was sent to an old priest who lived in a palm hut. The latter could show him only crude modern soapstone objects. (Actually, the modern idols were revered and just as holy as anything old, a fact Frobenius apparently never realized.) While chatting with the priest and offering him palm wine, the ethnologist suddenly noticed some fragments of a terra-cotta head lying half buried in the ground. He scratched them up. At last his hopes were rewarded. When he put them together, there was no doubt that the head was of a completely unique style. It showed a sophisticated craftsmanship and a power of idealization which could be compared to those of the Greeks. Nothing like it had ever been found in Africa.

Frobenius was in a state of high excitement. His man, Bida, redoubled his efforts. Frobenius was sure the Ifians knew where other objects were buried. He kept offering larger sums for something similar. Presently another head just as fine was offered—this time carved in granite!

"In my country is every old-time man big stone. . . ."

Before money could change hands, another message came saying the head had been offered for sale by mistake, and it was snatched away while the ethnologist gritted his teeth in desperation.

He obtained leave from the Oni to dig in the almost forgotten site of a near-by town, Modeke. Here he began to uncover excellent intact terra-cotta heads, a quartz crocodile, and some glass beads. (The manufacture of glass was supposedly unknown in Africa.) At last, after false alarms and much hesitation, he was led to the hut of another old priest. A boy appeared with a bag, and out of it rolled the most beautiful head of all, magnificently cast in bronze. Frobenius was sure that it represented Olokun, the African Poseidon, god of the sea.

He was allowed to buy the head for twenty shillings and a bottle of whisky. The Oni seemed to have no objection, but then, all at once, the hostile influences returned in full force. Somebody had complained to the English Colonial Secretary that Frobenius was wresting antiquities from the natives by force. There was talk of a law prohibiting their removal from the country. A complaint was made to the German consul. Then a messenger arrived and ordered Frobenius to return his finds to the Oni.

Frobenius was undoubtedly the victim of nationalist rivalries, political suspicion, and native intrigue. Police ordered him back to Ife. He quickly hid the best of his finds. British officials arrived, and an investigation ensued. Bida, his headman, was arrested and tortured. The Oni lied blandly. The officials allowed only Ifians to testify and refused to listen to Frobenius. He meanwhile read Goethe's novels to calm his mind. But one day, when some native policemen came poking into his living-quarters with a warrant, he seized a stick and beat them.

The affair ended in confusion, with the loss of a good many of the unfortunate anthropologist's specimens and considerable intensification of his sense of persecution.

He had, however, proved the contention he had held to for so many years. He had unearthed relics of a civilization whose art was nearer to the peaks of Mediterranean culture than anything ever before discovered in Africa.

His interpretation of his find was a combination of diffusionist method and pure romanticism. The culture of Nigeria and the Atlantic shore was older than the Islamic influence from the north or the slight Christian influence in Portuguese Angola. The Ifian religion could be compared only to that of the Etruscans. Glass beads, a certain type of water-storage, and architecture were all similar to the achievements of the Etruscans. The latter could easily have voyaged to the African coast and planted a colony there. Then there was the half-mythical tradition of Atlantis, "the home of Poseidon's posterity, the sea god, by them named Olokun . . . Atlantis whose walls, Solon informs us, held within them Poseidon's castle where there was a wealth of luxuriant vegetation . . . elephants lived there, bronze or brass was won there . . . the natives wore dark blue garments . . ." Like another Schliemann, Frobenius announced: "I have discovered Atlantis!"

Frobenius made many subsequent trips to Africa and in 1930 tried to prove that the custom of killing the king, found in South Africa, was the signature of a culture complex which stemmed from India. Most important of all, he discovered many ancient Bushman rock-paintings which proved that a Stone Age culture had existed in many parts of Africa. Some of the pictures were almost identical in style with those of the Spanish caves.

He founded a fine collection of reproductions of these paintings in the Frankfurt Museum and did more to arouse interest in African culture, past and present, than any scholar before him. In 1932 he obtained a professorship in the University of Frankfurt and became head of its museum in 1935.

An episode which occurred in 1905 throws light on the theory that the ancient cave art had a magical purpose. While traveling in the Congo with several pygmies for guides, he requested that they shoot an antelope for meat. They told him they could not without certain preparations. At dawn of the following day he was able to watch their rites. One of the pygmies drew a picture of an antelope in the earth. Just as the sun's rays fell on it, he shot an arrow into it while his wife stretched her arms to the sun, shouting an incantation. Frobenius was not allowed to photograph the picture. An antelope was then successfully shot with bow and arrow. The pygmies returned, smeared the picture with some of the animal's blood and hair, and then erased it. Without these precautions the blood of the beast would have destroyed them.

Erratic and emotional as Frobenius was, his work on Africa was another step in the study of diffusion. He was followed by the classic exponent of the school, Robert Fritz Graebner.

281

Chapter 28

IN TIME AND SPACE

Concerning Robert Fritz Graebner,

Father Wilhelm Schmidt, Grafton Elliot Smith,

William H. R. Rivers, Clark Wissler,

Robert H. Lowie, Paul Radin, Erland Nordenskjöld

■ In 1899 a young history student with some background in botany applied for a job as assistant in the Berlin Ethnological Museum, then headed by Professor von Luschan, who had been Frobenius's employer in the Bremen Museum. Robert Fritz Graebner (1877–1934) had no training in ethnology, but he needed money. Von Luschan said: "History is no mean preparation for ethnology" and gave him the job. He was assigned to cataloguing exhibits. He became acquainted with artifacts from many different areas and began to observe likenesses and differences. In 1904 he gave a lecture on culture areas of Melanesia to which Frobenius listened and with which he disagreed. Graebner continued to study the collections at his disposal, and in 1906 was called to Cologne to the Rautenstrauch Joest Museum of Ethnology. Later he became professor of ethnology at Bonn. Graebner made himself an expert on the South Seas, although he never visited the area, and is said to have astonished people who had lived there by his intimate knowledge of the natives. Oddly enough, the man whose work on diffusion was to influence ethnology all over the world was so poor a teacher that his only candidate for a doctor's degree was refused a position at Bonn on the basis of insufficient qualifications.

In 1911 Graebner wrote his *Methode der Ethnologie* (*Ethnological Method*), a work which became the definitive statement of the diffusionist point of view. It must be remembered, however, that by this time Franz Boas was already developing a more or less diffusionist school in the United States.

During the year following the publication of his book, Graebner was invited to an international anthropological congress in Australia. A leading English diffusionist who disagreed with him completely, Grafton Elliot Smith (whom we shall discuss later), was also present, but history has not recorded their meeting. In fact, World War I broke out just as Graebner arrived, and he was interned by the British. The unfortunate scholar had made the mistake of hiding a Baedecker map of the South Seas in his shoe. This was interpreted as an attempt at flight, and he was put in solitary confinement for some time. Later he was allowed materials for study and was thus able to write a couple of scientific papers during his five-year imprisonment. After the war he continued teaching in Germany. In 1928 he suffered a stroke, and produced little of importance in his final years.

We have already indicated that diffusionism dealt some sharp critical blows at the classic evolutionary picture of the origins of religion and marriage. Graebner attacked the evolutionary method systematically. Bastian, Tylor, and McLennan saw cultures as universal stages of human development arranged in a series from the simple to the complex. But, said Graebner, there was no way of proving that the music bow was derived from the hunting bow or vice versa. He quoted Boas on the derivation of abstract primitive designs from animal forms. Boas had shown that the series might be arranged in reverse, and that, alternatively, the two styles might have influenced each other.

Graebner demanded a radical revision of method. Ethnology up to his time had been unscientific. Evidence, whether in the form of material objects or written reports, must be treated as critically and classified as carefully as any other biological material. Each object had to be checked for authenticity. Reports must be examined for the bias of the observer or faulty command of the native language. His book outlined painstaking techniques for the scrutiny of basic materials which reflected (too much so, said his opponents) his museum training.

The study of diffusion raised an important question. Had the significant elements in human culture been discovered independently in many different parts of the world or were they invented only once? Adolph Bastian, the champion of elementary ideas, believed men's minds were so constructed that different peoples were bound to hit upon the same inventions in different areas. K. T. Preuss, a disciple of Marett, coined the term *Urdummheit* or "primitive stupidity" because he felt that savages were unimaginative and that great inventions were made only once. Graebner insisted that independent invention in different areas must not be accepted until, in every specific case, efforts had been made to determine whether the device or idea had spread from a single source.

Adolph Bastian had vaguely discussed what he called *culture areas*. Frobenius also had used the term. Graebner defined and discussed the term more exhaustively. In the Caribbean, for instance, Arawak speech, the use of the hammock, and the cultivation of tobacco went together. In Polynesia, Polynesian speech, the use of an instrument known as the coconut-scraper, and a certain type of head rest were everywhere correlated. First we must study such a group of elements or *culture complex*, said Graebner, to make sure they are organically related. Then, if we find the same interwoven group elsewhere with modifications, we can assume it has been borrowed.

The comparison of isolated traits was unsound, for, unless they were studied in relation to a complex, there was no way of knowing whether they had the same meaning in different areas. Frazer was particularly prone to snatch facts out of context and to relate them on a basis of superficial resemblance.

Graebner also believed that the time sequence could be worked out in certain areas. Young culture traits were sharper and more clearly defined. He felt that archeological chronology would help in the task of tracing the points of origin of specific cultural complexes. The study of physical anthropology, particularly of skeletal remains, could help define the migrations of peoples in the past, while contemporary physical anthropology, by investigating racial mixtures, could help to clear up recent population movements.

Graebner's method was largely that of the natural scientist who studied the range of a species of bird or animal. When all of the species and families of culture had been identified and the interrelationships worked out, then the evolutionary process could be clarified. The unity of man would be the last problem resolved. Until then, talk of elementary ideas was mysticism.

After Graebner's death in 1934, the Rautenstrauch Joest Museum, in which he arranged exhibits according to his method, was taken over by two students who had no academic degrees and no other qualification except membership in the Nazi Party. In an official document they criticized the method of display as Marxist. Graebner in his writings had made the mistake of attacking the Nordic myth.

Graebner again and again emphasized the importance of strict, factual, closely reasoned method. His followers promptly became guilty of excesses of subjectivity quite as extreme as those of the evolutionists whom they sought to displace.

Father Wilhelm Schmidt (1868–1954), a Westphalian, began his studies for the priesthood in 1875 and was ordained in 1890. His life has been spent teaching in Catholic schools and in the University of Vienna. After considerable training in linguistics, he turned to ethnology, proclaimed himself a follower of Graebner, founded the publication *Antropos*, and gathered a diffusionist school about him.

Although, like Graebner, he did no field work, he began by a study of South American culture. The great work to which his life has been devoted was *Der Ursprung der Gottesidee*, (*The Origin of the Idea of God*), in eleven volumes, published from 1912 to 1954.

Schmidt announced that "the evolutionist method . . . is really no method at all." The school of Ratzel, Frobenius, and Graebner "is able to lift even the unwritten monuments of culture out of the featureless plane where they lay side by side and arrange them one behind the other in a sequence extending far back."

This contention was premature.

Schmidt, for obvious reasons, was attracted to Lang's theory of a single, ethical, superhuman deity, credited with creating the world, as the earliest type of religion among the most primitive peoples. He fully agreed with Lang that such a type of monotheism was the origin of all religion. All other practices such as ancestor-worship, fetishism, preanimism, polygamy, and magic were a "degeneration." Schmidt criticized all his predecessors in the field of religion except Lang and was particularly violent against Freud because of the "revolting origin" that the latter posited for religion, morality, and society.

Schmidt set out to document Lang. The eleven volumes of his *Origin of the Idea of God* were a compilation of all the material so far collected on primitive religion all over the world, area by area. The basis of his theory was the religion of the pygmy or Negrito tribes, which he considered the oldest human groups. As they were found in the Andaman Islands, the Philippines, and various regions of Africa, he maintained that they formed a belt around the world. All, he said, revered a single, moral creator of the world. But in most pygmy cultures ancestor-worship, magic, and nature-worship were also present. These he explained away by saying that they were "not very concrete" or "not very strong." R. H. Lowie, the American diffusionist, was not convinced, and commented: "The occurrence of a creative personality among people so lowly as the Andamanese and the Semang is a phenomenon of the greatest psychological interest, even though we must divest it of the monotheistic halo with which Lang and Schmidt surround it." However, Schmidt's biographer, Wilhelm Oehl, comments happily: "The incalculable significance of this study for culture history and also for theology is obvious. Genesis and Christendom, basing themselves upon it, have hereby won wonderful support from the profane science of ethnology."

On the whole, Schmidt's thesis seems just as biased and colored by special pleading as that of the Communist Robert Briffault. When not riding his hobby, he is considered a capable analyst of ethnological material, and, as in the case of Frazer, his monumental work is a rich source for other scholars.

The well-known English diffusionist Grafton Elliot Smith (1871–1937) was a Cambridge anatomist of distinction who was led into anthropology through a study of the brain capacity of man. He took a trip to Egypt to investigate the skulls of mummies and became deeply impressed by what he saw of that ancient civilization. When he returned to Cambridge he discovered some Malayan skulls similar to those of the Egyptian mummies. He had read Graebner and Schmidt and had labeled their work superficial. By looking at a map, he discovered that a complex consisting of sun-worship, large stone monuments, and mummification could be seen all over the world—or at least in several places. To this he added the symbol of the swastika, serpent-worship, head-deformation, ear-piercing, tattooing of women's chins, the deluge myth, and couvade.

Mummification was a complicated and difficult process much too elaborate to be invented more than once. It must have begun in Egypt. Then in the ninth century diffusion occurred. Along with sun-worship and stone monuments, it was brought to India, from India to Malaysia, from Malaysia to the South Seas, from the South Seas to North and South America. While working on his scheme of world diffusion he met E. J. Perry, who was an expert on the Malay area. He converted Perry and used his material to prove his contention that Malaysia was an intermediate step in the travels of his pet culture complex. Smith seems to have been a persuasive personality, for he also met and converted William H. R. Rivers, who was writing a book on Melanesia.

G. Elliot Smith wrote, in 1912, in a state of high indignation (most other ethnologists opposed him) a treatise, *The Migrations of Early Cultures: A Study of the Significance of the Geographical Distribution of the Practise of Mummification as Evidence of the Migrations of Peoples and the Spread of Certain Customs and Beliefs*. His explanation of the origin of mummification is typical of his logic. When burial in the earth was supplanted by the use of stone coffins in which valuables were placed, grave-robbery occurred. The Egyptians, amazed to discover that bodies disappeared from stone coffins, decided that stone must have the property of consuming flesh. To prove this, Smith cited the literal meaning of the Greek word *sarcophagus*, which is "flesh-eater." Mummification was therefore invented to protect the dead from their stone coffins!

Contradictions of chronology were ignored, as were the obstacles of navigation over such distances. It was easy to draw arrows on a map indicating the magical journeys of sun-worship and stone monuments. Fifteen centuries later, he stated firmly, the swastika and chin-tattooing were added to the voyaging culture complex.

Robert Lowie wrote that the evidence for all this was precisely nil. Even Father Schmidt said of Elliot Smith and Perry: "Their lack of any real method is so complete that it can bring only discredit on the new movement." Although these British diffusionists had little influence on their anthropological confreres, Perry's

theories have been of some value in the study of European prehistory.

William Halsey R. Rivers (1864–1922), a brilliant doctor and
nerve specialist who founded the *British Journal of Psychology* in
1904 and who, as we have seen, was drawn into the Torres Straits
expedition and anthropology by Alfred Haddon, also has a place
in the diffusionist school. Rivers produced a useful field work, *The
Todas,* in 1907, a study of that much-debated group of Indian
polyandrists. He continued to take an interest in Melanesia and, as
a result of the Percy Slade Trust Expedition to the Banks Islands,
published his two-volume work *The History of Melanesian Society* in 1914. Rivers's attempt to relate psychology to anthropology
will be discussed elsewhere. *Melanesian Society* is his contribution
to diffusionism. The first volume had been written several years
earlier under the influence of Morgan. Investigating kinship, Rivers
discovered that the Melanesian tribes tended to be divided into two
exogamous halves or moieties. He noticed that in some cases there
was a marked hostility between the two groups. Furthermore, each
group seemed to have different terms for the same relationships.
These observations, coupled with indoctrination by Elliot Smith,
led him to announce his conversion to diffusionism in 1911 and also
to the belief that there were two racial stocks in Melanesia. The
first buried their dead in a sitting position and were notable for the
ceremonial drinking of the juice of a root called *kava.* Native myths
spoke of dark and light peoples, and the myths of the two moieties
dealt with different types of heroes and totems. He concluded that
the dark-skinned people were the aboriginals. They probably had
outrigger canoes and were more primitive than the lighter-skinned
invaders. The latter came in small groups without women. Their
culture was higher, but their morals were lower than those of the
aboriginals. Because they were without family ties they instituted
sexual communism and later became an autocracy of old men.
They also brought with them elaborate secret societies. Some part
of their invasion, perhaps a second wave, brought stone monuments
and sun-worship. These light-skinned invaders were, of course,
Elliot Smith's voyaging complex-carriers.

Rivers seems to have completely disregarded the fact that a few
individuals of a higher culture isolated among a larger more primitive population often degenerate and lose their identity. Waitz had
pointed this out decades before, with reference to the Portuguese

in the Congo. Rivers's diffusionist labors contained too many gaps, too much superficial interpretation, and too many guesses to make much impression on other anthropologists. He never learned the lessons that Graebner had tried to teach.

In America diffusionism had a different history. For some decades, perhaps because the factual down-to-earth approach was particularly attractive to the technologically minded new world, it dominated American anthropological thinking. We have seen that Boas in the nineties was already, to some extent, a diffusionist. Thanks to him, however, the new approach was combined with a tradition of careful field work. The criticisms that his pupil Robert H. Lowie leveled at the older theorists in the field of marriage and religion were based, as we have indicated, on a background of comparative studies made among North American Indian tribes. Indeed, Lowie made solid contributions to the solution of almost all the major anthropological problems.

Born in 1883 in Vienna, Lowie was educated in City College, Dartmouth, and Columbia. He taught for many years in the University of California and in Yale in 1937. His point of concentration was the Crow Indians, whose culture was still very much alive when he was working among them. He was thus able to record a society that had been in contact with the white men for a long period and consequently exhibited early examples of acculturation. *The Crow Indians* was published in 1935. In 1937 he wrote *The History of Ethnological Theory*, a provocative sketch of theoretical trends spiced with plenty of controversial opinions.

An important theoretical elaboration of the diffusionist method was made by Edward Sapir in an article published in 1916 in the Geological Survey of Canada entitled *Time Perspective in American Aboriginal Culture*.

Sapir (1884–1939), a German-born scholar who taught at Yale, has been called Boas's most brilliant pupil. The bulk of his work was done in linguistics. As we shall see later, he was also a pioneer in uniting psychology and anthropology. His contribution to diffusion consisted in analyzing the types of evidence which could be used to determine the spread of cultural elements from their point of origin.

In the historical period, direct evidence included both written documents and oral tradition. For instance, documents dated the diffusion of the horse among the plains Indians after its introduction by the Europeans. Again, the earliest Norse sagas referred to Eskimo kayaks, showing that such boats were already in use in the Viking period. The Mayan monuments, whose dates had been deciphered and correlated with the European calendar, were of great use in studying the range and age of elements in Mayan culture.

Inferential evidence could be gleaned from deductive logic. If one process was necessary to the development of another, the first predated the second. For instance, skin-dressing and -suppling had to be invented before the plains tribes could develop the buffalo-hide tepee. Frequent reference to a custom throughout a people's myths would indicate that it was older than the myths. Whaling appeared in all northwestern myths and thus was assumed to be a very ancient practice. A trait that was connected with *all* the institutions of a culture was also likely to be old. An example was the fact that among the Pueblo Indians symbols for the four points of the compass appeared in myth and ritual, were used in magical sand painting, and were also employed in decorative designs on pots and utensils. When a culture complex could be shown radiating from a center, peoples in the middle of the area could be assumed to have had it longest. (The cautious Boas questioned this. He said the point of origin was not always the area of strongest development.)

On this point another American, Clark Wissler (1870–1947), who succeeded Boas in the American Museum of Natural History, sided with Sapir. Wissler mapped the culture areas of the new world on the basis of types of food. Adapting the radiation-from-a-center theory to this problem, he assumed that American corn or maize had been domesticated from a Mayan wild grass. Maize was cultivated with the digging-stick and the hoe. When gathered, it was ground on a stone metate. From the Mayan area the maize complex spread northward to the southwestern United States, where the ground grain was made into *piki* bread, thin as a wafer. In Central America and Mexico the maize produced the tortilla, a pancake-like food. The diffusion of spinning and weaving cotton could be correlated with the maize complex. "The future status of anthropology depends upon the establishment of a chronology for man and his culture based upon objective, verifiable data," he wrote. This is a good statement of the exclusively historical point of view of American diffusionism of his time.

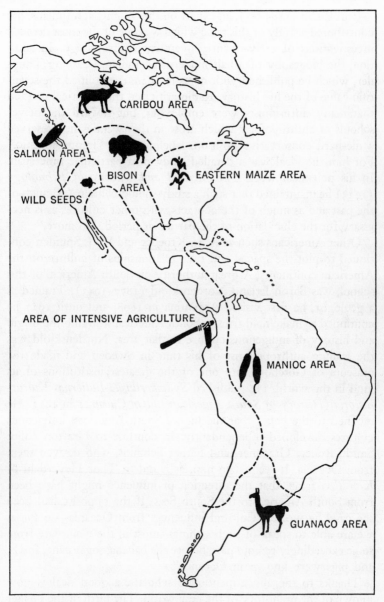

A food map of North and South America.

Paul Radin (1885–   ), an expert on the Winnebago Indians, has contributed a study of this tribe which was one of the most detailed investigations of early-twentieth-century anthropology. In addition, the biography of a half-modernized Indian, Crashing Thunder, which he published with notes in 1926, exemplified the scientific value of the life history. Radin criticized the statistical method that many diffusionists were employing, but toward the newer schools of anthropology which arose in the twenties he preserved a die-hard conservative position, labeling them "impressionistic." For him the ideal was a detailed study of a particular time span. In his polemical work *The Method and Theory of Ethnology* (1933) he maintained that such a study should contain "as much of the past and as much of the contacts with other cultures as is necessary for the elucidation of the particular period. No more."

Other Americans such as A. L. Kroeber and H. J. Spinden continued to plot the spacial and time relationships of culture on the American continents. A great authority on South America, of this school, was Baron Erland Nordenskjöld (1877–1933). Trained as a geologist, he first visited Argentina in 1898, and until 1927 he continued to make field trips to South America, studying the origin and history of indigenous culture in that area. Nordenskjöld was the leading anthropologist of his time in Sweden and made the museum of Göteborg into one of the greatest institutions of its kind in the world. He published *Sydamerikiska Indiernas Kulturhistoria* (*History of South American Indian Culture*) in 1912. He inclined to the belief that the higher South American indigenous cultures developed independently, in contrast to Grafton Elliot Smith, Robert Graebner, and Father Schmidt, who derived them from Oceania. It seemed to him, as it did to Thor Heyerdahl of *Kon-Tiki* fame, that the direction of influence might have been from South America to the South Seas. If the opposite had been the case, he wrote, "Cultural influences from Oceania—so far as we are able to speak of such a thing—must in the main date from some exceedingly remote past, before the banana, sugar cane, fowls, and pigs were known in Oceania."

Thanks to the above-mentioned scholars, a good deal is now known of the prehistory of the new world. The birth of the Geiger counter has, in the last few years, put a new tool in the hands of the archeologist. Objects containing carbon exhibit a certain amount of radioactivity which decreases in a calculable ratio over the centuries. By checking such objects in ancient sites, approximate dating can now be arrived at with much more certainty. Thus in American diffusionist studies anthropology has received considerable aid from the science of archeology.

On the whole, when it came to the origin of inventions, the older evolutionists believed that the same ideas occurred to different peoples at different times, while the diffusionists were skeptical and tried to trace important cultural devices to a single source. A. L. Kroeber, although he was of the Boas school, adopted a moderate position in his book *Anthropology*, published in 1923. He was willing to admit that the Mayans and the Hindus each developed the concept of zero. He also thought there was evidence that the exogamic-totemic complex might have arisen separately on different continents. The corbel arch appeared independently in Mycenae and Yucatán. On the other hand, it could be shown by factual evidence that the true keystone arch was invented in Babylonia around 3000 B.C. and from there traveled to Etruria about 700 B.C., from whence it entered Roman culture and eventually became a basic part of the medieval European church. Similarly, the phonetic alphabet was invented only once—by an unidentified Semitic people at approximately 1000 B.C. It was picked up by the Phoenicians and the Moabites. It next appeared in Carthage. The Greeks probably borrowed it from the Phoenicians.

Such ancient concepts as the fire drill and flint-chipping or animistic ideas were so early that it was impossible to establish any principle concerning their origin. On the whole, Kroeber believed that invention was rare because societies and individuals were conservative and opposed anything new. He summed up: "The most frequent process of cultural history therefore is one of diffusion in time and space, corresponding roughly to hereditary transmission in the field of organic life."

We have so far sketched the evolutionary school, which pioneered in the theoretical investigation of early cultural history, and the diffusionist school, which insisted on a stricter geographical and comparative method. In France the collectivist school, which acquired the name of sociology, is sometimes considered distinct from anthropology, but in many areas it overlaps the sister science.

Chapter 29

THE COLLECTIVE SOUL

Concerning Auguste Comte, Herbert Spencer,

Emile Durkheim, Lucien Lévy-Bruhl,

A. R. Radcliffe-Brown

■ The beginnings of sociology take us back once more to the early decades of the nineteenth century.

In 1821 a teacher of mathematics invited a group of Paris intellectuals, including Alexander von Humboldt, to attend a course of lectures which was to be the basis for a new philosophic system. Auguste Comte's method of composing lectures was highly eccentric. He used to meditate for days, staying awake all night drinking coffee and speaking to no one. After such a period of concentration, his ideas were so completely developed that he was able to put them on paper without changing a word.

The French savants came for three lectures. When they arrived for the fourth, they found the door closed, the shades down. Auguste Comte had had a nervous breakdown and was in an asylum.

The forces that caused the breakdown were complicated. Comte's family was provincial, royalist, and Roman Catholic. The boy's pious mother was fanatically anxious to keep him under her control, but by the time he went to Paris to study in the Ecole Polytechnique he was already losing his faith and becoming a champion of the cause of "reason and humanity." This, of course, caused painful tensions between him and his mother.

The French Revolution had intensified the currents of rationalism in French thought. With the advent of the Second Empire and the reactionary Louis XVIII, the intellectual world was split between those who would have liked to turn the clock back, such as Maistre and Gobineau, and the inheritors of the revolution, now largely social reformers, such as the utopian socialist Saint-Simon. Young Comte met the latter and wrote for his paper. Saint-Simon's circle was characterized by the same romantic enthusiasm concerning the regeneration of humanity, touched off by the industrial revolution, that had inspired Galton and Godwin in England. At the time of his unhappy eclipse, however, Comte was already disagreeing with Saint-Simon and indulging in controversies that were to end in a complete break. In addition, his personal life was acutely unhappy. He had recently married Caroline Massim, a girl with a history of prostitution, who was promptly unfaithful to him. It is not surprising that the development of Comte's philosophy was abruptly interrupted.

He was finally discharged from the asylum and fished out of the Seine after an attempt at suicide. Gradually he recovered his sanity, in spite of the conflicting ministrations of his mother and his wife. As soon as he was rational, he wrote a treatise on *Cerebral Irritation and Madness* and resumed his lectures, of which he gave seventy-two to the same undiscouraged group of scholars. Apparently the whole of his Positive Philosophy had remained intact in his mind during all of his harrowing experiences. It was this philosophy which included the new science of sociology, to which he gave a name.

Later in his career he rid himself of Caroline and formed a platonic relationship with a certain Clothilde de Vaux. Comte's love for her was on a high spiritual plane, and her Beatrice-like image became for him a symbol of benevolence which even turned up in his philosophy.

Comte was a gentle, sensitive man with one weak and drooping eye; his face was liable to nervous contortions. He is a curious example of a great intellect allied with mental instability. Indeed, the scope and pretentiousness of his philosophical system was accompanied by certain delusions of grandeur.

Sociology, before it became a true science, was therefore the product of the philosophical mind and was conceived as an all-embracing scheme for reorganizing society. Herbert Spencer, whose work in England paralleled that of Comte, also conceived sociology as an integrating philosophy of society.

Comte's great treatise *Positive Philosophy* begins by tracing the history and method of the sciences and criticizes their theory. All of the last book is devoted to "social physics." The concept of progress he maintained belonged exclusively to positivism. The classical societies lacked it because they worshipped the past and did not practice scientific observation. Christianity, the metaphysical stage, considered itself the ultimate perfection and thus allowed no room for further development. The French Revolution broke the power of the feudal system and the clergy and paved the way for a new social order. The early rationalists such as Montesquieu and Condorcet had freed themselves from theology and developed the idea of human perfectability. "The inevitable passage from the absolute to the relative is one of the most important philosophical results of each of the intellectual revolutions. . . ."

Comte's scheme of man's development was summary. Men began as fetish-worshippers and cannibals, progressed to star-worship with a priesthood, developed a military system, and finally, passing through the theological and metaphysical stages of recorded history, became positivists.

The basic lines of progress and development were subject to invariable laws. It was the duty of sociology to discover these by observation, experiment, and comparison. Reform would succeed only if it were in harmony with the general march of civilization. There was a certain leeway in which progress might be accelerated or modified, but only if the system of positivism were adopted.

The positivist circle counted among its members some ardent adherents in England, among them the bluestocking Harriet Martineau, who translated and abridged *Positive Philosophy*.

Herbert Spencer, working independently of Comte, read Miss Martineau's translation in 1853. With his usual egotism he commented: "The disciples of M. Comte think I am much indebted to him: and so I am but in a way widely unlike that which they mean. Save in the adoption of his word 'sociology' because there was no other available word (for both of which adoptions I have been blamed) the only indebtedness which I recognize is the indebtedness of antagonism. My pronounced opposition to his views led me to develop some of my own views."

Some money had accrued to Comte from the English translation, and when Spencer visited Paris in 1855 he undertook the task of bringing the French sociologist his royalties.

The meeting of these two neurotic geniuses was full of irony. Spencer wrote: "Certainly his appearance was not in the least impressive either in face or figure. One could say of his face only that, unattractive though it was, it was strongly marked; and in this way it was distinguished from the multitudes of meaningless faces one daily sees. Of our conversation I only remember that, hearing of my nervous disorder, he advised me to marry; saying that the sympathetic companionship of a wife would have a curative influence. This, by the way, was a point of agreement between him and one who differed from him in most things, Professor Huxley; who in afteryears suggested that I should try what he facetiously termed gyneopathy: admitting that it could not be left off if it proved unsuitable."

Spencer's progress in hypochondria had been rapid. He suffered continually from insomnia. Although he worked only five hours a day, he admitted that all of his spare time was spent thinking. "One morning after beginning to work, there commenced a sensation in my head—not pain, nor heat, nor fulness, nor tension but simply a sensation, bearable enough but abnormal." For eighteen months he could not bear much conversation and could read only in snatches without the "feeling in the head" occurring. For the last half of his life he was increasingly an invalid, flying from crowds, prostrated for weeks because he had run to catch a train, battling with his nervous disorder as he struggled to finish his multi-volume work *Synthetic Philosophy*.

He had already traced out his evolutionary point of view in biology and psychology. In 1867, while finishing his book on the latter science, he began preparations for writing *The Principles of Sociology*. He decided that this work would require an immense accumulation of facts from which to generalize. He therefore set several scholars to gather material on the uncivilized races, the extinct civilized races, and the present civilized races. The three volumes of *The Principles of Sociology* were published in the years 1876–96. In them Spencer developed the conception of society as an organism (an image also used by Adolph Bastian) or "the perpetually cited case of the polyp each part of which, when it is cut into several pieces, presently puts on polyp shape." In his view, progress resulted from an unknowable force that pushed evolution along the line of least resistance. Society was moving from an unspecialized, unorganized state in which all individuals were much alike to a highly organized condition of great specialization. Spencer's anthropological thinking followed the lines of Lewis Morgan and J. F. McLennan. He added the concept of military versus industrial society. The former was gradually being superseded by the latter, which would automatically and gradually bring about world peace. He, like Comte, believed that society should be studied scientifically, but that government in an industrial society should be chiefly negative.

Sociology, having started in France and taken root in England, continued to flower in France. Comte's inheritor was Emile Durkheim (1858–1911), the son of a Lorraine rabbi. After teaching philosophy in high school and lecturing at the University of Bordeaux, he studied with Wundt in Germany. He took his doctorate at the Sorbonne, where he began to teach philosophy in 1902. He was also the founder of the *Année Sociologique*. Durkheim possessed a sharp and orderly Gallic mind with a touch of poetry. The structure of his thought was clear-cut and its verbal expression beautifully organized. We have seen that Herbert Spencer and Auguste Comte hovered on the outskirts of anthropology. Durkheim made a foray into the closely related science to support his own scheme of thought and thus for the first time united the two studies.

Herbert Spencer had decided that a kind of Darwinian natural selection resulted in the formation of social groupings. Durkheim, disagreeing with this concept, developed a new one that was destined to be extremely important both for sociology and anthropology. He discovered the *collective conscience*, the latter word being used both in the French sense of consciousness and the more familiar English one meaning an inner moral check.

But what was this collective conscience, the key to human relationships?

Durkheim elaborated it in his most important work, *Les Formes élémentaires de la vie religieuse* (*Elementary Forms of Religious Life*) (1912), a book involving anthropology. Although France had colonies, her scholars had not taken an interest in anthropological field work; among them only Van Gennep had been much impressed by the work of the British evolutionary school. Durkheim, rather late in the day, when the school was already under attack, discovered the work of Tylor, Marett's preanimism, and particularly the communal meal of Robertson Smith, and Spencer's and Gillen's field work in Australia. In consequence, the anthropological base of his book was already somewhat dated. This accounts for the curious discrepancy between the value of his method and point of view and his specific contribution to anthropology.

He accepted Robertson Smith's theory of the social significance of the communal meal that involved eating the totem. He also assumed that the totemistic tribes of Australia practiced the earliest form of religion.

From this he went on to his own definition of religion: "Religion is a system of belief in sacred things with a church which morally unites a community." Religion was therefore a collective form of behavior. Magic he dismissed as a private affair. A magician had a clientele, but his practice did not include regularly repeated rites participated in by the group.

Religion was characterized by a sharp difference between the sacred and the profane. Totemistic practices made use of objects such as churingas and nurtunjas. These objects were symbols of sacredness, as were totem animals. Now, the concept of a sacred force ran all through primitive life. This force was called *mana* among the Melanesians, *wakan* by the Sioux, *orenda* by the Iroquois.

What was this sacred force? It was derived neither from fear of ancestors nor from personification of nature. It seemed to reside in totems or in totemistic objects that symbolized the tribal group itself.

Thoughts and feelings held by a social group had a different *quality* from private thoughts and emotions. There was a sort of self-hypnosis in crowd psychology. In revolutions, for instance, a perfectly average man could behave in a way impossible to him in ordinary situations and become a hero. Jeanne d'Arc was an embodiment of group thought and feeling, symbolized by her voices.

To return to the primitive, the need to express collective sentiments resulted in collective actions with a rhythmical character, such as dance and song. This of course led to ritual. In violent rituals the tribe became excited, its individuals were no longer themselves, they passed into a new world. This was the religious world, the sacred world opposed to the profane.

Religion was not *fear* of forces but a celebration of the strength and vitality that resulted from union with the mana inhabiting the ancestors or totemic protectors who were part and parcel of the group. The individual felt himself to be submitting, not to the group, but to his own nature. Religion, said Durkheim, *is* society.

The collective conscience was therefore an almost mystical participation and submission to the thought and feeling of the group. But it was also a real and material thing because the group was real.

In other words, the whole was different in essence from the sum of its parts. Social facts were not the same as individual facts. The collective conscience could never be understood through individual psychology. Durkheim also denied the supremacy of economic determininism, for response to the group aims and ideals could transcend self-interest.

In a sense Durkheim, who rejected psychology, was really foreshadowing that school which is known as *Gestalt*.

According to Durkheim, the concept of the individual soul was merely a fragmentation of the collective conscience or social soul. "It remains true that our nature is double; there is really a fragment of divinity in us because in us there is a part of the great ideas which are the soul of the collective."

The definition of the personality was something of a stumbling-block. He denied that it was merely the sum of an individual's sensations and perceptions. A man became a person in proportion as he freed himself from his senses and became capable of thinking and acting in terms of concepts. Concepts sprang from the collective conscience, but reached individual heights of symbolization in the separate members of the group.

His explanation of why the dead are sometimes thought to be hostile (his theory made them friendly) is elaborated with, apparently, no knowledge of Freud. In funeral rites, in which mob emotion became intense, the belief that death was caused by magic aroused anger and the feeling that the dead should be avenged. This almost unconscious desire for revenge resulted in self-mutilation in frenzied mourning. The primitive did not, in his calmer moments, really understand why he had hurt himself and blamed the departed. This was only temporary, and when the painful rites were over, the dead became beneficent again.

Similarly, the qualities of good and bad spirits arose from the rites connected with them. A joyful rite stemmed from a time of collective joy and was symbolized by a good spirit; an evil spirit was produced by a sad ritual.

Supreme gods were highly personalized fragments of the group soul. And, similarly, all idealisms of the more civilized groups were the products of the collective conscience in its highest form.

A philosophy, said Durkheim, could be created by an individual, but not a faith. Hence the failure of Comte's grand scheme to superimpose positivism on society.

The words *god* and *divine* can be substituted wherever Durkheim used the words *society* or *collective*. He was actually elaborating a religion that was at the same time idealist and (according to him) materialist.

He found a place in it for his own faith in logic, maintaining: "Scientific thought is only a more perfect form of religious thought." To think logically was always, in some measure, to think in an impersonal way. Scientific thought should be valid for all men, thus it was an achievement of the community and, in essence, the crowning expression of the collective conscience.

It will be seen that, in spite of his social point of view, Durkheim was fundamentally an evolutionist. His theory of religion was sharply criticized by Robert Lowie, who pointed out that among the plains Indians religion was distinctly an individual experience. A good deal of Durkheim's reasoning falls to the ground because investigation, which he disregarded, shows that many groups more primitive than the Australians have never developed totemism. Lowie also pointed out that the jump from the vague emotionalism of the crowd to the creation of actual ideas is a long one. Durkheim seemed to practically deny original invention, material or ideological, to the individual. Likewise, he failed to make a distinction between the behavior of the *mob* and the *group*. Groups do not always act in unison like a mob. In the normal life of groups there is certainly interaction between individual minds.

It cannot be denied that Durkheim's approach sparkled with insights. His insistence on the difference between individual psychology and mob psychology was important and opened up a new field for investigation. His statement that there are elements in the social scene which cannot be explained in terms of individual behavior has had an impact on anthropology which still continues, and by modern sociologists he is considered the real founder of their science.

One of the contributors to his periodical, *Année Sociologique*, was Lucien Lévy-Bruhl (1856–1939), who began his career as a student of philosophy and a follower of the philosopher Immanuel Kant. Among his early works were a study of positivism and a history of French philosophy. *Les Fonctions mentales dans les sociétés inférieurs* (*Mental Activity in Inferior Societies*), his most important contribution to anthropology, showed the influence of Durkheim. Rejecting psychology, as Durkheim had done, he nevertheless concerned himself with the mental processes of primitives and created his own system of psychological interpretation.

Other scientists had seen primitive man as a philosopher, an unsuccessful scientist, a good communist, a Christian monogamist, a fragment of the group soul. Lévy-Bruhl conceived him as a surrealist poet.

Like Durkheim an armchair anthropologist, he, too, made use of the data collected by the British school. He started from the same point as Durkheim: primitive minds were undifferentiated. Such minds were governed by waves of emotional force developed in ritual activities. But, beyond this, primitive thinking was completely different from that of civilized man.

Savages did not perceive in the same fashion as modern man, they did not analyze, they did not seek for explanations. Their world was dominated by "collective representations." What was a collective representation? When a savage looked at an object he saw it in terms of all the associations, superstitions, and prejudices of his group. Natives often objected to having their photographs taken. This was because the picture was identified with the real thing; the native saw it with all the associations supplied by the group.

The primitive conception of causality did not depend on sequence of time as in civilized logic—the act did not have to *follow* the cause. Instead, the connection was spacial. Because objects were seen together or events were spacially related, they affected each other. Even the sense of time was spacial. Omens could predict *after* the event. Likewise, divination could be practiced in regard to the past as well as the future.

There was another aspect of what the poet e. e. cummings would have called native "unthinking." This was participation. In totemism a man was himself and an animal at the same time. He did not perceive any contradiction; in fact, the logical law of contradiction was foreign to native "unthinking." In the same way, the photograph participated in the life of the original. The meaning of designs in primitive art was interpreted by this sense of participation—by their group meaning, not their appearance.

Then, too, many primitives believed that they had several souls. This indicated that they were entwined with all of life through these various copies of themselves. They were not really differentiated from the group consciousness, they pantheistically participated. Furthermore, the concept of *mana, wakan, orenda* was simply a means of indicating that all things possessed the same property, that they mystically participated in one another.

Among some groups, numbers were not thought of in sequence but in terms of their mystical properties; they, too, participated. Rituals performed in connection with hunting or fighting were not representations but actual participations in the real event. Sympathetic and contagious magic were both examples of participation; the magical action participated in the object, animal, or person to be affected.

A fairly accurate image of Lucien Lévy-Bruhl's conception of native thought would be a television screen with a multitude of superimpositions. Everything was everything else.

He also made the point that all native "pre-logical" thinking, as he called it, was based on emotions. Primitives did not personify natural objects or interpret the feelings of others, they simply felt toward them and projected their own feelings into them.

If he had read Freud, he would have found that the latter had anticipated him in this.

An example of the mechanism in action was a story of an old Tahitian who wore a garment that had belonged to a leper. When asked by a horrified white man if he was not afraid of contracting the disease, the old man laughed at him. The leper was a good friend of his, and he was in no danger.

Rituals and totemic ceremonies concerned with ancestors were performed to heighten participation. In the mind of the primitives, "the supernatural . . . though distinct from nature, is not separated. It is the part they feel most strongly and which occupies their spiritual life most often."

It is probable that Lévy-Bruhl would not have exaggerated his picture of native confusion to such an extent if he had engaged in field work. Men do not think the same way all the time. Even civilized man is wholly irrational in areas of prejudice. Boas made the point that beliefs collected from American college students were just as emotional as those of any South Sea islander.

Anthropologists have, on the whole, been cold to "pre-logical thinking," a term that has a patronizing tone (indeed, Lévy-Bruhl maintained it had to be abandoned before civilized thought could arise). If primitive man could be interpreted as a philosopher, an unsuccessful scientist, a good communist, a Christian monogamist, a fragment of the group soul, and a surrealist, civilized man can and has played all of these roles, too. Boas, who knew Eskimos and Indians personally, always stressed the fact that the potentialities were the same in all human beings.

We have so far traced three main schools of anthropological thought: the evolutionist, the diffusionist, and the sociological. Alfred Radcliffe-Brown (1881–1955) can be considered something of an eclectic. He studied with Haddon and was Rivers's first anthropology student after having worked with him for some years in psychology. All along he disagreed heartily with the latter's "conjectural method."

In 1908–9 Radcliffe-Brown undertook a field study of the Andaman Islanders (from which material on the dance has already been quoted). In the preface to the resulting book he announced his adherence to the French school. He also studied the Australian kinship systems and believed that, from an intimate knowledge of how they were worked out in specific groups, general laws might be deduced. *The Andaman Islanders*, published in 1914, is a classic piece of field work. In the introduction Radcliffe-Brown stated that "the study of culture is the study of adaptation to a particular environment." The work reveals him as one of the pioneers of the modern approach to field work, but subsequently he ceased to be active in the field and became a theorist and a teacher. In 1921 he was appointed to the chair of social anthropology in Cape Town University, where he played a pioneer role in developing social study in Africa. It was also here, among the Bantus, that Radcliffe-Brown initiated work in applied anthropology. In 1926 he was called to a newly instituted chair of social anthropology in the University of Sydney, and during the next five years he continued to develop the concept of applied anthropology in a course he gave to administrative officials. From 1931 to 1937 he taught in the University of Chicago and exercised some influence on the course of social study in the United States by championing Durkheim's point of view. He was finally called to the chair of anthropology at Oxford, at which university he established himself as one of the leaders of the modern British school in the late thirties and early forties. He retired from Oxford in 1946.

An example of a law which he formulated under the influence of Durkheim was the statement that all collective emotion tended to be expressed in ritual. "And in all ritual, again by a necessary law, some more or less concrete object is required which can act as a representative of the group." Such an object would be a totem or fetish.

The diffusionist Robert Lowie attacked laws of this kind as vague and subjective. In return, Radcliffe-Brown quoted a characterization of civilization as "a thing of shreds and patches." This, he said, was a typical failure on the part of the diffusionist to view culture as a living organism and to seek for scientific explanations.

Radcliffe-Brown made efforts to reconcile modified evolutionism with French sociology. He also held that the diffusionist or historical point of view could be combined with them. From the social point of view the real meaning of an institution could be determined. From the diffusionist method its relative age and range could be worked out. A combination of both might reveal its evolution.

As the science of anthropology grew older and wiser, it was beginning to be plain that schools of thought must borrow from one another. Radcliffe-Brown's rival in England was the founder of another species of anthropology which was somewhat different from evolutionism, diffusion, and sociology. The new school had come to be called *functionalism*. What is functionalism? The term, unfortunately, is one of those stiff, academic abstractions that must be translated if they are to be endowed with life. The man who gave it life, who also owed something to Radcliffe-Brown's concept of field work, was neither colorless nor academic, and was, in fact, one of the most widely known modern anthropologists. His name was Bronislaw Malinowski.

PART *Four*

Psychological Insight and Social Responsibility

Chapter 30

MAN THE MACHINE

Concerning Behaviorism and Anthropology

■ Malinowski belonged to a generation of anthropologists which followed that of Durkheim and could no longer ignore the latest developments in the science of the mind. Before discussing his work, therefore, it is necessary to glance at the interrelated study of psychology once more.

The earliest psychologists could not quite rid themselves of the notion of man philosophizing about his sensations. A closer look at man as an emotional animal showed that the greater portion of his life was governed by thoroughly non-rational impulses.

Some attempt to apply Freudian psychoanalysis to anthropology was made by W. H. R. Rivers, whose history of Melanesian society ranks him as a diffusionist. But Rivers was also a nerve specialist and during World War I was attached to British hospitals for shell-shocked soldiers. While engaged in therapy he read Freud and began to be interested in dreams. He squirmed away from the "objectionable" side of psychoanalysis, however, never really accepting the Oedipus complex, the notion of censorship, or the interpretation of dreams as suppressed wishes.

He decided that dreams were the result of a conflict in the mind and revealed an attempted solution. Instead of a Freudian censor, there were various layers of sleep, the deepest being infantile. Infantile processes in mature life had to be abandoned for practical reasons, and that was why the deepest meaning of dreams was normally not recognized by the dreamer.

Rivers made some effort to apply his psychology to primitive culture. Natives tended to dramatize their modes of thinking symbolically. Smoke could represent clouds; a beaten coconut shell, thunder; orange fruit strung on a creeper, lightning. According to Rivers, just as the psychologist could trace the conflict in a patient through layers of symbolism to its source, so the anthropologist could pursue a custom or institution in savage culture back through primitive symbolical thinking to its origin.

Since Rivers rejected the most essential part of Freud's doctrine, which dealt with sex, his attempt to link psychology and anthropology had no very lasting influence.

Other non-Freudian psychologists at the turn of the century got around the difficulty of non-rational human behavior by listing instincts. The urbane humanist William James, for instance, included such concepts as *shame, cleanliness,* and *modesty* among the instincts. (Yet Westermarck had pretty thoroughly destroyed any absolute standard of modesty.)

William McDougall, an Englishman who was a member of the Torres Straits expedition, taught at Oxford, and succeeded James at Harvard, and wrote on social psychology, listed seven instincts, none of which coincided with those of James. The concept of instinct was, on the whole, literary and vague.

Experimental psychology of the Wundt school, which had measured perception by the splitting-up process, had begun to seem rather a dead end. After taking the mind apart, the measurers never succeeded in putting it together again.

In Russia, however, experimental psychology had taken a new turn. As early as 1900, I. P. Pavlov was working with dogs. Dogs could not report their feelings or sensations, but their behavior could be observed. A remarkable phenomenon was discovered which Pavlov named the *conditioned reflex*. In a now famous experiment he rang a bell every time a dog was presented with food. The dog salivated at the sight of food. After considerable repetition the dog salivated when the bell was rung and no food offered. More investigation showed that many other stimuli could thus, by association, be made to produce the original reaction.

It was an epoch-making discovery, for it showed the *mechanics* of behavior in response to sensation and threw light on the process of learning. The dog did not associate by rational thought, nor was his final reaction an inborn "instinct." He became *conditioned* to the new stimulus.

John Broadus Watson, a hillbilly from South Carolina, arrived in Chicago in 1899 with fifty dollars in his pocket and some revolutionary ideas. He planned to complete his medical studies at the University of Chicago. Watson was aggressive and independent, and disliked philosophy. He obtained his doctor's degree in psychology and became an instructor in the university, where he remained until 1908. He worked with animals and endeavored to learn more about the nature of instincts. His work was interrupted by World War I, during which he ran an aviation examination board and quarreled with his superiors. After the war he continued his experiments, and in 1913, while an instructor at Columbia, he caused some consternation by stating that the recent discoveries in animal psychology could be applied to man. The human mind, he held, could be studied like a machine in terms of stimulus and response. He denied the existence of consciousness as a valid concept. Introspection he considered a hopeless method of psychologial investigation because, he maintained, there could be no objective check on subjective reports of an individual's sensations and feelings.

In 1919, in *Psychology from the Point of View of a Behaviorist*, he elaborated his doctrine. Taking an eleven-month-old child, Watson allowed him to touch a white rat, and at the same time the investigator struck a metal bar, producing a loud noise. The child's reaction to the sound was fear. After repetition, just as in the case of the dog, the child reacted fearfully whenever he touched fur.

Watson maintained that his experiments proved that there were no basic instincts other than fear, rage, and love. In babies fear was caused by loud noises and loss of physical support. All the mental processes were a matter of learned behavior built up by combining individual elements of conditioning.

Actually, he went too far in denying the existence of consciousness. The Freudians were able to compare many verbal reports of the feelings and ideas of their patients. On the basis of quantity, such subjective reports could have scientific value. From the common-sense point of view, consciousness existed and there was no use pretending to ignore it.

Watson was sure that if his method of upbringing were followed, the mental ills of mankind could be cured in a generation by conditioning. Behaviorism appealed to the mechanically oriented mentality of a technological culture and in the twenties became the most fashionable school of American psychology.

Ironically enough, after a well-publicized divorce proceeding, Watson resigned from Johns Hopkins, where he had been teaching, and went into the business world. It is not surprising that, with his practical theory of conditioning, he later became vice-president of a large advertising agency.

Bronislaw Malinowski, after a brief flirtation with psychoanalysis, incorporated a good deal of behavioristic thinking into his doctrine of functionalism. Behaviorism had disproved the contention that a whole series of human traits was mysteriously inborn. It now appeared that the child entered his world pretty much of a naked animal with only fear, anger, and love to guide him. His subsequent development and adaptation to his environment were shaped by what he learned from his parents and the institutions of his culture.

Chapter 31

THE MAGIC OF THE ISLANDS

Concerning Bronislaw Malinowski

■ In August 1914, Bronislaw Malinowski, a young Anglicized Pole, sailed past the southern coast of New Guinea, past steep, folded slopes covered with dense, rank jungle spotted here and there with brighter patches of grass, on his way to his first field assignment. The intense green contrasted with the azure of the sea and the sharp, bright beach. The mountains faded off into steamy tropical mists. Plastered on the slopes were big triangular clearings whose apexes pointed uphill. Villages were hidden on the foreshore in groves of trees through which, here and there, the glinting gold and purple of palm thatch could be seen. Malinowski's destination, however, was not New Guinea, but a group of coral islands lying slightly to the northeast. The ship entered a greenish sea broken only by sand banks, some of which were bare, some clothed in a few pandanus trees, their roots high in the sand. There were intricate passages into the lagoon of Boyawa, the main island of the Trobriands, which was to be Malinowski's base for several years—a peaceful oasis while the civilized world indulged in its first orgy of self-destruction.

Here the tangled matting of the jungle broke over the beaches, and in the interstices palm groves could be seen, their trunks seeming to support the green roof like pillars. Canoes were drawn high up on the beach, which was covered with mud and refuse. A closer view was less romantic than had been expected. The launch that had brought Malinowski chugged away and left him rather disconsolate on the beach. He made his way to the house of a trader and pearl-buyer, who took him into his compound. He had little time, however, to help the scientist interview the Melanesians of Boyawa.

Bronislaw Malinowski had been born in Cracow, Poland, in 1884. He received his Ph.D. in mathematics in 1908, and later devoted himself to work in chemistry and physics. Suddenly he was threatened with tuberculosis and obliged to discontinue his studies temporarily. He walked out of the college building of the medieval University of Cracow with the three green volumes of *The Golden Bough* under his arm, determined to read an English classic in the original to take his mind off his disappointment. "No sooner had I read this great work than I became immersed in it and enslaved by it. I realized then that anthropology, as presented by Sir James Frazer, is a great science, worthy of as much devotion as any of her elder and more exact sister studies and I became bound to the service of Frazerian anthropology."

Malinowski's health improved. In 1910 he went to London, studied in the London School of Economics, met and made friends with Frazer, and trained in anthropology under A. C. Haddon and C. G. Seligman.

The expatriate Pole often ridiculed English customs and preferred to spend his vacations on the Continent, but London became his home and the center of his intellectual life. His trip to the South Seas in 1914 was stimulated by Seligman (of the Torres Straits expedition) and financed by the Robert Mond Fund. With the outbreak of World War I he became an "enemy alien," for his birthplace, Cracow, made him a citizen of the Austrian Empire. He was interned, fortunately for anthropology, in the Trobriand Islands, where he spent four years.

Malinowski's life in Boyawa was the determining factor in all of his work. On his first visits to the village with the white trader, some of the natives flocked around him begging for tobacco. The older and more dignified remained seated before the gaily decorated house fronts. Malinowski made visits by himself, offered presents of tobacco, and asked the names of objects. He also tried to collect kinship terms and genealogies, but he found pidgin English a limited means of communication. Folklore data came out mangled and unintelligible. He felt that he had reached a dead end.

When he talked to the traders he found that, although they had lived in Boyawa for years, what little they knew of native life was garbled and inconsistent. Despairing of getting anything worth while in the space of a year, he went through a period of demoralization in which he read novels as another man might have taken to drink. Finally he decided on a drastic step. He put up a tent in the village and cut himself off from white men entirely, relearning a lesson that Boas had learned a couple of decades before.

Each morning he walked through the village, watching the dark-skinned, frizzy-haired islanders cooking, joking among themselves, playing with their children, sometimes quarreling, working at their domestic industries, fishing in the lagoon.

He rigorously schooled himself not to return to the white men for recreation. Instead, when he was lonely or bored, he forced himself to go on long walks by himself. He soon became glad of Melanesian companionship.

His informants became so accustomed to his presence among them that they ceased to be self-conscious. He poked his nose into everything, and soon they regarded him "as a part and parcel of their life, a necessary evil or nuisance."

As he learned their language, he also learned good manners and discretion and was thus able to share in their occupations, their amusements, and their ceremonials. Rites, births, deaths took place under his scrutiny. Anything dramatic that happened he was able to investigate while the villagers were sufficiently interested to talk about it. Thus he captured their typical emotional attitudes and opinions.

Except for Boas, probably no other field worker had so saturated himself with native life. He did not have to depend on what his informants chose to tell him or on their interpretation of their culture: he was able to observe both theory and practice. Whatever remnants of Frazerian approach still lingered were swept away. He began to shape his theory of functionalism.

Boyawa was a predominantly flat island with a fertile plain on a low coral ridge. The village was built in concentric circles. The yam houses, with red, black, and white decorations on their gable ends, stood in the middle, marking off a central plaza; they played an important part in the economy and emotional life of the Melanesians. In a second ring were the dwelling-huts, in front of which families squatted and chattered. The women wore short, stiff palm-leaf skirts, the men nothing but the briefest of pubic leaves. The physical type ranged from a thick-lipped Negroid to a lighter, thin-featured people, some of whom were handsome and the men, in particular, were superbly built.

Outside the village, a low, dense jungle grew in a matted tangle, patches of which were cleared for the yam and taro and banana gardens. Early in the year the sprouting crops were bright green; at harvest time the ripe vines turned brown.

Yam storage bin.

About half of the natives' lives were spent in these gardens, and more than half of their interests and ambitions were connected with them. The key to Melanesian character was a desire for social approval, and social approval depended on successful gardens, liberality, fulfillment of complicated obligations, and conspicuous display of property. This matrilineal people raised twice as many yams as they needed, piled them up at certain feasts so that they could be admired, and distributed them ceremonially to clan relatives. Eventually a part of the crop was stored in the yam houses for food. Another portion was sometimes ceremonially exchanged with another village, at which time rivalry became intense. Part of the crop was simply allowed to rot.

Garden magic was a part of their digging-stick-and-hoe agriculture. Garden magicians were generally village headmen. These were specialists who were paid for their work. The people as a whole also took some part in the ceremonials. There were rites before cutting the scrub, before burning the ground, before planting and weeding, and to insure a good crop. The magic had emerged from the ground with their ancestors. Food presents were made to these ancestors, while the magician had to observe food taboos. Before cutting the scrub the spell went:

> *The belly of my garden leavens.*
> *The belly of my garden rises.*
> *The belly of my garden reclines.*
> *The belly of my garden grows to the size of a*
>   *bush hen's nest.*
> *The belly of my garden rises like an ant hill.*
> *The belly of my garden rises like an ironwood palm.*
> *The belly of my garden lies down.*
> *The belly of my garden swells.*
> *The belly of my garden swells as with child.*
> *I sweep away.*

The gardeners knew all about the qualities of soil and the need for weeding and cultivation, but the magic took care of possible abnormal situations. Exceptionally good, good, or bad luck arose from success or error in magic.

When the missionaries tried to tell the natives that divine service would make their gardens grow, the Melanesians suspected them, not of lying, but rather of a certain feeble-mindedness or, as Malinowski wrote mischievously, "as Professor Lévy-Bruhl would put it, of a prelogical mentality."

The repetitive patter of magic spells accompanied almost every island activity, from love-making to building a canoe. Next to their gardens, their canoes were their pride and joy. Small dugout canoes were used for lagoon fishing, and they also made large out-rigger craft with beautifully painted prows and sternboards which were propelled by both a sail and leaf-shaped paddles. The lateen sail, constructed by sewing pandanus leaves together, allowed them to voyage from island to island—a highly adventurous exploit, for they could not beat into the wind and a sudden shift of the wind easily capsized them.

These seagoing canoes were used for a curious semi-yearly cere-monial exchange voyage called the *kula*. This was undertaken at a time when the crops did not need attention and the winds were fairly steady. The kula objects were red shell necklaces and white

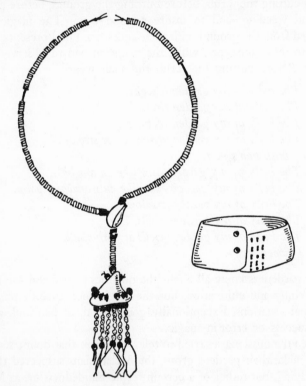

Kula bracelet and necklace.

shell bracelets. The necklaces (made in the south) traveled coun-terclockwise around the near-by islands, the bracelets (made in the north) traveled clockwise. Commoners had few kula partners, a chief might have hundreds. This relation was stylized: the partners were friends, patrons, allies. Kula objects might take from two to ten years to make the circle of the islands. Seldom worn, they had names and were considered historic heirlooms. They were symbols of conspicuous display, essential to status and prestige. The exchange took place on a sort of credit basis, each man promising additional objects which he did not yet own but hoped to get by a later transaction.

The weaving of magic began with the construction of the canoe, which was compared in the spells to a flying witch. (Certain women were supposed to be flying witches especially dangerous to sailors, for they endeavored to shipwreck them and feast on their bodies.) When the fleet was ready, the mariners dressed in their best, with hibiscus flowers in their helmets of frizzy hair. They equipped themselves with "beauty magic" to make them attractive to their kula partners, picnicked on the beach, and then all set sail together. "Sitting in the slender body while the canoe darts on with the float raised, the platform (across the outrigger) steeply slanting and the water constantly breaking over . . . the sail is hoisted, its stiff heavy folds of gold unroll with a characteristic swishing and crackling noise and the canoe begins to make way when the water rushes away below with a hiss and the yellow sail glows against the intense blue of the sea—then indeed the romance of sailing seems to open through a new vista."

The green-and-white waters were sprinkled with patches of brown seaweed. There were dangerous shoals whose origin was described in myth. Far away could be seen the cloud-wreathed mountains of other islands. As they sailed into new waters the mariners heard the cries of strange birds—the laughing jackass and the melancholy note of the South Sea crow, which never visited Boyawa. The sea became transparent, a pure blue in which they could see brilliant corals and multicolored fish that were not native to their lagoon. They passed volcanic islands with boiling springs, composed of dark obsidian rock, yellow ocher, and hills of ash. On such an island the mythical hero Kasabwayreta was marooned by his companions but escaped by climbing a tree to the sky. In the old days the Trobriand voyagers ran the risk of being attacked by cannibal neighbors; an unforeseen current might sweep them out to sea forever. Always their weak human voices were raised in monotonous spells to keep the winds favorable. In the midst of a squall, when the canoe tipped perilously, they were sure they could see flying witches hovering above the rigging, waiting to feast on their drowned corpses.

When the kula voyagers reached their destination, each partner vied with the other in exchanging fine necklaces of shells to the sound of conch trumpets. After a little subsidiary practical trading in pots, or whatever objects the neighboring islands produced, the fleet sailed home again.

The whole project combined romance, adventure, and the maintenance of prestige by which the Trobrianders lived.

As Malinowski scrutinized the lives of his Melanesian friends, he became convinced that anthropologists had been viewing life piecemeal and that their results were distorted and unreal.

He defined his new method as the study of "the influence on one another of various aspects of an institution, the study of the social and psychological mechanism on which the institution is based." Tylor, Robertson Smith, Hutton Webster, and Heinrich Schurtz were his precursors. "The magnificent title of the Functionalist School of Anthropology," he wrote, "has been bestowed by myself, in a way on myself, and to a large extent out of my own sense of irresponsibility." Remarks like this caused Malinowski's brother anthropologists to gnash their teeth at what they termed his egotism. Likewise, he tended to ignore Boas's and Radcliffe-Brown's contributions to functionalism.

Nevertheless, the method of complete immersion in the life of a group and intensive study of every aspect of its activities in relation to one another and to the environment has become the standard approach of field workers.

The coherence of his method is exemplified in his analysis of crime and punishment. The Trobrianders had no judicial or police system whatever. If any member of the village behaved badly, was stingy or unjust, the whole village knew of it and his behavior was discussed and condemned. If a more serious breach of custom and morals took place, such as one Malinowski witnessed when the son of a chief was discovered in adultery with another man's wife, the offended party and his clan relatives loudly and publicly accused and insulted the criminal in the village plaza. After this particular ritual of casting out, the transgressor left the village, and his father, the chief, suffered a great loss of prestige.

In another case, a man returned from fishing and found his wife in a compromising situation with the chief of a near-by village. Public opinion was against the adulterer, who was insulted and ridiculed. Shamed, he took fish poison—a halfway suicide measure, for the poison was not really lethal. He was given emetics, and he recovered and regained his prestige.

Actual suicide did take place. The younger wife of a chief was suspected by her elder (and less attractive) co-wife, who spied on her and caught her in adultery. The guilty wife was publicly harangued by the relatives of her husband. Her sense of shame was profound. She dressed in her best, climbed a palm tree, wailed aloud, and jumped from it. Another wife, falsely accused by her husband and beaten, also climbed a palm tree, proclaimed her innocence and her tragic shame, and cast herself to her death.

It was clear that the need for status and prestige and the compulsion to fulfill reciprocal obligations were the true source of moral sanctions, ruling, as they did, the whole emotional life of the Trobrianders. Petty offenses were held in check by social disapproval, the latter being ritualized in more serious cases by the public accusation. The individual, too deeply shamed, had no other resources than ending his or her life.

In a sense the morality of the Trobrianders therefore was the morality of the small group or village where everybody knew everybody's business and disapproval would be deeply felt. Even in a contemporary American village something similar occurs. Law-enforcement machinery has a minimum of cases and is scarcely necessary. The rare crime of violence is an abnormality and is very often the result of an intrusion from a larger, more impersonal community.

The family life of the Trobrianders was tied up with the clan system and called for many ceremonial exchanges of gifts between the wife's relatives and the husband. There was a strong brother-and-sister taboo; sex could never be mentioned between them.

Among the natives sex life began early and was remarkably uninhibited. Small children indulged in sex play when they felt like it, causing no stronger reaction in their elders than amusement. With the advent of adolescence, erotic adventures became a passion. The young men, now living in bachelor's houses, sometimes took their girls there, sometimes met them in corners of the yam houses. There was, however, a strong taboo against eating together in public. If any pair of young lovers did this, it was regarded as a serious breach of morality. Girls sometimes made up a party to visit a near-by village, where they paired off with the boys. These erotic adventures were conducted discreetly and surrounded with considerable romance. When a liaison became prolonged, the relationship generally culminated in marriage. After marriage, love affairs were supposed to cease. Chiefs, however, were traditionally polygamous.

Malinowski studied sex life in detail—the things said by lovers, the habits of courtship, the position used in intercourse, erotic folklore and myth. He freed himself completely from Victorian taboos and treated sex more frankly than any anthropologist before him.

In 1927, when he was analyzing family relationships, he was, for a period, interested in psychoanalytical theory. The Oedipus complex, he pointed out, was first observed in a strongly patriarchal European society. His Trobrianders were matriarchal. Were the findings of Freud universal or would a differently organized society throw new light on the Oedipus complex?

Pregnancy and nursing of children in civilized society, he felt, was rather a nuisance to the father, who, on the whole, was divorced from child-rearing and entered the picture only as a disciplinarian. Among the islanders, however, during the two-year nursing period, the father shared the care of the child with the mother, even to the Trobriand equivalent of diapering it, and was passionately fond of it. The mother, too, was relaxed and indulgent.

The natives, he was absolutely certain, did not recognize the physical mechanism of fatherhood. They insisted that the child was the reincarnated spirit of an ancestor who entered the womb of the mother. The father's role was merely to dilate the vagina. As the system was matriarchal, authority and social dominance rested with the mother's brother or the equivalent relative on the mother's side. The father was a stranger. Although a kind and valued friend, he was expected to earn the right to sexual privileges with his wife by giving her presents, which was also the case in a boy's relationship to his sweetheart.

As the boy grew up, the maternal uncle taught him the customs and restraints involved in clan kinship, magic and crafts, and par-

322

ticularly the sex taboos. Theirs was exclusively a formal relationship. Thus the uncle was much more like the European patriarchal father than the child's true father.

Malinowski noted that there was no period in which the young islander went through a surreptitious and pornographic interest in sex because, except for the sister taboo, he was at no time in his life taught that sex was evil or embarrassing.

The ethnologist also examined the dreams and myths of his Trobrianders. Most dreams that the islanders bothered to remember were "official," following certain magical patterns of divination. When he did get to the deeper layers of the subconscious he found interesting evidence. When asked if they dreamed of intercourse with their mothers, they simply looked at him incredulously. Only an idiot would have such a dream. When asked if they dreamed of sex with their sisters, they reacted with much emotion, embarrassment, anxiety, and angry denials. They often admitted that "other people" had such dreams. On the other hand, they were quite willing to admit dreams of intercourse with distant though prohibited female relatives. This sort of defiance of custom was considered piquant.

A myth described a cannibalistic ogre who began eating up the natives. All of the group he attacked fled except one girl who had a little son and who had hurt her foot. She was abandoned by her brothers. Bent on revenge for this criminal desertion, she brought her son up, taught him to kill the ogre, and when this feat was accomplished the boy presented the head of the monster, baked in a pudding, to his uncle. The uncle was shocked and horrified and tried to make atonement for his lapse by presenting the boy with his daughter for a wife. Malinowski interpreted this story as symbolical hostility toward the maternal uncle. He even thought the ogre was a symbol for the uncle. There was also a myth of a man who accidentally dropped love magic on his sister, pursued her, seduced her in a cave, and continued with erotic indulgence until they both died.

Malinowski thought the evidence indicated that the Oedipus complex did not apply to the Trobriand Islands culture, for here the maternal uncle replaced the patriarchal father and the area of sexual guilt involved not the mother but the sister. Freud's biographer-to-be, Ernest Jones, attacked Malinowski and tried to defend the universality of the Oedipus complex by saying that the savage had unconscious knowledge of the mechanics of paternity and repressed it and substituted his sister for his mother.

Malinowski retorted by rejecting Freud's theory of exogamy and totemism, which maintained that both arose from guilt as the result of the murder of the old male by a band of brothers. Was culture present when this tragedy took place, he asked, or did it develop afterward? If there was no culture and this was the origin of culture, how was the sense of guilt transmitted without a racial unconscious? Did the tragic act occur only once or did it happen in every group and horde? He saw no reason why young males should submit to voluntary sex starvation while getting up courage to steal their father's harem. "It is easy to perceive that the primitive horde has been equipped with all the bias, maladjustments and ill-tempers of a middle-class European family and then let loose in a prehistoric jungle to run riot in a most attractive but fantastic hypothesis."

Freud must have pondered this criticism, for, years later, when he restated his thesis in *Moses and Monotheism*, he rather shamefacedly admitted that his theory required a racial unconscious.

It is a pity Malinowski was handled so dogmatically by the orthodox Freudians, for he seems to have reacted strongly and dropped all of psychoanalysis because of his disagreement with Freud on the theory of origins. Psychoanalysis was, however, never an organic part of his method. Actually, his suggestion that the basic drives recognized by psychoanalysis could be modified in different cultures was to bear fruit and influence later generations of psychiatrists.

At any rate, Malinowski in later years defined his psychological approach as behaviorist. Cultural patterns were impressed on children by their parents; they were conditioning. This ruled out the group unconscious. The family and clan formed the key to the complicated network of responsibilities and privileges which held savage society together. Good manners and doing the right thing as defined by transmitted custom were the unwritten laws of primitive society and were just as binding on it as any judicial code or formal etiquette of their civilized brethren.

In contrast to Durkheim, whom he criticized, he believed that the primitive was neither an extreme collectivist nor an extreme individualist.

For the diffusionist school Malinowski had considerable scorn, calling Graebner "a museum mole." In a symposium on the diffusionist controversy, published in 1927, G. Elliot Smith announced that if he found a match in a primitive area, he would know it had been diffused by a white man, for it had been invented only once. Malinowski retorted that many modern inventions, including the telegraph, had been made simultaneously by several people. He added that if he found a match on the Trobriand Islands he would know it had been mechanically transported by a trader. Furthermore, when matches were scarce during the First World War, the Trobrianders went back to making fire by friction. They did not possess the chemistry to make matches, and the latter were decidedly not "diffused." After all, when it came to proving diffusion by comparison of objects, the function of the objects should first be exhaustively studied. A digging-stick, for example, could be used as a walking-stick or a punting-pole. Although the sticks might be identical in form, only the functionalist would know that they had no real connection with one another.

His view of social motivation was behavioristic in character. The will of God, the categorical imperative, Schmidt's supreme moral being, and Durkheim's collective soul were vague concepts. Moral behavior resulted from conditioning of the nervous system. Thus it was neither an instinct nor a logical desire for personal benefit, but was produced by gradual training within a set of cultural traditions. These traditions often conditioned behavior so that "man prefers death to surrender or compromise, pain to pleasure, abstention to satisfaction of desire."

But what set up the original cultural pattern? Some anthropologists consider this question unanswerable. Others are still doggedly seeking a solution.

In 1927 Malinowski was appointed to the first chair of anthropology created by the University of London. He was a stimulating teacher and a tireless worker, laboring at all hours of the day, in bed (his health was never good), out of bed, eating, or walking. His students learned to discuss their theses on the top of a bus or dodging market barrows on side streets as they followed him about London. Despite ill health, he wrote many books and articles. He early abandoned formal lecturing, ignored the prescribed curriculum, and conducted brilliant Socratic seminars, attended by colonial officials on leave, other university lecturers and amateurs, and undergraduates. His wit was proverbial, but it often made enemies, for it had a satirical bite. He was also deliberately theatrical and fond of playing the role of *enfant terrible*. He once wrote a letter to a missionary in language, said the recipient, "so terrible that I cannot let my secretary read it." The same missionary said that the letter had given him enough ideas to work on for a year.

Malinowski spent his summers in a villa in the Dolomites of northern Italy. There several of his students were accustomed to follow him. They lived in a pension near by, set out their writing-materials under trees, and worked all day in the open. In the afternoon they went up to the villa, where they had tea with him and his wife, and then went walking and discussed their work. After dinner they again gathered in the villa to read aloud some-times Malinowski's own manuscripts, sometimes the work of other anthropologists. Hortense Powdermaker recalls that one of the books they read was Radcliffe-Brown's study of the Andaman Islanders. Between these two men who were the leaders in their field in England there was a state of respectful hostility. Each one accepted the other's students without question. They indulged in brisk controversies in scientific journals and, despite the fact that their theoretical positions were not far apart, were always temperamentally at odds. Radcliffe-Brown, more formal and intensely British, tended to collect a compact group of followers. Malinowski encouraged individuality in his students, a rapid informal give-and-take that developed whatever originality they possessed.

Headstrong, dramatic, with the independence of the aristocrat (his family was an important one in Poland), he had the European intellectual's impatience with the mass methods of modern teaching. When giving a course in the New School for Social Research in 1929, he found himself confronted with about a hundred students. During the first week, by skillfully insulting those who he decided had joined the group for the wrong reasons, he reduced his class to about twenty-five serious scholars.

In 1934 Malinowski made a flying trip to Africa. He had already been writing on colonial problems for the publication *Africa*. When he was lecturing in America the following year, he received an honorary degree from Harvard University. Clyde Kluckhohn of Harvard, who was extremely sympathetic to Boas, echoed the sentiments of the Boas camp to the effect that Malinowski publicized the obvious and raised to a doctrinal level field practice which the Boas group had used for decades. "He could be," wrote Kluckhohn, "defiant, petulant, wilfully brilliant, contradictory in professional meetings and in writing."

His enemies considered him a pretentious messiah; the field workers who followed him felt he had given their science new life. Kluckhohn, however, acknowledged his great gifts as a writer. Indeed, his first and probably best book, *Argonauts of the Western Pacific* (1922), teems with vivid images and colorful re-creations of island life.

Because his field work was done in only one geographical area, his critics accused him of generalizing from too narrow a base of experience. He also failed to catalogue and describe his native informants and to record their life histories. His own theory of functionalism called for an integration of all his material into a comprehensive account of Trobriand culture. This task he never performed. Instead, it was said that *Coral Gardens and Their Magic* (1935) made all island life seem to center around gardening, while *The Sexual Life of Savages* (1929) made sex seem to be the key to primitive culture. During the last few years of his life, however, when he was on a sabbatical and teaching at Yale, he began studies of the marketing system in Oaxaca, Mexico. He planned to extend his study from the market into all phases of Mexican culture and to develop reports on the progress of the work each year. From this it is evident that he was striking out in a new area and might well have produced work that would have answered his critics. World War II found him still at Yale. He became an active antagonist of fascism and a defender of Poland, although up to this time he had not been identified with Polish nationalism. He died of a heart attack in 1942. In the years since, his influence has not decreased. Among the distinguished scholars trained by him were M. F. Ashley Montagu, Raymond Firth, H. L. Shapiro, Meyer Fortes, Max Gluckman, who wrote on primitive law, and Hortense Powdermaker. One of his most outstanding students is E. E. Evans-Pritchard, who now occupies the chair of anthropology at Oxford and continues the functionalist tradition combined with the sociological outlook of Emile Durkheim.

Like Frazer, Malinowski had the magical gift of making his

science popular. He pointed out that the study of man was concerned with living people and was not a compilation of facts for specialists. With Boas, he prepared the ground for the contemporary point of view that anthropology, if it is to justify itself, must take up the task of understanding and guiding social change.

Chapter 32

WHAT IS CULTURE?

Concerning A. L. Kroeber, Robert Redfield, Ralph Linton

■ What is culture? Anthropology, which had grown up pragmatically, in the early twenties began to realize that it was weak in theory. The various schools approached the study of man with different emphases and disagreed considerably in terminology. Even the concept of culture was imprecisely defined.

Tylor had formulated the classic definition, which included the material and non-material achievements of men living in a social relationship. This was a new and technical use of the word *culture*, which he had borrowed from the Germans. It had arisen only in the mid-nineteenth century. Before that, *culture* meant "refinement."

Culture, as we have seen, overlaps those two fields which have come to be called anthropology and sociology. Theoretically, anthropology is the study of culture, sociology that of society. But both culture and society are created by living people—the same people. We have seen that Malinowski insisted on the study of function—that is, the use and meaning of culture traits and institutions. This sounds suspiciously sociological. On the whole, as twentieth-century science became richer and more complex, the anthropologists began to perceive that their own science had many levels and that the analysis of culture was an extremely intricate problem.

Three Americans who achieved stature during the first decades of the twentieth century reflect in different ways the changing attitude toward culture and the study of man. They are Alfred Louis Kroeber (1876–   ), Robert Redfield (1897–1957), and Ralph Linton (1893–1953).

A. L. Kroeber, whom we have mentioned before in connection with diffusion, came of a German family that had settled in New York City. He entered Columbia University in 1892, came under the influence of Boas, and decided to become an anthropologist because he felt that the new study would have a liberating effect on the human mind. After taking his doctor's degree in anthropology at Columbia he became an instructor in the University of California, where he has remained ever since.

Throughout all his writing he shows an interest in defining culture and has vigorously maintained a specific point of view. Essentially a historian, he has always insisted that the proper sphere of anthropology is "cultural facts," not "social facts." Ants, he says, have a society but no culture. Man is distinct from the animals; his patterns of behavior are transmitted not by instinct, as among ants, but by learning. What is transmitted is culture, an abstraction. This is a restatement of the classic diffusionist position. It is not surprising, therefore, that Kroeber has done work in Mexican and South American archeology and that his major books are summations of material, attempting to define culture areas and patterns.

In 1919 he participated in a survey of the Southwest Zuni district which was published under the general direction of Clark Wissler, who, as we have seen, was a pioneer in establishing American culture areas. Kroeber's contribution was a potsherd study in which he classified types and tried to set up time sequences. His *Handbook of the Indians of California* (1925) was a thousand-page synthesis of all that is known of this area, both a descriptive record and an attempt to chart the spread of tribal cultures. By 1939 he had produced another monumental work, *Cultural and Natural Areas of Native North America*, which was an elaboration of Wissler's general scheme in the light of further data. Kroeber and Wissler diverged from Boas as early as 1906 in that they attempted to make historical reconstructions of the spread of culture in the past while Boas felt that the technique for such work was in its infancy and most time sequences were merely conjecture.

Despite a flirtation with psychoanalysis during which Kroeber became a lay analyst, he steadily rejected any linkage between anthropology and contemporary psychology. At times he has stated that a psychology of culture would be desirable, but he has made it clear that he finds no existing school satisfactory. Functionalism he considers "unhistorical" because it deals with a point in time, and he has used the same word to describe sociology. It is clear that he has been anxious to keep his own brand of anthropology apart from both. He has also at times deplored the lack of a theoretical basis for anthropology, but in 1953 he wrote: "A fully systematic, scientific theory of man, society, and culture, has yet to be created."

Kroeber has always been interested in large general patterns of history. Preoccupations similar to those of Spengler or Toynbee (whom he quotes) are exemplified by his book *Configurations of Culture Growth* (1944). In this work he described and charted the peaks or bursts of culture in all civilizations of the past, with particular emphasis on the grouping of geniuses in the arts and sciences. But as he has found no theory of history satisfactory and has developed none of his own, the book remains merely descriptive and the conclusions are extremely meager. He suggested that there might be a connection between the growth of population and wealth and such culture bursts, and that genius was not an isolated phenomenon but a symptom of a burst of culture.

On the whole, Kroeber commands respect because of the strictness of his method and the scope of his works. As chairman of the department of anthropology of the University of California, he created a great department and trained many important scholars. In the perspective of recent developments he seems to sum up the best in the diffusionist school. His final definition of culture as "an abstraction from behavior and the products of behavior" is far too narrow to cover the newest preoccupations of anthropology. For if culture is conceived as an abstraction, people are somehow left out of the picture. Culture, as Kroeber admits, is continually changing. The historian cannot be indifferent to the process of change. The scholars of the diffusionist school have preferred to infer change by comparing artifacts, by making quantitative studies of distribution, and by noting the results on maps. But culture is changed by living human beings, and if contemporary human behavior is not the province of anthropology, then the latter science is scarcely to be distinguished from archeology.

A significant symptom of the newer attitude was an article by Robert Redfield, Ralph Linton, and Melville Herskovits in the *American Anthropologist* in 1936 entitled "A Memorandum for the Study of Acculturation," which was written because the Social Science Research Council (of which we shall have more to say) had the year before set up a subcommittee on acculturation. The word had come into use about 1880 and had been defined by Graebner. The three Americans now redefined it as the study of direct contact between peoples with different cultural patterns resulting in change in one or both. This, of course, was concentrating on diffusion in the present and studying it in action. By 1946 a summary of the outstanding works on anthropology included 49 devoted to acculturation as against 111 of the classical diffusionist type.

The work of Robert Redfield both exemplifies this dynamic approach to culture and adds a new area to anthropological study. Redfield has been identified with the University of Chicago, where he took his first degree and where he has been chairman of the department of anthropology and Robert M. Hutchins Distinguished Service Professor of Anthropology. From 1926 to 1927, with the aid of a grant from the Social Science Research Council, he studied Mexican peasants. In the introduction to his book *Tepoztlán, A Mexican Village* (1930) he pointed out that he was interested in cultural *processes* and in changes *as they occurred*. His point of view reflects that of Malinowski and Radcliffe-Brown. (The latter was to teach at the University of Chicago from 1931 to 1937.) Turning away from studies of diffusion, Redfield found in Mexico, where an Indian race had been conquered by a European one and fusion was taking place, a living laboratory of cultural change.

Although the villagers were mostly of Indian stock, an interesting division had taken place. *Los tontos* (the fools), so-called by the better-educated, made up the group that was most Indian in culture; *los correctos* (the genteel) had had some contact with the city, were more likely to speak and read Spanish as well as the indigenous Nahuatl, and had some notion of the modern scientific world. Through them modern (and relatively more Spanish) culture was introduced.

The bulk of the population kept the ancient *metate* or maize-grinder and the *olla* or pot, and lived in one-room adobe houses, but used certain modern artifacts such as the kerosene stove, the china pitcher and saucer, the steel knife. The *rebozo*, worn over the women's heads, was originally a Spanish shawl, but the men's *sarape* was a fusion of the Indian cape and the Spanish blanket. The theory of disease was particularly interesting. The ancient Indian belief blamed sickness on *los aires* (the airs), and sacrifices were made to them; they were envisioned as little spirits. Since los correctos were gradually abandoning this magical notion, there was a drugstore in town. Los tontos sometimes bought medicines and combined them with magical propitiation of los aires, but a European doctor was unsuccessful in building up a practice and had to move away.

Actually, the villagers were no longer a truly primitive group; they had stabilized certain fused elements, although in other respects they were still changing. Redfield later came to see that such village groups as Tepoztlán could be compared with similar village or peasant groups in other parts of the world. His studies caused him to define and describe peasant culture as a new area for investigation. Peasant culture was a *partial* culture because, through certain key persons, it was hinged to the more complex urban culture representative of a nation, and between the two fusion was continuing.

In these later studies Redfield saw peasantry as a kind of society and culture connecting indigenous local humanity with civilization. He presented the peasant as an agriculturalist laboring in his fields to carry on, not a business, but a traditional way of life. The city sophisticates constituted an elite that sometimes dominated the peasant culture politically, sometimes offered a prestige example, sometimes did both. Although the peasants admitted that the urban elite was culturally superior, they nevertheless compensated by calling it effete and considered themselves hardier and more industrious. Redfield felt there was evidence that the Mayas of Mexico and Central America had already begun to develop a peasantry of their own before the coming of the Spaniards.

Illiteracy was a key characteristic of peasant culture. In Tepoztlán los correctos could read, but the majority of the villagers could not, and popular literature consisted of ballads known as *corridos*. These dealt with personalities such as the revolutionary hero Zapata and made them into legendary figures, satirized contemporary politics, or recounted tales of murder, calamity, and love affairs. Corridos were sometimes printed and sold for a few centavos. The current love songs were ceasing to be folk songs and falling into the classification of commercial popular art.

Redfield made two studies of another Mexican group, the Mayan village of Chan Kom in Yucatán. In this case his interest was aroused by a conscious effort on the part of the citizens of Chan Kom to modernize themselves. A few scattered families in 1925 decided to turn themselves into a pueblo or village. They applied for a survey, got title to their lands, and in 1927 cleared the ground, blasted rocks, and made a plaza around which they built their houses. About this time a college student, Alfonso Villa Rojas, became their schoolteacher. Villa Rojas, who was later to become an anthropologist, proceeded to learn Maya; he won their confidence and became their counselor. In 1930–3, the period during which these villagers were studied by Redfield, Sylvanus Morley was excavating the near-by ruin of Chichén Itzá. The nurse accompanying this expedition made friends with the villagers, who were at first anti-American. Young Villa Rojas read Morley's books. The rest of the village began to hear of modern hygiene, built a new road, and spoke of becoming like a North American town.

Next came North American Protestant missionaries. The majority of the villagers (who were nominally Catholic but who retained much of the old Mayan religion) embraced the new cult for a time. When Redfield came back to Chan Kom in 1948 he found that the village had several masonry houses, a church, a Protestant chapel, two outdoor theaters, two gristmills, four stores, and a baseball diamond.

What was the meaning of Chan Kom's achievement? Were the villagers pleased with their success and did they still follow the same goal of progress?

They were still, he found, a peasant people dependent on agriculture, and books were still a rarity although a few citizens were semi-literate. The leading families owned masonry houses on the plaza. Most villages still had kitchens made of pole and thatch. There were no privies, no mosquito netting, and two outdoor showers, which the schoolteacher had persuaded them to build, were no longer in use. The theaters, which a "cultural mission" from Mexico City had prompted them to build, were also not used. Most of the men had made the change from white drawers and apron to long trousers. Most of the women still wore the native blouse, the *huipil*, though on certain occasions some wore dresses. Shoes, the ultimate step in sophistication, were rare.

As in Tepoztlán there was an elite with which the villagers had some connection. Mexicans who wore citified clothes were called *dzules*. Their only resident dzul, however, had been the teacher.

Returning in 1948, Redfield found that since 1933 there had been a slow regression. The conversion to Protestantism had come about partly because of a religious and social rivalry between two prominent families. The one which felt itself to be losing out took to the new religion as a protest. Then the whole village, except for the rival family, began to be swept by the movement, identifying it with the idea of progress. The rival family remained obstinately Catholic and took the village saint into its house. The missionaries, however, were dogmatic and insisted not only that all colorful Catholic ritual must go but also that the villagers must cease to dance their local folk dance, the *jarana*, which was the principal social outlet. Some of the converts became puritan extremists; there was hard feeling between them and the Catholic minority. Then, one night, just after a prayer meeting, the Catholics put on a gay jarana fiesta. Gradually the converts drifted over to it. The next morning the majority resigned from the Protestant church. The few who were left began, in an impulse to regain a lost sense of village unity, to modify their worship until it approached Catholicism.

With the swing back from Protestantism the ancient Mayan religion, never abandoned, came back strongly and the rain ceremony was regularly practiced. When Redfield returned in 1948, some of the cattle had hoof-and-mouth disease. The villagers were divided between using injections of serum and resorting to pagan prayer and magic.

The Mayans of Chan Kom had taken from the modern world only those elements of progress which did not disturb their inherited culture too much. They accepted a few novelties because they thought these changes would make them more prosperous. When they saw there was no end to change, they drew back. They did not like the new freedom between boys and girls which arose from going to school together. They were afraid of what they considered the vices of town life—the eventual arrival of movies and a tavern. A little reading and writing was good and arithmetic was practical. "But," said one of their leaders, who was a fairly literate man, "in the city, where there are so many books, people are always talking about their problems, wondering how to solve them. Out here, even if we do not use books, we have some way to solve every difficulty."

Chan Kom was a fascinating and unusual example of a technically backward group trying to cope with modern civilization. Every such group will face the same problems when the inevitable change comes to it. As Redfield pointed out, the leaders of Chan Kom had a moral integrity based on survivals of their ancient religion as long as they remained a self-contained unit. Their descendants will consciously have to join the outside world. This world will take the old moral integrity from them and give them more comforts and more science in return. We ourselves are still trying to balance this equation.

Redfield's work on peasant culture has helped to channel the interest of scholars away from the remote little primitive tribe. Now studies are undertaken of similar peasant areas in many parts of the world. His books, embodying a more or less functionalist approach, are agreeably written and can be read with pleasure by the general public.

If anthropology was learning that cultural change could be studied anywhere among living people, the problem of putting its own house in order still remained. Ralph Linton's greatest achievement was an attempt to synthesize the scholarly attitudes toward the study of man which existed in the late twenties.

Linton, who came of Philadelphia Quaker stock, received his master's degree in archeology from Swarthmore in 1916 and worked in the ruins of Quiriguá, Guatemala. After serving in World War I he was sent by the Bernice Bishop Museum of Honolulu in 1920 to the Marquesas Islands to study native archeology. He published a report on the material culture of the islands, but by this time he had discovered that living societies were more interesting than dead ones. He went on another field trip, this time to Madagascar as a one-man Marshall Field expedition in 1925. He received his doctor's degree in anthropology from Harvard the same year and, after more field work in Madagascar and Africa, joined the faculty of the University of Wisconsin in 1928. During the following years he prepared what he considered his magnum opus, *The Study of Man*, which was published in 1936. The next year he succeeded Boas as head of the anthropology department of Columbia University.

The Study of Man, which was used as a textbook in Columbia, embodied unconventional approaches to most of the subjects that anthropologists had been considering for decades. In comparison, Kroeber's *Anthropology*, which was published in 1923 and also used as a text, seems like a handbook of diffusion. Linton spent almost half of his book on a discussion of race and society. The other half was concerned with culture, but diffusion and historical reconstruction got only two chapters. In his introduction he wrote that he was willing "to go part way with any one of the competing schools but not all the way with any one." The multiplicity of schools he blamed on the youth of the science.

In many cases Linton abandoned current terminology and invented some of his own. When he spoke of the unity of society he called it *esprit de corps*. He made it clear that by this he meant a sacrifice of personal inclination in favor of a good deal of voluntary co-operation. This "sharing of ideas and emotional responses" was really a much reduced form of Durkheim's *collective conscience*. Perhaps his most important contribution was his elaboration of the sociological concepts of *status* and *role*. Every society, he said, had a pattern of reciprocal behavior between groups or individuals. Status was position in this pattern involving rights and duties. Any individual might have several statuses. When a man played his role he acted in accordance with the rights and duties that went with his status. Statuses could be ascribed or achieved. The Brahmin caste in India, for instance, was an ascribed status and had nothing to do with ability or individuality. On the other hand, a man achieved the status of President of the United States. The kinds of status which society prescribed for its members and their distribution among age and sex groupings determined the character of the society. Castes and classes within a society also had their internal systems of status. He pointed out that highly organized societies abounded in ascribed status—a situation difficult for Americans to understand, for they prized achieved status above anything else. He added: "Membership in a rigidly organized society may deprive an individual of opportunities to exercise his particular gifts but it gives him an emotional security which is almost unknown among ourselves."

Linton introduced a new perspective into the problems which had traditionally been discussed in terms of matriarchy and patriarchy. In the first place, he pointed out that marriage and the family, though often confused, were not the same concept. One particular group, the Nayar of India, had reduced marriage to a formality that lasted only a few days. After that the husband departed, the wife took lovers, and her children were raised by her kin. There were actually two types of family: the consanguine, which was organized around the blood relationships of either husband or wife, and the conjugal, which was organized around the biologically reproducing unit, the married pair. Whether the husband went to live with the wife's family or vice versa had little significance if both families lived close together. If they did, the two members of either type of marriage remained closely attached to their own consanguine groups. As both individuals had the support of their relatives, such marriages were easily broken up. It was only when one marriage partner had to take up residence at a distance that the alien was in an inferior position and had a serious problem of adjustment. Patriarchal or matriarchal systems seemed to Linton merely a matter of legal emphasis. In no case were women really dominant because in the human species the males were, on the average, larger and stronger. Even in matriarchal societies the woman's male kin were the real rulers. Linton was inclined to think that the two systems were produced by economic factors. The sex involved in the most important economic activity would be the one which had property to transmit. In general, he said, male-supported societies tended to be patrilineal, female-supported ones matrilineal.

Marriage, according to Linton's view, in most societies was a legal contract between two individuals or between their respective families. In few areas did it have anything to do with romantic love, and even the religious aspect was subordinate. This was the reason (and here he was close to Briffault) for the many types of marriage by purchase. The bride price was a compensation for loss of services.

Linton's concept of cultural study had profited from functionalism, and consequently he did not shrink from an analysis of society. "To understand cultural process," he wrote, "we must know content and observe this content in action." In a later book he insisted that the anthropologist should follow through on problems, using every technique, and without fear of crossing the boundaries between the different sciences.

Linton went on to discuss the relation between the individual personality and role. He remarked that psychologists had written a good deal about the presumed effects of childhood experience on the adult personality and that studies of infant care in different societies might prove or disprove this contention. A year after *The Study of Man* was published, he began joint seminars with the psychoanalyst Abram Kardiner in which they investigated this very problem. He and Kardiner then collaborated in writing two books. This study leads to another trend in anthropology which will be discussed in the next chapter.

In 1940 Linton edited a study of acculturation among American Indians which indicated his continued interest in this subject. In his summation he stressed the fact that accultural study led to the investigation of the destructive effect of enforced cultural change among colonial peoples and also to a consideration of the problem of the Negro minority in the United States. In 1944 he helped René d'Harnoncourt to arrange an exhibition of South Sea primitive art in New York's Museum of Modern Art which did much to popularize primitive art among the general public. Linton's attitude toward the immediate future of society was, in contrast to that of many social scientists, pessimistic. He foresaw a period of totalitarian darkness and stagnation after which the constructive forces in mankind would start to build once more. For this reason he dedicated his book *The Study of Man* to "the next civilization."

Within his own character there was conflict and contradiction. He had strong likes and was fond of meeting new people, but his dislikes were just as strong and often fairly irrational. Shortly before he died he wrote in an autobiographical sketch: "I consider as my greatest accomplishment that I am an adopted member of the Comanche tribe, was accepted as a master carver by the Marquesas natives, . . . am a member of the native church of North America (Peyote) according to the Quapaw rite, became a properly accredited *ombiasy nkazo* (medicine man) in Madagascar, and was even invited to join the Rotary Club of a middle western city."

Chapter **33**

THE CHILD IS FATHER TO THE MAN

Concerning Margaret Mead

■ To the classical anthropologist the suggestion that he should study children would have been completely bewildering. But, then, all the classical anthropologists were men. In the late twenties a woman entered the field of anthropology and helped to create an important new trend. The woman was Margaret Mead. The new direction that resulted from several interacting influences was the trend toward the integration of the social sciences and the study of personality. Most important for the study of personality, or individual character, was the rearing of children, for, according to psychoanalytical theory, the personality was formed by the age of five.

Up to this time the individual had not been recognized in anthropology. Society was composed of institutions, traits, culture complexes, not people. However, Boas, whose interests were many, had taken some steps in the study of the individual, for he had encouraged the recording of Indian life histories. As we have seen, his attitude toward the psychoanalytical movement was ambivalent. Nevertheless, Boas's pupils played the most important role in bringing anthropology and the psychiatrists together.

It will be remembered that A. L. Kroeber reviewed the English edition of *Totem and Taboo* somewhat sympathetically in 1920. In his own works, however, he always ignored psychoanalytical concepts. Another Boas pupil, Edward Sapir, whom we have mentioned in connection with diffusion, was a remarkably well-rounded person. He published poetry, played the piano, even composed a sonata. He also wrote for such sophisticated magazines as the *Dial*. In 1917 we find him reviewing a book on the psychoanalytical method in that magazine. Although the review echoed some of Boas's criticisms of Freudian excesses, Sapir showed that he was seriously interested in the movement and ended by saying that it was the most fruitful direction psychology had taken in recent years. Sapir also reviewed Rivers's *Instinct and the Unconscious* favorably in the *Freeman* in 1921. In 1923 he reviewed Jung's *Psychological Types* in the same magazine and indicated that he had read the latter's earlier book, published in 1916, which set forth the concept of two psychological types—the introvert and the extrovert. Although Sapir wrote no extended works dealing with psychology or the study of personality, his short essays and reviews bristle with insights, and he must be considered an important influence in developing the new outlook.

Margaret Mead (1903–) became interested in psychoanalytical thinking at about the same time, for when she was an undergraduate at Columbia in 1920 she took a course given by the sociologist William Ogburn in which all of the available literature, including works by Freud, Jung, Adler, and Rivers, was studied. The youthful Mead was at this time specializing in anthropology under Boas. She was destined to become the leading exponent of the personality school and, together with Ruth Benedict (who was Boas's assistant at the time) and Sapir, to do most to crystallize the new direction in anthropology.

Other straws in the wind indicated that a need was felt for a closer rapprochement among the social sciences. The formation of the Social Science Research Council in 1923, which united the official organizations of anthropology, sociology, history, statistics, psychology, economics, and political science, was an organizational move that brought these groups together for a yearly meeting and promoted joint research. In 1927 William Ogburn, with the anthropologist Alexander Goldenweiser, edited *The Social Sciences and Their Interrelations*, in which experts from the fields of economics, psychology, history, political science, and sociology tried to define the relations among their sciences. It is interesting to note, however, that, despite Ogburn's interest in psychoanalysis (he had been analyzed), the psychological contributions to the book were mostly behavioristic. Freud's name is mentioned only once, in a footnote. Psychoanalysis was not yet officially recognized in academic circles. It was not until some years later that joint seminars were held by anthropologists and Freudian psychiatrists.

Nevertheless, while such tentative moves toward integration were being made, Mead worked steadily in the field *applying* the insights of Freudian psychiatry. For this reason her first book, *Coming of Age in Samoa,* is a pioneer effort and indeed a landmark in anthropological literature.

Mead, aside from her study of psychoanalytical writing, had personal contact with Edward Sapir (and with C. G. Seligman of the Torres Straits expedition, who was also interested in psychiatric concepts) and studied with Benedict. Mead's graduate work was done on Polynesia. In 1925, when she was ready for her first field assignment, Boas encouraged her to do a study on adolescence. Educators believed that adolescence was unavoidably a period of emotional tension. Mead's problem was to find out if this was a universal truth or was true only of western civilization. A careful study of the upbringing of girls in a primitive group could serve as a basis of comparison.

Boas inclined toward an Indian tribe, but Mead preferred the islanders of the South Seas, whom she had studied in the library and who seemed less likely to be corrupted by western influences. For a young girl just out of college, in a period when women had scarcely begun to enter the field of anthropology, to go off alone to the haunts of cannibals was a truly revolutionary step. But the early twenties were also the period when women were beginning to assert themselves and demand equal rights with men. Margaret Mead has always been interested in the capabilities of women and was later to compare the male and female temperaments.

Boas, who could be extremely stubborn, objected to the whole idea. An anthropologist had been murdered in the Philippines, others had died of tropical diseases. South Sea islands were not safe for students. The indomitable Mead set out to convince her own family that she was right. Fortunately for the project, her father was an economist and her mother a sociologist. Indeed, the first wedding she ever attended was an Italian one, for her mother was studying Italian immigrants in America. With this social-science background in her family, it is no wonder that she obtained sympathetic support. Her father offered to supply the balance of the funds necessary for the trip if she could obtain a National Research Council fellowship.

After this victory she went back to Boas and reproached him for being a tyrant. Boas could not bear to see himself in this role. He gave in and recommended her for the fellowship, but stipulated that she must choose an island at which a boat stopped every three weeks. Samoa, of which little was known, happened to fill the bill.

Oddly enough, though picked at random, Samoa could not have been a better choice for her study, as the girls of that island received an upbringing radically different from the practices of western civilization. Margaret Mead's Samoan project was also a pioneer undertaking from another angle. Until her time (there were still very few field workers in the twenties) no woman had studied the primitive members of her own sex and taken advantage of the fact that she could gather confidential material which would have been very difficult for men to obtain.

Mead, like Malinowski, immersed herself in the life of the village. She took care to learn the language and customs. She participated in the activities of the women and gained their friendship. Her material was thus obtained by a combination of observation and informal interviews.

She wrote: "The life of the day begins at dawn, or if the moon has shown until daylight, the shouts of the young men may be heard before dawn from the hillside. Uneasy in the night, populous with ghosts, they shout lustily to one another as they hasten to their work. As the dawn begins to fall among the soft brown roofs and the slender palm trees stand out against the colorless gleaming sea, lovers slip home from trysts beneath the palm trees or in the shadow of beached canoes, that the light may find each sleeper in his appointed place. Cocks crow negligently, and a shrill-voiced bird cries from the breadfruit trees. The insistent roar of the reef seems muted to an undertone for the sounds of the waking village."

In this charming and gracious setting she studied the behavior of children and found that, on the whole, the island system of upbringing did not cause repressions. Babies were nursed for two or three years, pacified in this way whenever they cried. After being weaned, the young children were turned over to the older girls, who had to see to it that they did not annoy the adults. Elders seldom punished children. The restrictions were mostly a few practical avoidances enforced by slaps from the young nurse-maids. When the girls neared puberty they were relieved of baby-tending and began to learn such tasks as weaving and cooking.

Samoan society was not one in which intense competition was encouraged. Proficiency without the desire to excel was the ideal, although there were hierarchies of rank with special duties and privileges.

The younger boys and girls had little to do with each other, but after adolescence a series of sex relationships was normal (childish experiments were merely laughed at). These were finally terminated by marriage. With a few exceptions there was no crisis in adolescence; it was simply a period in which interests and activities slowly matured. "The girls' minds were perplexed by no conflicts, troubled by no philosophical queries, beset by no remote ambitions. To live as a girl with many lovers as long as possible and then to marry in one's own village, near one's own relatives and to have many children, these were a uniform and satisfying ambition." Such sex experimentation was possible be-cause in adolescence there was a period of non-fertility (this was also true of the Trobriand Islanders).

M. F. Ashley Montagu has pointed out that, contrary to popular opinion, menstruation often does not occur until about the age of seventeen in the tropics. He also demonstrates from animal and human statistics that there tends to be a natural period of sterility lasting for some time after the onset of puberty. This period he considers to be an automatic protection of the immature organism against too early pregnancy.

Mead's conclusion was that the American child, the center of many conflicts and conflicting currents of religious, social, and sexual theory, must be prepared for free choice. "Unhampered by prejudices, unvexed by too-early conditioning to any one stand-ard, they must come clear-eyed to the choices that lie before them." This, to a large extent, coincided with the prevailing theories of progressive education.

In 1928 *Coming of Age in Samoa* was a popular book, coming as it did just when the sexual revolution in western culture was being earnestly discussed. The Freudian analyst A. A. Brill hailed it as a great contribution to psychology. It was also engagingly written. The general public learned, for perhaps the first time, that anthropology could shed light on its own problems and that primitive peoples in some departments of life were better adjusted than modern civilized man.

Mead returned to the South Seas to study child development in Manus, a field trip that resulted in the book *Growing Up in New Guinea* (1930). In 1931 she again visited New Guinea for her investigation of sex and temperament. All during this period of the thirties the study of personality and culture was becoming the preoccupation of more and more leading social thinkers. Not all were convinced, however. Paul Radin, as we have seen, damned the new school as impressionistic. Alexander Salomonovich Goldenweiser (1880–1940), a leading Boas pupil and a cultivated intellectual who had written on totemism, published, in 1933, *History, Psychology, and Culture*, which contained a readable summary and criticism of past and present social theory. Goldenweiser was unsympathetic to Durkheim's sociology, but presented J. Teggart's theory of history (which credited human progress to the clash of idea systems) favorably. When it came to Freud, Goldenweiser felt that the new psychology had no place for such idealistic traits as courage and kindness. He rejected what has now come to be called the "just-so story"—the primal patricide and cannibal meal—but showed some interest in Freud's elaboration of the omnipotence of thought in both primitive and abnormal psychology.

One of those favoring the new school was Lawrence K. Frank, then of the Education Board of the Rockefeller Foundation. Frank had been interested in culture and personality and child development from the time of World War I, and in 1927 he sponsored a conference on the study of personality under the auspices of the Social Science Research Council.

Edward Sapir, too, had published several more articles in which he tossed off provocative suggestions. In one which appeared in 1934 he remarked that anthropology must concern itself with such familiar matters as child upbringing and note whether the relationship to the father was strict and formal or warm and loving. This, of course, was just what Mead had done in *Coming of Age*. This basic concept—that the parent-child relationship shaped the adult personality—Sapir had perhaps learned from Harry Stack Sullivan, with whom he had long discussions. Sapir's assistant at Yale, who worked with him in a seminar in 1933, was John Dollard, a neo-Freudian social scientist. Thus the trend toward personality-study and that toward the integration of the social sciences were interacting. They culminated in the formation of the Yale University Institute of Human Relations in 1929.

Meanwhile, the orthodox Freudian point of view continued to flourish, and the doctrines of *Totem and Taboo* found a new disciple in the Hungarian Géza Róheim. The latter was a practicing psychoanalyst from Budapest who obtained private financing for a trip around the world in 1927, during which he did anthropological field work in Africa and Australia. In Australian totemic mythology he decided he found support for all of Freud's basic anthropological ideas. Freud, too, continued to apply his theories to society, analyzed religion as an infantile institution, and also contributed a study of group reaction to the leader. The essay which his follower Géza Róheim wrote after his trip, *The Psychograph of a Primitive People*, published in 1932, was read by Mead while she was studying the Arapesh in New Guinea and, she acknowledges, influenced her thinking.

Mead's project was related to the already noted cultural revolution in the civilized world, the change in the attitude toward sex and the shift in the relationship between men and women. World War I had put women into industry to take the place of the absent soldiers. Once gainfully employed, they refused to give up the advantages they had won. In return, men, or spokesmen for men, were deploring the break-up of the home and accusing the mother of distorting her personality or adding to juvenile delinquency. Was it true that women were temperamentally suited to certain activities and men better equipped for others? Was there a feminine temperament and a male temperament, each immutably a part of basic human nature?

It is not surprising that Margaret Mead, herself a woman who had pioneered in a field that had been the province of men (except for the work of Mary Kingsly, Elsie Clews Parsons, and Ruth Benedict), set out to investigate this problem in terms of certain primitive New Guinea tribes. Three tribes, all within a hundred-mile area, were chosen, and it was not known in advance what would be found. Mead discovered that they exhibited an amazing variation in standards of behavior for the two sexes.

The mountain Arapesh lived in isolated family groups, raised a few pigs, and tilled the scarce, infertile soil. The Arapesh did not think in terms of owning land; rather, they belonged to it and cultivated the yam gardens in small co-operative groups. The relationship between mother and child was prolonged with a great deal of gentle play and warm bodily contact as the child was carried about before it could walk. Arapesh boys were not encouraged to be aggressive; injuring others was considered the greatest sin. Men were also responsible for the care of children and were as patient as women in handling them. The Arapesh scarcely ever fought. Men and women were gentle and sensitive, both sexes being very much alike in personality. The aggressive members of both sexes were the deviants and tended to be neurotic. On this contrast to western civilized behavior, Mead commented: "It is hard to judge which seems to us the most utopian, to say that there are no differences between men and women, or to say that both men and women are naturally maternal, gentle, responsive and unaggressive."

The second group studied was the Mundugumor, a tribe which lived on a branch of the Sepik River and whose head-hunting and cannibalism had been prohibited only three years before with the consolidation of British control. Although they lived on the river, they were not used to it; the river had shifted, so they were now located on its banks. They fished and traded tobacco and coconuts for household articles produced by other tribes. Neighboring tribes feared them with good reason, for hostility was the key to their society. Mudugumor men were polygamous and were supposed to exchange their sisters for wives. Those with no sisters had to take wives by force. Sons hated their fathers, for they often saw their mothers ill-treated—sometimes even beaten with a crocodile jaw. Then, too, because old men often married young women, there was fierce competition even between sons and fathers for the same women. Both husband and wife detested pregnancy, fretting at the taboos connected with it which decreed sexual deprivation. Children had no prestige value and were not loved. Indeed, some, at birth, were bundled up in palm leaves and tossed into the river. While babies, they were kept in uncomfortable baskets, and were suckled only when their crying became unendurable. They were crossly weaned and later surrounded by harsh taboos.

In this society, women grew up as aggressive, jealous, individualistic, and violent as the men. They did the hard work, such as fishing and collecting coconuts, while the men (who were good artists, in contrast to the artistically undeveloped Arapesh) carried on theatrical rituals and hunted heads. Thus in this society, which exaggerated in both sexes all the characteristics known to the west as "masculine," the gentle people were the deviants and neurotics.

The third group studied, the Tschambuli, lived on a lake connected with the Sepik River by various waterways. Surrounded by small sharp hills, the almost black waters of the lake were covered with pink and white lotuses and deep-blue water lilies, among which stood white ospreys and blue herons like figures in a Japanese painting. In this exotic setting the natives built ceremonial houses on each of whose high gable ends a huge red-and-white face was carved in low relief surmounted by a high thatched steeple ornamented by a wooden bird and the figure of a man. These were the famous men's clubhouses that we have met in the pages of Hutton Webster and Heinrich Schurtz.

Food was abundant, for the Tschambuli lived on fish and sage. Without agriculture or hunting to occupy them, they had time for a rich ceremonial life. Boys and girls were similarly educated during their early years. They were treated in a relaxed way, continually fed to stop their crying and weaned rather casually. At puberty, however, the boys were put through a painful and upsetting initiatory scarification. From then on, like the Victorian female, the boy was left to grow up a frivolous butterfly, joining with the others in the men's houses to perfect his dancing, painting, or flute-playing. Girls, on the other hand, became hard-working responsible citizens, for the adult women ran the society. They were co-operative, they fished, traded, and carried on domestic manufactures. Meanwhile, the men, who were nominally in control because the society was patriarchal, busied themselves with theatrical representation and turned into coy charmers who spent much time making themselves attractive to the women. The women were therefore the more aggressive in sexual matters, while the men, caught in the conflict between their nominal dominance and actual submission, were highly neurotic and even given to maniacal outbursts. Truly dominant men and unaggressive women were the unhappy and maladjusted in this society.

The German functionalist Richard Thurnwald attacked Mead's *Sex and Temperament* on the basis that the material had been gathered hurriedly and that there were inconsistencies in the data which did not support the conclusions. On the whole, however, the material drawn from these three groups vividly demonstrated the malleability of human nature and the fact that many of the temperamental characteristics which the west traditionally assigned to each sex were not inherent or at least could be imposed on each sex by a culture that was determined to do so. It also showed that in any culture the official sex patterns were bound to impose too great restrictions on the drives of many individuals, who therefore became maladjusted deviants. Mead subsequently applied the same point of view in a study of contemporary American sex standards.

Sex and Temperament in Primitive Societies was published in 1935. By that year the study of personality had made further strides. The psychiatrists Eric Fromm, Karen Horney, and Franz Alexander were in the United States developing analytical viewpoints that differed somewhat from that of the orthodox Freudians and showed the influence of Malinowski's criticism. Fromm, notably, was applying his theories to an analysis of the rise of German fascism. The intolerance of the latter regime was to force some of the best German psychologists into exile and residence in the United States. At Yale University an entente was being worked out between Clark Hull's behaviorist theories of learning, psychoanalysis, championed by John Dollard, and comparative studies of culture. Abram Kardiner, another neo-Freudian, more or less of the Fromm-Horney camp, quite independently started a joint seminar with the anthropologist Ralph Linton at Columbia University in 1937. Their work was based on Linton's field studies in the Marquesas and Madagascar. In 1939 Kardiner published *The Individual and His Society: The Psychodynamics of Primitive Social Organization*. In this work he stressed the influence of the cultural pattern upon the individual and tried to show (following Malinowski's lead) how polyandry and scarcity of food in the Marquesas Islands conditioned and modified the basic drives established by Freud. Although Kardiner attempted to elaborate a general thesis for studying primitive groups from a psychoanalytical point of view, he was actually only putting in more theoretical form insights that Mead had been employing for ten years.

Indeed, through all of this period in which so many scholars were interested in fusing what is now known as *psychology in depth* with anthropology, the field work of Mead sums up the many interacting influences. For instance, a German analyst of the Freudian school, Erik Erikson, working at the Harvard Psychological Clinic, first became acquainted with personality study when he encountered Mead, Scudder Makeel, and Benedict. He developed and presented at Harvard a series of modal *zonal charts*, intended to facilitate the study of pregenital sexuality in children, in 1935. (Freud maintained that the child's first erotic areas were the mouth and anus.) These charts were, in turn, used by Mead in her field work. Erikson's influence is most noticeable in Mead's Balinese studies, which took place during a field trip from 1936 to 1938 with further work in 1939. Here, because she felt her earlier approach to cultural study could be criticized as literary and imprecise, she tried the method (in collaboration with her husband, Gregory Bateson) of making a photographic record of behavior of children and adults with a textual commentary. The amount of space devoted to the oral behavior of children and their attitude toward elimination suggests her debt to Erikson. Mead found that Balinese women indulged in a great deal of sexual play with their children, teasing them physically but eventually not responding to them. This, she felt, resulted in a frustrated, withdrawn personality prone to fall into trances that were eventually ritualized in Balinese trance dancing. In Bali, Mead also used motion pictures to record her findings.

Thus the study of personality made use of every technological device to record the actual behavior of individuals. Above all, the psychoanalytical approach had taught the investigator the importance of examining the personality of his informant from the standpoint of reliability. In the past it had been assumed that any primitive was typical of his group. The new attitude made it clear that biographies of informants were necessary in order to indicate their attitudes toward their own culture. Mead had started supplying such histories of her informants in *Coming of Age*. In the thirties many anthropological field workers underwent training analyses themselves and learned how to use free-association techniques in interviews. In this way they were able to probe much deeper into the personalities of their informants. Mead, however, although she is the anthropologist best known to psychiatrists, has never been analyzed.

As we have seen, the emphasis on children has run through all of Mead's work. Children are the hope of the future. What is the relation between the way we bring them up and the pattern of our society and social change?

Mead's studies of the cultures of Samoa, New Guinea, and Bali showed that methods of child-training in primitive society differed as much as the patterns of adult society to which the children eventually had to adapt themselves. In her early field trip (1928) to the Manus of the Admiralty Islands, near New Guinea, her findings touched on the very pertinent role of progressive education in social change. The modern educators of the first half of the twentieth century, stimulated by Freudian thinking and the social-reformist sociology of the nineteenth century, had hoped by bringing up children free of complexes and inhibitions and offering them a less rigid and more socially oriented educational program to produce healthier-minded and more enlightened citizens. Could hostility and aggression be sublimated into constructive effort? Could exploitation give way to co-operation through education?

The revolutionary-minded said no. Change the institution and the individual will automatically change.

To the anthropologists the societies they studied were laboratories in which to test these dogmas. Conditions among the Manus seemed to show that the educators were naïve. The children of this South Sea people were brought up without cramping inhibitions. They were as gay, spontaneous, unacquisitive, generous, and friendly as any hopeful reformer could wish. Unfortunately, the society in which they were trapped when they grew up was taboo-ridden and driven by an exaggerated ceremonial economic system of conspicuous wealth. There were investments in marriages, a piling up of debts, a continuous competition in ritual accumulation which bred quarrels, tensions, and anger. Backing up the system was the authority of the family ghost, a skull hanging from the rooftree, who communicated, in seances, by whistling and visited illness upon the family for the slightest transgression. Fear of failure in economic obligations kept the adults in a state of perpetual tension. In addition the ghost, like any Puritan divine, considered sex to be evil. Marriage, which was a web of economic and sexual sanctions, created a family in which there could be no tenderness or friendship.

The happy, carefree children turned into tense, quarrelsome adults.

In 1953 Margaret Mead revisited the Manus after the catastophic events of a second world war had ripped apart their small, isolated society. She found that a fascinating and unlooked-for revolution had taken place. The Manus had suddenly come in contact with American technology on a large scale. Thousands of soldiers, with a fairly democratic attitude and armed with the magical tools of modern science, had shown them for the first time what the world outside was like. Catholic missions had given them some inkling of a set of ethical values different from the pronouncements of the skull on the roofbeam. American movies and observation of Australian officials (they were under Australian mandate) had taught them that women were not hedged in by taboos in other parts of the world.

Out of this cultural contact came first an orgiastic religious movement in which the Manus had visions of magical cargoes arriving on planes and ships, bringing them the blessings of modern civilization. To prepare for this millennium, they flung their dogtooth and shell money, dancing costumes, spears, pottery, all of their old life, into the sea. The movement had some parallel to the Ghost Dance which spread like wildfire through the Sioux Indians at the time when their culture was disintegrating. In the Admiralty Islands, however, an exceptional native leader arose who channeled the desire for change into constructive effort. He broke with Catholicism (which had not encouraged modernization) and promulgated a native version of Christianity which made anger the chief sin. He strove to bring democratic procedures into their lives: native courts, village councils, schools, the philosophy of majority decision. He tried to unify the islands politically. He advocated the equality of women and a more relaxed sex code, and abolished the old hampering taboos and avoidances.

When Margaret Mead came back to the Manus she found them pathetically struggling, despite a lack of trained leaders and officials and material resources, to adhere to the New Way. In a space of ten years they had responded to the currents of nationalism in the world and were trying to bridge a gap of thousands of years which stood between them and modern civilization. The adjustment was precarious and partial, but it was also heartening. The Manus were leading a much freer existence. There was less quarreling. The younger people were determinedly learning to read and write. The old burden of ceremonial wealth was gone. They took great pride in their village meetings, at which even women spoke. They doggedly fought to control their tempers and submitted to fines when they failed. It was true that their sex lives, though less constricted, were not free from hostility, for the Christian concept of sin had replaced the prohibitions of the family ghost, showing that puritanism died hard. The exciting fact, however, was the amazing will to change, the vitality and initiative suddenly awakened in a people who for centuries had stuck fast in the Stone Age. One more nail had been driven in the coffin of the doctrine of inferior races.

How had the change come about?

The upbringing of the children had something to do with it. The young Manus were trained from babyhood to be independent. Walking, swimming, manual dexterity were skillfully encouraged as soon as the babies showed any initiative. From their earliest years they were on their own, paddling their own little canoes in the shallow water, loudly demanding what they wanted and getting it. This made them active, energetic individuals, quick to accept and perfect new skills. On the other hand, Mead had noted on her first trip that they never played at adult activities. The harried, complicated, ritualized commercial world of their elders did not exist for them. Neither did they come under the jurisdiction of the family ghost. In this they differed from most youngsters of other primitive tribes, who normally played at being grown-up.

Mead concluded that they identified with their parents, sensed their elders' rebellion against the too heavy obligations of their culture, and ignored this culture as long as possible. Indeed, one of the patterns of youthful evasion was running away to take a job with the white men.

Thus the potential forces for change already existed. The typical personality was independent, alert, able to accept new techniques, and energetic. At the same time, there was a deep dissatisfaction with the restrictions of society. What was needed was a catalyst. The abrupt contact with the Americans had provided just this. Without the contributions of an exceptional leader the result might have been only disintegration, as in the case of the aftermath of the Ghost Dance.

Change, in this case, was brought about by adults, but the way was paved by the type of upbringing which produced dynamic individuals.

Margaret Mead has been a member of the department of anthropology of the American Museum of Natural History since

1926 and associate curator since 1943. In 1954 she became Adjunct Professor of Anthropology at Columbia University. Her books, like those of Malinowski and Robert Redfield, are extremely readable and convey a vivid picture of the life of the people she has investigated—unlike most diffusionist studies, which are of interest only to specialists. Although she has been accused of too hasty generalizations and of being too ready with interpretation, these are the defects of an imaginative mind. The trend of contemporary field work is toward a more synthetic approach to both culture and society. In all of Mead's books one feels that she is attempting to capture the character of the people she is investigating. This is not accidental. Mead's friend and teacher, Ruth Benedict, was the first anthropologist to develop the "configuration" theory of culture. This point of view drew some of its inspiration from still another development in psychology. It is known as the *Gestalt* theory and is a school distinct from both behaviorism and psychoanalysis.

Chapter 34

PATTERNS

Concerning Ruth Benedict, Clyde Kluckhohn,

A. Irving Hallowell

■ If a series of sketches of a horse galloping are drawn on cards, capturing the successive positions of the legs in its stride, and if these are placed in sequence and ruffled so that the eye passes rapidly from one to another, the horse appears to gallop.

Around 1910 a German psychologist, dissatisfied with the doctrines of Wilhelm Wundt, began to examine this peculiar effect. It had generally been explained physiologically on the basis that the retina retained one image and blended it with the next.

But, said Max Wertheimer, what did this mean psychologically? The end result was not a mere sum of the different drawings but something perceived by the mind which everyone recognized as motion.

Wundt had analyzed perception by breaking it down into component parts and assumed that the mind put sensations together in order to form concepts. This did not explain why motion was a *quality*, a mysterious something that was not the sum of a number of static images.

In another area of perception, that of sound, it had already been pointed out that when a melody was transposed into another key the tune could still be recognized although all the notes were different. The tune, or *arrangement*, had an identity of its own.

Certain lines, drawn against a background with spaces between them, were always seen in groups; the eye could not separate them.

A square or a triangle was certainly not seen as the sum of its line, but had a *shape*.

On a clear night when men looked up at the stars they saw them in groups—sharply defined groups that from ancient times had been given names. The Big Dipper and Orion were firmly rooted in human thinking.

After all, if the neural units merely put sensations together, why was not every perception unique? Why did everyone agree on the squareness of a square or the treeness of a tree?

Max Wertheimer (1880–   ), Wolfgang Kohler (1887–   ), and Kurt Koffka (1886–   ) all worked together in Frankfurt and later became colleagues in the Psychological Institute of Berlin. Wertheimer published his first important paper in 1912, and in 1920, with *Drei Abhandlungen der Gestalt Theorie* (*Three Treatments of Gestalt Theory*), he formulated the new school of psychology.

He and his co-workers believed that the Wundt school was completely wrong about perception. The mind, they said, perceives structures or units of experience which in German are called *Gestalten* (*Gestalt* is the word for "form" or "shape"). This was a fundamental fact of human psychology. It meant that the whole was not the sum of its parts but something *different*.

It was a return to the common-sense view of experience, yet it could be backed up by experiment. The *Gestalt* theorists even pointed to certain significant tendencies in nature. Solar systems were *Gestalten*. If a film of oil on water was punctured by dropping a loop of thread into it, the loop always formed a complete circle. This was in line with the definition that a *Gestalt* tended toward completeness.

Wertheimer attacked both Wundt and the behaviorists. (Watson's theory made the learning process a mechanical summing up of conditioned habits in which consciousness played no part.)

Kohler, interned during World War I on the island of Teneriffe, spent his time applying *Gestalt* theory to apes. An ape which was accustomed to use a stick to reach bananas left outside his cage was deprived of the stick. After a time he broke a branch from a tree in his cage and used it as a stick.

What did this mean? According to Kohler, it represented an insight. It was neither trial and error, conditioning, nor putting together single units of sensation. Two different *Gestalten* had coalesced to form a new one. The ape perceived the stick and the tree as wholes, but the effort of will brought the two elements together.

Why was effort necessary? Because one psychic process was working against another. A *Gestalt* tended toward completeness, toward equilibrium. At first the data concerning the tree and the data dealing with the stick would not coalesce. When they did, equilibrium was regained and the sense of strain disappeared. This was the *Gestalt* contribution to the learning process, which, at higher levels, was an effort of consciousness, not mere conditioning.

Memory was composed of *Gestalten*. Any element of a *Gestalt* could call up the whole.

Analysis into component parts was, for Wertheimer and his co-workers, a more sophisticated process. It was an "and connection," dividing up and putting things together intellectually. Thus the primitive tended to think in *Gestalten*, the fundamental form of consciousness, while the civilized thinker made use of "and connections."

Within the individual there were certain stress systems (or predispositions) that tended toward the completion of specific *Gestalten*. It was these stress systems which determined the personality.

Wertheimer's theory was compared to Plato's "ideas." Although the theory was criticized as vaguely defined, it did depend on observed facts, it was both psychic and material, and it did not violate the everyday view of the world.

Wertheimer and Koffka lectured in America (all three of the *Gestalt* psychologists were teaching in the United States by 1935) and fought diplomatically and effectively for their school. They were less dogmatic than the behaviorists. Watson had waved away psychoanalysis, saying that "with the advent of behaviorism the mind-body problem disappeared. . . . There can be no festering spot in the substratum of mind because there is no mind." Koffka, however, found a place for the unconscious. "Complexes" were analogous to *Gestalten*, and both *Gestalt* theory and psychoanalysis agreed that the unconscious, and indeed the whole personality, had innate structure. He criticized Freud for separating the conscious and unconscious too sharply. For him they were essentially the same, consciousness being merely an added property.

The higher intellectual processes, according to *Gestalt* theory, were interpretation. Although perception of form was fundamental, the ideas resulting from it might differ. In other words, a group of stars was clearly perceived as a pattern, but it might be a great bear to one, a big dipper to another.

Gestalt theory did not immediately penetrate the social sciences. It was, however, a symptom of the intellectual trend of the times.

Edward Sapir, as we have already indicated, showed a keen interest in psychological points of view in the early twenties. In 1924 he was pointing out that cultural groups acted in accordance with traditional and instinctive forms. He went on to speak of what was often called "the genius of a nation." The French, for instance, had a reputation for rationalism and aesthetic vanguardism. It is clear that he was moving toward the concept of the intrinsic character of a culture. As we have seen, he also knew Margaret Mead and Ruth Benedict personally. It was Ruth Fulton Benedict (1887–1948) who crystallized the search for a more synthetic point of view. The trend toward integration was expressed in Mead's work through the use of psychoanalytical concepts. Benedict also was interested in psychological types, but, unlike most anthropologists, she had a literary background. A Vassar graduate, she married Dr. Stanley Benedict in 1914. She hoped to have children and spent the first few years of her married life experimenting with various branches of culture. She taught English in a secondary school, published poetry, studied dancing, and tried social work. Courses in anthropology at the New School for Social Research with Elsie Clews Parsons and A. S. Goldenweiser turned her toward anthropology. She took her doctor's degree under Boas and did some field work in American Indian religion with A. L. Kroeber. The discovery, during the twenties, that she could not expect to have children impelled her to undertake anthropological work with a new intensity. She acted as Boas's assistant from 1922 to 1923, and in 1927, while on a field trip to Pima, Arizona, she began to develop the idea that the pattern of a culture was a projection of the personality of those who created it. Benedict had read the psychologist William Stern, who insisted that the whole personality of the individual must be studied in order to form any picture of the mind. She was also familiar, through Sapir, with Oswald Spengler's *Decline of the West*, in which he described and characterized the cultures of history. Still another influence on Benedict was a concept of Friedrich

Nietzsche's. In discussing Greek tragedy, Nietzsche had described two types of character. The Apollonian personality sought for order, restraint, and unity. The Dionysian tried to break through the boundaries imposed by the five senses in order to reach another order of existence. The Dionysian was prone to drunkenness and frenzy, and his rites were ecstatic and individualistic. Those of the Apollonian were formal and communal. (We have already seen that the psychoanalyst Jung had identified these two categories with his concepts of extrovert and introvert.)

In 1928 Benedict read a paper at the Congress of Americanists in which she applied the Nietzschean concepts to Indian cultures. If the diffusionist saw culture as a creeping blanket of vegetation and the French sociologist pictured it as a living polyp, Benedict's image was a piece of weaving in which the colored strands formed a distinct and recognizable pattern. This she called a "configuration."

Mourning rites among the Pueblos, who were *Apollonian*, were restrained. There were quiet prayers, ritual feeding of the dead, and seclusion of the mourners, with ritual fasting. There was no destructive activity or outward emotionalism.

The *Dionysian* Plains Indians reacted violently to death. They wailed and refused to eat. Women sometimes committed suicide at the death of their children. A dead man's lodge was pulled down and given away. His favorite horses were killed. Female relatives often gashed their heads or cut off their fingers.

As can be seen from her examples, the configuration of a culture could not be revealed by an exhaustive enumeration of detail. To capture such a pattern, selection was necessary; the anthropologist came close to being an artist. A configuration, according to Benedict, had the same relation to group behavior as the individual personality to items of individual behavior. Abnormal psychology had defined such specific emotional types as *cycloid* and *schizoid*. Cultures projected individual psychological types on a large screen.

Benedict's orientation was definitely literary and humanistic. In a paper delivered before the American Anthropological Association the year before she died, she stated that her training in Shakespearean criticism and her reading of George Santayana's philosophy had prepared her for anthropological study. She also maintained that the humanistic tradition was a corrective to the natural-science approach which had prevailed for so long in anthropology.

In 1934 she published her famous book, *Patterns of Culture*, in which she developed her point of view in terms of three primitive cultures: the Zuni, the Dobu, and the Kwakiutl. By this time she had become acquainted with *Gestalt* psychology, which coincided with her own insights. Referring to the work of Koffka and Kohler, she wrote: "Gestalt psychologists have shown that in the simplest sense-perception no analysis of the separate percepts can account for the total experience."

Boas, in his introduction to her book, pointed out that her approach differed from the functionalist in that it did not try to unite every cultural item but was concerned with fundamental attitudes which showed the relation between the individual and his society.

The Zuni were Benedict's example of an Apollonian or restrained culture. Their whole life was taken up with ceremonial. They had hierarchies of *katchinas* (masked gods), some of which were impersonated in dances and some worshipped in ritual. The whole emphasis was on perfection of ritual. It was strictly forbidden for a man serving as a priest to feel anger, for this detracted from his religious concentration.

Marriage was a personal affair with almost no ceremony, and divorce was even easier. In this matrilineal society, when a wife became tired of her husband, she put his bundle of belongings on the doorstep. When he came home, he shed a tear or two and went home to his mother. Adultery caused little commotion. In one case when a wife felt that her husband's extramarital affair had gone on too long, she refrained from washing his clothes. The unspoken reproach was enough, for he gave up the other woman.

Dreams were avoided rather than sought, for they were considered omens of death. There were no visions or hallucinatory experiences in the Zuni religion, which called for hour-long prayers that had to be repeated without a slip. Aggressive, ambitious individuals were frowned on or even suspected of sorcery, which the Zuni feared. The ideal type was an easygoing, socially poised individual who made everybody feel comfortable.

The Dobuans of Melanesia had been studied by Reo Fortune. They were a part of the *kula* ring described by Bronislaw Malinowski, but, unlike the genial Trobrianders, they were a people of endless antagonisms and hostility. In their yam-cultivation they used charms to defend their own crops and harm those of their competitors. If they were outdone in gardening, they ascribed it to evil magic. All of life was full of secret and treacherous rivalry. Adultery was common, with violent jealous outbursts. The injured husband broke his wife's cooking-pots, the wife beat her husband's dog. In extreme cases the husband committed semi-suicide with the non-fatal fish poison also used by Malinowski's Trobrianders.

Patterns of culture: Zuni, Dobu, Kwakiutl.

The Dobuans were specialists in incantations to cause disease in those whom they disliked. Every man and woman possessed several specific charms for certain diseases, complete with the antidotal spell. Some people even had a monopoly on the power to cause certain specific diseases and were sole owners of the cure. They used these charms to protect their property; by means of them they could infect trespassers or thieves.

The names of supernatural powers were secret, known only to those who paid for the information or inherited it. Thus religion was private property. Even in the kula exchange hostile rivalry continued. The man who possessed a successful beauty magic that made him irresistible to his kula partner was hated, and sorcery was used in an attempt to kill him.

Death was always attributed to magic, and women were particularly suspect, for they might be flying witches. When one member of a married pair died, the other was generally considered the magical murderer. Consequently, mourning went on in an atmosphere of suspicion and hatred. The Dobuans, who were sour people generally, disapproved of laughter, for they believed that gaiety during gardening would prevent the yams from growing. The ideal personality was one who had cheated, stolen, charmed, or even poisoned his way to Melanesian eminence. All existence was a struggle to the death, with suspicion and cruelty the most trusted weapons. The Dobuans seemed intent on proving how far men will go to make life unbearable.

The third contrasting culture was that of the Kwakiutl, which had been definitively studied by Franz Boas. These Indians, who lived on a narrow strip of the Alaskan coast, were a wealthy people fed by the products of the sea: salmon, cod, seal, and even whales. Technically, they surpassed the other two groups, working wood without metal tools. They built houses and ceremonial halls of cedar planks, and raised great totem poles. Running through their culture—painted on the house fronts, carved on implements, and even sketched on their bodies—ran a bold stylized pattern of decoration based on animal motifs such as the bear, the killer whale, and the raven.

The values of their culture were Dionysian to an exaggerated degree. We have already referred to their dancing, which was ecstatic. The leader, at the high point of his performance, foamed at the mouth and was supposed to go quite mad; in one dance he even threw burning coals among the spectators. The cannibal-society dance involved a corpse and an initiate, who reached such a point that he bit the spectators and swallowed their flesh with loathing. Their distaste for human flesh was particularly significant, for by engaging in this necrophilic rite they tapped the supernatural power that was supposed to reside in a ghastly defiance of their own instincts.

Their attitude toward property was just as violent. Wealth, valued for display rather than use, was regarded as other societies regard family heirlooms. It consisted of cedar-bark blankets and *coppers*—etched sheets of copper which were equivalent to thousands of blankets. Canoes and shell money were also a part of this conspicuous wealth, which they lent out at interest. This lending out, or distribution with obligatory reimbursement, began with the children. It was analogous to the economic exchanges of the Manus and other South Sea tribes. When a youth, financed by his family, acquired enough property he was ready for his first *potlatch*. This was a ritual event, a feast and a battle of wealth. A man of property either heaped a rival with so many gifts that the rival would never be able to repay him, or engaged in a wild destruction contest, endeavoring to burn up more goods than his guest, all the while reciting megalomaniac hymns of self-glorification. While the host at a potlatch destroyed blankets, coppers, valuable candlefish oil, and even broke up his canoes and tossed them on the bonfire, he heaped scorn and insults on his guests. If the guest could not repay or destroy as much as his host had expended, he was forever shamed in this orgy of conspicuous waste.

The same pattern held good in marriage. The bridegroom's party might try to overpower the father of the bride with heaps of gifts; the latter, in turn, might build a roaring fire and pour so much candlefish oil on it that the bridal party, forced to sit close to it without flinching, were actually scorched.

There were ritual forms of revenge by which perfectly innocent parties were killed to avenge natural deaths. A woman accused of adultery and sent home was likely to commit suicide. A boy who was struck by his father had to distribute property, go head-hunting, or commit suicide to wipe out the shame. Thus the ideal character in the Kwakiutl society was close to the civilized definition of paranoia. (This picture of Kwakiutl society has since been criticized by Helen Codere, who has discovered evidence of burlesque potlatches, proving that this people was not without humor and indicating that its culture was not so integrated as Benedict believed.)

There was an area of agreement between Benedict's and Durkheim's points of view to the extent that both felt the pattern of a culture was more than the sum of its parts. Although a culture was made up of individuals, there was some element in group relationship which molded the psychic processes of individuals.

Tendencies that certain cultures stressed and shaped into ideals were probably the common property of human nature, but why did a group of traits receive social approval in one part of the world and not in another? Environment did not explain everything, for even in Europe the population was prone to mystic and ecstatic behavior in the Middle Ages but became hard-headed commercialists in the nineteenth century without any related change in the environment or any alteration in racial composition. Benedict seemed to feel that the cause of change was a crisis. "Revision comes, but it comes by way of revolution or of breakdown," she wrote.

We have seen from Mead's two visits to the Manus that something more can be learned about the processes of social change, however, and this strengthens the hope that progress can be made in this area.

The study of culture patterns has great comparative value, even if it is only to show us our own social rivalry and anxiety reflected, as in a Coney Island distorting mirror, in the manic property contests of the Kwakiutl.

Ruth Benedict's formulation of culture configuration had considerable influence on her contemporaries. As we have seen, Margaret Mead in her South Sea books was attempting to seize the character of each society. The pattern approach was just as clear in *Co-operation and Competition among Primitive Peoples*, edited and partly written by Mead in 1937.

This study covered twelve different tribes in different parts of the world. Margaret Mead wrote the chapters on South Sea peoples, while various specialists contributed descriptions of the other groups. The problem investigated was a general one that cut across institutions and made it necessary to paint the portrait of each group in order to show to what extent its pattern tended toward either type of behavior. The groups ran the gamut of the scale from the insanely competitive Kwakiutl and the self-sufficient Eskimos (a people whose family economies were so isolated that there was little cohesion among them) to the mild and communally oriented Arapesh and Zuni.

In general, in the more co-operative societies an individual achieved status and prestige by a sense of belonging. Society was organized so that each member derived a feeling of security by being certain of his place in it, whether high or low, and certain of the obligations which he owed and which were owed to him. In competitive groups the individual fought for status, there was an emphasis on personal experience, and the society was organized around his drive and initiative.

The desire for prestige gained by owning, giving away, displaying, or destroying property ran through all of the groups and accentuated the fact that property functions as a symbol just as often as it functions as a fulfillment of biological needs.

Co-operation and Competition draws some of its concepts from the work of Radcliffe-Brown, Gregory Bateson, and Fromm and, together with Benedict's configuration point of view, shows the spread of an approach to the wholeness of cultures.

When Boas retired from the chairmanship of the department of anthropology at Columbia in 1937, Benedict became acting head. At this time she wrote a book on the race problem, continuing Boas's fight for enlightenment in this area. During World War II she worked in Washington, where she studied foreign cultures, a task that culminated in a book on Japan and touched off a new interest in the investigation of national character. After the war she organized research in contemporary cultures under the Office of Naval Research. During a trip to Europe she died of a heart attack in 1948.

Ruth Benedict was a warm, sensitive person who inspired great affection in her students and associates. She brought into anthropology an awareness of culture as an aesthetic phenomenon, and her point of view captured an audience for the science of man which had hitherto not been attracted by the traditionally more austere approach.

While neither belongs actually to the configurationist school, the work of both A. Irving Hallowell (1892–   ) and Clyde Kluckhohn (1905–   ) embodies a modern integrated approach to culture with an emphasis on the individual. Kluckhohn, chairman of the department of anthropology at Harvard, is something of an eclectic. He acknowledges his indebtedness to R. R. Marett of Oxford and Father Schmidt of Vienna, and also owes something to Ralph Linton. Sympathetic to the historical point of view, he has also been quick to adopt insights from the personality-and-culture school. He is an expert on the Navaho Indians, and he and his wife, Dorothy Leighton (1908–   ), have published two books on this tribe under the joint auspices of the University of Chicago and the United States Office of Indian Affairs. The first, *The Navaho* (1946), is a historical and descriptive study that synthesizes firsthand investigation with other material in the field. It consists of a detailed description of the contemporary state of the Navahos' culture with an emphasis on their view of life and also includes a discussion of their present problems of acculturation. This work is supplemented by *Children of the People* (1947), in which the Kluckhohns study child development and personality, using the contemporary psychological approach. Kluckhohn's breadth of interest is also indicated by a popular work describing the uses of applied anthropology, *Mirror for Man* (1949).

Irving Hallowell, who teaches in the University of Pennsylvania, published in 1955 a book, *Culture and Experience*, that outlines his own method of cultural study in terms of his particular field, the Ojibway of Canada (of the same stock as Schoolcraft's Chippewa). Hallowell uses the Rorschach test as a means of recording personality data. In contrast to the personality-and-culture school, however, which puts so much emphasis on the unconscious, Hallowell emphasizes that ego and self-awareness also deserve study. In fact, he makes the study of these the integrating factor in his own ethnological method. The response to the roles of other people, he points out, is a part of awareness of self and one's own role. The awareness of self in space and time is an important boundary of a group's view of life. The Ojibway, for instance, believe that certain supernatural characters can be met in dreams and in real life, but examination of their self-awareness shows that they know very well when they are dreaming. This kind of analysis proves the error in the classical belief that the savage cannot tell the difference between dream and reality. Ethical judgments, likewise, says Hallowell, cannot be understood except from the point of view of the self because it is the ego which feels guilt, and the desire for prestige is certainly based on self-awareness. Hallowell uses the time sense of the Ojibway as another illustration of the need for understanding ego orientation. Being a hunting people, they eat irregularly and consequently have no sense of morning and afternoon, early or late. When he wished to speak to one of his informants in the morning, he told him to come after he had lifted his fishnets, for this was generally a morning activity. He summed up: "If we assume the point of view of the self in its behavioral environment, it is likewise possible to gain a more direct insight into the psychological field of the individual as he expresses it than a purely objective description affords."

It is necessary to go backward a few decades to pick up another thread in the contemporary anthropological pattern. The period between the two world wars was in many ways a time of intellectual ferment. As we have seen, in the social sciences there was a trend toward integration and a greater awareness of the role of the individual in culture. As a result, a new hope was shaping—a hope that something concrete could be learned about how and why men created the intricate forms of society in which they lived together.

World War I had failed to lead to the regeneration of society, as some had hoped in the early twenties. No one could cling to the happy belief of Herbert Spencer that industrialism would automatically bring international peace. The onrush of technological invention had put increasingly dangerous tools into men's hands along with increasingly miraculous comforts and means of dominating the physical world. At the same time, the old pictures of man and the universe no longer seemed to apply. The two extremes of fascism and communism were challenging all the ideals that the nineteenth-century western individualist had kept before him as a guide to progress. In such an atmosphere, anthropology could no longer remain the study of remote little exotic tribes, or a picture-puzzle game of matching culture trait to culture trait. Many scholars had begun to feel that nothing certain could ever be known of the remote past. Instead, the present and the future loudly claimed the attention of social thinking.

The point of view of the man in the street was inevitably: *We are all in a mess—what has your science got to say about it?* The question that naturally followed was: *Why can't the anthropologist look around him?*

He could and did.

Chapter 35

1924
1935

PRIMITIVE LIFE IN AMERICA

Concerning Robert and Helen Lynd,

W. Lloyd Warner, Hortense Powdermaker,

John Dollard, Geoffrey Gorer

■ As anthropologists grew more sophisticated they discovered that the primitive's mind was not so different from that of his civilized brethren as it had at first seemed. When the same scientists turned their attention to contemporary civilized society they discovered that modern man was far more primitive than he cared to admit.

In 1924 Robert S. Lynd and his wife, Helen Lynd, descended with a staff of field workers on a moderate-sized midwestern city whose identity they protected by calling it "Middletown." Although the Lynds had been trained as sociologists at Columbia University, they embarked on a truly anthropological study. As Clark Wissler pointed out in his introduction to their book *Middletown*, theirs was a pioneer attempt to study an American community by approaching it as an anthropologist approached a primitive tribe. Modern society had theoretically been the province of the sociologist, who tended to work with statistics, engaged in "sampling" studies, and most often attacked limited and isolated problems. The Lynd project differed, being an exhaustive study of a single group's institutions and cultural habits. Their work was one more proof that no rigid boundary could be drawn between anthropology and sociology.

They picked a community of less than fifty thousand, composed mostly of Americans whose ancestors were of English stock and had first settled in New England or the South. The Lynds and their staff interviewed leaders and average citizens. They employed questionnaires, studied statistics, investigated schools, churches, and clubs, and went to parties.

The town's industrial history dated from 1871, when some operators drilling for coal were suddenly overcome by a foul odor and heard a roaring sound in the bowels of the earth. They hastily plugged up the hole, and the rumor got around that they had accidentally invaded the devil's domain. A decade later, when natural gas was discovered in near-by towns, the citizens realized they could harness their own supply for industrial use. The town went wild. Real-estate values jumped. Forty factories were set up. One of the most important was a plant that made fruit jars, owned by a family which the Lynds kept incognito with the designation X.

As every school child knows, two beliefs are fundamental in the United States: that all men are equal, and that success is within any man's reach. The first stems from the philosophy of the makers of the American Revolution, the second from the historical fact of pioneering, when immigrants from an old and rigid society were able to shape their own careers in an unsettled country.

In four decades Middletown had jumped from a slow-paced, horse-and-buggy settlement of the pioneer age into the modern technological era.

The Lynds were interested in the relation among belief, behavior, and factual reality. Primitives exhibited complicated or, from the civilized point of view, fantastic adjustments to their environment. Modern man was supposedly more logical.

In the first place, the Lynds found that, although all Americans were theoretically equal, the almost classless society of the frontier had hardened into two distinct groups, the business people and the workers, the latter group being two and a half times as large as the first.

All subscribed to the philosophy of success, which was envisioned in terms of more material possessions and an easier life. For the workers, in particular, the advent of machines had deprived factory employment of craft satisfaction. Education was believed to be the key to getting ahead. Between 1890 and 1920 the white population of the state had increased by twenty-five per cent, but the state university enrollment had increased by seven hundred per cent.

The businessman, too, subscribed to the theory of unrestricted opportunity and believed that anyone could get work. At the same time, they kept want ads from other towns out of the local papers for fear the local labor supply would be drained off. The whole area was strongly Republican and anti-labor-union.

The Lynds felt that the child born into the business class had distinctly better opportunities for achieving the popular notion of success than a child of the working class. In addition, there were other types of discrimination. The Ku Klux Klan had been imported by the business group as a weapon against the minority Democratic party. It became a workers' organization through which a sense of frustration had been turned into prejudice against the Catholics and a small Jewish retail-merchant group. The latter were members of some of the smaller civic clubs, but not of Rotary. The few Negroes were strictly confined to the working class. They attended the schools, but not the larger motion-picture houses, the Y.M.C.A., or the "white" churches.

There was therefore a considerable gap between official equilatarian beliefs and the realities of the situation. The frontier had disappeared, but it still existed in men's minds.

Cultural change was taking place, however, in two areas of behavior: sexual customs and religious activity.

The official religious views were the same as in 1890. A questionnaire that asked if the theory of evolution offered a more accurate picture of the origin and history of mankind than a literal interpretation of Genesis was submitted to the juniors and seniors in high school. Only nineteen per cent chose the theory of evolution. At the same time, religious practice had declined sharply. In 1890 the whole community had attended church at least once on Sunday and secular activities were frowned on. By 1924 the various clubs, movies, and golf had invaded Sunday. Only eleven men and about eighteen women per hundred attended church regularly. The churches were trying to drum up business by organizing clubs and social activities. Questioning seemed to show that to the workers, and especially to their wives, religion was a source of consolation for frustrations. Among the business class, belief in heaven and hell had definitely weakened. In the nineties there had been a small percentage of active questioning of and dissent from orthodox Christianity. In 1924 there was merely indifference.

We have already noted the re-evaluation of traditional sex attitudes reflected in Mead's first book, which was published one year earlier than Lynd's study. *Middletown* (1929) documents what had been happening. Officially, monogamous marriage based on romantic love was the ideal. Although the taboo against pre-marital relations was strong, various forces were weakening it. Women, generally considered illogical and intellectually inferior to men, were beginning to work. A knowledge of contraceptives had spread among the business group, but not among the workers. The automobile, now becoming common, acted as a kind of catalyst. It was viewed by moralists as "a house of prostitution on wheels." Also significant was the fact that in 1890 there had been from twenty to twenty-five houses of prostitution and in 1924 there were scarcely any. The growing independence of children also affected the situation. They were accused of staying up too late, going to too many parties, demanding too much money. A large percentage indulged in petting. Use of the automobile had tended to put adolescent youth out of the reach of family authority, and the movies, in this period beginning to exploit erotic themes, were considered a bad influence. Thus the authority of the traditional patriarchal system was weakening, and parents, growing unsure of themselves, began to yearn for professional advice.

The recreational activities of the Middletowners were more social than intellectual. Reading had declined among the business group since 1890 but increased slightly among the worker class. The automobile allowed all groups to spend time traveling to dances, restaurants, or parties. Music lessons were on the wane, as a result of the rise of radio and recordings. Movies, of course, were the greatest single entertainment device; three hundred performances were available each week. Concerts were not well supported, and there were only eight live plays per year as against one hundred and twenty-five in 1890.

Clubs and ritualized groups were dominant in the social structure, as much so as in any primitive tribe. School children were organized into clubs and teams; their fathers joined booster clubs, political and civic associations, and lodges. The women of the business class occupied their free time with clubs, many of which imported lecturers and busied themselves with culture. It was these women's clubs, the Lynds felt, which kept intellectual traditions alive.

The Lynds were impressed by the gap between the traditional ideologies and the rapid changes brought about by industrialism. There was a tremendous urge to conform. Material progress set up acquisitive standards of conformity, while folk belief clung to traditional ethical and spiritual ideals.

The anthropologists reflected the critical mentality of the east at a time when American writers were beginning to deplore standardization and cultural barrenness. H. L. Mencken praised their book, calling Middletown "a city in Moronia." The Middletowners were flattered to be chosen as a typical community, irritated by much of the criticism—which they absorbed secondhand, for few read the book—and simmered down to the attitude that the anthropologists were "cynical."

The Lynds went back to Middletown in 1935 to discover what had happened to the conflicts they saw in its society after a war and a depression.

In the meantime, another anthropologist had set out to study a typical small New England manufacturing town. William Lloyd Warner (1898–   ) came to Yankee City (Newburyport, Massachusetts) with a background of Australian field work. He had worked with Robert Lowie in the University of California and later with Radcliffe-Brown in Chicago. He had also encountered Malinowski when the latter lectured in the United States. His background therefore included diffusion, functionalism, and Durkheim's sociology, the latter being the strongest influence. In 1935 he joined the anthropology department of the University of Chicago. His book *A Black Civilization* (1937) was an authoritative treatise on the northern tribes of Australia which Spencer had discussed decades before. Warner, influenced by psychoanalysis (he was in touch with the contemporary study of personality), tried to avoid cross-questioning his informants and used the free-association method. The Australian network of classes, groups, and kinship relationships made a strong impression upon him, affecting the orientation of his later work.

The impetus to investigate an American group came from the

psychiatrist Elton Mayo, who had already in 1933 studied the social behavior of the factory worker in the Western Electric plant at Hawthorne, Illinois. Warner decided that the worker could be understood only in terms of his whole community. Under the auspices of the Yale Institute of Human Relations, he recruited a staff of thirty for his project.

He chose a Massachusetts community with a population of under twenty thousand. Yankee City had a longer history than Middletown because the eastern seaboard was settled much earlier. A clipper-ship importing-and-exporting tradition preceded the shoe industry that was in 1933 the dominant activity. Thus there had been time for an aristocracy of "family" to crystallize. Immigration from Europe had then brought in succeeding waves of ethnic groups. Yankee City was a typical "melting-pot."

Warner's chief interest, born of his Australian experience, was in the role of social groupings in the structure and folkways of the town. The four volumes he published between 1941 and 1947 dealt with the social classes, the status system, the ethnic groups, and the natural history of a strike. The final volumes deal with symbolic thinking and supplementary data.

Yankee City, in contrast to prairie-bound Middletown, was situated on a harbor. Its streets bordered a river, climbing to higher ground as they receded from the bank. Clamming was a minor industry, the refuge of the lowest economic group. The configuration of the land was curiously symbolic of social position. The river's edge was inhabited by the lower-lower economic group, consisting generally of the most recently arrived foreigners. The middle class lived halfway up the hill. The upper class had mansions surrounded by old shade trees on its summit. The situation was not rigid, however. As each foreign group became Americanized and acquired goods and status, its individuals moved into a better area. The native American (of Yankee stock) ranked highest; next, in order, came the Irish, French Canadians, Jews, Armenians, Greeks, Poles, and Russians. Negroes were at the bottom of the social order.

Warner's team detected three well-defined classes, which he subdivided. The upper-upper class consisted of old families. A certain amount of money was necessary for membership, but ancestry and a certain type of behavior were the most important qualifications. This group belonged to certain exclusive clubs, the children went to certain preparatory schools, and a percentage of the men did not work. Thus a leisure class was forming. The upper-upper class had taste, furnished their homes with antiques, and prized heirlooms and genealogy. The daughters of this class were afraid of marrying out of their group, and endogamic cousin marriage was common. Because of a lack of eligible men, this group had the largest percentage of spinsters.

The lower-upper class had possessed wealth for a short time, were acquiring upper-upper behavior, and were trying to move up. They were the "new" people. They had the best of everything, but the best was new and shiny. Their daughters, as they gradually acquired polish, were able to marry above themselves.

The upper-middle group sometimes got into upper-upper clubs, but, as a whole, were more interested in money and comfort than in the struggle for status. The lower-middle class were strong believers in conventional morality. The middle group as a whole had more security than the classes just above and below them.

The upper-upper had the security of tradition; the lower-lower had given up status, lived for the moment, and did not care. The upper-lower were struggling for more comfort and education just as the lower-upper were trying to gain status. Both groups produced children who were often maladjusted and neurotic.

Warner and his thirty field workers decided that the social groupings were more intricate than those of the Australians. They began investigations by securing introductions to prominent men, who, in turn, put them in contact with everyone they needed to meet. Most people, they discovered, could not understand and did not even try to find out what they were doing. They became all things to all men: to old ladies they were genealogists; businessmen accepted them as economists; schoolteachers saw them as specialists in education; at parties they were just young men having a good time. Questionnaires they avoided; statistics and documents from social agencies were used, newspapers were studied, and biographies of individuals were collected. Their interview technique was psychoanalytical. Because the investigators schooled themselves never to show boredom, their informants were simply delighted to talk. (Anthropology was almost in the position of furnishing free therapy.) Eventually they compiled personality cards for all the seventeen thousand inhabitants above the age of infancy.

Warner and his aides wrote fictional episodes to show individuals reacting along class lines. The lower-class Irish were drawn as sloppy housekeepers, bitterly resentful of the pretensions of the "lace-curtain" Irish who had climbed from manual labor to upper-middle or lower-upper status. To compensate, they fantasied about their glorious old-country origins. An upper-middle Irish professional was shown torn by conflicts. He could not accept birth control, but he could not afford to have more children. In consequence, he took a mistress. A lower-upper Irish family, residing on the hill, was mingling with the upper-upper group and affected by Protestant behavior and folk habits. The children had gone to the right schools, and the daughter became engaged to a man from an old Yankee family. Torn by the religious issue, she decided to have two marriage ceremonies and to put off the conflict over the education of children by not having any for five years. The oversensitive son was violently anti-Catholic, had had a nervous breakdown, had written a novel about a sensitive boy in his own situation, and was thoroughly bitter and unstable.

The Irish groups were further advanced socially because they had arrived in America first (it took them eighty years to reach Hill Street), but the lower groups were moving from class to class in the same pattern. When they first arrived, the men formed ethnic clubs. Then came an ethnic church and stores. As the European patriarchal form began to give way to contemporary attitudes that granted more freedom to women and children, conflicts arose. The children defied their parents and rejected the old ethnic ways. In a new synagogue, for example, the younger people rebelled against the segregation of women and finally compromised by seating the progressives together in the middle while the traditionalist men and women sat segregated on either side.

As the ethnic families acquired property and were able to join some of the civic and philanthropic organizations, they individually moved away from their ethnic village into a better position up the hill.

Most of the ethnic families had come from rural feudal backgrounds. As members of the peasant class, the gulf between them and the ruling class had been fixed. In America, when they discovered that they were free to move up, they exhibited a burst of energy and ambition.

The American ideal was complete democracy. The anthropologist, however, was aware of a "pecking or butting order." Animals kept in a group worked out hierarchies. The most dominant individual pecked or butted the others away from the trough. The next strongest tyrannized over the others, and so on down. This system was accepted and adhered to by the group.

There was, therefore, a biological tendency that ran counter to the abstract American ideal. Significantly enough, the Lynds found the pecking order emerging more sharply when they returned to Middletown in 1935. During the depression an attempt was made by the A. F. of L. to organize unions. Poorly handled, it failed, and left the workers more keenly aware of their poorer chance of getting ahead.

At the same time, many of the smaller industries had gone under during the depression, while the X family, owners of the fruit-jar factory, had prospered. A group of brothers, they had got their start during the natural-gas boom. In 1935 two of the older generation, both men in their seventies, were left. They were good examples of the pioneer industrialist, alert, "democratic," capable, consciously Christian, patrons of art, education, religion, and charity, and rugged individualists. After the bank holiday the brothers merged Middletown's banks and from then on became the reigning family, the first hereditary aristocracy.

By 1935 they owned the largest department store, the milk company, and the beer company. While speculating in real estate they developed a new residential section and created a state teachers' college. They retained the best law firms, and no one could hold the post of secretary of the Chamber of Commerce without their approval. They saw to it that Bertrand Russell's *Marriage and Morals* and John Dos Passos's *1919* were taken out of the college library, considering them cynical or immoral books. Their influence barred eastern liberal thinking from the Y.M.C.A., and the clergymen bowed to their wishes in the pulpit. Local politics had been poorly run. One member of the X family became a Republican committee chairman, another became a state Democratic leader. The one independent local editor said it was "heads they win, tails you lose." They controlled the largest daily paper, and the memorial hospital was their gift.

They paid substandard wages, fought unions, employed their sons and sons-in-law in the business, and could not understand why their employees did not see how carefully the X's looked after the employees' welfare.

The workers considered the family a symbol of oppression. A liberal clergyman said that they would do better to turn some of their profits into wages and engage in somewhat less conspicuous philanthropy.

Enforced leisure and government-supported education, as a result of the W.P.A., had produced a temporary increase in cultural activity such as painting as a hobby and the formation of local orchestras. This suggested that when the road to material success was blocked, energy could be channeled in other directions. On the whole, the townspeople seemed culturally adrift, living by outworn symbols. *Middletown in Transition* was published in 1937.

In the thirties a third geographical area entered the anthropological picture. Hortense Powdermaker and John Dollard both engaged in studies of a Mississippi town. The former conducted independent investigations sponsored by the Yale Institute of Human Relations, the latter was inspired by Warner's work in Yankee City. Powdermaker (1903–) had come from field work in the Melanesian area of New Ireland. She had been a friend and pupil of Malinowski. In 1929 she took up residence in the native village of Lesu, showed her neighbors pictures in anthropology books, and told them that her status at home depended on her learning their customs and manners. Her neighbor, the chief's wife, announced that Miss Powdermaker was her sister. Thus taken into the clan, she was given an instructor in their language and beliefs. Her people put powdered lime in their hair, painted a yellow ring around one eye, and staged wonderfully dramatic dances in which a man moved inside the effigy of a crocodile. The girls were supposed to be chaste before marriage (marriage took place immediately after menstruation), but every young matron, in order to be socially successful, took as many lovers as possible. On the whole, they were an amiable, friendly group of ex-cannibals.

With the detached point of view developed in Lesu, Powdermaker came, in 1936, to Cottonville. Here the greatest gap of all between democratic opportunity, equalitarian ideals, and reality was apparent. In addition to the existence of classes, a rigid caste system blocked a whole ethnic group in their efforts to better themselves. If Australian marriage regulations seemed illogical and hampering to a western observer, an Australian would have found the sex code of Cottonville quite inexplicable. Here sex had been raised to a symbolic importance greater than in any primitive tribe.

Powdermaker was introduced to the highest Negro education official in the county and, through him, met Negro teachers and educators and gained access to all types of social and church groups. She used questionnaires, interviews, and statistical material. Although she lived in a white boardinghouse, she did not discuss the difficulties of her position while studying both Negro and white groups. John Dollard (1900–), who worked in the same town in 1937, did. He was psychoanalytically trained, had been analyzed, and used the new technique of free association in interviews. He also collected life histories, but did not rely on statistics. The Negroes, he found, felt a certain solidarity with the north, hoped for pressure from that area in their behalf, and were very willing to talk. Among the whites his presence aroused nervousness for fear he might "stir up trouble." He had difficulty in finding a place in which to work. The house he lived in was owned by a white family; Negroes who came there would have had to use the back door. Visiting the houses of Negroes would have embarrassed the Negroes and raised the suspicions of the whites, who were quick to attribute sexual relations to white men and Negro women. He solved his difficulty by renting an office in a business building.

Nevertheless, he often felt like the last of the carpetbaggers, for the whites suspected him of antagonistic northern attitudes, and when he tried to outline a neutral position they immediately showed hostility.

This led him to search his own soul in discussing the question of objectivity. He had to admit that he shared the prejudices of his area and had a sneaking desire to "show up" the injustices of the situation. He decided that he must try as much as possible to compensate for being a northerner.

Both Dollard and Powdermaker agreed that the class situation was intensified by the caste line, posited on color of skin.

The lowest class consisted, of course, of Negroes, but also contained poor whites. These "rednecks" were of native stock, blond descendants of English settlers, undernourished, low in vitality, spiritless in outlook, and in far worse condition culturally and economically than the middle-class Negroes. Thanks to the caste line, however, the white cotton-planters could not apply the same authoritarian treatment to the rednecks that they did to the Negroes. Hence, according to Powdermaker, they preferred to hire

Negroes, and this bred among the rednecks an intense hatred toward both upper-class whites and Negroes, with the Negroes as scapegoats. Thus the poor whites became the raw material of lynch mobs.

Both investigators agreed on the pattern of the situation. The railroad track was the dividing-line. On the "wrong" side lived all of the Negroes: the well-kept home of a college graduate could stand next to the shack of a simple laundress who believed in voodoo.

A cultural form had been set up to preserve the former pattern of the plantation slave society. Economic considerations, a Negro majority in the state, resentment dating back to reconstruction after the Civil War (when for a time Negroes under northern protection had had some political power) had crystallized the attitude of the whites. Sex was the symbol of the caste situation. White men had sexual access to women of both races. Negro men must never, never raise their eyes to the women of the dominant white caste.

The use of conventional signs of equality between whites and blacks, such as shaking hands and the title of Mr. or Mrs., was utterly and magically taboo. "Jim Crow," or segregation, was another type of ceremonial restriction.

In this cotton-picking area, the town sprawling around the dark waters of a bayou, there was only one white-pillared mansion left from the aristocratic pre-Civil War days. Yet the folk beliefs were molded on pre-Civil War conditions. As the local psychology was officially based on survivals of the slavery situation, middle-class whites descended from small farmers who never owned a slave pictured themselves in their fantasies as plantation aristocrats. The middle class, which in Yankee City or Middletown would have done such small jobs as lawn-mowing for themselves, never did manual labor but always employed Negroes. All through their ideology ran a feudal attitude to which they had no hereditary right.

All classes of whites firmly believed that Negroes were racially inferior. A symbolic system of stereotypes was fabricated to justify the *status quo.* Negroes were shiftless, lazy liars, unable to control their passions, brutally lustful, and no Negro woman was ever chaste. On the whole, they were supposed to be a cross between children and animals.

All agreed that white men and black women did mate, but the black concubine was no longer kept openly and her children acknowledged as in the days of slavery. Liaisons were kept secret. Among the young whites religious sanctions and sex taboos were weakening (as in Middletown), and there was, as a result, less taking of black mistresses.

Black and white children could play together. At this age the taboo against a Negro showing any hostility toward a white was weaker. Later such contradictions arose as that of a white woman, who had loved a Negro nurse, shuddering if she saw a black man at her door after dark. There was distrust and dislike of light Negroes, Negroes who had lived in the north, and educated Negroes in general, for the small group of white employers had no desire to see their manual workers educated out of submissive behavior and acceptance of low wages. From this arose the ambivalent attitude that lynching was, of course, a bad thing but perhaps necessary to "keep the Negroes down."

A more liberal state of mind, a firm opposition to lynching, a general humanitarian feeling toward Negroes prevailed among the remnants of the actual southern aristocracy, which was a much more secure group than the fantasying middle class.

Meanwhile, the Negroes adopted the white Protestant folkways as their goal. The upper class, which contained some landowners, businessmen, professionals, and, above all, teachers, upheld a puritanical sexual ideal and a standard of good manners and taste in the hope of combatting the white folklore. Psychiatry showed that they sometimes indulged in the fantasy of becoming white. Middleclass Negroes, less burdened with assumed Puritanical repression (historically as unreal as the middle-class-white plantation fantasy), were less interested in status. Marriages were less stable. The lower class had no pretense to monogamy at all.

Radio and the movies had brought national attitudes more commonly into the local situation (also true of Middletown), but there was no labor organization. As Powdermaker summed up, "The situation bred conflict deeply felt by every person, black or white, in the Cottonville community; conflict of race against race, of class against class, of individual against individual, and of each individual within himself."

Dollard was more interested in psychoanalytical speculations. He noticed the exaggerated myth of the utter purity of white women maintained in the mint-julep tradition as a concomitant of the other myth of unlimited lewdness among Negro women and men. The white man increased his sense of mastery by taking the black woman. She, in turn, perhaps felt a certain triumph in pulling him down to her level and getting even with his wife. Folklore clustered around the lustful male Negro: his sex organs were supposed to be larger than the white's, and his vitality excessive. White women were never, never supposed to feel attracted to Negro men. Dollard suspected that such attraction did exist and that often the cry of rape was a hysterical rationalization. Lynching might contain a special element of punishment for the Negro because the white man unconsciously suspected this fact. Another element in lynching would be projected hostility resulting from the white man's own sense of guilt.

To sum up, the Negroes all felt more or less under sentence of death if they made a misstep, while the whites were always susceptible to panic.

In this group, therefore, sex had assumed a symbolical importance at variance with biological function, similar to the exaggerated role of property among the Melanesians or Kwakiutls.

There were several possible attitudes for the Negroes caught in the caste situation. Individual hostility led to lynching or the electric chair. The Gandhi-like method of bus boycotts had not been thought of in 1937. (It is probable that the need to pacify Oriental colored groups in the cold war which brought about the Supreme Court desegregation order has given the Negroes a new strength. They now feel a solidarity with struggling ethnic groups all over the world.) Among the lower-class Negroes a passive indifference was common. Yet even the passive group felt that the upper class, actively struggling for status, spoke for them. Some frustrated aggression undoubtedly found expression within the caste group. Another reason for the shooting, stabbing, and wife-beating among lower-class Negroes was the white attitude that it didn't matter. White law-enforcement felt little need to step in. There was also an outlet through a source of experience other than that defined by white values. Colored preachers who catered to the middle- and lower-class Negroes were dramatic actors, a cross between witch doctors and political spellbinders. Dollard found that he was excited emotionally by their technique and, when asked to speak, himself experienced a remarkable rapport with the audience. It was notable that such preachers were not particularly moral in their private lives and, though they preached against sin, it was the orgiastic experience (Dollard cited Durkheim) which was important to the congregation. This experience led to shouting, singing, and trances more allied to West African religion than to the Protestant forms whose terminology the preachers employed.

Compensations were not enough. Even among the older generation of Negroes the assumption of the smiling deferential "Uncle Tom" attitude was often shrewd play-acting that hid disrespect and bitterness. The younger, well-educated Negroes tended to emigrate to the north or to keep well apart from the whites in order to avoid being forced to play a submissive role.

Dollard felt that the "conflict between the dominant American mores, which are expressed formally in the Declaration of Independence, and the regional mores of the South which have to deal with Negroes . . . has done more than any other to wrack the American constitutional system and is still one of the major sources of imbalance in our social life."

From an anthropological point of view, the rigid taboos and the magical thinking untouched by modern scientific knowledge, together with sex as an instrument of status, constituted a regression to a state of affairs worse than the tribal.

If Cottonville had not changed greatly during the depression, its cotton economy remaining static, its caste system shielding men's minds like a protective screen, Middletown had been temporarily rocked by the setback to the philosophy of success.

When the depression was seen to be neither a bad dream nor something which could be driven away by magical slogans (much as primitives shouted at a hurricane), the business people became frightened. With the bank failures of 1933 they began to think the end had come. Local relief agencies, hampered by conflicting self-interests, failed to handle the situation. The unemployed, disgusted with such fumbling, organized a Council of the Unemployed. The terrified business group sent in saboteurs and broke it up, but already people were talking of the red menace.

When Roosevelt was elected, the business group endured the experiments of the N.R.A. and welcomed federal relief. Out of W.P.A. activities the town got a sewer system, new roads, improvements in public parks, a swimming-pool. Poor local government and distrust of planning had deprived the city of all these things in the past. When business picked up in 1933, the General Motors plant came back in search of an open-shop town and the business group returned to their old psychology. They also increased their police force to make sure that unions stayed out of Middletown.

The trend toward sexual freedom continued, and sex experience before marriage was now fairly general. An automobile culture had erased the sharp line between paid prostitution and sex for fun. Use of lipstick and nail-painting now began in grade school. Yet, together with this premature sophistication in the young, groups still existed who prohibited drinking and card-playing, and in school the girl who was not allowed to date sat beside the up-to-date adolescent who necked and knew how to handle boys.

Although the faith in education had been shaken by the fact that too many young people graduated from college and found no jobs, nothing had developed to replace the success philosophy. Thanks to the state teachers' college, the ideas of progressive education had begun to penetrate the school system, but they had little relation to the prevailing Middletown mentality. Thus the school had become another area of confusion, for it preached liberalism and independent judgment instead of passing on the community folk belief. As a result, the Daughters of the American Revolution were beginning to exert pressure to stamp out radicalism among teachers. (The relation between the ingroup-outgroup morality and the magical use of the scapegoat and red-baiting in later decades would make an illuminating anthropological study.)

Religion had continued to wane. No revival of faith took place as a result of the depression. Lip service was still paid to churchgoing, but attendance had declined still more, and Sunday was completely secularized. The local radio had tried religious music on the Sabbath, but had given it up. Indeed, the gap between official religious belief and practice was so great that religion had become a mere survival, a form of symbolical thinking used to allay confusion in a complicated world.

The small conscious aristocracy now indulged in riding-clubs and private airplanes and collected paintings. In order to bolster the old slogans of rugged individualism and freedom to achieve success, they had skillfully blamed the Roosevelt Administration for meddling, ignored the social gains from federal aid and the ensuing centralization, and maintained that the economic disruption would have automatically righted itself.

In essence, Middletown had not changed as a result of the depression. The trend toward conformity was stronger than ever. Individual dissenters or deviants either were tolerated as oddities or moved away to larger towns. A dissenting group would have been persecuted. Conformity was to mass-produced, materialist patterns and to folk belief more and more divorced from reality.

The Lynds felt that such thinking, thanks to the rise of mass communications, could be manipulated by demagogues and easily used to bolster a fascistic trend.

In Yankee City, however, as a result of the depression, a revolution took place. "On a cold March day in the worst of the depression all the workers in all the factories of Yankee City walked out."

There had been depressions before without strikes, and there had been strikes when business was good. Warner felt, therefore, that a purely economic explanation did not cover the event. His staff investigated both sides and busily collected data.

When the upper classes failed to handle the unemployment situation, the workers grew indignant. Stimulated by organizers from a near-by town, they walked out spontaneously, joined the union, conducted an orderly strike without violence—for the mayor was impartial and the police force friendly—and won most of their demands. Management, amazed and confused, fought for a time, but finally bowed to the inevitable.

What were the social elements other than purely economic ones behind the strike?

Historically, shoemaking had been a skilled craft. It arose in Yankee City in the eighteenth century and became dominant when the harbor proved too shallow for steamships. The paternalist, capitalist Yankees who founded it cherished ideals similar to those of the X family in Middletown, but the development of industry in the two areas was different. The shoe industry preceded the advent of the machine and, as a craft, created a social form. The plants were small; the founders knew their workers by name and took a personal interest in them. The workers were adjusted to the role their employers played in the community, in government, in the moral and cultural life of the town, and considered them their leaders. As more and more machinery entered the shoe business, the old skills went out, hierarchies of craftsmanship disappeared, the situation became impersonal. There was less emotional satisfaction in the work, and, as the plants grew larger, the succeeding generations of employers lost touch with their men. With the loss of craft prestige and the rise of the foreman, who was not a craftsman but merely an unsympathetic boss, the social pattern was broken. Yet, at the same time that the worker felt dissatisfied because he did not count and no longer belonged to a social pattern that had meaning for him, he fantasied the old founders into godlike figures who would never have let him down. The new generation of management (often absentee owners) succumbed to the same kind of thinking and felt confused and inadequate when faced with what seemed to it to be ingratitude. A second element in the situation was the bitter disappointment of the ethnic groups that had advanced up the hill and now saw economic conditions, personified by the upper classes, depriving them of their hard-won status and driving them back toward the river.

Taken together, these elements made the workers behave like a primitive group whose culture is shattered on contact with western civilization. The strike, to Warner, was a wave of emotion equivalent to the cargo cult of the Manus or the ghost dance of the Sioux. When the union leaders took charge, they channeled it into a new social form. The union offered the workers hierarchies, status, a sense of belonging. Thus technical development had created a new social pattern.

The workers of Middletown had not felt the shock of a changed industrial form, nor did they show the vitality of the ethnic groups newly freed from rigid European class systems. This perhaps explained their failure to organize when faced with the conditions of the depression. In the south the cotton economy was also static and the caste system was maintained by violence or threat of violence.

Another important element in sharpening the gulf between industrial management and the workers was the trend toward monopoly, absentee control by the banks. The shoe industry had already partially succumbed to this during the strike, and the Lynds noted that some of the capital in the X family concerns was held by the banks.

So far all the anthropological data discussed show that the equalitarian idea so significant in American ideology is largely negated by the existence of classes, and that the gulf between the lower and the higher classes has become more sharply defined in recent years. Warner felt that this was compensated for by the ability of the American to move from one class to another. When advancement seemed less easy through work opportunities, the typical American fell back on education. Unfortunately, statistics that Warner quoted in 1953 were not very heartening. Studies in the last decades have shown that 41 per cent of children from the lower economic levels do not finish grammar school and 60 per cent do not finish high school. In addition, intelligence tests show that there is no particular difference in mental ability between those who stay in and those who drop out. A further disquieting fact is the failure of the colleges to expand sufficiently or to plan for the children of the war generation who will swell the number of applicants for entrance in the next few years.

Anthropologists see danger signals if the road to advancement through education is blocked or if enthusiasm for education weakens. Disillusionment concerning the equalitarian formula seems likely to breed serious social demoralization.

Margaret Mead, who wrote a book on the American scene during World War II, felt that the success philosophy had had a profound effect on child-rearing. Americans misapplied the merely descriptive standards of achievement set up by child-psychology manuals. These became goals to work for. Anxious parents created guilts in their offspring, who were made to feel they would not be loved if they did not reach the proper norm. Thus the American conscience was created by "conditional love"; it was a sense of guilt in which the superego was cast in the image of the parent. A difficult type of morality was created, not shared by a large part of the world which lived by supernatural and external sanctions. American guilt was a driving force that kept the individual going, but it also caused deep anxieties. Indeed, the typical successful businessman, according to Warner, identified with his superiors and derived his satisfactions from ceaseless achievement, but revealed, by the prevalence of ulcers, his fear of failure.

If the drive to success was continuing in spite of an increasing number of obstacles, what other forms of social solidarity sustained the equalitarian ideal?

Warner investigated a midwest Republican stronghold in 1945.

In Jonesville he studied particularly the effect of the war and its aftermath.

Americans do not hate war, he concluded. Communities such as Jonesville responded to the war with enthusiasm. The average civilian got a great stimulus from new activities. Mead had commented on the American's rejection of kinship ties, a drastic breaking away from deep-rooted social bonds, which created great individual loneliness. The war helped the isolated individual to feel that he belonged. All local antagonisms could be projected against a common enemy. Patriotic symbols and ritual activities were a source of great emotional satisfaction. Out of war experiences had come veterans' organizations and cults of the dead, and in the twentieth century the unknown soldier was established as an equalitarian symbol, the personification of the common man. To this was added myth. Lincoln-worship was important in Memorial Day ceremonies. Although Lincoln, at the time he became president, had joined the industrialist upper class, he was dramatized as a railsplitter in American legends. His assassination at the close of a war also served as a symbol of unification. He became a Christlike figure, an offering on the altar of unity, a more and more divine image.

At the same time, actual veterans of World War II showed very little understanding of what they had officially been fighting for. Orientation courses had had only the vaguest effect. The average soldier had tended to respond to a surge of group emotion.

"Just as the totemic symbol system of the Australians represents the idealized clan and the African ancestral worship symbolizes the family and state, so the Memorial Day rites symbolize and express the sentiments the people have for the total community and the state."

This interpretation, based on Durkheim's doctrines, could be carried further, for in authoritarian communities such symbols and such state rituals are developed to a much higher degree than in democracies.

An English anthropologist, Geoffrey Gorer (1905–   ), also examined American character, his approach stemming from the outlook of Margaret Mead and John Dollard, who were his teachers. In *The American People* (1948) Gorer developed an image of father-rejection and compared the American colonists' revolt against Brit-

ish authority to Freud's "just-so story" of the band of brothers killing their father. This tendency to reject the past and instinctively to
reject authority, he felt, continued through succeeding generations.
To compensate, maternal authority became extremely important in
America, the mother, the female schoolteacher, and, later, women's
clubs setting the general ethical standards. These maternal standards were, he maintained, the only bulwark against the cynicism of
profits and the desire for an alcoholic good time. Gorer drew a
picture of a very oral people, obsessed by child-rearing and indulging in unique experiments in this area which produced a good
deal of parental anxiety and tension. He credited the maternal
orientation of the American with causing the commercial breast
fetishism that runs through advertising and popular literature.

The anthropological picture of America shows that—unlike societies in the past which have changed slowly, both materially and
ideologically, with centuries of elbow room to adjust the two departments of life to each other—ever accelerating technological
advance has created a widening gap between thinking and reality.
There is too much allegiance to outworn symbolic ideas which are
retained for emotional consolation but which actually hinder adjustment to other individuals, perception of reality, and social
progress.

If Warner is right in his belief that war was welcomed as a stimulus to social solidarity, that veterans' organizations are cults of
the dead, and that celebrations in honor of war dead are rituals to
express group consciousness, this is indeed a grim symptom. To
use national symbols based on war memories to achieve solidarity
is a step backward. Emphasis on war is likely to lead to intensifying
of the ingroup-outgroup dual morality, outlined by Boas, which
leads only to greater international antagonism.

The anthropological profile of America sketched by the scholars
just discussed documents the evidence presented by serious and
critical novelists and playwrights. *Main Street* and *Babbitt* by Sin-
clair Lewis and *1919* by John Dos Passos approximate Middletown. John Steinbeck recorded the tensions of the depression. Jean
Stafford's *Boston Adventure* and some of the novels of John P.
Marquand illustrate New England class structure; indeed, his *Point
of No Return is* Yankee City. The novels of William Faulkner and
Erskine Caldwell, and Lillian Smith's *Strange Fruit* parallel the
work of Dollard and Powdermaker. Such plays as *Belt Line* and

1931 by the Siftons are fictional studies of industrial tension like that of Yankee City. A novel like Norman Mailer's *The Naked and the Dead* stresses the passivity of the citizen soldier.

The writers of fiction, employing their own background and rebelling against it, are found guilty of satire and bitterness. The anthropologists, who make use of data based on quantity and who attempt to be objective, cannot perhaps be so easily shrugged off as "cynical."

Educators would do well to ponder this picture of the American scene. In the schoolroom the rationalism of the eighteenth and nineteenth centuries still persists. It is assumed that the average individual can be taught to think logically about the data presented by the curriculum. Techniques of education are intended to prepare the child to make independent decisions.

Modern child psychology has made use of Freudian insights to liberate the developing individual from cramping inhibitions and compulsions and to promote social health. But, according to Warner, a study of attitudes toward child-rearing indicates that such methods have penetrated only as far down as the upper middle class and even there more in theory than in practice. Over half of the population is thinking symbolically or even as magically as any Australian tribesman. How many homes, affected by the conflicts just sketched—by new obstacles to success, by the insecurities of shifting class structure—and dependent on the emotionally consolatory inconsistencies of folk belief that harks back to another era, will produce children able to exercise independent judgment?

The example of the Manus indicates that education must enable individuals to change if they are to survive a social crisis. If the pattern of our society is not to degenerate into negative conformity —and in the last few years such sociologists as David Riesman in *The Lonely Crowd* (1950) and C. Wright Mills in *The Power Elite* (1956) have continued to warn Americans of this danger—it behooves us to take the criticisms of social science seriously.

Indeed, William A. Whyte in *The Organization Man* (1956), another appraisal of contemporary American society, points out the manner in which the point of view and theory of social science itself is often misused in order to strengthen an anti-individualist, collectivist tendency that, in his opinion, leads to sterile bureaucracy.

Chapter 36

___

MORE BLESSED TO GIVE THAN TO RECEIVE

Concerning Claude Lévi-strauss

___

■ Scarcely anybody is indifferent to sex and marriage, and we have seen that anthropologists are not exceptions. Although controversies over the latter institution died out in the early twentieth century, the interest in social structure—which always, among primitives, involves kinship and marriage—is still very much alive. We have seen that W. H. R. Rivers began as a follower of Morgan. More recently A. R. Radcliffe-Brown analyzed Australian kinship, and his pupil Evans-Pritchard has also been concerned with social organization. A comparative approach was used by George P. Murdoch in his book *Social Structure* (1949). (Murdoch, who worked in the Yale Institute of Human Relations, also initiated the establishment of a massive set of files at Yale in 1937, dealing with the cultures of primitive peoples from all parts of the earth, which was called The Cross-Cultural Survey. Ethnologies from various continents were analyzed according to a standard outline. Murdoch and his associates wrote handbooks for the navy during World War II and built up files from the Pacific area. After the war, in 1949, the project became the Human Relations Area Files, an inter-university organization that now has sixteen university members and, under the presidency of Clellan S. Ford, is occupied in processing the material from all the societies of the world. The files are intended to be a storehouse of information for all social scientists.)

The most recent contribution of importance to the theory of social structure, however, comes from France, and the book elaborating it is, appropriately enough, dedicated to Lewis Henry Morgan. Indeed, the work of Claude Lévi-strauss (1908–   ), for brilliance and penetration, may well be compared to that of the American pioneer. Although Lévi-strauss stems from the sociological school of Durkheim, he wrote his book in the United States with the aid of a Rockefeller grant. He is linked with Durkheim through the work of Marcel Mauss (1872–1950), the latter's nephew. A treatise by Mauss, *Essai sur le don* (*Essay on the Gift*), contains the germ of Lévi-strauss's book, *Les Structures élémentaires de la parenté* (*The Elementary Structures of Kinship*) (1949).

Culture, says Lévi-strauss, is not superimposed on life, but "in a sense is substituted for life." Little, he felt, could be learned about society from animal behavior because animal behavior is generalized and not stabilized by rules. Nature is general, culture is the particular. Since the incest taboo is general, common to all groups (for all have some marriage regulations) and also takes particular forms and is subject to rules, it marks the transition from nature to culture and must originate on the very threshold of society. In consequence, Lévi-strauss made a new effort to resolve the much-discussed problem of incest. Finding none of the old theories satisfactory, he proceeded to outline one of his own.

Food and love among primitives, he said, were of equal emotional importance. Therefore, it was possible to draw some parallels between the treatment of food and the treatment of women. To begin with, food, being a basic social element among primitives, was often surrounded with ritual. In the family group, game was often divided up according to strict rules, each relative of the hunter receiving a specific portion (as Fison and Howitt discovered long ago in Australia). In the case of famine, however, among the Eskimos, all the community *shared* in the catch. Thus there was a conflict between the rights of the family and the rights of the social group. In contrast, on a higher social level, as among Malinowski's Trobrianders, there was elaborate ritual exchange of gifts. And, as we have seen, among the Kwakiutl this became an intense rivalry. There was no doubt that almost all over the world exchange of gifts had a strong spiritual significance. The philosophy of exchange, as Mauss had pointed out, was not economic but total—religious, moral, sentimental: it was a great primitive and human fact. The Trobriand kula exchange, for example, was an adventure. Even the exchange of Christmas presents and cards in the United States was a sort of national potlatch; there was rivalry as to who should send the most beautiful or original cards, and those received were displayed on the mantelpiece.

The *duty* of ceremonial exchange was akin to the duty of sharing food in time of famine. Between strangers or alien groups the exchange of presents was the beginning of social intercourse, an easing of the tension between foreigners. Even modern individuals often initiated a conversation by offering cigarettes.

Thus the idea of *reciprocity* was one of the most basic organizing factors in society. The behavior of children was also significant (Lévi-strauss was familiar with the American culture-and-personality school). At first children desire to own everything they see, are unwilling to share, and try to secure one another's property by violence. They must be gradually taught to accept arbitration. From this they finally realize that if they can not have everything, they can at least be equal, and the principle of reciprocity is established.

Something like this, Lévi-strauss believed, must have happened at the beginning of social organization when the value of reciprocity was learned by experience. Love and food were not in separate categories, and in most primitive societies women were classed as property—in fact, the most valuable property; it followed, therefore, that the rules of reciprocity applied to them. Although the number of individuals of each sex might be equal, there were always some women *more desirable* than others. This made for social tensions. The social group would feel it to be unfair that the attractive women should be the exclusive property of the males of their family. From this, Lévi-strauss argued, the group would begin to insist on rules of reciprocity (an idea that accorded well with Talcott Parsons's analysis of the relation between the individual's need drives and the social norm). If, said Lévi-strauss, a man was forced to give up sexual access to his own daughter or sister, he, in turn, was given access to someone else's daughter or sister. When this principle was established, the institution of marriage came into existence.

The incest taboo, then, was not an instinctive aversion, a eugenic desire to avoid inbreeding, or a lack of sexual interest in housemates, but simply the ingrained normative rule of the group reinforced by ritual and religious sanctions.

Having arrived at this basic principle, which resolved many problems that had been puzzling anthropologists for decades, Lévi-strauss proceeded to analyze many types of marriage exhaustively and to compare kinship systems. The simplest type of reciprocity was a tribe split into two halves which exchanged daughters and sisters. Exogamy was, of course, exchange between alien groups. In every case, he felt, he could reveal the basic principle of reciprocity. The curious complications of some systems he viewed as an instinctive effort to work out exchanges in which the intellectual process had not been clarified. Matrilineal societies and matrilocal marriage, for him, reflected a time "when husbands and brothers-in-law had not resolved their conflicting roles of takers of wives and givers of sisters." Cross-cousin marriage—a form in which a man's son married his sister's daughter, with variations—was a shining example of reciprocity, for it was notable that all varieties of this form of marriage resulted in a man marrying a woman descended *from another male line.*

Lévi-strauss's reasoning is original and provocative and seems to fit the facts better than any previous solution of kinship problems. Indeed, he has been called the Darwin of kinship structure.

He has pointed out that the reciprocity principle can be carried to pathological lengths when purchase of women is substituted for direct exchange. In some cases the compensation involves a fantastic system of loans and debts, as among the Manus of New Guinea.

On the other hand, the truly worth-while social principle, "It is more blessed to give than to receive," inherent in the primitive obligation to share and exchange food, has been lost in the modern development of the profit system. In sex matters we moderns remain primitive, however; our incest taboo continues intact, and we preserve the ancient law of the group, which is, according to Lévi-strauss: "In the field of sex relations you may not do as you like."

Chapter 37

A PICTURE OF SOCIETY

Concerning Talcott Parsons, Gregory Bateson,

M. F. Ashley Montagu

■ Looking back over the decades of study just outlined leaves an impression of many brilliant and provocative insights, a colorful mass of data, and great diversity. It is as if a symphony were being played by an orchestra without a conductor. Where is the promised synthesis?

It is true that organizational steps have been taken to unite the social sciences, that they have begun to learn from one another, but theory has not developed as rapidly as descriptive field work and historical investigation. Can anthropology concern itself with shaping a unified view of human behavior?

One of the most recent answers to this question comes from a thinker whose training took place in other fields.

Talcott Parsons (1902–   ), son of a Congregationalist minister, began his intellectual career with the study of biology when an undergraduate at Amherst. By the time he was graduated in 1924 his interest had shifted to economics, which he studied in the London School of Economics in 1924–5. Here he encountered Malinowski and was introduced to the functionalist point of view. A scholarship for study in Germany led to an acquaintance with the work of Max Weber, a sociologist who died in 1920. Back in Amherst as an instructor in economics, Parsons translated Weber's great work, *The Protestant Ethic and the Spirit of Capitalism.* Thanks in some measure to Parsons, Weber's reputation has been steadily growing in the English-speaking world. Malinowski's functionalism, combined with certain elements in Weber's thought, inspired Parsons to undertake investigations in the theory of the social sciences. In the ideas of Emile Durkheim he found still another stimulus.

For Talcott Parsons there was no satisfactory unified point of view in the various sciences that deal with human behavior.

The nineteenth-century scholars had sought for absolute laws. In the social sciences they had never succeeded in finding any which seemed generally valid. The monolinear evolutionary idea had succumbed under the weight of concrete data. Boas, as we have seen, was highly skeptical concerning the possibility of discovering any laws at all.

Twentieth-century science, however, has tried to arrive at truth in a new way. At one time Euclidean geometry was considered final, an absolute and proved picture of a part of the world. But recently mathematicians have ·devised other types of geometry. Consistent in themselves, these various types are useful when tested practically, but there is no way of deciding which are "true."

Such geometrical systems, therefore, are tools, free creations of the human mind which throw light on the data of the senses. They are not absolutes but systems of relationships, methods of working (subject to criticism and revision).

Applying this new point of view, even if there are no laws in social behavior as seemingly universal as the arithmetical statement $2 + 2 = 4$, is it not possible to find an adequate and systematic *way of thinking* about society and culture?

Talcott Parsons first analyzed the problem historically. The individualist culture of the western world had taken a mechanical view of social action. Nineteenth-century thinkers divided society into individuals, each pursuing a selfish goal. In an imagined primitive horde these goals were all in conflict with one another. How did social unity arise?

Darwin's doctrine of the survival of the fittest through natural selection, as we have seen earlier, was quickly applied to the social field. What held society together, according to this theory, was simply the automatic domination of the fittest, and the goals pursued by the successful. This was a mechanical process. Society was analogous to natural environment. This explanation threw little light on the meaning of institutions or on why some goals were considered good and some bad. Human motivation was reduced to instinct. The theory was, however, reinforced by the prevailing capitalist mentality and a faith in the automatic virtues of competition. It was the position of the sociologist Herbert Spencer.

A variation of this type of thinking ascribed individual motivation to the desire for pleasure and avoidance of pain. But, said Parsons, why are some actions productive of pleasure and others not? Likewise, although there are maximums of pleasure, individuals continue with social actions after biological needs are satisfied. Pleasure in this context was not a real category. It was simply a *measure* of gratification, not a goal.

Trapped in this kind of thinking, anthropological scholars could only pile up concrete facts or indulge in intuitive theories. The actual picture of society remained full of contradictions. On the other hand, attempts to formulate theories in the economic field, on a more or less mathematical basis, indicated that there were nonlogical elements at work.

The contribution of Max Weber presented a new insight into the problem. On the basis of statistics and comparisons between western society and that of other peoples, he attempted to show that the capitalist system was correlated with Protestantism. The goal of capitalism, he said, was not acquisition for use, because acquisition had no limits and was considered an end in itself. Work was ethically regarded. The system produced a dedicated bureaucracy that had certain ascetic elements. These latter he correlated with the Protestant theological idea. As good works were a sign of grace, the most successful man was most likely to achieve a state of grace. Catholicism had turned ascetic drives toward monastic life; Protestant ideology, in which each man was the keeper of his own soul, translated them into a dedication to acquisition.

Assuming that Weber was right (he attempted to show that Chinese and Hindu religions did not provide a basis for the development of capitalism), his work tended to prove that ideas, emotions—judgments of value, in short—played a fundamental role in shaping social action. Although he agreed with Marx that profitmaking was a compulsive necessity of the capitalist system, he disagreed with Marx's insistence that all value-judgment and culture were an indirect reflection of economic drives.

The connection between individual goals and social goals was, however, still not clear. If the intellectual and emotional life of the individual played an active part in his social behavior, what held together a group of people whose individual desires and needs were bound to conflict?

Parsons found an epoch-making insight in Durkheim's collective conscience. The French word *conscience* contains more meaning than the English one. It can signify both awareness and conscience and, in Durkheim's thought, does. This collective conscience, the French thinker insisted, was different in quality from individual psychic activity, and to it he at times ascribed an almost mystical significance. Parsons analyzed the concept more exhaustively. It was actually a set of standards for social behavior, or, as Parsons put it, *normative* rules. These rules shaped the goals of individuals in the group and harmonized them.

A completely isolated man would be forced by biological urges to satisfy his needs. He would be governed by pleasure, pain, or utility. But his acts would have no meaning except for himself. As soon as he lived in a group and his acts came into relation to other individuals' acts, they acquired social meaning. The constraints forced on him by adjustment to the conflicting goals of others changed his character and were passed on to his children in the form of *learning*. Thus the collective conscience came into being and continually perpetuated itself. Religious rituals symbolized, and emotionally reinforced, these sets of normative rules.

Parsons's most important book, *The Structure of Social Action* (1937), published when he was an instructor at Harvard, contained all of this historical analysis and suggested a further development which he called *the theory of action*.

Durkheim, as has been pointed out, became so obsessed with the collective conscience and the deification of society that he practically negated individual freedom of action. He seemed to feel that ideas were born of collective, ritual excitement. But we know that individuals do exist and that they have social meaning.

Parsons analyzed this problem and added some important insights.

In his view, the individual personality is a system of action. Society is also a system of action. It is possible to study the interrelation between the two, but it must be studied *in terms of action*.

The word *action* is highly significant. Parsons' point of view is *dramatic*. Fundamentally his insights are those of the playwright couched in philosophical and scientific terms.

In 1946 Parsons became chairman of a new department of social relations at Harvard, an organization parallel to the Yale Institute of Human Relations. This was also an attempt to unite anthropology, sociology, and clinical psychology. It showed that his thinking had begun to bear fruit.

In the fall of 1948 he and a group of sociologists, anthropologists, and psychologists, including Edward Shils, Clyde Kluckhohn, Gordon Allport, Henry Murray, Robert B. Sears, Edward Tolman, Richard Stouffer, and Richard Sheldon, contributed to a symposium, *Toward a General Theory of Action*, published in 1952. In this study they combined under his leadership to set up basic principles of a method on which they could all agree. It was an attempt to find a common ground among the three sciences, to thrash out a series of working concepts and a terminology based on the proposition "action is the basic unit with which social science deals."

Starting with the individual, the personality of the child was a system of action based on what Parsons termed *need dispositions*. These were complexes based on the drives for food, sex, or love and social approval. These need dispositions caused the individual to act toward goals, to seek gratification. In a social situation, in conflict with other sets of need dispositions, he was obliged to orient himself, to choose a course of action and strike a balance between gratification and deprivation.

Parsons made it clear that there was always a certain amount of leeway between the system of action which constituted the individual and that which constituted society. For instance, the normative rule might constrain a man to wear a necktie and a jacket, but it was possible for him to rebel against the rule.

These rules that made up the collective conscience were absorbed by the individual through imitation (learning) and through identification.

Here Parsons (whose thinking can be harmonized with personality study) made use of a Freudian concept. Freud had described the mechanism of identification. The child tended to identify with a parent, to seek to be like him or her in order to win the parent's love. This created what Freud called the superego, a built-in emotional and moral guide. In other words, the collective conscience became *internalized*. Thus Freud and Durkheim, starting from different premises, arrived at the same result.

As a part of his analysis, Parsons attacked the distinction between society and culture from the standpoint of action. Benedict, in her concept of culture patterns, had little room for action and change. She tended to see society and personality as almost the same thing, with the culture of a group as a projection of individual personality. The image illustrating her thought was a textile with a pattern. The diffusionists saw culture as a creeping blanket of vegetation. Spencer viewed society as an organism, a polyp.

Action was the key, said Parsons. Perhaps the nearest image to make concrete his thought is a chess game. Individuals are the pieces in the social chess game. Culture is an abstraction, the rulebook of the game; it contains the shoulds and oughts.

Although the personality (the individual) had considerable freedom of action in the social situation at a given moment, his social behavior was conditioned by his *role*. (Parsons no doubt owed a good deal to Linton's analysis of role.) The individual's role derived from his status, based on age, sex, position, office, etc. Here it should be noted that there was also a certain freedom in enacting the role, just as actors, with different personalities, in playing the same part speak the same lines but create different effects. The concept of role, however, made possible mutual expectation of reactions between individuals. These expectations, though not exact, connected within limits. These expectations of reaction also conditioned the goals of the individual, his value orientations in a situation, and the amount of gratification or deprivation he could aim at. According to Parsons, the individual was constrained to seek, not for the *greatest amount* of gratification, but for the *best compromise possible* between his need dispositions and those of others in his social group, within the cultural pattern.

In this process, variables came into play. Because choice (not instinct, natural selection, or pleasure-pain) was the organizing principle of society, in order to gratify need dispositions the individual had to orient himself toward situations in five ways. These five variables, according to Parsons, covered all the alternatives needed for action toward a goal. They were the tools by which the scientist could analyze social behavior, and Parsons hoped that they would make it possible to describe the value orientations of different societies.

1. In any social situation the actor must decide whether to accept an opportunity for gratification or to consider the consequences. For instance, if there is very little food on the table, a mother may decide to deprive herself in order to leave more for her children. She may think of the consequences to their health if they are not well nourished.

2. The actor must decide on the act with reference to its personal significance for him or her as against its significance for the group and the group's moral code. Again, the mother chooses between her own hunger and the effect on the group. The children may cry and complain if they go hungry. She also takes into account her moral feelings about the duty of a mother, which is an internalized collective value.

3. The actor must choose between evaluating an act or object in terms of its general meaning and evaluating it in terms of its specific meaning in relation to the actor. For instance, if a beggar who seems to be starving arrives while the mother is making her decision, she must choose between (a) the values of blood kinship and her feeling of love for her children and (b) her sense of responsibility toward society and her general sense of humanity before she gives him some of the food.

4. The actor must view the object of the action (in this case, the beggar) as a composite of ascribed qualities or as a composite of actions. In other words, the mother may consider the beggar to be starving and worthy of charity because he is old, looks pale and ill, and seems scarcely able to stand on his feet, or she may be more critical and insist on hearing his hard-luck story (the history of his actions) in order to learn if he is really in need.

5. The actor must choose whether he shall have a limited specific relation to the object or a diffuse, general involvement with it. In the above example, the mother must decide whether she will give the beggar some food and send him on his way or whether she will direct him to a relief agency, keep in touch with him, help him to get a job, and, in general, become responsible for his rehabilitation.

It should be noted that in these situations the terms *mother*, *child*, and *beggar* all indicate social roles which arouse expectations.

An example of a specific study will give an idea of the application of one of the variables. A questionnaire was given to 648 Harvard students to test their behavior in terms of the third variable.

A man driving a car, accompanied by a close friend, goes thirty-five miles an hour in a twenty-mile-an-hour zone and has an accident. There is no witness except his friend. If the friend testifies under oath that the driver was going only twenty miles an hour, he may save him from serious consequences. Should he do so out of personal loyalty to the friend or testify honestly? Of the Harvard students, twenty-six per cent gave the particularistic response that the witness should testify falsely.

It is Parsons's contention that the individual must find a balance between his need dispositions and the prevailing cultural pattern. When such a balance is maintained, both the personality of the individual and society are integrated. On the other hand, creative change must derive from that part of the individual personality which has room to deviate from the cultural pattern. Too much deviation in the individual produces crime or mental ill-health, in society, instability. Society must therefore strike a balance and tolerate only a certain amount of dissent.

Cultural symbols such as art, literature, and religious ritual are a set of signs, a language that arouses the patterned reaction, an emotional reinforcement of the normative rules of society.

According to the theory of action, psychology must deal with the personality of the individual, anthropology with culture, and sociology with theory and method. Of course the theory allows for interchange of data and also for the inclusion of history and economics in the method.

The theory of action has been formulated so recently that it has scarcely been tested. It is clear that Parsons is a brilliant analyst and that he has contributed important new insights which can be tried out by other scholars in the social sciences.

From the culture-and-personality school comes another attempt at synthesis. In 1951, C. Jurgen Ruesch, a psychiatrist, and Gregory Bateson (1904–), an anthropologist who has collaborated with Margaret Mead, published *Communication: The Social Matrix of Psychiatry*. Much of the thinking of these writers is influenced by a new study called Cybernetics, which deals with communication and control. Cybernetics considers man in terms of some of the more complicated modern machines. One of the characteristics exhibited by the so-called "thinking machines" is that of *feedback*. In the case of feedback, a machine incorporates data from past performance into its system of control in such a way that they modify future performance. Similarly, an experimental animal, traversing a maze to find food, modifies its behavior on the feedback principle. Learning can therefore be considered a highly complicated form of feedback, and thus Cybernetics applies the insights of engineering to society. (Bateson had used engineering images as early as 1934 in discussing a society with two symmetrically interacting systems within it. He felt that there might be an equation which could describe the ensuing build-up of tension through a chain of variables.)

Ruesch and Bateson held that communication was the only concept which could be used to explain all the aspects of events within one system. The earlier analysts of culture and society were content to take reports of informants on their face value. The communication-oriented scientist ideally gathers together experts from different fields, such as statisticians, semanticists, economists, psychiatrists, social anthropologists, to help analyze the personality of the informant, the data furnished by him, and the background and character of the investigator.

Just as the insane individual is unable to communicate and come into constructive contact with his fellows, so the semantic distortion and falsification of propaganda which destroys healthy communication between groups is a symptom of social madness. Hence, according to Ruesch and Bateson, it is the duty of the social scientist to analyze and evaluate communication. The social scientist who has trained himself to be objective and to allow for the predispositions of his own culture can be of great use in mediating between individual cultures, which tend to be closed systems of communication often mutually incomprehensible.

Bateson makes an interesting comparison between the insights of the artist and those of the social scientist. The artist contributes an emotionally integrated perception of the world, but, according to Bateson, does not know what he is saying. The modern social scientist wishes to include perceptions as integrated as those of the artist, but at the same time tries to define *what he is saying* and also studies himself in the role of observer. He further tests his perceptions against *repeated observation*, thus introducing quantitative analysis. While the artist's concepts are swift, intuitive insights which are also aesthetically pleasing, the scientist works slowly and clumsily and is preoccupied with terminology and definitions in the hope of avoiding semantic confusion.

Bateson's recognition of the relationship between art and social science is a fruitful one, for all through the evolution of social anthropology, as we have noted, there has been an oscillation between semi-literary insights and a desire to reduce the study of society and culture to the formal accuracy of the physical or mathematical sciences. With the tendency of modern scientific thinking to abandon rigid systems, perhaps this uneasy dichotomy will disappear. As the historian Crane Brinton puts it, scientists now seek for useful conceptual schemes that will enable them to make statements about phenomena. The social scientist from now on should feel free to use insights borrowed from literature, engineering, or psychiatry, and will seek for conceptual schemes to reconcile them.

Although Talcott Parsons and Ruesch and Bateson stress different images of society, their approaches are not incompatible. Systems of communication are also systems of expressive action. Parsons is interested in the process of choice and in value-judgments. Ruesch and Bateson direct our attention toward the content of expression and analysis of control. Parsons and his associates stress the conscious aspects of behavior, Ruesch and Bateson the unconscious. The thinking of neither group is isolated; both draw on many specialized contributions of their contemporaries.

Another approach to a synthetic view of society is found in M. F. Ashley Montagu's *The Direction of Human Development*. Born in England in 1905, Ashley Montagu was trained by both Malinowski and Boas, and thus his work is a link between the functionalist and culture-and-personality schools. Additional background in biology and physical anthropology has helped to mold what might best be described as a socio-biological approach that relates him to Westermarck. As a corrective to the nineteenth-century Darwinian concept of the competitive struggle for survival, Ashley Montagu traces the co-operative element in life forms and in society in detail. An organism, he points out, is a society of many cells. Indeed, the cells of certain sponges, when separated, tend to regroup and reconstitute the organism. This tendency toward association he considers to be a basic force that operates at all levels of evolution and modifies evolution. The individual in many cases has a better chance of survival when part of a group. Ashley Montagu cites the small and vanishing number of predatory and solitary animals as against the large numbers of those which associate in groups. He goes on to develop this principle in terms of psychoanalytical thinking, the lack of love (love defined as reciprocal co-operation) being the cause of social illness: neurosis, crime, and international hostility. Animals and simple non-literate societies such as those of the Eskimos or the Australians teach us that the basic co-operative urge is a potential for social harmony and can be developed.

Ideas of this sort, which stem from contemporary developments in social science, are symptomatic of a revolution in modern thinking, a revolution perhaps more important than the technological one. For the first time we are truly beginning to view man as a social animal, to assess the individual's aspirations and capabilities, not in terms of supernatural motivations or intuitive philosophy, but in a perspective of social meaning. As Ashley Montagu puts it, "From the point of view of the social situation there are no individuals. . . . A creature apart from a social group is nothing but an organic being, the member of a social group is a person." Depending on how it is interpreted and applied, this trend can lead to unthinking conformity or to new and rational social harmony.

On the whole, such efforts to unify social theory are a healthy sign that social science is assuming more responsibility in the search for a synthetic point of view.

These are recent developments in theory, but meanwhile anthropology has not stood still in more practical areas. In the social sphere the need for action has begun to seem more and more imperative. To this need anthropology has not turned a deaf ear.

Chapter 38

MAKING THE WORLD SAFE FOR HUMANITY

Concerning Homer Barnett, Ruth Benedict,

Margaret Mead, Allan R. Holmberg, Sol Tax,

Alfred and Rhoda Metraux

■ We have seen anthropology turn to the contemporary scene as an observer. Can it play a still more active role in shaping human relations? To answer this question we must go back to a minor colonial war of the last century.

In the interior of the Gold Coast of West Africa lies the Negro kingdom of Ashanti, now a part of Ghana. In the eighteenth century a certain magician announced that God had empowered him to make the Ashanti a great and powerful nation. In the presence of the king and a great multitude he drew down from heaven a black cloud from which issued rumblings of thunder, and a wooden stool partially covered with gold sank slowly through the air until it rested on the king's knees. The people were told that their power, their wealth, their honor were bound up with the stool.

Once a year the stool was carried in a solemn procession under its own umbrella, followed by more attendants than there were in the king's train.

The Ashanti prospered. They defeated neighboring tribes. One of these had the audacity to make a replica of the stool. The

Ashanti added the gold from the conquered stool to their own. Their sovereignty finally extended to the seacoast, where, in the late nineteenth century, the British had already built forts. Conflicts took place. In 1873 the British burned the Negro capital of Kumasi and concluded a treaty with the king. A later and prouder king refused a British protectorate and refused to put a stop to his people's coastal raids. In 1896 Kumasi was once more occupied, the king banished, and the kingdom made a protectorate.

The stool vanished. The British, who considered it a symbol of sovereignty, for years made efforts to find it. In 1899 a young traitor to his tribe offered to lead the British to it. A captain and a detachment of soldiers accompanied him. He was disguised as a British soldier, for the whites feared reprisals. The boy lost his nerve on the trip, ran away, and told a local chief the story. The British captain tried to pretend that his guide was mad. By threats and persuasion they got the traitor to lead them another twenty-five miles. Finally he refused flatly to go farther. They were obliged to return empty-handed.

A few months later the British governor, Sir Frederick Hodgson, called the chief and the people to a great meeting at Kumasi. Already rumors of the attempted treachery had got about, and all that was needed was a spark. Hodgson set off the spark.

The words of his speech bring to the eye a vivid picture of a pompous Colonel Blimp haranguing the black fellows. "Where is the golden stool?" Sir Frederick demanded. "Why am I not sitting on the golden stool at this moment? I am the representative of the paramount power; why have you relegated me to this chair? Why did you not take this opportunity of my coming to bring me the golden stool and give it to me to sit upon?" In his bureaucratic stubbornness he ignored the fact that no king had ever sat on it.

The same captain and the same young African were again sent to look for the stool. They failed to find it, and on their way back they were ambushed and massacred. Kumasi was besieged.

The British sent reinforcements. Three months later the governor, the women, and twenty-nine other Europeans were got out of the Ashanti town, leaving three officers and a hundred Hausa troops behind with only a week's rations. A month later, nearly dead from starvation, they were relieved. Fighting went on for another five months. The British lost about a thousand men. No one knows the extent of the Ashanti casualties.

It was a huge price to pay for a blunder.

Ashanti was annexed. Nothing further was said about the stool. Twenty years later a quarrel took place in the village where the stool was hidden. A British officer made an inspection. Once more the stool was spirited away.

In 1920 a road was begun between this village and the next. The overseer decided, on the spur of the moment, to change its direction. Danso, the head of the road crew, became very much agitated; it was he who was in charge of the stool, and now he was not quite sure where he had buried it. Sure enough, one of the workmen drove his pick into the box containing it. The headman diverted his workmen with a story that the box contained a smallpox fetish.

That night Danso hid the stool in a tin box in a friend's house. A former stool-bearer, now a Christian, whose morals had not improved with his conversion, persuaded Danso to plunder the stool of its gold and to divide the loot.

The chiefs discovered the theft. The people became aroused. Tension increased. The whites began to fear a new uprising. The culprits were put in jail to prevent the Ashanti from tearing them to pieces. The chiefs decreed the death penalty. Finally the British succeeded in softening the punishment to banishment.

Before this took place a ceremony was carried out in which two golden bells, belonging to the stool, were carried forth under a ceremonial umbrella. Suspects were obliged to touch them and swear they possessed none of the stolen gold. They were told that if they lied, the fetish would kill them.

The whole incident passed off without bloodshed because a capable anthropologist, appointed as adviser in this area, had been investigating the case of the stool. He discovered that every native believed that an ordinary wooden stool was the repository of his soul. The Ashanti even put miniature fetters on such stools to chain the soul to them. Similarly, the famous golden stool was the collective soul of the Ashanti nation. They were ready to fight to the death to preserve it. Rattray, the anthropologist, explained the situation to the British authorities and also explained to the natives that the British would never interfere again. There would be no further need to hide the cherished symbol.

When Princess Mary was married, the Ashanti queens sent her a silver replica of the stool used by their queen mother, saying:

"It does not contain our soul, but it does contain all the love of us queen mothers and of our women."

This episode is perhaps the earliest dramatization of applied anthropology. It showed that the knowledge of the specialist could be used to prevent social misunderstanding and conflict.

The British heeded the lesson. Actually, the functionalist point of view of Malinowski and Radcliffe-Brown was needed before anthropology could go into action. In the publication *Africa*, in 1928, Malinowski expressed the view that the anthropologist should be guided by the colonial administrator in his choice of research problems. If the practical man would state what he needed to know about savage law, religion, or economics, the scientist could provide him with the facts. Three years later, in the same publication, he launched an amusing tirade that is as revealing of his own character as of the new point of view. "Science is the worst nuisance and the greatest calamity of our days," he wrote rebelliously. "It has made us into robots, into standardized interchangeable parts of an enormous mechanism. It pushes us with a relentless persistence and a terrible acceleration towards new forms of existence . . . an ever-increasing speed in communication; accessibility of superficial knowledge and meretricious art; endless opportunities in cheap and mean forms of amusement, leisure to do a thousand irrelevant things—these, from the side of human consumption and enjoyment, are the benefits of our modern civilization. . . . Anthropology, to me at least, was a romantic escape from our over-standardized culture. On the islands of the Pacific, though I was pursued by the products of the Standard Oil Co., weekly editions, cotton goods, cheap detective stories, and the internal combustion engine in the ubiquitous motor launch, I was still able with but a little effort to relive and reconstruct a type of life moulded by the implements of the stone age—and now, after twenty years of anthropology I find myself, to my disgust, attempting to make anthropology into a real science."

If he appreciated the romantic side of anthropology, he was still able to scold his colleagues and himself for their self-indulgence. It was, after all, ridiculous that they knew so much about little tribes in Australia, about some natives from Tierra del Fuego, about one or two atolls in the Pacific, about a few Veddas huddled in an inaccessible cave of the Ceylon jungle, while they had ignored the Orient, the problem of detribalized natives, and the conflicts of acculturation when white civilization overcame primitive societies. Gradually scientists and administrators began to work together. (The Dutch were pioneers and started training colonial administrators in anthropology in 1899.)

In one case the anthropologist undertook to present a picture of the native concept of justice in order to prevent misconceptions when the official applied the British system.

In another area in Africa attempts to stabilize land ownership failed. The anthropologist pointed out that when a man moved, as he often did for fear of witchcraft, his coffee trees reverted to the village and were assigned to another owner. The scientist suggested that British law award the original owner a percentage of the crop when the new owner took over.

In Papua the British frowned on the use of a human victim in a fertility rite. An anthropologist appointed after World War I managed to substitute the body of a pig for a man and a football to replace a spear in discharging hostility.

When new sources of quinine were being sought in Ecuador, anthropologists made the first contact with the head-hunting Indians of the interior and smoothed the way for the botanists.

Anthropologists were the first to establish friendly relations with the northwest Indians when the Alcan Highway was built to Alaska.

These examples show that if anthropology had been applied decades earlier, the ugly story of colonization might have been somewhat different. In the United States in particular, the application of such knowledge might have prevented untold loss of property and human life in the clash between European culture and that of the American Indians. Actually, despite Schoolcraft's efforts, it was not until 1934 under John Collier that the Indian Bureau systematically began to use the services of anthropology and serious efforts were at last made to preserve Indian languages and culture.

There are many problems to be resolved between administrators and scientists, however. As Homer Barnett (1906–   ), staff anthropologist for the United States Trust Territory of the Pacific Islands in 1951–3, has pointed out, if the anthropologist makes specific recommendations he is often criticized for abandoning the impartiality of the scientific attitude. On the other hand, officials often accuse the scientist of being naïve and without practical experience. On the whole, the British school tends to see the function of the ethnologist as one of supplying information, while the Americans prefer to play a more active role. Barnett's book *Anthropology in Administration* (1956) sums up the history of work in this area and discusses the problems in detail.

As we have already seen, anthropology has begun to concern itself with modern civilization as well as the primitives. In this area, too, social scholars have found ways of applying their science. Reference has been made to Elton Mayo, who influenced Warner by his study of industrial workers. This particular study was a pioneer effort. Mayo was a psychiatrist and a friend of Malinowski and Radcliffe-Brown. In 1933 he decided to investigate the problem of fatigue among industrial workers who were supposed to be affected by obsessive thinking. A group of girls in the Western Electric plant at Hawthorne were picked for the study. Various changes in their working environment were tried, such as modification of the lighting and temperature, and different types of rest periods. To the investigators' amazement, no matter *what* changes were tried, good or bad, the production of the group went up. Finally it became clear that the increased production was the result of better morale. It was the first time anyone had paid any attention to this group of girls!

The study was broadened, and an observer was stationed in the room to record the social organization of the group and its relation to their personalities and their output, much as if they had been a primitive tribe. In addition, the individuals were interviewed. The interviews had such a cathartic effect that once more production went up. As a result of the study, a psychological counseling system was set up by the plant.

Having got over their nostalgia for the vanishing primitive, anthropologists dug in and scrutinized labor relations. They tried to reduce tensions between employer and employees. They studied ways in which individual personalities could better fit into the social groupings of industrial organizations.

A pioneer in this field is Eliot D. Chapple, who in 1941 founded the *Journal of Applied Anthropology*. The Society for Applied Anthropology now maintains its headquarters at the New York State School of Industrial and Labor Relations at Cornell University.

The Second World War was a tremendous stimulus to the practical application of anthropology. Not only were all the resources of science called on to aid in the struggle, but also it soon became apparent that sweeping cultural changes, unlike anything before envisioned in human society, were bound to result from it. In 1939 Margaret Mead, returning from a field trip, wrote: "I came home to a world on the brink of war, convinced that the next task was to apply what we knew as best we could to the problems of our own society. . . . Anthropology was made for man, not man for anthropology."

As soon as the tide turned in the Pacific, American soldiers were thrown into contact with Stone Age peoples of the islands and military authorities were faced with the job of administration. The anthropologist John Embree, who was employed by the Office of War Information, found that he had to explain to American officers why natives did not respond to American hearty good-nature. The officials decided, when the islanders did not laugh at American jokes, that they had no sense of humor. They did not know that to the islanders it was the height of bad manners to laugh in the presence of a superior. An American officer mortally offended a native chief by playfully tousling his hair. He did not know that taboos prohibited the touching of the head, and that his action was roughly equivalent to unbuttoning another man's fly in public. The old mistakes were made in regard to leaders. Natives were "elected," under American supervision, to chieftainships to which they had no hereditary right. As a result, they could not discharge their duties. At one time six minor native officials were imprisoned because they protested that their women were obliged to do coolie work for a high-ranking officer. On the island, social custom did not allow women to perform such work. When the members of an imprisoned murderer's family flung themselves hysterically at the feet of an American officer, crying: "Why don't you kill us?" he was bewildered. He did not know that in this culture the family group was supposed to suffer for the crimes of any member. The American GI was amazed to discover that amiable shouts of greeting, slaps on the back, and attempts to teach married women American dance steps evoked violent discontent and complaints from native men.

Even more significant use of anthropology was made in regard to the Japanese. The Americans were astonished to find that the fanatical Japanese soldier, so prone to suicidal actions, was often willing, after he had been captured, to broadcast for the Americans and sometimes even offered to join the American army. American generals had avoided taking Japanese prisoners on the theory that they would be treacherous. It took the anthropologists to explain that Japanese ethics were situational. The soldiers had been told by their leaders that no Japanese patriot could surrender. As a result, prisoners, when taken, appeared to be unconscious regardless of the circumstances of their capture. Once captured, they considered themselves dead to their own society and were quite ready to adjust to a new set of circumstances.

It became clear to the Americans that the Japanese were the most alien enemy they had ever fought. In 1944, as we have seen, Ruth Benedict was assigned to study Japanese culture by the Office of War Information. Her work led to a more general project, Research in Contemporary Cultures, which will be discussed presently. Her analysis of Japanese character, *The Chrysanthemum and the Sword* (1946), was prepared without, of course, a visit to the field; Benedict studied documents, literature, journalism, and movies, and checked her conclusions with Japanese Americans. That some of the latter defended and some hated their traditional national culture was all the more useful. After the occupation her book was discussed by Japanese anthropologists in one of their periodicals. While they criticized details, on the whole they accorded her great praise for the objectivity and acuteness of her insights.

One of the objects of such study was the crucial question of the surrender. Was the Emperor to be retained or forced to abdicate? Anthropologists pointed out (it was Geoffrey Gorer's memorandum that made the specific recommendation) that many Japanese considered him a symbol of peace. He was all things to all men, a key culture symbol, far more like a Polynesian sacred chief than a western dictator. The scientists argued that his prestige alone could cause all the far-flung unconquered groups of fanatic soldiers to surrender at the same time. Their view prevailed, and they were right. After the Emperor's broadcast the Japanese army laid down its arms as one man, and the astonished Americans were greeted by a cheerful, co-operative people who cherished no desire for revenge, indulged in no guerrilla warfare, and were quite ready to accept the occupation.

A wrong decision in this case would have sacrificed countless lives.

The key to Japanese culture, Benedict decided, was a deep feeling for hierarchical organization—a place for everyone and everyone in his place. This probably harked back to the clan system and was closer to the kinship psychology of the South Seas than to western culture.

America saw Japan's entry into the war as willful aggression. Japan argued that she was only maintaining her "proper place" as a leader of the Orient in the international hierarchy.

Part of Japan's peculiar culture could be understood from her history. Just at the crucial period when the merchant class began to develop in the seventeenth century, their rise to power was checked by the Shogunate, a military dictatorship set up by a leading general, which turned the emperor into a puppet. Trade with Europe was forcibly cut off. Western ideas were shut out. In this way feudal structure was preserved for two hundred years, and the merchant class had no opportunity to break it up as their European counterparts did. The philosophy of individualism did not develop.

The warrior class, or Samurai, were not allowed to acquire property, but were kept as salaried retainers, dependent on their feudal lords. Japan's economy was one of scarcity, and this militated against an ideal of material acquisition. As a result, the Samurai class made a virtue of certain non-material values such as honor and self-discipline. As peace was maintained for long periods, these same warriors, who alone were permitted to wear swords, filled their leisure with an interest in the drama, rituals such as the tea ceremony, a conscious aestheticism based on borrowed Chinese forms.

During this period the population remained almost static. The sense of proper place was so ingrained that all psychic life revolved around it. Peasants, for instance, were supposed to have the right to present petitions. Occasionally peasant leaders did offer such petitions to the feudal elite. Although these were sometimes acted upon favorably, the leaders who presented them were executed for stepping out of their proper place. The peasants, in turn, accepted this as right and proper, and honored the dead leaders as martyrs.

The only way an individual could move out of his class was by adoption (again harking back to kinship customs). Thus a merchant's son might be adopted into a Samurai family. This, too, prevented the break-up of feudalism by tying together the merchant and Samurai classes.

The advent of Commodore Perry (who dealt with the Shogun and did not suspect that he was not the emperor) forced the Japanese to reopen trade with the west. This made some adjustments imperative. In 1880, when there was a move toward reform, it did not come from below. In planning national industrial development the Samurai-merchant group (the merchants were dominated by a few monopolistic families) actually consulted the British sage Herbert Spencer. Spencer informed them that their hierarchy system was their strength and advised them to adhere to it. The Samurai-merchant elite constructed a kind of planned economy based on the old feudalism and reinforced by a state worship, called Shinto, which was grafted onto local cults. Japan was thus able to develop a heavy industry without changing her handicraft consumer-goods economy and her traditional social patterns.

Beginning with the family and extending to all of society, the pattern continued to be a series of obligations. (Again the parallel with Oceania is striking.) The supreme obligation was to the emperor, and laws were obeyed out of respect for him. Next, obligation was owed to superiors in station. The wife was indebted to her husband, children to their parents. A Japanese felt that his obligation toward his deceased parents could be fulfilled toward his children.

This sense of obligation differed from either western or Chinese concepts because it was *unconditional.* Even though the parent, superior, or ruler might be cruel and unjust, this did not relieve the Japanese individual of his duty.

Thus the Japanese sense of honor and duty was not at all like western reciprocal affection. Obligation to relatives could be easily accepted, for relatives were a part of the individual who was receiving, but a favor from a casual stranger was humiliating. For this reason the Japanese way of saying "Thank you" means "I am insulted and ashamed to have received such a great benefit." This ambivalent sense of honor and duty made for a curious psychology. Failure to fulfill a duty caused intense shame. A Japanese student, for example, did best when measuring himself against his own record. Open competition with other students was avoided, for it caused deterioration through fear of failure and even led to suicidal moods. Suicide was historically an honorable way for a Samurai to avoid punishment. In modern Japan (as in the Trobriand Islands) it was the only escape from an intolerable sense of shame.

Westerners thought the Japanese submissive, Japanese found the westerners lawless.

The Japanese had no sense of abstract evil. In personal life they accepted and cultivated sensual pleasures. Sexual enjoyment was sought with prostitutes. Wives were instruments of procreation. On the other hand, these same people practiced austerities to harden the spirit. The cultivation of self-discipline, such as going without food and bathing in icy water, made a man able to overcome enormous obstacles. The techniques for this resembled yoga and were supposed to produce a highly efficient individual.

It followed that saving life was unimportant in war, for it interfered with heroism, the opportunity to conquer through the spirit. A propaganda story to raise the morale of the troops went as follows: A captain returned to headquarters after an engagement, made his report, and dropped like a stone. When examined, his body was found to be already cold. He had made his report *after* death.

The ideal personality was therefore a man so controlled that he felt no tensions, yet so poised that he could act with complete efficiency—to the west a kind of super-zombie.

This mentality coupled with the desire for "everything in its place" made it possible for Japan's military caste to challenge a power many times superior in resources, in the belief that the spirit would conquer. Defeats were described as "withdrawal according to plan." Up to the end everything was still in its place.

To the anthropologist, trained to understand kinship complexities and the magical point of view of the South Sea peoples, all this made sense. But it was painfully clear that without the mediation of anthropologists the average Japanese and the average westerner could only be utterly incomprehensible to each other.

It was a dramatic example of a basic international problem.

Another contribution along the same lines resulting from the war effort was Margaret Mead's pamphlet *American Troops in a British Community*, published in England in 1945. Mead was married to a British anthropologist and thus understood which aspects of Yankee character the British would find puzzling. She

415

explained historically the American's tendency to brag, his disrespect for things old, and his casual dating habits. The British, she warned, would have to break through their code of manners and ask personal questions if they hoped to get to know their allies.

The techniques evolved for studying inaccessible countries with which the United States was at war, and those such as Red China and the Soviet Union in which there were barriers to travel, led to the idea that a general method for the study of culture at a distance might be worked out and eventually to a new interest in the concept of national character. With the aid of a grant from the Human Resources Division of the Office of Naval Research, Ruth Benedict inaugurated the project Research in Contemporary Cultures in 1947. This work was carried on in successive projects under the auspices of Naval Research and the Massachusetts Institute of Technology. The report edited by Margaret Mead and Rhoda Metraux in 1953, *The Study of Culture at a Distance,* reveals how important the concept of collective effort has become in contemporary social study. To list only some of the scholars involved, Geoffrey Gorer and Margaret Mead co-ordinated the work on Russia, Rhoda Metraux that on France, Conrad Arensberg and Mead that on Jewish culture; Ruth Bunzel headed the work on China, Martha Wolfenstein contributed material on child study, Gregory Bateson analyzed a Nazi film. The Jewish study was an attempt to use the method to learn something of small Jewish communities in Europe which no longer existed. The project on the whole was a significant application of fresh developments in methods of field work. Written and oral literature and films were analyzed, informants were interviewed, life histories were taken down, psychological tests were given. The approach used reflects Ruesch's and Bateson's theory of communication, which we have elsewhere discussed. In addition, techniques for analyzing content owed much to the work of Harold Lasswell and Nathan Leites. Lasswell, in particular, had used psychoanalysis in studying the aggressive behavior of public-relief clients as early as 1934. He elaborated a method for investigating the symbolic data in documents from a psychoanalytical point of view in a book, *Analyzing the Content of Mass Communications,* in 1941. Nathan C. Leites and I. Pool were the authors of a study, *On Content Analysis,* published in 1942.

In *The Study of Culture at a Distance* material on such specific themes as a Pole's attitude toward responsibility, Russian sensory images, a Frenchman's conception of friendship was recorded. Various experts analyzed this material for its conscious and unconscious content. Films typifying national points of view yielded such fantasies as the French split father image (half a sexually attractive protector, half a prowler who menaced the home from outside it) and the Italian image of the sexually bad woman, destroyer of men. In this way insight could be gained into national attitudes toward the family, sex relations, ethical concepts—all the various elements which make for contrast between cultures and which, when not interpreted by objective scholarship, are productive of antagonisms and semantic confusions between peoples.

Further examples of this trend are Geoffrey Gorer's report *The People of Russia* (1950), the result of a co-operative effort, and *Soviet Attitudes toward Authority* (1951), a group study by a research team, edited by Margaret Mead.

Mead's conclusions sketch a series of contradictions. She saw the traditional pre-revolutionary Russian as an individual given to violent changes of mood and requiring external controls to keep him within bounds. He was a prey to a deep general sense of sin, but lacked a keen awareness of individual responsibility. This picture (which evidently owed much to Chekhov and Dostoevski) was not entirely erased by the new regime. The new rulers, still unsure of the structure set up on the old base, devised very rigid controls. They distrusted the talkativeness of the old intelligentsia and wanted to substitute action.

Their state theology, which demanded unconditional obedience to the Party, depended on a sort of Puritan religious dogma. Soviet justice held everyone guilty for mistakes or crimes, and there was much blundering in an attempt to make agencies and groups responsible for individual acts. Party leaders were credited with a kind of papal infallibility. By a supposedly scientific but actually magical process, they became aware of the "correct line." The correct line interpreted the true course of future events. Although infallible, the leaders were, in theory, responsible to self-criticism and to criticism from below. Also any Party member, regardless of ability, was theoretically able to rise to leadership through Party virtue. This was something like the American success philosophy held by individuals whose incomes would remain the same all their lives.

417

As the leaders were not infallible in actual fact, they had to be repudiated completely when they failed. Thus any individual was capable of changing from a completely virtuous friend to a wholly evil enemy at any time. The west believed that there was some consistency in human character. A man was neither all good nor all bad. His record could be taken into account in assessing him. From the Russian point of view, with a couple of shifts in the line, a man could go from all good to all bad and then become all good again. Of course, in relation to external policy, the rightness of the line and the doctrine that it alone would result in international social good allowed for retreat (or shifts when someone erred) but no real compromise.

Falsification of events and ritual dramas such as the famous trials occurred because reality had to be re-created so as to accord with the line. According to Soviet philosophy, what should happen must happen, or have happened.

Despite the existence of a secret police that was supposedly a dedicated priesthood, above politics, whose duty was to root out error (rather like the Inquisition), the official goal of Soviet society was to lead the people in the correct direction by arousing their enthusiasm. Might was not right, in the Soviet view. A leader should inspire love and respect. On the other hand, ruthlessness could be employed with a good conscience because the end—a good society—justified the means.

Mead's analysis indicated that repeated western charges of hypocrisy and deep-dyed duplicity merely reflected conventional western moral slogans. The present Soviet society was as different from the west as that of the Japanese. To adjust to its consistent inconsistency realistically and to try to assess the possibilities of change would be a wiser course than to hurl insults.

Time alone would tell if this—to the west—highly contradictory view of human character would result in deep-seated demoralization. The new generation of school children were urged to be imaginative and full of the joy of life and at the same time eternally self-critical, somewhat as pious Christians in the past were expected to search their consciences continually for sin. Rigid control, however, was incompatible with creativeness and imagination, and if the Soviet Union wished to forge ahead on both scientific and cultural fronts, apparently it would be confronted with a dilemma.

The contradictions in the Soviet Russian ethic, it was clear, resulted in a good deal of cheating and conniving and covering up of dishonesty. Likewise, the attempt to cut down the power of agencies by overloading them with contradictory functions resulted in inefficiency and confusion.

On the whole, if the citizens were to continue to be dedicated to the state and the future and to accept the Party's power of life and death over them, would they not demand more material rewards? The Russians, after all, had no yoga-like tradition of self-discipline like that of the Japanese. Their history was closer to that of the west. In other words, would not the long-promised increase in production of consumer goods be demanded more articulately by the people at large as time went on?

Mead predicted that, to solve these conflicts and contradictions, there might be less talk of capitalist attack, a relaxation of police vigilance, and a closer correlation between real guilt and punishment.

The study of culture at a distance is of course influenced by Benedict's effort to grasp the character of a social group. Recently UNESCO, in order to promote international understanding, has undertaken a number of studies of national culture which are prepared by teams consisting of an anthropologist and a psychologist.

International relations are, however, only a part of human relations. The Society for Applied Anthropology has set up a code of ethics for its members. Those who subscribe to it take responsibility for their recommendations. They do not consider themselves technicians unconcerned with ends. Ends cannot be used to justify means. The applied anthropologist aims to promote a dynamic equilibrium in social groups whose potentialities for change will result in greater well-being for the individuals in the group. He must always work in accordance with this code of values and must test the code scientifically. He is pledged not to work for a special-interest group if he feels its activities will have a destructive effect on the whole community. He works to prevent loss of life or health and irreversible damage to the natural environment. Above all, he tries to advance relationships that will contribute to the integrity of the individual human being, he respects human personality and cultural values, and he shares new discoveries and methods with his colleagues.

With this end in view, it is not surprising that applied anthropology has found in the U.N. a most important institution through which to work. Aside from promoting descriptive studies and studies of the tensions that produce war, and combating distorted racist views (Ashley Montagu was Rapporteur of the committee which drafted the UNESCO statement on race), the United Nations has begun to recognize that anthropology must co-operate to meet the greatest challenge of all, the absorption of the technically backward peoples into the modern world. In the words of Margaret Mead, introducing a book on the subject which she edited for UNESCO, "How can technical change be introduced with such regard for the cultural pattern that human values are preserved?"

Since the Second World War there has been an upsurge of nationalism, a stirring in the non-European cultures such as has never been known before. Two great powers are bidding for the support of these peoples and offering them different solutions. The colored races have inherited a legacy of hatred and suspicion from the colonial past. A chaos of tensions and wasteful cross-purposes divides mankind.

Yet somehow the strong must help the weak. Somehow the riches that science has given us must be shared. Somehow diverse societies must discover common goals.

Although there are no all-embracing solutions, the United Nations exists as a symbol of intention, an act of affirmation, however imperfectly it has been implemented. Among its activities, one small UNESCO project is symbolic of what can be done and, above all, of how essential anthropology is to an attack on the problem.

The Haitian Pilot Project, started in 1948 at the request of the Haitian Republic, was set up in the Marbial Valley, under the direction of Dr. Alfred Metraux, an anthropologist on the UNESCO staff. This valley was suffering from all the worst problems of backward areas: overpopulation, land hunger, deforestation, drought and soil erosion, sickness, poverty and intermittent famine, widespread illiteracy, and a declining agriculture. The valley was a horrible example of how not to live.

Even while the initial anthropological survey was in progress, the investigators realized that some constructive steps must be taken at once. They began with the schools.

The valley schools were practically without books. The teachers had had almost no training and contented themselves with making the children, who did not understand French, parrot French grammar by rote. The malnourished students were sleepy and inattentive.

The survey's language experts recommended that the lower grades be taught in Creole. They prepared special textbooks to help teach French to Creole-speaking natives. Some new teachers were brought in, and a school canteen was set up which provided three meals a week for the children. Attendance of course improved at once. Next the government's illiteracy campaign took on new energy in the area. The experts provided new textbooks in Creole and accompanying filmstrips. To help mass-produce the books, UNESCO sent a small multigraph press to Haiti. The education experts reorganized teaching methods and introduced supervised games in recreation periods. The increased energy and alertness of the children was astonishing. The Catholic school alone refused UNESCO aid and advice.

UNESCO built a headquarters and a community center to which the peasants immediately came for advice, to express their needs, and for general catharsis. At this center, charts, posters, and filmstrips were prepared. The need for anthropological advice was demonstrated in the reaction to a poster designed for the literacy campaign. It was an artistic success, but the natives insisted it was a picture of a wedding ceremony.

Attempts were made to improve soil-conservation methods. A hillside was terraced, ditches were dug, and rows of sisal cactus were planted to hold the soil in place and serve also as a productive crop.

Experts were brought in to teach the weaving of sisal fiber and cotton and the techniques of working cow's horn and leather. The peasants used their own designs, working on a co-operative basis. Their products sold in Port-au-Prince, and some samples, sent to the United States, showed export possibilities. The ceramics department of the University of Southern California made it possible for a kiln to be built at the UNESCO center, where some of the natives of the valley learned to make both useful and decorative pottery.

A small medical clinic was swamped with patients as soon as it was opened. The response showed clearly that the natives were anxious for the benefits of modern medicine when they found it within their reach.

All these activities were only tentative, but showed what could be done.

A more recent effort of the same type was initiated in Peru in 1952. This was not under UNESCO auspices but was a collaboration between Cornell University and the Indigenous Institute of Peru, aided by funds from the Carnegie Corporation. A couple of hundred miles north of Lima, in a narrow valley paralleling the highest mountain range in the country, topped by snowcapped Huascarán, the second-highest peak in South America, some 2,250 Quechua Indians lived on the Hacienda Vicos. The hacienda, or estate, to which they owed a certain amount of unpaid labor, had been owned by the Peruvian government since the seventeenth century. It was generally leased for exploitation to the highest bidder. The Indians owned no land themselves, but were allowed to cultivate small subsistence plots. They were more or less in the position of our southern sharecroppers. They inhabited small, dark, circular, thatched adobe huts. Only two per cent were literate. Their only relaxation was drunkenness at fiestas. They were looked down on by the *cholos* or halfbreeds, and exploited by them whenever possible. The women wore felt hats and many layers of skirts. They plodded about submissively with wood, babies, or provisions in carrying-cloths on their backs. The Quechua are a short, brown-skinned, Mongoloid people. In such depressed areas their skins are dirty and scabby, children suffer from sore eyes, the women look old at thirty, and the low hygienic level of the community is obvious to the most casual observer. For centuries they have nourished a kind of passive antagonism against the whites and the better-off cholos which dates back to the Spanish conquest.

When Allan Holmberg of Cornell set up the project, blight had twice ruined the potato crop and the corn crop had also failed. The vicosinos were reduced to eating their seed potatoes and seed corn.

Holmberg (1909–   ) had a considerable background of work in South America. He is best known for a study, *Nomads of the Long Bow* (1950), in which he investigated a primitive hunting people of Bolivia who suffered continually from a scarcity of food, but whose sex lives were almost entirely uninhibited. He found that their anxieties and neuroses were largely based on hunger, not sex, and, just as food could become a surrogate for sex among the civilized, so sex among these primitives was often an outlet for the frustration of hunger. Interestingly enough, these conclusions seem to document Lévi-strauss's equating of food and love.

Holmberg had studied the Quechua Indians of Peru in association with the Smithsonian Institution and with the local University of San Marcos. The Vicos area had also been studied for five years in preparation for the project. The aim of the anthropologists was to see what could be done to stimulate self-help within the framework of the local culture and also, at the same time, to make a contribution to the methods of applied anthropology. Thus Vicos, which was representative of the condition of the Indians who make up half the population of Peru, became a laboratory of social change.

Only a fraction of the land on the steep mountainsides was under cultivation; the rest was used for grazing cattle. The scientists began by supplying blight-resistant potato seed and suggesting better techniques of irrigation, fertilizing, and combating insects. At the beginning there was a heritage of suspicion to overcome. Peru has a sad history of venal and inefficient government and palace revolutions which makes the average Indian distrustful of official help. The United States anthropologists had the co-operation of Mario Vasquez, a young Peruvian student from the University of San Marcos, who lived on the hacienda with his family and helped to break down the barrier of distrust. The first year only seventeen families enrolled in the project. Their potato crop, thanks to the new seed and new methods, was doubled. Since they had been supplied with seed on a sharecropping basis, the harvest was divided into two equal parts and they were given their choice. This was new and surprising to the Indians, for they were used to being cheated. The second year eighty-five families joined, including one of the *mayorales*, or headmen. By 1955 the vicosinos had all the seed they needed, and the sharecropping system was dropped.

The hacienda had a miserable hut for a school, and, despite a compulsory-education law, less than five per cent of the children attended it. The scientists brought in a contractor and a few skilled craftsmen, the Indians supplied the manual labor, and by 1953 a new six-room school was built. The following year three more rooms, a kitchen, and a school-lunch program were added, the school being staffed by the Peruvian government.

Stimulated by the anthropologists, the regional public-health service set up a clinic, which examined all school children. In a short time the clinic was serving the whole neighborhood.

The Quechua of this particular area were highly individualistic, and one of the local problems was a series of quarrels over the ownership of cattle. Cattle were a desirable form of wealth, and apparently some cattle-rustling went on. A great deal of time and money was wasted settling such disputes. Each mayoral presided over a *casta* or kinship group and fulfilled certain religious and social functions. The anthropologists began to promote initiative among the mayorales by turning the weekly *mando* (a meeting at which they were given their orders) into a discussion group. The Americans suggested to this group of headmen that branding the cattle might solve their problem. The mayorales accepted the idea. At first the people in general did not respond. Then one of the mayorales shrewdly suggested that the biggest owners had not accepted branding because they had got their herds by rustling. Immediately the largest cattle-owner of all, thus put on his mettle, branded his cattle. The rest followed suit, and by the following year there were no more disputes over cattle.

The goal of the experiment was to improve the vicosinos' technique for living and getting their living, without a large capital outlay, to a point where they would be able to take over the hacienda themselves. The project has been so successful that many students from both Cornell and the University of San Marcos have studied it as a model. Indeed, all such pioneer efforts are models for the rest of the world.

Dr. Holmberg has summed up the role of the applied anthropologist who "intervenes," and at the same time studies the process he initiates, by comparing it to that of the psychoanalyst. He deals with people who desire to change but who have been held back by social obstacles. Like the psychoanalyst, the anthropologist initiates a process of self-enlightenment and helps the patient to cure himself.

A different type of problem was discussed at a symposium held at the University of Chicago during a meeting of the Central States Anthropological Society in 1956. Sol Tax, chairman of the university's department of anthropology, reported on a project that he had headed. This was a study of the Fox Indians intended to find ways in which they could adjust to the surrounding white civilization without abandoning their own culture.

The question of social change has been studied theoretically by Homer Barnett, whom we have mentioned in connection with applied anthropology in administration. In a book, *Innovation* (1953), he advanced the theory that change was the result of identification of elements in two configurations (or they might be called *Gestalts*). The elements thus felt to be equivalent, though never precisely similar, bring together non-equivalent elements in the two configurations, and something new results. We are reminded of Kohler's ape that substituted a tree branch for a stick to get its bananas. The length and the shape of both tree branch and stick were equivalents, but the use of the stick to get bananas brought in an element foreign to the concept of the branch growing on a tree.

The impulse to create an innovation invariably crystalizes in an *individual*, and may result from such drives as boredom; the desire for release from restraint, irritation, or unpleasantness; the desire for certainty, efficiency, or accuracy. In order for a *people* to accept something new, they must find elements in the new which they can identify with their own culture; otherwise, the psychological barrier is too great. Likewise, the innovation must have advocates with sufficient prestige to promote it successfully.

Sol Tax and his associates endeavored to create a group of educated Fox Indians who could mediate between the two cultures. In the case of the Vicos Quechua, the educated foreigners enjoyed a high prestige. The anthropologists, on their part, tried to suggest useful innovations that could be linked to something familiar.

The Vicos experiment was not an isolated one for Cornell. The university has a second project in Thailand, under the direction of Lauriston Sharp, and has run a third among the Navajo, under Alexander Leighton. Indeed, Cornell is playing a major role in developing this anthropological trend.

Vast areas of the world face the same problems as the Haitians of the Marbial Valley and the vicosinos of Peru. Poor, lacking modern knowledge and initiative, they need a catalyst.

In contrast, the Manus, as we have seen, are an example of a people who do not lack initiative and who deeply desire change. In their case there is a divided administration policy to contend with, a holdover from colonialism. Some elements in authority do not welcome their wish for self-government and distrust their ability to modernize themselves. Commercial interests are not anxious to see them become economically independent. Their leader, by rejecting vested western religious interests, created further antagonisms. They therefore are in danger of failing through lack of understanding on the part of the dominant west.

Once more the lesson is driven home that, in our era, education is our weapon against demoralization. Anthropology can both guide this education in underdeveloped areas and quicken the modern nations' awareness of the needs of the suffering world. Progress must be achieved *by* the people, not *for* them. In no other way can they preserve their self-respect and self-reliance.

Lawrence K. Frank, a pioneer in stimulating child-development study, has suggested a Center for Cultural Dynamics sponsored by UNESCO which would not only contribute plans for approaching and aiding the technically backward peoples of the world but would also act as a central agency enlisting "the aid of scholars, artists, poets, dramatists, novelists, musicians, all those who can assist in revealing the basic goals of their own people . . . and can further their translation into the basic forms of communication."

Not only must there be no more golden-stool incidents, but understanding between peoples must become a constructive force. Thus, tentatively at first but more and more rapidly, anthropology, like its sister science psychology, is playing an active role in the everyday affairs of men. As the earth shrinks under the restless advance of the machine, men are forced to face the fact that they must either head toward self-destruction or learn to live together. All of our social sciences can contribute toward the constructive solution, and among these anthropology must take the lead.

In a little more than a hundred years social anthropology has come a long way from the first half-curious, half-contemptuous awareness of the variety of human behavior on this planet.

Slowly, picking his way through a fog of his own prejudices, the student of society, at first merely a dilettante historian, has come to realize that he has raised most of the great questions man asks about himself. What is the relation between freedom and authority? How shall we solve the conflict between the individual and society? What, after all, is culture? What in our heritage is good and what should be discarded? Why do we choose one way of life instead of another?

The concept of anthropology as a science unconcerned with

contemporary life is untenable. If the idea of democracy is to endure, if the majority is to retain the right to make decisions, the majority must understand the choices it is making.

The modern mind tends to rely less and less on ancient dogmas for its standards of authority. Anthropology itself has shown that many of these dogmas are rationalizations of local vanity or shields against fear. In the past it has been easier to set up a painted and scowling deity in the image of its creator than to face the darkness of the unknown. We have eaten of the apple and there is no going back. The trend toward increasing awareness is not reversible. And thus it is clear that in the future the social scholar must undertake the study of values. It is a new and heavier burden from which he can not shrink. It is his responsibility to clarify the ideals for which men struggle or for which they think they struggle.

In the future the social scholar will continue to record and compare cultures and to fill in the gaps that still remain in their history. He will continue to theorize, define, seek for laws, and revise his own theories. All this is a part of the scientific approach. But, fortunately, the study of man has always had a pragmatic side. The field worker goes among people. He participates in their joys and sorrows. Without a sympathetic concern for their daily problems he could never hope to understand them. The most distinguished leaders in the field of social anthropology have been men of profound humanity and wisdom. They have created a tradition of responsibility. Thanks to them, the scholars of today have responded to the call of the average man and are endeavoring to help him in his desperate struggle to orient himself in a world of bewildering transformation and terrifying multiplicity.

The human animal will never achieve utopia. He need not fear this ultimate boredom. With unforeseen catastrophe, with the perils of nature, with the search for the meaning of life and the immanence of death he will always have to contend. Man's inhumanity to man, however—the countless tragedies of ignorance and misunderstanding—is preventable and he should try to prevent it if he is to continue to look away from the ape and toward the angel.

Anthropology, the science of man, is shaping weapons to reduce the inhumanity, to lessen the tragic ignorance of this world. It remains to be seen whether we are willing to use them.

Bibliography

(containing some titles not mentioned in the text)

General

Goldenweiser, Alexander: *History, Psychology, and Culture* (New York, 1933).

Haddon, Alfred C.: *History of Anthropology* (London, 1934).

Herskovits, Melville: *Man and His Works* (New York, 1948).

Lowie, Robert H.: *History of Ethnological Theory* (New York, 1937).

Muhlman, Emil William: *Geschichte der Anthropologie* (Bonn, 1948).

Penniman, Thomas Kenneth: *One Hundred Years of Anthropology* (London, 1952).

Chapter 1

Schoolcraft, Henry Rowe: *Algic Researches*, 2 vols. (New York, 1839).

——: *Historical and Statistical Information Respecting the Indian Tribes of the United States*, 6 vols. Philadelphia, 1855–8.

——: *Notes on the Iroquois* (Albany, 1847).

——: *Oneonta: The Indian in His Wigwam* (New York, 1844).

——: *Personal Memoirs of a Residence of Thirty Years with the Indians* (Philadelphia, 1851).

——: *Plan for the Investigation of American Ethnology* (Washington, 1846).

Chapter 2

Morgan, Lewis: *The League of the Iroquois* (Buffalo, 1919) (First Edition, 1851).

Stern, Bernhardt: *Lewis Morgan, Social Evolutionist* (Chicago, 1931).

Chapter 3

Darwin, Charles: *The Origin of Species* (London, 1859).

Macbride, W. W.: *Huxley* (London, 1934).

Moore, Ruth: *Man, Time, and Fossils* (New York, 1953).

Bibliography

Spencer, Herbert: *An Autobiography*, 2 vols. (New York, 1904).
——: *Principles of Psychology*, 2 vols. (London, 1870–2).
Ward, Henshawe: *Charles Darwin* (New York, 1909).

Chapter 4

Bachofen, Johan Jacob: *Das Mutterrecht* (Berlin, 1861).
Maine, Sir Henry: *Ancient Law: Its Connection with the Early History of Society and Its Relations to Modern Ideas* (London, 1861).
McLennan, John Joseph: *Primitive Marriage* (London, 1865).

Chapter 5

Morgan, Lewis: *Ancient Society* (New York, 1877).
——: *Systems of Consanguinity of the Human Family*, Smithsonian Contributions to Knowledge (Washington, 1870).

Chapter 6

Lubbock, Sir John: *The Origin of Civilization* (London, 1870).
——: *Prehistoric Times* (London, 1865).
Tylor, Sir Edward Burnett: *Researches into the Early History of Mankind and the Development of Civilization* (London, 1865).

Chapter 7

Marett, Robert Ranulph: *Tylor* (London, 1936).
Tylor, Sir Edward Burnett: *Anahuac or Mexico and the Mexicans Ancient and Modern* (London, 1860).

Chapter 8

Tylor, Sir Edward Burnett: *Primitive Culture*, 2 vols. (London, 1871).

Chapter 9

Max Mueller, Friedrich: *Chips from a German Workshop*, vol. 2 (London, 1867–75).
Tylor, Sir Edward Burnett: *Anthropology* (London, 1881).
——: "On a Method of Investigating the Development of Institutions Applied to the Laws of Marriage and Descent," *The Journal of the Anthropological Institute*, vol. 18 (1888), p. 245.

Chapter 10

Fison, Lorimer, and Howitt, A. W.: *The Kamileroi and the Kurnai* (Sidney, 1880).
Frazer, Sir James G.: "Fison and Howitt," *Folklore*, vol. 20 (1907), no. 2.
Howitt, A. W.: *The Native Tribes of South East Australia* (London, 1904).
Marett, R. R., and Penniman, T. K., eds.: *Spencer's Last Journey* (Oxford, 1931).
——: *Spencer's Scientific Correspondence* (Oxford, 1932).
Spencer, Sir Baldwin: *The Arunta: A Stone Age People* (London, 1927).
——: *Wanderings in Wild Australia* (London, 1928).
Spencer, Sir Baldwin, and Gillen, F. J.: *Across Australia* (London, 1912).
——: *The Native Tribes of Central Australia* (London, 1899).
——: *The Northern Tribes of Central Australia* (London, 1904).
Stern, Bernhardt, ed.: "Selections from the Letters of Lorimer Fison and A .W. Howitt," *American Anthropologist*, vol. 32 (1930), no. 2.

Chapter 11

Haddon, Alfred Cort: *Headhunters, Black, White, and Brown* (London, 1901).
——: *Magic and Fetichism* (London, 1910).
——: *The Study of Man* (London, 1898).
——: *The Wanderings of Peoples* (London, 1912).
——: *Reports of the Cambridge Expedition to the Torres Straits*, 6 vols. (Cambridge, 1901–35).
Quiggin, A. H.: *Haddon, the Headhunter* (Cambridge, 1942).

Chapter 12

Black, J. S., and Chrystal, G. W.: *Lectures and Essays of William Robertson Smith* (London, 1912).
Chrystal, George W.: *The Life of William Robertson Smith* (London, 1912).
Smith, William Robertson: *Kinship and Marriage in Early Arabia* (London, 1885).
——: *Lectures on the Religion of the Semites* (London, 1889).

Chapter 13

Downie, R. Angus: *James George Frazer* (London, 1940).
Frazer, Sir James George: *The Belief in Immortality and the Worship of the Dead*, 3 vols. (London, 1913–24).
——: *Folklore in the Old Testament* (New York, 1925).
——: *The Golden Bough*, 2 vols. (London, 1890).
——: *The Task of Psyche* (London, 1909).

Bibliography

Chapter 14

Green, Roger Lancelyn: *Andrew Lang* (Leicester, 1946).
Lang, Andrew: *Custom and Myth* (London, 1885).
——: *Magic and Religion* (London, 1901).
——: *The Making of Religion* (London, 1909).

Chapter 15

Crawley, Alfred Ernest: *The Idea of the Soul* (London, 1909).
——: *The Tree of Life* (London, 1905).
Lowie, Robert H.: *Primitive Religion* (New York, 1924).
Marett, Robert Ranulph: *A Jerseyman at Oxford* (London, 1941).
——: *The Threshold of Religion* (New York, 1914).

Chapter 16

Adam, L.: *Primitive Art* (Harmondsworth, 1940).
Balfour, Henry: *The Evolution of Decorative Art* (London, 1893).
Boas, Franz: *Primitive Art* (Oslo, 1927).
Cushing, Frank Hamilton: "A Study of Pueblo Pottery," *U.S. Bureau of Ethnology, Annual Report No. 4* (Washington, 1886).
Haddon, A. C.: *Evolution in Art* (London, 1895).
Holmes, W. H.: "The Origin and Development of Form and Ornament in Ceramic Art," *U.S. Bureau of Ethnology, Annual Report No. 4* (Washington, 1886).
Marsh, O. T.: *The Origins of Invention* (London, 1895).
Read, Herbert: *Art and Society* (London, 1937).
Stolpe, Knut Hjalmar: *Collected Essays,* translated by Mrs. C. Marsh (Stockholm, 1927).
Weltfish, Gene: *The Origin of Art* (Indianapolis, 1953).

Chapter 17

Westermarck, Edward: *Marriage Ceremonies in Morocco* (London, 1914).
——: *Memories of My Life* (New York, 1929).
——: *The Origin and Development of the Moral Ideas,* 2 vols. (London, 1906).
——: *Ritual and Belief in Morocco* (London, 1920).

Chapter 18

Briffault, Robert: *The Mothers,* 3 vols. (London, 1927).
Crawley, A. E.: *The Mystic Rose: A Study of Primitive Marriage* (New York, 1902).

Lowie, Robert H.: *Primitive Society* (New York, 1925).

Westermarck, Edward: *The History of Human Marriage* (London, 1891).

Chapter 19

Balfour, Robert: *The History of the Musical Bow* (London, 1889).

Boas, Franciska, ed.: *The Function of the Dance in Human Society: A Seminar* (The Boas School, New York, 1944).

De Zoete, Beryl, and Spies, Walter: *Dance and Drama in Bali* (London, 1939).

Evans-Pritchard, E. E.: "The Dance," *Africa*, vol. 1 (1928), no. 4.

Grosse, Ernst: *Der Anfang der Kunst* (Berlin, 1894).

Hambly, Wilfred Dyson: *Tribal Dancing and Social Development* (London, 1920).

Harrison, Jane: *Themis: A Study of the Social Origins of Greek Tragedy* (Cambridge, 1927).

Hawkins, E. W.: *The Dance Festivals of the Alaskan Eskimo*, University Museum Anthropological Publications, vol. 6, no. 2 (Philadelphia, 1914).

Herskovits, Melville: *Dahomey: An Ancient West African Kingdom* (New York, 1938).

Michelson, Truman: *The Buffalo Head Dance of the Thunder Gens of the Fox Indians*, Bureau of American Ethnology Bulletin No. 87 (Washington, 1928).

Radcliffe-Brown, A. R.: *The Andaman Islanders* (London, 1914).

Ridgeway, William: *The Drama and Dramatic Dances of Non-European Races with Special Reference to the Origin of Greek Tragedy* (Cambridge, 1915).

Sachs, Curt: *World History of the Dance*, translated by Bessie Schönberg (New York, 1937).

Seligman, C. G. and Brenda S.: *The Veddas* (Cambridge, 1911).

Wallaschek, Richard: *Primitive Music* (London, 1893).

Wissler, Clark, ed.: *Societies of the Plains Indians*, Anthropological Papers of the Museum of Natural History, vol. 11 (New York, 1916).

Chapter 20

Schurtz, Heinrich: *Altersklasse und Männerbunde, eine Darstellung der Grundforme der Gesellschaft* (Berlin, 1902).

Van Gennep, Arnold: *En Algérie* (Paris, 1914).

——: *Etudes d'ethnographie Algérienne*, 2 vols. (Paris, 1912–14).

——: *Les Rites de passage* (Paris, 1909).

——: *Tabou et totémisme à Madagascar* (Paris, 1904).

——: *Totémisme et méthode comparée* (Paris, 1908).

Webster, Hutton: *Primitive Secret Societies* (New York, 1908).

Bibliography

Chapter 21

Hall, C. Stanley: *Founders of Modern Psychology* (New York, 1912).
Jones, Ernest: *Life and Work of Sigmund Freud,* vols. 1 and 2 (New York, 1953–5).
Murphy, Gardner: *The History of Modern Psychology* (New York, 1949).
Puner, Helen Walker: *Freud: His Life and Mind* (New York, 1947).
Winkler, John, and Bromberg, Walter: *Mind Explorers* (New York, 1939).

Chapter 22

Boas, Franz: "The Origin of Totemism," *American Anthropologist,* vol. 18 (1916), no. 2.
Frazer, Sir James: *Totemism and Exogamy,* 4 vols. (London, 1910).
Freud, Sigmund: *Totem and Taboo* (London, 1912).
Goldenweiser, Alexander: *History, Psychology, and Culture* (New York, 1933).
Kroeber, A. L.: "Totem and Taboo," *American Anthropologist,* vol. 22 (1920), no. 1.
Lang, Andrew: *The Secret of the Totem* (London, 1905).

Chapter 23

Boas, Franz: "The Central Eskimo," *Bureau of the American Ethnological Association, Third Annual Report* (1888).
——: "A Journey in Cumberland Sound and on the West Shore of Davis Strait in 1883 and 1884," *Journal of the American Geographical Society of New York,* vol. 14 (1884).

Chapter 24

Agassiz, Louis: "The Diversity of Origin of the Human Race," *Christian Examiner,* July 1850 (reprint).
Gobineau, Conte Joseph Arthur de: *Essai sur l'inégalité des races,* 2 vols. (Paris, 1853–5).
Klemm, G. F.: *Allgemeine Culturgeschichte der Menschheit,* 10 vols. (Berlin, 1843–52).
Ratzel, Friedrich: *The History of Mankind,* translated by A. J. Butler (New York, 1895).
Waitz, Theodor: *Anthropologie der Naturvölker,* 5 vols. (Berlin, 1859–72).

Chapter 25

Bastian, Adolph: *Ein Besuch in San Salvador, ein Beitrag zur Mythologie und Psychologie* (Bremen, 1859).

Bastian, Adolph: *Ethnische Elementärgedanken in der Lehre vom Menschen* (Berlin, 1895).
——: *Die Kulturländer des Alten Amerika* (Leipzig, 1878).
——: *Der Mensch in der Geschichte, zur Begründing einer Psychologischen Weltanshauung* (Leipzig, 1860).
——: *Die Volker Oestlichen Asiens* (Leipzig, 1868).

Chapter 26

Boas, Franz: *Contributions to the Ethnology of the Kwakiutls,* Columbia University Contributions to Anthropology, III (New York, 1925).
——: "Ethnology of the Kwakiutl," *35th Annual Report of the Bureau of American Ethnology* (Washington, 1921).
——: *The Mind of Primitive Man* (New York, 1944).
——: *Race and a Democratic Society* (New York, 1945).
——: *The Religion of the Kwakiutls,* Columbia University Contributions to Anthropology, X (New York, 1930).
——, ed.: *The Jesup North Pacific Expedition Publications,* Memoirs of the American Museum of Natural History, 15 vols. (New York, 1900–30).
Herskovits, Melville: *Franz Boas: The Science of Man in the Making* (New York, 1953).
Kroeber, A. L., Benedict, Ruth, Emeneau, Murray B., and others: *Franz Boas,* Memoirs of the American Anthropological Association, vol. 61 (Washington, 1943).

Chapter 27

Frobenius, Leo: *Erythräea, Länder und Zeite der Heiligen Königes Mordes* (Berlin, 1930).
——: *Prehistoric Rock Pictures, in Europe and Africa,* from Material in the Archives of the Research Institute for the Morphology of Civilization, Frankfurt on Main (New York, 1937).
——: *Der Ursprung der Kultur,* vol. 1, *Afrikanische Kultur* (Berlin, 1898).
——: *The Voice of Africa,* 2 vols., translated by Rudolph Blind (London, 1913).

Chapter 28

Graebner, Robert Fritz: *Methode der Ethnologie* (Heidelberg, 1911).
——: *Das Weltbild der Primitiven* (Munich, 1924).
Lowie, Robert H.: *The Crow Indians* (New York, 1935).
Nordenskjöld, Baron Erland: *Sydamerikiska Indiernas Kulturhistoria* (Gothenburg, 1912).
Perry, W. J.: *Children of the Sun* (London, 1929).

Bibliography

Radin, Paul: *Culture of the Winnebago, as Described by Themselves*, Indiana University Publications in Anthropology and Linguistics (Bloomington, 1950).

——: *Method and Theory of Ethnology* (New York, 1933).

——: *Primitive Man as Philosopher* (New York, 1927).

——: *Social Anthropology* (New York, 1932).

Rivers, William Halsey R.: *The History of Melanesian Society*, 2 vols. (London, 1912).

——: *Social Organization* (London, 1924).

Sapir, Edward: *Language* (New York, 1921).

——: *Time Perspective in American Aboriginal Culture*, Memoir 90, Anthropological Series No. 13 of the Geological Survey, Canadian Department of Mines (Ottawa, 1916).

Schmidt, William: *The Origin and Growth of Religion* (New York, 1931).

——: *Der Ursprung der Gottesidee*, 11 vols. (Münster, 1912-54).

Smith, Grafton Elliot: *Human History* (London, 1929).

——: *The Migrations of Early Cultures* (London, 1912).

Wissler, Clark: *The American Indian* (New York, 1925).

Chapter 29

Comte, Auguste: *Positive Philosophy*, translated by Harriet Martineau (London, 1893).

Durkheim, Emile: *De la division du travail social* (Paris, 1893).

——: *Les Formes élémentaires de la vie religeuse* (Paris, 1912).

——: *Les Règles de la méthode sociologique* (Paris, 1895).

——: *Suicide* (Paris, 1897).

Lévy-Bruhl, Lucien: *Les Fonctions mentales dans les sociétés inférieures* (Paris, 1910).

——: *La Mentalité primitive* (Paris, 1912).

——: *Le Surnaturel et la nature* (Paris, 1931).

Radcliffe-Brown, Alfred Reginald: *Structure and Function in Primitive Society* (London, 1952).

Spencer, Herbert: *The Principles of Sociology*, 3 vols. (London, 1876-96).

——: *Social Statistics* (London, 1850).

——: *The Study of Sociology* (New York, 1896).

Chapter 30

Heidbreder, Edna: *Seven Psychologies* (New York, 1933).

——, Child, C. M., Koffka, Kurt, and others: *The Unconscious: A Symposium* (New York, 1937).

Chapter 31

Malinowski, Bronislaw: *Argonauts of the Western Pacific* (London, 1922).

——: *Coral·Gardens and Their Magic* (London, 1935).

Malinowski, Bronislaw: *Crime and Custom in Savage Society* (London, 1926).

———: "Culture," *The Encyclopedia of Social Sciences,* vol. 3–4 (New York, 1942).

———: *Magic, Science and Religion* (Glencoe, 1948).

———: *A Scientific Theory of Culture and Other Essays* (New York, 1944).

———: *Sex and Repression in Savage Society* (London, 1926).

———: *The Sexual Life of Savages* (London, 1929).

Chapter 32

Kroeber, A. L.: *Configurations of Culture Growth* (Berkeley, 1944).

———: *Cultural and Natural Areas of Native North America,* University of California Publications in Anthropology, Archeology, and Ethnology, vol. 38 (Berkeley, 1939).

———: *Handbook of the Indians of California,* United States Bureau of American Ethnology Bulletin No. 78 (Washington, 1925).

———: *The Nature of Culture* (Chicago, 1952).

———: *A Survey of the Southwest Zuni District,* Anthropological Papers of the American Museum of Natural History, vol. 18, (New York, 1919).

Linton, Ralph: *The Cultural Background of Personality* (New York, 1945).

———: *The Material Culture and Archeology of the Marquesas Islands,* Bernice Bishop Museum Memoirs, vol. 8 (Honolulu, 1923).

———: *The Study of Man* (New York, 1936).

———: *The Tanala,* Field Museum of Natural History, Anthropological Series, vol. 22 (Chicago, 1933).

Redfield, Robert: *The Folk Culture of Yucatan* (Chicago, 1941).

———: *Peasant Society and Civilized Culture* (Chicago, 1956).

———: *The Primitive World and Its Transformations* (Ithaca, 1952).

———: *Tepoztlán, A Mexican Village: A Study of Folk Life* (Chicago, 1930).

———: *A Village That Chose Progress: Chan Kom Revisited* (Chicago, 1950).

Redfield, R., Linton, R., and Herskovits, M.: "A Memorandum for the Study of Acculturation," *American Anthropologist,* vol. 38 (1936), no. 1.

Redfield, Robert, and Villa Rojas, Alfonso: *Chan Kom: A Mayan Village,* Carnegie Institute of Washington Publication No. 448 (Washington, 1934).

Chapter 33

Ashley Montagu, M. F.: *Coming into Being among the Australian Aborigines* (London, 1937).

Erikson, Erik: *Childhood and Society* (New York, 1950).

———: *Observations on the Yurok, Childhood and World Image,* University of California Publications in American Anthropology, Archeology, and Ethnology, vol. 35 (Berkeley, 1943).

Bibliography

Kardiner, Abraham: *The Individual and His Society* (New York, 1939).
Kluckhohn, Clyde: *Psychiatry and Anthropology: One Hundred Years of American Psychiatry* (American Psychiatric Association, New York, 1945).
Mead, Margaret: *Coming of Age in Samoa* (New York, 1928).
——: *Growing Up in New Guinea* (New York, 1930).
——: *New Lives for Old* (New York, 1956).
——: *Sex and Temperament in Primitive Societies* (New York, 1935).
Mead, Margaret, and Bateson, Gregory: *Balinese Character* (New York, 1942).
Mead, Margaret, and Macgregor, Frances Cooke: *Growth and Culture* (New York, 1951).
Ogburn, William: *The Social Sciences and Their Interrelations* (New York, 1928).

Chapter 34

Benedict, Ruth Fulton: "Configurations of Culture in North America," *American Anthropologist*, vol. 34 (1932), no. 1.
——: *The Conflict of Cultures in North America*, Proceedings of the American Congress of Americanists, vol. 23 (1928).
——: *Patterns of Culture* (New York, 1934).
Codere, Helen: "The Amiable Side of Kwakiutl Life," *American Anthropologist*, vol. 58 (1956), no. 2.
Foch, Mildred: *What Is Gestalt Theory?* (New York, 1935).
Hallowell, A. Irving: *Culture and Experience* (Philadelphia, 1955).
Kluckhohn, Clyde: *Beyond the Rainbow* (Boston, 1933).
——: *Mirror for Man* (New York, 1949).
Kluckhohn, Clyde, and Leighton, Dorothy: *Children of the People* (Cambridge, 1947).
——: *The Navajo* (Cambridge, 1946).
Mead, Margaret, ed.: *Co-operation and Competition among Primitive Peoples* (New York, 1937).

Chapter 35

Dollard, John: *Caste and Class in a Southern Town* (New Haven, 1937).
——: *The Changing Function of the American Family* (Chicago, 1931).
——: *Criteria for the Life History with Analysis of Six Notable Documents* (New Haven, 1935).
——: *Social Learning and Imitation* (New York, 1941).
——: *Victory over Fear* (New York, 1942).
Gorer, Geoffrey: *The American People* (New York, 1948).
Lynd, Robert S., and Lynd, Helen: *Middletown* (New York, 1929).
——: *Middletown in Transition* (New York, 1937).

Mills, C. Wright: *The Power Elite* (New York, 1956).
Powdermaker, Hortense: *After Freedom* (New York, 1939).
——: *Hollywood: The Dream Factory* (Boston, 1950).
——: *Life in Lesu* (New York, 1933).
Riesman, David: *Faces in the Crowd* (New Haven, 1952).
——: *The Lonely Crowd* (New Haven, 1950).
Warner, William Lloyd: *A Black Civilization* (New York, 1937).
Warner, William Lloyd, and Lunt, Paul S.: *The Social Life of a Modern Community*, Yankee City Series, vols. 1–3 (New Haven, 1941–2).
Warner, William Lloyd, and others: *American Life: Dream and Reality* (Chicago, 1953).
——: *Democracy in Jonesville* (New York, 1949).
Whyte, William A.: *The Organization Man* (New York, 1956).

Chapter 36

Lévi-strauss, Claude: *Les Structures élémentaires de la parenté* (Paris, 1949).
Mauss, Marcel: *The Gift: Forms and Functions of Exchange in Archaic Societies*, translated by Ian Cunnison (London, 1954).
Murdoch, George P.: *Social Structure* (New York, 1949).

Chapter 37

Ashley Montagu, M. F.: *The Direction of Human Development* (New York, 1955).
Parsons, Talcott: *Essays in Sociological Theory* (Glencoe, 1949).
——: *The Structure of Social Action* (New York, 1937).
Parsons, Talcott, and Shils, Edward, eds.: *Toward a General Theory of Action* (Cambridge, 1952).
Ruesch, C. Jurgen, and Bateson, Gregory: *Communication: The Social Matrix of Psychiatry* (New York, 1951).

Chapter 38

Barnett, Homer: *Anthropology in Administration* (Evanston, 1956).
——: *Innovation* (New York, 1953).
Benedict, Ruth F.: *The Chrysanthemum and the Sword* (New York, 1946).
Brown, C. Gordon, and Hutt, Alexander: *Anthropology in Action* (Oxford, 1935).
Collier, John and Mary: "An Experiment in Applied Anthropology," *Scientific American*, vol. 96 (1957), no. 1.
Frank, Lawrence K.: "Education for World Community through Cultural Dynamics," *Aryan Path*, July 1943.
Gorer, Geoffrey, ed.: *The People of Russia* (New York, 1950).
The Haitian Pilot Project, Monographs on Fundamental Education No. 4 (UNESCO, Paris, 1951).

Bibliography

Holmberg, Allan R.: "Experimental Intervention in the Field," *Human Organization*, vol. 14 (1955), no. 1.

——: *Nomads of the Long Bow*, Publications of the Institute of Social Anthropology, Smithsonian Institution, Monograph 10 (Washington, 1951).

Kroeber, A. L., ed.: *Anthropology Today: An Encyclopedic Inventory* (Chicago, 1953).

Lasswell, Harold: *Analyzing the Content of Mass Communication* (Washington, 1941).

Leites, Nathan C., and Pool, I.: *On Content Analysis* (Washington, 1941).

Malinowski, Bronislaw: "The Rationalization of Anthropology in Administration," *Africa*, vol. 3 (1930), no. 4.

Mead, Margaret, ed.: *Cultural Patterns and Technical Change* (UNESCO, Paris, 1955).

——: *Soviet Attitudes toward Authority* (New York, 1951).

Mead, Margaret, and Metraux, Rhoda, eds: *The Study of Culture at a Distance* (Chicago, 1953).

Smith, Edwin W.: *The Golden Stool: Some Aspects of the Conflict of Culture in Modern Africa* (London, 1926).

Tax, Sol: "The Freedom to Make Mistakes," *America Indigena*, vol. 16 (1956).

Index

A Note on the Author

■ H. R. Hays spent five years in the reading and research that preceded the writing of *From Ape to Angel*. Fascinated by the complexity of primitive societies, he developed an insatiable appetite for the works of the pioneers in the relatively new science of social anthropology. Mr. Hays, who is best known for *Lie Down in Darkness* (1944), *The Takers of the City* (1947), and other novels, is married and divides his time between New York City and eastern Long Island. His articles and poetry have appeared in the *Kenyon Review*, *Poetry*, *Accent*, *New Directions*, and elsewhere, and many of his plays have appeared on television.